Data Equals

Data Equals

Democratic Equality and Technological Hierarchy

COLIN KOOPMAN

The University of Chicago Press
Chicago and London

The University of Chicago Press, Chicago 60637
The University of Chicago Press, Ltd., London
© 2025 by Colin Koopman
All rights reserved. No part of this book may be used or reproduced in any manner
whatsoever without written permission, except in the case of brief quotations in
critical articles and reviews. For more information, contact the University of Chicago
Press, 1427 E. 60th St., Chicago, IL 60637.
Published 2025
Printed in the United States of America

34 33 32 31 30 29 28 27 26 25   1 2 3 4 5

ISBN-13: 978-0-226-84224-0 (cloth)
ISBN-13: 978-0-226-84225-7 (paper)
ISBN-13: 978-0-226-84226-4 (ebook)
DOI: https://doi.org/10.7208/chicago/9780226842264.001.0001

Library of Congress Cataloging-in-Publication Data

Names: Koopman, Colin, author.
Title: Data equals : democratic equality and technological hierarchy / Colin
    Koopman.
Description: Chicago : The University of Chicago Press, 2025. | Includes bibliographi-
    cal references and index.
Identifiers: LCCN 2025001942 | ISBN 9780226842240 (cloth) | ISBN 9780226842257
    (paperback) | ISBN 9780226842264 (ebook)
Subjects: LCSH: Digital divide—United States. | Big data—Social aspects—United
    States. | Electronic data processing—Social aspects—United States. | Equality—
    United States. | Democracy—United States.
Classification: LCC HM851 .K6665 2025 | DDC 303.48/340973—dc23/eng/20250331
LC record available at https://lccn.loc.gov/2025001942

♾ This paper meets the requirements of ANSI/NISO Z39.48-1992
(Permanence of Paper)

Authorized Representative for EU General Product Safety Regulation (GSPR)
queries: **Easy Access System Europe**—Mustamäe tee 50, 10621 Tallinn, Estonia,
gpsr.requests@easproject.com
Any other queries: https://press.uchicago.edu/press/contact.html

Contents

Introduction

Reconstructing Democratic Equality in Data Technology from Paper Records to Artificial Intelligence

The paramount problem facing democracies today is that of social and political separation. We too often find ourselves cleaved from each other—split apart and increasingly estranged. As the separation between us spreads, democracy is destabilized.

Democracy totters, yet data prospers. This is no mere coincidence. We are not just separate, we are separated. Prominent among the causes of our separation, and so of democracy's decay, is the unmistakable fact of our increasing enmeshment in data technologies from social media to automated prediction to generative artificial intelligence. Such data-driven innovations increasingly operate as what I call *technologies of separation*. Wrapped up in these technologies, we find ourselves swaddled in data that insulate us all and over time isolate us from each other.

Swaddled in data? It can truly be said today that one is born into flesh but is everywhere in data. Our activities from the most mundane to the most monumental are conducted through and transacted within data. Our everyday shopping: recorded by merchants, financial institutions, payment processors, all of whom resell iterations of those data to brokers who then repackage them and sell them at scale to other merchants and bankers looking to capture slivers of a future expenditure. Our movement: tracked by governments at those data-dense checkpoints known as borders, but equally datafied in quotidian commutes and even on ritual jogs as real-time locations are reported to the tech corporations loaded onto personal devices. Our education: from our first grade-school assessments to final degrees, all recorded in increasingly standardized education dossiers that register grades, tests, qualifications, and behaviors. All of this and so much more traces back to the natal event of each of our births—there too, within minutes of our fleshy entry into the world, each of us was registered into multiple databases including, at minimum, a hospital health records system, a governmental birth registration database, a health insurance data portal, and typically many other systems besides (consider today's newborns whose proud parents push out notices across the internet via emails, texts, and social media updates that establish the first series in what promises to be a lifelong stream of identifying data points).

At some level, each of our actions is configured, mediated, or (to use a term whose sense will become clear over the course of this book) formatted by data. Try to think of just one of your ordinary activities that is not in some sense configured by data. The exceptions are slim and in every plausible instance grate against the edges of an impressive informational apparatus. Even your solitary walk in the woods is facilitated by the GPS in your pocket, or at least the one in the car that brought you to the trailhead. My point is not that our every moment is lived entirely within data. It is that at every moment our data help condition and structure what we can do. Data are among the most common infrastructures of our most ordinary actions. And as our actions are ensconced in data, so too are we; for if what we do is designed in part by data, then who we are and even who we can be is, in significant respects, a function of the designs that data hold for us.

As ordinary as data are, we are told time and again that they are extraordinary. The largest data conglomerates (which also happen to be the largest corporations in human history) dazzle us with the promise of what their data (which they freely announce is our data too) can do. In most cases, the promises are hyperbole. Yet often enough, the credit extended by the promise gets cashed in, and the payouts are huge—mostly for the tech elite and those who bought shares in their vision. The internet gets transformed from a phonebook-like directory into a searchable all-purpose repository (circa 2000). The telephone, once a simple voice communication appliance, gets replaced by a handheld data-retrieval, -collection, and -analytics device (circa 2007). The device becomes powerful enough to carry around the internet in one's pocket thereby fueling a suite of social media platforms becoming a cultural obsession (circa 2012). The gigantic text database that the internet has since become gets leveraged into a massive model of human language that forms the functional basis for generative artificial intelligence (circa 2022). It is as if the extraordinariness of data has itself become ordinary.

Yet what are the unfulfilled promises that have been made on behalf of all these data-driven devices and designs? We have been told that data will connect us to each other, strengthen our friendships, and even enrich debate on pressing public matters. These and other promises by data's biggest boosters have not quite been lies. But they have been distractions. Social media have been presented for more than two decades as technologies of connection, but have all the while been formatting us in datafications that tend to drive us apart. Some of us have been pushed toward outright political polarization, while others have been more modestly nudged toward lives of isolation prepared for enmity. Data have become technologies for "organized loneliness," to adopt a phrase from Hannah Arendt's chilling study of the reemergence of authoritarianism in technological societies in the middle decades of the twentieth century.[1]

The organized loneliness of our contemporary technological moment is widely discussed across a range of academic disciplines as well as a variety of more popular narrative genres.[2] Yet the social and political effects flowing from today's most prominent deployments of data technology are still poorly understood. In the face of all this observed separation, suspicion, and division, this book provisions a vocabulary for making sense of what we so plainly see yet struggle to understand in our technologies of separation.

How shall we comprehend our technologies of separation so that we may better counteract the threats they pose to our democratic equality? To meet a moment in which democracy's inadvertent adversaries are the designs of megacap technology corporations, this book argues that we need to reconstitute democratic equality within our designs and implementations of data technology. This means becoming equals to each other with respect to our data—or becoming data equals. Data equality requires redesigning and reregulating our data technologies so that they better serve our democratic engagements with each other. It also requires reconstructing sites and practices of democratic engagement—perhaps most prominently those of education—so that technologies of separation do not undermine the very sustenance of democratic ways of living.

Our Obligation to Data

Why should it matter so much if our data technology leaves us separated from each other? Far from merely occasional and accidental, the separateness enacted through data more and more defines how we are able to relate to each other. Data's separations seem increasingly unavoidable. Consider the extent to which we are today obligated to act through and with our data. The obligation to allow oneself to be loaded into a database is of course not that of physical necessity or moral duty. The obligation is practical. In our contemporary moment, this is what one must do and how one must act in order to do the so many other things that are central to one's purposes—both in the sense of one's banal daily purposes and also in the more meaningful sense of one's fuller plan of life.

It is with a view to our data being obligatory for what we do and how we live that we have become our data. We have become what I call *informational persons*, a concept I developed in my previous book, *How We Became Our Data*.[3] That book details how an extensive network of obligations to data emerged across the first decades of the twentieth century. Prior to the turn of the twentieth century, most people conducted most of their lives without coming into enduring contact with information systems. Only a few decades later, vast swaths of citizens (especially in industrialized democracies like the United States) found themselves compelled to conduct increasingly many of their affairs in coordination with databases that at the time typically took the form of paper-and-cabinet records systems. Many donned data such as government identifiers (like the US Social Security number), formalized legal name requirements, education dossiers, property records, psychological assessments, vocational licensure, and so much more. Nearly everyone in prior generations (excepting the rich and the royal) had lived and died with hardly any paper traces beyond the private ephemera of family Bibles and epistolary imprints. Then, by the end of 1930s, nearly everyone's affairs were borne along by databases, beginning with a birth certificate and ending with a death record. This is when we became our data—that is, became obligated to data. These obligations persist today. Techniques for recording and analyzing data have migrated from paper forms to computational machinery powered by artificial intelligence, but the underlying technology of datafication has remained remarkably constant. An extensive datafication is today as obligatory as it is ordinary.

That data technology is obligatory is not in itself bad, but it is certainly fraught with danger. Data's dangers can be divided into two basic kinds. The first kind, and the one that commands the most attention in discussions about the politics and ethics of data, involves threats to our *liberty*. A paradigmatic data danger in this vein is mass surveillance and its concomitant threat to individual privacy. The concern here is that our being tracked, collected, and datafied in so many ways amounts to coercion that limits what would otherwise be free pursuits by individuals unencumbered by data. Threats to liberty are real dangers that deserve our attention. But equally important is a second kind of data danger. This concerns *equality*, and in particular those inequalities that flow from our obligations to data. Consider that for any concern we might have about being loaded onto a database, the object of concern impacts different segments of society unevenly. Some of us are more burdened by the damages that data inflict. Others are much more the beneficiaries of data systems that, say, keep certain groups from being entered into a database that confirms a particular right (such as a right to legally work, or to receive certain forms of state assistance). In connection with these inequalities in the distribution of social goods, data technology has also come to undermine a more basic sense of equality: being equal to each other. Where data technology polarizes and separates us from each other, it undermines our ability to relate as equals in a democracy.

Much attention has been given to concerns about data in defense of values of liberty, autonomy, and noninterference. But concerns about inequality are actually more important insofar as they are more central to democratic political societies. The most pressing problems we face when we confront data technologies are problems of hierarchy or inequality. Data hierarchy is so vexing because it operates on a terrain that is unavoidable in light of our obligations to data.

It is in the context of what is obligatory that inequality has its greatest force. If those who are burdened could simply opt out, the relevant inequality would dissipate over time. But where the burdened cannot exit, inequality is exacerbated, as it gets reproduced over and again. This is what we are witnessing today in data. We are witnessing intensifying inequalities of data—compounding, of course, with other forms of inequality or hierarchy in which we are already saturated.

There is nothing inevitable about any of this. The obligatory terrain that data have become could also become a site for equality. Data technology could be used to much more effectively build up facilities for more-equal treatment. Data could be leveraged for the sake of egalitarianism.

Approaching Data Equality (beyond Alignment and Fairness)

In light of these observations about our ordinary obligations to data, this book builds an argument for a fuller pursuit of democratic equality in data technology. The argument can be approached through a set of three frames for the *problem*, *potentiality*, and *peril* of data, forming a triptych for the chapters that follow.

The first frame involves a concept for a *problem*, or what can be described as a set of challenges we face in light of our having become informational persons whose activities and relations are increasingly organized through data. That data have become obligatory to who we are—that we have become our data—sets for us deep challenges, including, most importantly, those of democratic inequality. One prominent term for such challenges taken in the abstract is that of *value alignment*, or just *alignment*.[4] This term circulates more widely in industry circles invested in artificial intelligence than in scholarly research, but the basic idea is right enough, for the problem that alignment

speaks to is that of finding ways to implement our data technologies in service of our values.

A second frame comes into view here concerning the *potentiality* or *promise* of data; in particular, that of realizing equality in and through our data.
This involves actually becoming data equals—that is, equals to each other
with respect to our data. This requires data technologies that at the very least
mitigate, and preferably even repair, existing inequalities. It may appear that
data equality in this sense is just one more form the alignment problem can
take. Yet data equality actually comes prior to value alignment, as a kind of
operational presupposition for it. Equality matters not only in its own right,
but also derivatively wherever we face deep conflicts among values held by
those with a stake in data technology. Where value conflicts run deep, efforts
in alignment cannot presume what is all too often simply assumed by tech
industry proponents—namely that alignment is achievable by way of realizing values we all endorse.[5] If values are in conflict, our alignment problems
are not, in any straightforward sense, solvable. That conflicts of values may
well be a pervasive feature of modern moral and political life has long been
affirmed in philosophical discussions of value pluralism; and, in any event,
conflicts of values are certainly widely present today.[6] Rather than singular
solutions for all, what is needed in the face of conflicting values are robust
practices of equality, and in particular of equality as understood through the
lens of democracy. It is in virtue of relations of democratic equality that societies hold themselves together in the face of persistent disagreements over
discordant values.

This speaks to the other side of data's challenge: its danger, or what we
might call the *peril* of data. The data threat we face above all others is that
of extending inegalitarian hierarchies through our data technology. In short,
the peril is the decay of democracy into data-driven hierarchy. Such technological hierarchy forms conditions for all manner of exploits, ranging from
disinformation and polarization to mass-scale dataveillance and always-on
personalization.

This triptych frames an argument for data equality. The argument holds
that we ought to, where possible, reconstruct our data technologies so that
they are more fully expressive of data equality and thereby more resolutely
resistant to data hierarchy. A conception of data equality is needed in the
face of aspirational accounts that emphasize values proximate to, yet always
somehow short of, equality. One prominent such value widely forwarded in
the field of data ethics is commonly referred to as *algorithmic fairness*. This
ideal has become something of a consensus concept not only in academic
scholarship (including much of the scholarship that presents itself as more

critical) but also in many corners of corporate and governmental influence.[7] The central idea of algorithmic fairness is that an algorithm is unfair when some who are subject to it are more burdened than they would have been if a less-biased algorithmic procedure had been implemented. This claim is true enough so far as it goes. But it does not, I argue, go nearly far enough. In some respects, it is even a distraction.

What is wrong with algorithmic fairness? Just two things—first is its exclusive focus on algorithms, and second is its exclusive attention to fairness. With respect to both of its two main ideas, the ideal of algorithmic fairness gets something right, and yet is disconcertingly limited. We need far more than what the ideal of algorithmic fairness can deliver.

What we need is a fuller concept of data equality. Computational systems never run on algorithms alone but always require data structures, or what I call *formats*, to constitute those very data that serve as inputs for algorithmic processing. Further, a fuller conception of equality requires not only a concern with fairness in how personal data are processed but also a difference-sensitive notion of *equity* concerned with how data situates persons at entry into a procedure of treatment.[8] On each point, the perspective afforded by algorithmic fairness misses something that is structurally prior to algorithmic processing and procedural fairness. A conception of data equality brings this fuller perspective into clearer view.

Although data equality is a more robust standard than algorithmic fairness, it is also more pragmatically achievable. This may seem counterintuitive. Consider, then, how data equality's focus on formats (like database schema and classification taxonomies) helps make data technologies more tractable to more people in contrast to the sense of inaccessibility cultivated by algorithm-centric approaches. Formats almost always involve conceptual materials that are more comprehensible to most people in contrast to the impenetrability of algorithmic procedures wrapped up in complex statistical formulae encoded in programming and scripting languages. Consider, further, how the more robust account of equality central for data equality does not so much set a higher and more unattainable bar as it sets a different bar. Data equality as I present it in this book is situated within a family of egalitarian concerns focused on how well we relate to each other as equals. Its goal is to foster data technologies that enable us to engage each other as equals rather than serving to separate us. In theory, this could be a goal for algorithmic fairness. But as currently conceived and implemented in practice, algorithmic fairness most often assumes the form of tweaking algorithmic weightings in contexts of zero-sum competitions over biases. This assumes operational contexts in which people are pitted against each other in ways that intensify comparative hierarchies. Algorithmic fairness thereby tends to lead to inegalitarian conditions of hierarchy that undermine the very efforts at fairness motivating it in the first place.

In the face of data hierarchy, we need a reconstruction of our familiar concept of equality, one that is more usable for computational contexts of data technology. As I envision it, what I call *reconstruction* begins with a concept that already widely circulates in the penumbra of a problem yet fails to effectively address the problem's core. Reconstruction then reengineers, reformulates, and remobilizes that concept (as well as companion conceptions) so that it may better meet the moment of its problem. Normative reconstruction ought not seek values cut of wholly new cloth, but rather should excavate existing values in order to facilitate their transition into a transformed context of deployment. A reconstruction of data egalitarianism is needed because it is by no means obvious what needs to be done to achieve equality (a well-established value) in data (a relatively newer problematic).

Reconstructing equality for data technology requires simultaneous interventions across at least three contexts: legal regulation, technological design, and public education. Regulation, design, and education are the operative contexts on which the promise of a technological democracy is premised— the three-legged stool upon which data egalitarianism balances. This reflects a crucial aspect of reconstruction: it always seeks to meet its problematic in multiple ways. The idea of reconstruction is not to aim at singular one-off solutions but to orient inquiry to the plurality of problematic situations where intervention can lead to improvement. This book thus engages each of the three legs of data equality, but education also plays the leading role throughout.

What, then, is equality as suitably reconstructed for data technology? Central to a reconstructed conception of data egalitarianism is a distinction between two concepts of equality. One concept, familiarly referred to as *distributive equality*, takes equality to be a feature of the distribution of social goods—for example, a resource like income or an opportunity like an educational pursuit. Do some persons have more or less of some social good than others, and if so, is this inequality justifiable or is it unjustifiably arbitrary? This distributive question speaks to serious issues. Yet the question itself is normatively derivative of a concern for another kind of equality with a much wider bearing. This second concept of equality, that of *relational equality* (also often called *democratic equality*), is focused on equality as a feature of how persons can and do relate, or interact, with each other. Are persons able to relate as equals, or are they put in a position where they can regard each other only as inferiors or superiors? Are we able to convene and collaborate, or are we so separated from each other that we cannot find ways of working together? Recent philosophical developments of the idea of relational equality show this concept to be both wider and deeper than purely distributive equality.[9]

Democratic or relational equality is wider than distributive equality in that it brings into view non-distributive issues, such as whether and how well citizens are able to collaborate as equals in democratic projects of self-governance. For example, relational equality speaks to issues of political polarization and social separation. That social media silos so many of us implicates problems that are hardly intelligible as matters of maldistribution. For a different kind of example, explored later in the book, consider education technology that delivers highly personalized curriculum to students in ways that leave them ill equipped to relate to each other as equals in the course of learning. The inequalities engendered in learner segregation are not issues of maldistribution, though these relational inequalities can sometimes lead to distributive inequalities later on.

Democratic or relational equality is also deeper than distributive equality in that it is capable of holding distributive concerns in view alongside its focus on non-distributive inequalities of hierarchy. Indeed, on an even stronger interpretation, relational equality is a necessary component in any viable justification for distributive equality. Without an expectation of relational equality between two parties, there could never arise a serious question concerning the justifiability of a distributive equality between them. Where two parties are unequal in status, such as an ordinary person and a rudimentary robot, there can be no plausible justification for a claim to distributive equality between them. But where status equality ought to hold, as between two persons, there is already in place a justification for at least some form of distributive equality—namely, a distribution of benefits and burdens that is required for the two to be able to relate as equals.

Contemporary liberal democracies are riven by a staggering and growing level of wealth inequality. This disparity is nowhere more visible than in the municipal hubs of the biggest Big Tech palaces, like San Francisco and Seattle. Surely one of the most urgent needs of contemporary liberal democracies is a more-equal distribution of basic assets—affordable housing, health care, and access to higher education. The idea of relational equality both underwrites a justification for such distributive equalization and also offers a plausible explanation for why justified claims to redistribution remain widely unmet. Surely one reason we are so sorely lacking in distributive equality is because a host of persistent relational inequalities, or social hierarchies, stand in the way. Many liberal democracies find themselves increasingly divided along lines of urbanity and rurality; people separated by geography feel themselves deeply at odds with each other. The same societies are also plagued by entrenched hierarchies of race, gender, sexuality, and ability that can demotivate efforts to fulfill justified claims for redistribution. Wealth inequalities are widely acknowledged to matter greatly, and yet these divisions remain intact in no small part because of how they are fortified by relational inequalities of hierarchy.

The distinction between relational and distributive conceptions of equality has been prominent in political philosophy for more than two decades. Yet outside of political philosophy, this distinction often goes unrecognized. It is certainly ignored in data ethics scholarship on algorithmic fairness. Without even really reflecting on it as a choice, proponents of algorithmic fairness adopt as a default the framework of distributive equality; they just assume that problems of distribution are the only equality-relevant problem that algorithmic systems need solve for. It is as if concerns over relational equality have never even entered into consideration. This is probably because for almost all proponents of algorithmic fairness they actually never have entered into explicit consideration. This is not so much a shortcoming on the part of proponents of algorithmic fairness as it is a function of the separating silos in which are incubated much of data ethics scholarship. It may also be a function of certain structural incentives that cultivate these separations in the interests of maintaining inertial tendencies.

Centering a conception of democratic or relational equality in the way we approach questions concerning value in data technology dramatically transforms how we approach equality as a value to pursue with and within data technology. To preview arguments developed in later chapters, consider an important implication of relational equality for data technology. Relational equality's central concern with how people are situated in relation to each other enables us to attend to how they are entered into a system, not just on how the protocols of a system differentially distribute goods. How people are related to each other by system inputs can significantly impact their ability to relate as equals. People channeled into a space through different doors may come to perceive themselves as importantly different from each other once inside that space. Doors differentiating people as superior or inferior will generate impediments in their relating as equals on the other side of the threshold. Equity in entry is therefore every bit as important as fairness in processing. In the context of computational systems, this means attending to entry conditions established by the formats configuring input data instead of focusing only on those data-processing protocols commonly referred to as algorithms. How people are channeled into a computational system is always structured by the formats that define them for that system.

With these implications of relational equality in the foreground, it is worth considering what in the background motivates the view in the first place. Why should relational equality be considered so important? Here the synonymy of relational equality and democratic equality is revealing. Democracy is the very paradigm for the practice and virtue of relating as equals. By contrast, a purely distributive conception of equality need not implicate an endorsement of democratic politics (as exampled by political regimes that aspire to authoritarian programs of equal resource distribution). This point draws our attention to how the underlying distribution-centric assumptions that inform the ideal of algorithmic fairness are perfectly compatible with nondemocratic forms of political order. Of course, few proponents of algorithmic fairness seek to support the decline of democracy. Yet it is striking that our current technological configuration is one in which data technology is assisting democracy's decay and in which the leading ethical ideal being applied to data technology is an ideal of algorithmic fairness that does almost nothing to strengthen our democratic commitments. Proponents of algorithmic fairness may not be hoping for democracy's decline, but the idea of algorithmic fairness in service of purely distributive forms of equality does little to sustain democracy.

One way of stating the difference between a democratic equality view and the current consensus has to do with the research fields that have incubated these ideas. Algorithmic fairness is largely the product of an emerging scholarly field often referred to as *data ethics*. Though I sometimes use that term endorsingly, this book is more centrally concerned with *data politics*. This contrast brings attention to how some ideals forwarded under the banner of data ethics bear the mark of structural influences flowing from megacap data technology corporations.

The technology anthropologist Rodrigo Ochigame has documented in detail how "the majority of well-funded work on 'ethical AI' is aligned with the tech lobby's agenda" of self-regulation rather than legal restriction.[10] He shows how initial investments by the tech industry in data ethics incubators at MIT and Harvard led to a bloom of institutes and centers all benefiting from the same largesse. This includes spaces widely regarded as leading the field: "The Data & Society Research Institute is directed by a Microsoft researcher and initially funded by a Microsoft grant; New York University's AI Now Institute was co-founded by another Microsoft researcher and partially funded by Microsoft, Google, and DeepMind."[11] As Ochigame documents, the corporations that seed-funded these centers soon after adopted voluntary codes of ethics that drew on ideas nurtured at the very shops they had incubated: "In January 2018, Microsoft published its 'ethical principles' for

AI, starting with 'fairness.' In May, Facebook announced its 'commitment to the ethical development and deployment of AI' and a tool to 'search for bias' called 'Fairness Flow.' In June, Google published its 'responsible practices' for AI research and development. In September, IBM announced a tool called 'AI Fairness 360,' designed to 'check for unwanted bias in datasets and machine learning models.'"[12]

Anyone who has followed these fields over the past decade will be keenly aware of the general patterns Ochigame describes, as well as at least a few representative episodes. What is probably the most disturbing case was first reported in *Politico* by the journalist Alexandra Levine in January 2022, and soon after at *Vice* by the tech writer Joanne McNeil (whose recent novel *Wrong Way* poignantly captures the desperate loneliness of a gig worker at a tech firm ever on the cusp of transforming humanity).[13] McNeil's piece details the role played by a prominent data ethics scholar from a well-known data ethics research institute (Data & Society) in brokering a deal to share text message data sent to a suicide crisis text line (Crisis Text Line) with its own for-profit sentiment analytics spin-off firm (Loris.ai).[14] That this affair involved an extremely influential data ethics scholar is deeply disappointing; that the data ethics research community has responded with an almost total lack of concern feels scandalous.[15] Yet the majority of data ethicists, and even many critical data studies scholars, routinely ignore discomfiting facts about the field's funding and sponsorship arrangements. Corporate-backed research in just about any other field is usually dismissed out of hand, as in the case of climate-change think tanks funded by Big Oil. Yet numerous Big Tech firms (perhaps most prominently Microsoft, whose market capitalization breached $3 trillion in early 2024) continue to directly sponsor research on data ethics that nearly everyone in the scholarly community holds in high regard.[16] Ethics research shops funded by corporations whose market capitalizations are in the trillions have every incentive not to pursue real equality and instead to proffer thin conceptions of fairness that are fully consistent with the ongoing reproduction of existing inequalities.

It is not a reach for Ochigame to describe algorithmic fairness scholarship as "a new corporate-sponsored field of research" that conceives of fairness as "a mathematical property of algorithms and their outputs."[17] In the face of growing calls for legal regulations, he notes, "corporations are hard at work to evade and contain regulatory efforts, and to prescribe technical definitions of fairness for strategic purposes."[18] What Ochigame describes of fairness also holds for the other half of algorithmic fairness—namely, the algorithm itself. On the heels of major investments in academic research by Big Tech conglomerates and roughly simultaneous with marketing campaigns by these corporations touting the power of their algorithms, there occurred a large uptick in academic research on algorithms beginning in the early 2010s. Much of this work is critical in intent, and some of it has been genuinely valuable. However, the unstated assumption of this work has always been a faith in the enormous power of the algorithm, which is exactly the line sponsored by the major tech industry firms. All of this has recently reached a fever pitch in the simultaneous corporate and academic campaigns for work on one subclass of algorithms: machine learning, or artificial intelligence. In this space too there has been valuable work. But we ought to be able to recognize that critical scholarship has been channeled in this direction by the very corporations producing the wares that the critics take as their object of criticism. What commands the attention of scholars in data technology is not accidental. Gaps in data technology scholarship tend to overlap strongly with gaps in the marketing campaigns purveyed by technology firms.

In light of the alignments between academic research and industry interests, a distinction needs be made between data ethics as a field and a different sort of research program whose focus is on data politics. A more political focus drives this book. That said, the criticisms of algorithmic fairness I have documented so far concern external dynamics, such as how funding arrangements can steer what might otherwise be good ideals in the wrong direction. What still needs further consideration is an internal account of the flaws inside the idea of algorithmic fairness, regardless of its provenance. The chapters that follow, where they are critical, are focused on internal critiques of just this type. For now, my hope is that the evidence offered of Big Tech's leading role in funding data ethics research seeds sufficient suspicion.

Once we are suspicious of something, we must make ourselves ready to move out of the skeptical mood in order to take up the work of building pragmatic possibilities for its reconstruction. This book furthers a line of thinking emerging among a small but growing number of data scholars working to assemble conceptions that reach beyond the limits of the current consensus.[19] In this and other ways, a reconstructive effort, rather than a suspicious temper, forms the animating impulse at the center of this book.

Developing Data Equality (with Pragmatism)

This book is informed by multiple perspectives, but the methodological center of the reconstructive approach I take is most fully within the orbit of philosophical pragmatism.

A natural next question to ask is: what is pragmatism? The philosophical version of pragmatism is not all that different from the colloquial sense of the term. Pragmatist philosophy is focused on working toward what betterment can be achieved (and not letting the perfect be the enemy of the good). This hopeful commitment implicates a number of companion ideas—for instance, an attentiveness to practices or actions, as well as a focus on processes or transitions rather than idealized visions of eternal repose.[20]

In light of pragmatism's prioritization of what can be done, another natural question to consider is: how does pragmatism proceed? How pragmatism does its work has already been referred to above—pragmatism reconstructs.[21] Reconstruction involves excavating concepts that serve as substrate for our ordinary practices and reconfiguring them so that they might be remobilized where practices are transforming.[22] In this book, reconstruction is sought with respect to a particular value (equality) with the intent of remobilizing that value in a context undergoing transformation (data technology).

Why think that pragmatist reconstruction is suited to the particular purposes of data egalitarianism? One reason has to do with pragmatism's political commitment to democracy and the democratic inflection it thereby offers to equality—this is particularly needful in the face of technologies of inequality inflicting separation, isolation, and polarization on the public. Another reason concerns pragmatism's metaphilosophical orientation toward processes and transitions. Not only are we in a time of rapid technological transformation, but our transformative technologies are themselves processing technologies, as in the case of computational machinery whose very operation involves processing vast flows of data. A third reason for pragmatism's special relevance to questions of values in data technology concerns its concepts of thought and intelligence. Pragmatism helps us relax our grip when it comes to efforts to fortify a divide between a uniquely human intelligence and the artificial intelligence of learning machines. In doing so, pragmatism enables us to focus instead on the distinction that really matters here: that between better (problem-solving) and worse (problem-exacerbating) thinking. This feature is worth considering at some length as a means of introducing some general features of philosophical pragmatism.

Thought, on the pragmatist perspective, is an act of inquiry. Thinking is a practice of learning or education. Through this conception, pragmatism establishes continuity between the potentialities of human thinking and those of machine learning, or artificial intelligence. To affirm continuities between human thinkers and thinking machines carries enormous advantages where we pursue questions of value concerning technology. Such continuities locate the human inquirer as adjacent to, and sometimes even internal within, the data technologies whose values are under survey. This positions the inquirer to pose questions about the forms of educability for computational machines without having already decided in advance that computers could never learn. This does not mean, however, that all learning machines will learn in ways that will help realize values of equality and democracy. In more ways than we typically expect, our machines are just like us. Not all human thinkers further values of equality and democracy; some are very much caught up in the work of purveying hierarchy. And so too with intelligent machines. A pragmatist approach helps us not be hung up so much on drawing a rigid line between humans and technologies so that we can focus instead on distinguishing pursuits of hierarchy from pursuits of democracy, regardless of whether humans or machines are doing the pursuing. The point is not, however, to endorse transhumanist or posthumanist ontologies.[23] Rather, the purpose is to shift concern away from unresolvable ontological debates in order to focus on more-relevant considerations concerning the values purveyed by those data technologies being increasingly wielded by humans who are themselves increasingly datafied.

A perspective that assumes our proximity to data technologies is decisively advantaged over both transhumanist views that collapse together human and machine as well as more critical reflexes that refuse to even entertain the possibility of intelligent artifice. A common critical cliché has it that there is something elusive in human thinking that simply cannot be expressed by a machine. Many critics deny that machines exhibit whatever it is we are pleased to call "intelligence." Others counterpose a refined quality of "thought" or "reason" to an unrefined property of intelligence that is viewed with no small suspicion. Still others locate the power of mind in its modes of "intuition," "imagination," or "creativity," which remain inaccessible to machines. What all these critics share is the conviction that artificial intelligence must miss what is most essential to human thinking. But this perspective is unhelpful when it comes to questions of value concerning technology, for the critical posture can only ever take a skeptical stance. Such stances neglect the complexity not only of our artifice, but also of our relations to it.

When it comes to pragmatism's preparedness to affirm continuities between human and computer thinking, much can be gleaned from an argument made by the French philosopher Catherine Malabou in her 2017 book *Morphing Intelligence*. Malabou's claim is that "intelligence is always already artificial."[24] Rather than mount a "defense against the modern scientific concept of intelligence,"[25] Malabou argues that a critical confrontation with artificial intelligence must be "set up in the heart of the concept of intelligence" in a manner that requires the kind of continuity pragmatism affirms.[26] Indeed, in order to establish continuities between human and machine thinking,

Malabou sources insights from the early-twentieth-century pragmatist phi-losopher John Dewey.[27] She finds in Dewey a conception of intelligence as dynamic, transitional, and even "automating" in its pragmatic operations—"automatic" not in the sense of mere repetition but rather of self-movement.[28] The automatic quality of intelligent thought is at its highest pitch in expres-sions of recursiveness and reflexiveness—thought moving by bending back on itself. A crucial implication of this pragmatist view is its separation of normative achievements of intelligence, learning, and knowledge from a cri-terion of conscious awareness.[29] A conception of intelligent thought as a pro-cess of reflexive movement need not involve appeals to consciousness, which remains a mysterious philosophical notion that both fails to explain much and also institutes ontological barriers between that which is conscious (like a human) and that which is not (like a computer).

A formulation of intelligence as automatic might seem unexpected to seasoned readers of Dewey, but I find Malabou's interpretation both precise and compelling. In his 1925 *Experience and Nature*, considered by many his masterwork, Dewey presents a conception of mind as "a moving stream, a constant change which nevertheless has axis and direction, linkages, asso-ciations as well as initiations, hesitations and conclusions."[30] In light of this conception, which I have elsewhere described in terms of a focus on *transi-tions*, what Dewey praises as fecund in thought is not the mere application of a predefined routine, but rather the process of inquiry reflexively extending itself: "The more an organism learns, the more it has to learn, in order to keep itself going."[31] Intelligence refers to that within action which propels reflexive (that is, reflective) processes of practical self-transformation.

"One acts . . . for the sake of learning," Dewey says, in observation of how action reflexively aims for, but is never guaranteed, an extending of intel-ligence.[32] Pragmatism's emphasis on learning as the seat of thinking is enor-mously consequential. Malabou rightly observes that "the natural automatism of intelligence reveals its collective, that is, social, nature."[33] This follows from two ideas: first, that intelligence is exemplified above all in learning, and sec-ond, that learning always begins as a collaborative endeavor.[34] This second idea does not mean there cannot be learning in isolation; what it means is that learning can neither begin nor subsist entirely in isolation. Learning in isolation always presupposes prior sociality in learning.

Dewey's philosophy of democracy expresses well just how much this soci-ality matters. The very heart of democracy is the social process of education, a view developed in exquisite detail in Dewey's 1916 *Democracy and Edu-cation*.[35] But Dewey's connection between democratic sociality and reflexive intelligence raises a crucial question that he himself left unresolved: what is it about the sociality of education that makes the difference for processes of reflexive intelligence?

On Malabou's view, Dewey's analysis of the social quality of intelligence leads to a requirement that "ideas be shared and communicated," such that "we might conclude that there is no collective intelligence without community expression."[36] This formulation diligently follows one line in Dewey's vision of democracy—indeed, a prominent one among his interpreters—as a shared communicative and deliberative endeavor in "connected dialogue."[37] But I hesitate to place too much faith in deliberative democracy, for it is difficult to not be skeptical about the sufficiency (though I fully endorse the necessity) of a deliberative or communicative conception of democracy in contexts where our political problematics are driven, even if only in part, by those data systems and information technologies that promise to make communication more connected.[38] This is an argument I have explored in detail in discussions of Dewey's and Jürgen Habermas's deliberativism in my previous book on data politics, so I shall only summarize it here.[39] The gist of the concern is that deliberation can begin only once data are given, and yet it is in the way that data are made (and not just in the way they are communicated once they have been constituted) that they are of paramount political concern. Communicative interaction is ill equipped to resolve political problems stemming from misinformation and disinformation—that is, problems of political contexts that no longer accommodate a shared sense of what Arendt describes as the basic "factual truths" of the everyday world.[40] Where we confront such contexts—and surely we do in the face of off-the-shelf generative artificial intelligence tools and unmoderated social media shares—deliberative democracy is no longer a self-sufficient normative force. We need communicative democracy, to be sure; but we need much more than communicative democracy.

In contrast to the communicativist approach, yet still consistent with its animating impulse, the arguments of this book focus on what I take to be the central normative commitment of democracy and therefore of democratic education: equality between persons. Democracy is the idea that government can be self-regulated, and even self-propelled, among people who relate to each other as equals. Communication is often a valuable means to democratic equality. But it could never be its core in a context where the information presupposed by any communication is already a terrain of inequality (an idea that I explain in later chapters as a problem of inequality within data). By declining to travel too far with deliberativist democratic theory, this book refocuses the thrust of pragmatist democracy around its robust commitments to equality. Democratic equality includes communicative democracy as one of its aspects. But it also requires much else, as its best instantiations in education show. What it also requires is collaborative equality across a plurality of forms in how we treat each other. This surely includes for us today our interactions as mediated by data technologies like social media, predictive algorithms, and learning platforms.

Situating Data Equality (with and beyond Philosophy)

Pragmatist perspectives on equality, democracy, education, intelligence, and technology are central to the arguments I pursue in this book. Though I have started with Dewey and Malabou, I look sideways to a contemporary of each to really get the argument going. I first consider Dewey's contemporary W. E. B. Du Bois—specifically, his pragmatist reconstructions of early efforts in data analysis—to better motivate and justify a concern with equality in data technology (chapter 2).[41] I then move forward to a contemporary of Malabou's (and ours), the pragmatist political philosopher Elizabeth Anderson, in particular her democratic view of equality as concerned with how well we are able to relate to each other as equals (chapter 3).[42] Dewey's concepts and arguments eventually return to a more central place when I mobilize data equality in the context of education technology (chapter 7). Along the way I pull insights from numerous other self-described pragmatists, including Danielle Allen and Philip Kitcher (both of whom ably explain educational equality from pragmatist perspectives), as well as some other pragmatists who have sometimes resisted the label, including Ian Hacking and Barry Allen (both of whom offer needed insights concerning our intimacies with our techniques and technologies).[43]

In engaging pragmatists past and present, I pull mostly on the common thread of their pragmatist method for inquiry. Reconstructive method is the beating heart of pragmatism. The methodological center that defines a philosophy can be distinguished from the particular concepts that practitioners of that philosophy have come to endorse, articulate, and mobilize. Pragmatist concepts of democracy and equality matter much to my argument, but they come to matter here only insofar as I reshape or reconstruct them. My conception of data equality is therefore a reconstruction, rather than a rote repetition, of preceding pragmatist concepts. Consider that, despite living through the early-twentieth-century advent of mass-scale datafication, Dewey never wrote anything significant about data technology. More or less the same can be said of almost all pragmatists preceding and following him.[44] This is not to fault Dewey. It is only to observe the limits of concepts he crafted (and reconstructed) for contexts now in the past. By pressing inherited concepts through the mill of the present by way of pragmatism's reconstructive methodology, concepts like democratic equality can be remobilized in the transformed conditions of today. In this way, pragmatism propels itself ever onward.

No pragmatist should be content to be only a pragmatist. I draw much in this book from other philosophical perspectives that are not significantly within the orbit of pragmatism. These include considerations about equality and hierarchy in analytic political philosophy, especially those of Bernard Williams, T. M. Scanlon, and more recently Niko Kolodny.[45] Another constellation on which I rely is a lineage in recent French philosophy that includes the political philosopher Michel Foucault and the philosopher of technology Gilbert Simondon.[46]

Beyond the direct influences that bear on the arguments I develop in this book, there are numerous other fields of scholarship that also inform, partially anticipate, or instructively contrast to my pragmatist argument for data equality. Two are worth noting at the outset.

My general approach—applying conceptual resources mined from political philosophy to pressing problematics in contemporary data technology—is by no means unique. Over the past five years or so, there has emerged a literature in what might be called the political and social philosophy of data. Among the many scholars contributing to this burgeoning field, I have learned much from work by Shannon Vallor, Mathias Risse, Carlos Montemayor, Luciano Floridi, Mark Coeckelbergh, Davide Panagia, and Bernard Harcourt.[47] These precedents influence not only the questions I ask here, but also how I ask these questions, as well as how I respond to them. That said, none of these works pose the specific questions that I take to be most urgent in this space: questions of democratic data equality. The arguments most proximate to mine are those of Risse and Montemayor in their pursuit of liberal democratic conceptions of human rights appropriate to an era of artificial intelligence.[48] My argument for the value of democratic equality in technology is conceptually intimate with a defense of rights in the face of technology—for surely democracy is needed to sustain such liberal strategies as human rights, the rule of law, and public reason in the face of onslaughts of hierarchizing technologies. At the same time, equality also goes well beyond these strategies in instantiating a much wider suite of democratic practices, including practices of education.

Although an increasing number of recent contributions in political philosophy develop valuable insights about data technology, almost all this philosophical work is preceded by a substantial interdisciplinary literature on data that includes contributions from a range of fields, including communications, anthropology, sociology, history, and literary studies, and transdisciplinary fields such as new media studies. Various labels have been applied to describe the central concerns uniting all this work. One label that seems both sufficiently descriptive and possessed of some stickiness is "critical data studies."[49] Many of the central arguments I develop here, though enriched by more recent philosophy, first came into view through engaging the work of critical data studies scholars including Wendy Hui Kyong Chun, Ruha Benjamin, Virginia Eubanks, Louise Amoore, Alexander Galloway, and others cited in the chapters to follow.[50] Also influential for the chapters on education were writings by critical education technology scholars like Neil Selwyn and Ben Williamson.[51]

This book, in a sense, is like me. It finds itself inveterately caught between a few different crowds. This can be a difficult position from which, and to which, to write. But it is also where all the action is.

The Plan of the Book

A complete account of data equality involves numerous elements, including a theory of equality as a feature of how we relate to each other (chapter 3), an account of how equality understood in this way is to be enacted in operative data technologies (chapter 4), an understanding of the functional operation of data technologies as involving not only the algorithms that process data but also the formats that structure those data so they can be subject to processing (chapter 5), and methodologies for interrogating and evaluating data systems (chapter 6). The chapters that follow detail these and other elements requisite for a full presentation of data equality. To orient the reader at the outset, I offer a brief overview of each part, followed by a more detailed overview of each chapter.

The book is divided into four parts. The first part presents some initial openings that help motivate the concept of data equality as well as some major obstacles to realizing it. The second part develops and defends a conception of equality. The third part provisions a detailed conception of data technology. And the fourth part mobilizes all these pieces within a domain that should be egalitarian in democratic societies if anything is (namely, education). Each part consists of a pair of chapters. The central theoretical arguments of the book are advanced in parts 2 and 3, both of which are arranged so that the first chapter in the pair presents arguments for a specific conception (of equality and data, respectively) and the second then develops methodological implications of that conception.

Part 1 sets the stakes for the arguments that follow by describing obstacles to and openings for data equality. Chapter 1 begins with two general obstacles and one more specific impediment to equality in data. The first obstacle is data hierarchy. Hierarchies can be so deeply entrenched that they form an effective, and often invisible, part of our social structures. Where hierarchy is entrenched in data apparatus, achieving equality in data requires more than the minimum of not making things worse, but an active pursuit of equality against hierarchy. Unfortunately, minimal standards tend to dominate our visions of technology. This is exemplified in a second general obstacle to data equality, the idea of technological neutrality. According to this idealization, technologies are by default neither good nor bad, but are only neutral tools whose effects for better or worse are the responsibility of their users. This is an incoherent idea—at least, in any context where technologies are deployed against the background of entrenched hierarchy. Adding neutrality to hierarchy can only reproduce hierarchy. One specific idea that appears to serve data equality, but actually ends up furthering the ends of hierarchy by falling back on tech neutrality, is the aforementioned ideal of algorithmic fairness. Algorithmic fairness is crucially necessary for data equality but also problematically limited in proffering a thin conception of equality (as requiring only fairness) and a narrow conception of data computation (as requiring only algorithms).

Chapter 2 considers an alternative response to entrenched data hierarchies in the form of the active pursuit of equality in data. A good place to start exploring equality in data is with the historical precedent of the data work of Du Bois. Though he is widely embraced today as a theorist of racial equality, Du Bois is still not often acknowledged for his innovative work on racial datafication. The discussion in chapter 2 aims to recover Du Bois as a motivating precedent for the needed work of designing equality into data.

The arguments developed in both chapters of part 1 adopt a structural approach to political and social matters. According to this approach, political problems are not primarily problems of individual psychology (like the beliefs or attitudes a person may hold) but are in the first place effects of social structure (such as institutional policies and the affordances of technological designs). Part 1 thus presents an outline of a structural conception of data equality. Parts 2 and 3 then develop the details of that structural approach with respect to the two focal concepts of data equality, namely equality and data.

Part 2 presents, develops, and defends a structural conception of equality. Chapter 3 begins with Anderson's concept of relational equality (or democratic equality) as contrasting to purely distributive ideas of equality. Relational equality both provides a justification for distributive equality and brings into view non-distributive forms of inequality. This chapter develops an interpretation of democratic equal relations that builds out some of the more pragmatist insights that underlie the view but which nevertheless get left to the side in Anderson's own account. Specifically, it articulates a structural conception of relational equality according to which equality is primarily a feature of how social structures position people as able (or unable) to relate to each other as equals.

Chapter 4 describes how equality can be enacted according to my structural model of relational equality. A focal idea for equality is equal treatment or, more precisely, treating people as equals. This chapter develops a conceptual anatomy of equal treatment that affords two crucial insights. First, equal treatment is a process with distinct stages in which equality assumes different desiderata at different stages. This helps show why equal treatment involves two distinct conditions: equity in entry and fairness in processing. Second, processes of equal treatment conceived in this way are parallel in form to computational systems, which also have an entry stage (of data inputs) and a processing stage (of algorithmic data analysis). This parallel prepares the way for understanding how equal treatment can serve as a mechanism for equality in data technologies.

Part 3 explores the parallel between equal treatment and computational programs from the other side of data technology. Chapter 5 explains what data are and why we should assess them according to a valuational standard such as equality. It is common to think of social structures as consisting only of institutions (like governmental agencies or regulatory policies). But technologies too are a part of social structures, for they dispose our actions in significant ways. It follows that we need precise accounts of how specific data technologies dispose or configure us. Such precision must begin with the fact that data technologies consist of two jointly necessary operational elements: algorithmic processors and formats. Formats (or data structures) are structural technologies for the same reason that algorithms are: they also configure and dispose us. Data designs help design what we can and cannot do (regardless of whether we protest or submit). Accordingly, this chapter argues, formats (and not just algorithms) ought to be subject to evaluation according to the values we expect more broadly of our social structures.

Chapter 6 presents a methodology for inquiry into formats—specifically, into how formats structure our actions and interactions. The methodology for data dissection presented here is one I call an *anatomy of formats*. A format anatomy offers a way to interrogate formats in their simultaneous conceptual and technical functions—that is, as bearers of concepts and as operational vectors for computational techniques. Format anatomies are contrasted with, but also described as potential companions to, the already-prominent methodology of algorithmic audits.

Part 4 mobilizes the theory and methodology developed in preceding chapters. Education is a worthy exemplar for mobilizing the concept of data equality for two reasons. First, as much as any other social domain, we broadly expect education to reflect democratic values of equality, which is to say that education is itself already internal to the concept of democracy itself. If data equality is to get off the ground anywhere, then it should be able to get off the ground in the context of education. Second, some of the most democratic aspects of education are currently under significant stress due to the disruptive transformations sought by upstart education technologies that would dispense with collaborative-learning practices in favor of personalized-learning trajectories designed for solitary students staring at individual screens. Chapter 7 describes how artificial intelligence is now being leveraged for the development of highly personalized–learning experiences. The methodology of format anatomies shows how an unreflective reliance on data formats is fostering such personalization. This chapter specifically surveys the data stores collected on students that are used as the inputs for the learner models (or personalized profiles of individual students) generated by machine-learning approaches. This anatomy shows that these data rely on an implicit conceptualization of students as isolated learners.

Chapter 8 then offers an evaluative assessment on the basis of the format anatomy conducted in the previous chapter. If Dewey's vision of education in democracy involves the social bonds of students collaborating with each other, many students' leading collaborators in education technology today assume the form of cartoonish avatars miming vapid words of support. There are countless such proprietary coaches stalking the education technology platforms being placed in the hands of students worldwide today. One of the most famous is Duolingo's Duo, a wide-eyed little green owl who is quickly becoming a pedagogical partner to entire cohorts of students who are thereby no longer afforded sufficient opportunities for developing skills for collaborating with each other. Data technologies are organizing learning as an isolated, and too often lonely, activity. Students are separated from each other. Yet, data technology could be turned toward more-equal pursuits. This chapter concludes with a consideration of recent projects leveraging data analytics toward the support of collaborative educational practices.

The arc of the book on the whole aims at a conception of data equality that can be effectively mobilized as a part of reconstructive interventions where technologies of separation are being selected over technologies of collaboration. Where separation edges out collaboration, we witness the erosion of crucial conditions for democracy. Creating collaborative alternatives to the data technologies that separate us requires becoming equals to one another with respect to the data increasingly defining our lives. Sustaining our democracy requires our becoming data equals.

PART 1

Data Equality

Data Hierarchy, Technological Neutrality, and Algorithmic Fairness
Some Obstacles

When confronting the political, social, and ethical implications of our tech-nologies, we can pursue one of two paths. We can build data technologies that further entrench the manifold histories of hierarchy that continue to structure current social arrangements. Or we can cultivate data technologies that actively resist the inertia of hierarchies in the interest of creating more-egalitarian orders. Hierarchy and equality are our only two options.

Faced with this choice, it is sometimes proclaimed that a third way is pos-sible: the path of presumptive technological neutrality. With respect to data technologies, this view is often presented through arguments that statistical algorithms and artificial intelligence are not themselves tilted toward either hierarchy or equality. When unequal outcomes follow from uses of data tech-nologies, this argument holds that they are largely the fault of historical pat-terns of inequality that shape the datasets that algorithms and other artifices are run over.

To assess these three views of data technology—and indeed, technology writ large—the first half of this chapter develops two related arguments. The first explicates just what is wrong with hierarchy, technological or otherwise. This argument is unlikely to meet with vigorous objection. Who truly holds hierarchy in high esteem? Yet the implications of the rejection of hierarchy are not as widely understood as the rejection itself. Considering hierarchy more carefully can bring into better view the historical inequalities that continue to structure our present. This sets up the second argument, which shows that the presumptive path of tech neutrality is an idealization—that is, a fantasy. Tech neutrality attempts to say something meaningful about tech-nology without ever seriously considering the situations in which technology is used.

These two arguments concern admittedly abstract ideas: hierarchy, neutrality, equality. The second half of the chapter places these ideas and arguments on a more concrete level, in the context of an ideal for data ethics that currently enjoys near-consensus endorsement across industry, government, and (most of) academia. The ideal of algorithmic fairness certainly gets something right. But it also leaves out much that is important. Widespread endorsement of this ideal thus institutes an obstacle to a more fulsome pursuit of equality. Clarifying how algorithmic fairness embraces a subtle form of tech neutrality, and thereby exposes itself to data hierarchy, helps frame the need for a fuller concept of data equality, which I then turn to in the next chapter, and the rest of the book after that.

Hierarchy in and beyond Data

What is hierarchy, and why does it matter for equality?[1] Hierarchy as I bring it into focus here consists in status inequalities according to which people are unable to relate as equals. According to this view, hierarchy is (or at least seems) wrong. We all ought to be able to look each other in the eye as equals without having to bow and scrape.

Is hierarchy really always wrong? What about vertical relations of authority—say, between a judge on the bench and a defendant on trial, or between a municipal bureaucrat and a resident? The view I adopt regards hierarchy as a default wrong that always stands in need of justification to be righted. Justifications of rightful hierarchy can be supplied by what Niko Kolodny refers to as "tempering factors" for disparities and asymmetries.[2] For instance, a real inequality of status may be confined to a context (the judge cannot make rulings about the defendant after court has been dismissed and they find themselves together out on the street) or to a content (the bureaucrat may insist that the client follow protocol to achieve a particular end, but they cannot insist that the client must pursue that end in the first place). Absent such tempering justifications, hierarchy is by default wrong. But tempering factors are real, and so there are cases of rightful hierarchy. It is helpful to have a distinguishing term for these, so I shall refer to *authority* where tempering factors justify status inequalities, thus reserving *hierarchy* for instances where it is wrong (including presumptively wrong).

Why begin with hierarchy rather than inequality? One reason has to do with the fact that inequality, like equality, admits of multiple understandings. Two concepts of inequality are particularly prominent in contemporary egalitarian theory: inequality in distributions of goods (distributive inequality) and inequality in relations among persons (relational inequality, often also called democratic equality).[3] If relational inequality is central for any justifiable conception of equality (a claim I develop below, in chapter 3), then it follows that a concern about inequality requires a corollary focus on hierarchy. A second reason to start with hierarchy rather than a more general notion of inequality is that inequality just is the absence of equality. But what makes equality go missing? Hierarchy helps explain the presence of equality's absence. Hierarchy refers not so much to those social relations that take root after democracy dissipates, but rather to how prior social processes actively root out relations of democratic equality, recasting fellow citizens as superiors or inferiors.

A general hierarchical style is increasingly prominent today. In its more extreme executions, hierarchy works to institute requirements vertically, unassailably, and divisively. In these extreme forms, hierarchy exhibits as authoritarianism.[4] Specific qualities of authoritarianism include the rigidity and fixity of its requirements, the unquestionability of those requirements, the expectation of unquestioning commitment on the part of the obedient, and often (though certainly not always) the overwhelming scale of its operation. Authoritarianism spawns a multiplicity of harms. Among them are separation and exclusion—an observation that proves crucial from the perspective of a democratic aspiration to equality as a feature of our relations with each other.

It is important that authoritarianism not be confused for other concepts of political organization with which it can sometimes commingle, such as autocracy or tyranny. *Autocracy* refers to the consolidation of all power in a single person or position. *Tyranny* refers to a condition in which power thus consolidated is implemented in ways that are especially cruel. *Authoritarianism* is conceptually distinct from both, though it can of course partake in the consolidation of power or the use of power for cruelty. Unlike autocracy, authoritarianism involves an institution of conditional requirements, rather than a consolidated employment of power, to achieve some end. The autocrat forbids their subjects from some activity (such as prayer to their own god) or makes their subjects partake in some activity (such as praise for the leader). The authoritarian is a less-empowered figure who simply institutes distinctions that divide people along lines of those who follow and those who do not. And unlike tyranny, authoritarianism need not be cruel, though it often can be. These differences are important not because the authoritarian can never exhibit the qualities of the autocrat or the tyrant. The differences matter, rather, for the sake of conceptual clarity that helps us recognize authoritarianism when it is in action.

What, then, does authoritarianism look like in practice? Consider the authoritarian political figure. The paradigmatic authoritarians of the contemporary moment do not always wield power in a way that compels all citizens to act in specified ways. Rather, authoritarians institute requirements that people can often either choose to follow or not—that is to say, the authoritarian institutes requirements that are incumbent on those within their party, their movement, their network, their platform, their clubhouse, or what some describe as their cult. The authoritarian thereby divides a people. The authoritarian leader often does not make everyone do the same thing for the simple reason that they frequently do not have the capacity to compel (and just as frequently, they are aware of this and will even publicly vocalize it as a presentation of their own presumptive victimization). Rather than the coercion of the autocrat or tyrant, what authoritarians fundamentally achieve in practice is illiberal division and enmity among a people. People who do what the authoritarian says are those who obediently follow what they believe the authoritarian would otherwise compel them to do. Those who do not obediently follow are not often compelled to follow, but they are demonized, mocked, belittled, or in many cases simply disregarded or left to languish. When such divisions are instituted, a path is prepared for autocracy or tyranny, but these are a distinct step.

Next, consider hierarchy, including its extreme forms of authoritarianism, as it operates in data technology. Think of the requirements for joining a digital platform (whether devoted to connecting friends or conveying property). The operators of these platforms institute requirements for participation, but they do not directly compel participation itself. There is not a requirement, nor even an explicit injunction, to participate. But networks operating at scale often introduce practical obligations that make nonparticipation too costly, whether in the form of time costs or social exclusion penalties. At a certain point, the holdout who refuses to get a social media account or a smartphone ends up an unintended burden to others who now have to go out of their way (to communicate, or to give directions, or to share an image from a family gathering). There is in any event no such thing as a holdout from data as such. We are all enrolled in multiple data systems. For those who do participate in the data technologies of platforms, there are strict requirements constituting the protocols for participation. Consider the templatization of the social media profile. All users are vertically compelled to present themselves through the same informational categories consisting of similar sets of variables and sequenced in the same way. We might greet this charge of verticalism with some surprise, thinking that there is no other way it could be. But consider the alternatives, including some of the technologically most-proximate alternatives—someone who presents themselves not on social media but on a handmade website is in certain respects subject to less verticalization. Whatever other vices and virtues may attend to each technology of presentation, one is decidedly less verticalized than the other and thereby exhibits a less-hierarchical structure.

Rigidified requirements, incontestable exclusions, and verticalized protocols are among the many techniques of authoritarian hierarchy. What leads to the adoption and acceptance of such techniques? Although there can be no single answer to this question, one consistent thread running through all authoritarianisms is that of epistemological overconfidence. Authoritarians are convinced that they know things that more circumspect observers affirm as unknowable. This epistemic conviction often originates in some prior success—a killer technological innovation or a booming business model. The authoritarian style makes much hay of such successes. Impressed by the bluster and bravado of a leader who claims on that basis to know something special, followers come to devotedly share the faith—indeed, so much so that they dismiss and even eventually demonize those who fail to see the same. Thereby is social division sown. Soon after sprouts a rampant hierarchy.

A distinguishing mark of authoritarianism is its idealizing tendency to overgeneralize its earlier successes. The epistemological error of overconfidence involves a failure to see both the sheer luck that contributed to whatever went well before and the improbability of applying at scale what worked in one domain at one time to drastically different circumstances. Missing in authoritarianism is the epistemological fallibilism that has long been a cornerstone for humbled tolerance in political matters. Thus does authoritarianism manifest in a politics of hubris that cuts against both the progressive vision in pluralistic democracy as well as the conservative caution in free-market capitalism that stands resolutely opposed to the excessive confidence exhibited not only by zealous state actors but also monopolistic corporate enterprises.[5] And thus does authoritarianism similarly manifest in technology in such forms as the unbridled pursuit of disruption for its own sake, neglecting to consider both the wider social values our technologies should serve as well as the unanticipated collateral losses involved in sweeping away current socio-technical configurations.

These hierarchical tendencies as they are made manifest particularly in data technology can be more precisely conceptualized by way of the triptych framing I laid out in the introduction specifying the *problematic, potentiality,* and *peril* of data technology. I begin with the problem, noting that this term does not refer to the bad side of data technology (which is the peril of data hierarchy) but rather to the fraught challenges and instabilities that condition our relationships to data technology.

My previous book, *How We Became Our Data*, develops an account of the problematic of data technologies in terms of a general tendency in data systems whereby people become fastened to their data, and more specifically to the formats that configure any participation in and use of a data technology.[6] *Fastening* refers to the process of tying ourselves, and each other, to specific formats (often referred to as *data structures*) in a way that also speeds up our participation with each other. *Formatting* refers to the process of assembling data structures (such as information ontologies, database rules, technologically instantiated conceptual requirements) to which people can be, and also often are, fastened. A central argument in my previous book is that observing the work of fastening enacted through ensembles of formats helps bring into view the political power of data. Data are more than innocent little technological devices. Data are in fact urgent political and ethical phenomena in that they pin down and default set us as subjects. This constitutes what I call the *infopolitics* of our contemporary moment, in reference to the political problematic in which we as *informational persons* have been enrolled.

The infopolitics of fastening, I argue, can take many forms. Not all of them are bad, and certainly not all are good. Overall, infopolitics constitutes a horizon, or a terrain, of action. This terrain is the problematization within which we must act, if we act at all. Infopolitics is a condition of action for our contemporary world that carries dangers as well as opportunities. *Data equality* refers to the potentiality inherent in more-equal data regimes. *Data hierarchy* points to the perils of the divided data society we increasingly find ourselves in.

In the face of being obligatorily fastened to our formats, we informational persons need distinguish between better and worse forms of fastening. Hierarchical iterations of fastening are at the current moment running rampant—this is data hierarchy. As data hierarchy scales the ladder toward its authoritarian extremes, it enacts an increasingly verticalized fastening that operates through ever more rigid and fixed formats. But data hierarchy is not enacted, as it were, all at once. It is often slow in its accumulation and quiet in its operation. Its processes involve probabilities rather than absolutes. Thus, better, because more-equal, forms of data fastening are possible and therefore ought to be cultivated—this is data equality.

The most problematic, or most concerning, form of inequality enacted by hierarchy is not the most obvious. Hierarchy often consists in certain notable differentials in status—for example, between a leader and the people, or between a corporative executive and a user of their platform. These differentials are often concerning in themselves. But they should not be our primary concern. What is most problematic about hierarchy, both in its authoritarian extreme but also in its more humble ordinary manifestations, is its tendency to produce inequalities of relations throughout the populace (or the user base). What is concerning about hierarchical structures is the divisive inequality between persons (or users) that they foment.

A leading technological example is the polarization abetted by social media platforms.[7] What is most concerning about online polarization is its fomentation as a form of hierarchy within the platform—an issue that is separate from the hierarchy in the relationship between corporate platform designs and users subject to those designs. As more and more of our lives migrate toward social media shares and other verticalized information ecologies, we find ourselves at increasingly deeper odds with each other. This kind of polarization is a partial effect of data technologies that engineer division into their basic computational functioning—for example, through the division between one's "friends" and everyone else on the platform who is therefore implicitly defined as "not a friend." Looking at these platforms from the outside, we might be disinclined to think of such forms of social sorting as hierarchical. Yet when looked at from within, the polarization internal to these platforms appears hierarchical in the tendency of separate groups to view themselves as in some ways better than others, often in the sense of supposedly knowing something important that those outside of the group do not know. What matters here are assumed hierarchies operative within a platform, even if those looking at the platform from the outside can see no status differentials.

If there is anything surprising about all of this, it is only that the corporations purveying social media have successively done so under the slogan of connecting people, when in fact their technologies are very well designed (though perhaps not always intentionally) to drive people apart. Data hierarchy's enactment of technological separation is visible not only in polarization but also in other significant effects of data technologies, including segmentation on the basis of prediction, competition as incentivized by gamification, declining trust in online interactions; online disinformation, and (as discussed in detail below, in part 4) data-driven personalization.

To resist these and other data hierarchies in which we find ourselves increasingly enmeshed, and to repel the data authoritarianism toward which those hierarchies are tending, we need a fuller pursuit of data egalitarianism. The egalitarian alternative to data hierarchy—that more-democratic path forward in a technological society heavily reliant on data—is focused on democratic relations between and among all those subject to data.

Rather than instituting requirements in a vertical fashion from the top, what requirements there are would be achieved horizontally, that is, collaboratively. Those requirements would therefore be subject to ongoing negotiation and contestation rather than being templatized. The requirements to which users of more-egalitarian systems would be fastened would not be fixed, but rather would be temporary outcomes of ongoing democratic processes. The data systems themselves would not be overwhelming to those who are subject to them but would be sites of collaborative participation among people who can and do relate to each other as equals.

A pressing question for the contemporary moment thus concerns the persistence of the hierarchical style as an obstacle to more-egalitarian alternatives. How does hierarchy hold in place within technologies, and even within data systems whose designers ostensibly seek the path of social good through data? A starting point for answering this question can be found in the historical patterns that underlie persisting hierarchies. Such patterns are widely recognized by more than just critical academic scholars. They are also frequently acknowledged by corporate leaders and technology researchers, who eagerly draw our attention to them as the explanatory variable whenever a new machine-learning implementation leads to unexpectedly undesirable results. The algorithm's bias is a function of biases in the historical data, they say. At the heart of this defense is an obdurate fact: computational systems that analyze data are, as Shannon Vallor notes of artificial intelligence, "built to *conserve* the patterns of the past and extend them into our futures."[8] As data technologies spread throughout society over the past century and more, they became ever more entrenched in multiple extant hierarchies. And as those data technologies became entrenched in inequalities, those same inequalities became ever more embedded in data.

Consider a figure in whose legacy is condensed the complicated configurations of historical hierarchy. The Victorian polymath Francis Galton is a profoundly impactful predecessor for today's technological hierarchies.[9] Galton remains for us today a paradigm of hierarchy in light of his prominent role in white supremacist projects like racial eugenics. "It is in the most unqualified manner that I object to pretensions of natural equality," he once wrote, summing up his effortless elitism.[10] Of further interest is that Galton pursued his hierarchical visions through a multitude of data technologies that he himself innovated, such as the technique of statistical correlation.[11] Undeniable is Galton's sheer genius in having developed techniques of informational manipulation that remain among the fundamental tools of statistical analysis today. Galton is so interesting because he was so complicated. And that matters insofar as things are also complicated for us too.[12]

That which is complicated is so often simplistically approached. Galton's odious racist beliefs are, well, odious by our lights today. It is therefore often thought, and even more often just assumed, that we can simply disclaim Galton's racism and thereby sever his data technology from its data hierarchies. Galton put his innovations in statistical correlation, percentile ranking, and regression to the mean to undeniably cruel uses. But we need not put them to bad use today, for there is no meaningful sense in which eugenic aspirations lurk furtively inside statistical correlation as such. This truism noted, on one prominent version of this line of thinking we need not worry ourselves over these techniques and technologies at all, insofar as they are essentially neutral. Yet a faith in tech neutrality fails to counter the inertia of historical hierarchy, and in fact tends to reproduce it by simply allowing inequalities to remain in place.

Neutrality about Technology

The view that technologies are value-neutral appears to many observers to extend easily across a vast range of technologies, from statistical regression analyses to generative artificial intelligence.[13] Tech neutrality sounds like good common sense: the tool itself cannot cause harm because someone must first wield it before it can do anything at all. However, this view is only a simplification staring in the face of a complication. It is not so much that the view is wrong as that it is wrong-headed.

The thesis of tech neutrality is on the ascendant today in that it helps underwrite all manner of contemporary techno-enthusiasms: techno-optimism, techno-solutionism, techno-utopianism. To be sure, such buoyant outlooks often stray from strict tech neutrality by regarding technologies as inevitably beneficial. Yet tech neutrality serves as a kind of guarantee for these views by giving them something to fall back on when things go unexpectedly wrong. Failures can be laid at the feet of failing users, leaving the technology ensconced in its promised beneficence.

The thesis of tech neutrality makes its mistake in running together two distinct claims. One of these claims is straightforward enough: technologies can be used for good or for ill. I endorse this claim, but only with reference to particular technologies. Some technologies, such as biological weapon delivery systems, are not in any meaningful sense capable of being used for good. Other technologies, like statistical correlation, afford both good and bad uses. By endorsing this first claim, my view diverges from an argument commonly asserted by techno-pessimist critics of tech neutrality—namely, that there are furtive codes of hierarchy inevitably inscribed within our technologies that render those technologies necessarily oppressive. Some might think statistical correlation is necessarily and surreptitiously hierarchical in light of its contingent entanglements in Galton's strident pursuit of racial hierarchy. This is a weak argument. I accept the contrasting claim, subject to empirical scrutiny, that statistical correlation can be drafted into service both on behalf of racist data predictions but also on behalf of valuable projects, like quantitative analyses of the racially disparate impacts of social policies.

The claim that tools can be used for good or for ill is true enough so far as it goes, but it also does not get us nearly as far as adherents of tech neutrality think. Where this first claim certainly does not get us is to a second claim on behalf of a much stronger conclusion. This second claim is that technologies, or at least some specified class of technologies, are themselves neutral, that is, neither good nor bad. This claim is the heart of any robust statement of tech neutrality. Yet this strong supposition does not follow at all from straightforward observations of good and bad use.

TECHNOLOGICAL NEUTRALITY AND ACTUAL TECHNOLOGICAL OPERATION

The strong conclusion on behalf of tech neutrality can be motivated in one of two ways. The first, which results in what I will call *context neutrality*, relies on the belief that technologies can be neutrally deployed in contexts that are themselves neutral. The second, which yields what I will call *tool neutrality*, involves the claim that technologies can be evaluated independent of their actual deployments. Both views share a common logical strategy—they move from the observation that something can be used either for good or for ill to an imagined ideal of something being used for neither good nor ill. My objection to this strategy can be stated somewhat technically as follows: ambivalence does not entail indeterminacy (that x can be either true or false does not entail that x can be neither true nor false). Stated less technically, the crux of my argument is that the possibility of something being used for good or bad does not somehow whisk into existence a third possibility for which we have no evidence—namely, that it can be used for neither good nor bad. To spell out the details of my argument, I will start with context neutrality, for it is the simpler view of the two (and is also the position that tool neutrality often ends up falling back on).

Context neutrality holds that technologies can be neutral when deployed in contexts that are themselves neutral. For example, a responsible application of statistical correlation in social contexts that are themselves neutral is taken to leave things as they are without inflicting significant harm. The problem with this view is that there are few, if any, contexts of deployment that admit of neutrality. Consider a society characterized by deep racial inequalities. Statistical correlation could be used to deepen these inequalities (in, say, discriminatory predictive policing) or to lessen it (in, say, disparate impact analyses that prove the existence of illegal discrimination). But what is not possible is for statistical correlation to be actually deployed at scale in a way that is itself neutral by being neither discriminatory nor antidiscriminatory. Actual cases of use are going to fall out one way or the other. There is in an already-unequal society no third option of an actual use that is going to be neither good nor bad. This is because deploying even the most facially neutral instrument in a society characterized by inequality can at best only serve the reproduction of extant inequalities. The argument implicit in context neutrality relies on an unrealistic idealization: that society is somehow itself already sufficiently neutral. But a society is a fraught order, holding in balance an enormous number of underlying conflicts, strategies, and hierarchies that cannot be assumed away. We can disinter Galton's technique of statistical correlation from the hierarchical uses to which he put it, yes; but we cannot on that basis alone expect to deploy this technique in a social context from which histories of hierarchy have been erased. Those histories still structure social practices today.

Next, consider tool neutrality. On the basis of evaluating a tool independent of its use, this view understands the tool as neither good nor bad. This view wrongly moves from the idea of a technology conceived independent of its uses to the quite separate idea that someone could ever actually wield that technology as a neutral tool. One way to see the error here is to consider what kind of question neutrality is supposed to answer. The presumed third status of technologies as neither good nor bad is an evaluative status answering an evaluating question. Concepts appropriate for evaluation arise only in a context where some entity is in some way responsible. Responsibility in turn implies some degree of agency. Where there is no agency over technology, there is no responsibility over technology, and there can therefore be no relevant question of an evaluation of neutrality. But wherever someone (or something) is related to a technology as an agent, the elusive third status cannot be attributed, for the operation of a technology by an agent can only ever be either good or bad, but never neither good nor bad. This last point follows from the rejection of context neutrality. Since tool neutrality cannot fall back on context neutrality, the only way to salvage the view is to assert that a tool can be evaluated appropriately without respect to any of its possible uses. The argument in tool neutrality thus ends up relying on the idealization that evaluation can function appropriately independent of actual operations, uses, and impacts.[14]

In both of its two forms, the running common sense of tech neutrality involves what comes down to much the same idealization. Context neutrality idealizes a conception of a neutral social context. Tool neutrality idealizes a conception of a tool independent of its practical deployment. Idealizing social context disregards or ignores actual social practice. Idealizing tool use similarly disregards actual social practice. And only by ignoring actual social practice can we move from tools being either good or bad to tools being neither good nor bad. But where actual practice is taken to matter, we can recognize that certain technologies can be either good or bad (and sometimes both, in some degree), yet never neither.

HOW TECHNOLOGICAL NEUTRALITY PERPETUATES DATA HIERARCHY

Both forms of tech neutrality involve a failure to recognize the extent to which the forces that structure actually existing contemporary society today are heavily entrenched in histories of hierarchy. One way of denying the reality of structural patterns of hierarchy is to just neglect entirely the project of assessing or describing social context at a structural level. The neglect or denial of social structure is often motivated by assuming that a different kind of question is more pertinent, most typically a question about beliefs.

In introducing Galton's statistical techniques above, I noted that a common reaction today to his work on eugenics is to disclaim it in hopes of thereby assuming a position of default neutrality with respect to the continued use of statistical correlation today. This fits a more general pattern according to which those professing the neutrality of data technology tend to take enormous pride in data while they think of themselves as having disowned any attitudes of hierarchy. They do this by declining to consider inequalities as features of social structure, focusing instead on forms of inequality that can be made sense of in terms of individual attitudes like prejudice or bias. In short, the pattern relies on neglecting structural analyses focused on social conditions in favor of attitudinal analyses focused on the beliefs held by those who design, deploy, or use technologies. By attending to attitudes, those endorsing tech neutrality proudly regard themselves as possessing morally upright views. Galton's eugenics are disclaimed as odious in a way that is meant to secure for statisticians a presumption of moral neutrality. But the presumption simply does not follow. The reason is not because statisticians assessing themselves as unprejudiced are wrong about themselves—it is rather because they are asking quite the wrong question. They are asking about the attitudes (beliefs, desires, and hopes) of individuals like themselves when what is really at stake are the operative social structures within which individuals act.

At the heart of the neutrality thesis is a tendency to neglect those structural conditions that configure how technologies actually operate in favor of a focus on attitudinal statuses in virtue of which agents appear praiseworthy or blameworthy. But prioritizing attitude over structure is mistaken for purposes of evaluation—at least, with respect to such evaluative notions as equality, justice, and fairness, which do not refer to properties of direct relations between people but to properties of general social structures. Neglecting structure thus effectively adds to the inertia of whatever social structures are currently entrenched and, along with them, whatever inequalities and injustices those structures tend to propagate.

Algorithmic Fairness and Its Limits

Hierarchy and neutrality are general ideas. I turn now to a more specific ideal. Where a normative assessment of data technology is at issue, the ideal of algorithmic fairness stands out as particularly prominent. But algorithmic fairness is beset by a number of interrelated problems. One particularly notable problem is that this ideal often functions unexpectedly as a mechanism for attributing neutrality to algorithms (specifically those algorithms that have been shown to be fair) in a way that enables computational systems employing these algorithms to reproduce historical hierarchies. Seeing this takes some showing.

The problem with algorithmic fairness is not that it is wrong (like hierarchy) or that it is wrong-headed (like neutrality). In fact, algorithmic fairness is, within certain limitations, quite right. The problem is just these limitations. Algorithmic fairness is often presented as the singular solution to problems of inequality in data technology. Yet the limits of this ideal make it unsuitable as a complete concept of equality in data. Algorithmic fairness is necessary, but insufficient, for data equality.

A survey of the limits of algorithmic fairness is needed insofar as this ideal has become something of a consensus concept among academic researchers, industry professionals, and policy analysts focused on data ethics.[15] This consensus poses both an opportunity and a problem. The problem is that algorithmic fairness now dominates discussions in data ethics to the exclusion of other ideas. But if algorithmic fairness is insufficient for data equality, as I will show, then other ideas are needed. The opportunity here is that algorithmic fairness can be reconceived as an initial first step toward a more robust approach to data equality. My argument is that those who have already taken that first step can and ought to take a step beyond the limits of algorithmic fairness.

My argument develops an internal critique of algorithmic fairness—that is, a critique that delineates problematic implications and erroneous assumptions internal to the idea itself. This argument builds on the skeptical case about algorithmic fairness I considered in the introduction: the technology anthropologist Rodrigo Ochigame's account of the influence of the tech industry on the development of much of the scholarly research in support of algorithmic fairness.[16] One reply to Ochigame could always be that the ignoble origins of algorithmic fairness do not prove that the idea itself is flawed. Maybe an industry can fund research on the ethics of its products in a way that actually gets it right. The probability of this is far lower than many scholars of data ethics would like to think. But surely there is an abstract possibility here. An internal critique of algorithmic fairness is thus needed to show why advocates for ethical data technology should not count on this possibility.

Before limning the limits of the ideal of algorithmic fairness, it first needs to be defined. Although data ethics is quite recent as a stable research field, algorithmic fairness has already emerged as a leading concept. As Luke Stark, Daniel Greene, and Anna Lauren Hoffmann observe with respect to the field of artificial intelligence, "Technical tools for mitigating bias in AI systems have coalesced around strategies for ensuring fairness."[17] This consensus view is animated by a conception of fairness as aiming toward, or at least exhibiting the qualities of, what is frequently labeled "formal fairness" or "mathematical fairness." Fairness so conceived provides a response to what is widely taken to be the root problem in these systems: statistically discoverable forms of unjustifiable bias due to algorithmic processing.[18]

One reason there is such deep agreement in support of algorithmic fairness is that there is wide latitude when interpreting this idea. Deborah Hellman observes that the field is "littered with a multitude of measures" of algorithmic fairness.[19] Sahil Verma and Julia Rubin count twenty competing conceptions.[20] The many metrics of fairness are often grouped into three broad classes: statistical (or group-based) fairness, individual (or similarity-based) fairness, and causal fairness.[21] Such a multiplicity of measures is not in and of itself a problem if we can coordinate them with methodologies that determine which measures are appropriate for which circumstances. Deirdre Mulligan and colleagues have taken steps toward developing such a methodology.[22] Yet confusion persists.

In addition to all this confusion, recent scholarship leveraging statistical reasoning has posed some serious technical challenges to algorithmic fairness. Two are particularly notable. The first is the well-known finding that some leading measures of fairness are mutually incompatible, often referred to as the "impossibility of fairness" results.[23] If the mere presence of multiple measures causes confusion about which one to choose, the fact that certain pairings cannot be satisfied appears to cast doubt on the reliability of the very concept of fairness itself. A second technical challenge—much more recent, and so as yet undigested by most scholarship—is even more concerning for standard approaches to fairness in binary classification algorithms. A recent finding by A. Feder Cooper and colleagues shows that when training predictive models, the simple work of harnessing different subsamples of those data to build a training set results in levels of statistical variance that are so high as to effectively make prediction arbitrary for a significant share of cases.[24] This argument deals a major blow to current approaches to algorithmic fairness, insofar as this research typically relies on evaluating the fairness of a single model rather than evaluating "distributions over possible models for a given learning process" that can be generated by taking multiple subsamples.[25]

Despite these technical challenges, a continuing consensus in favor of algorithmic fairness persists, at least for now. There is some indication that concerns are beginning to take root even within the machine-learning community itself.[26] And if we cast a wider net including scholarship about machine learning by researchers in adjacent critical fields, then there are clear signs of serious concerns about algorithmic fairness.[27] My argument advances two important lines of criticism emerging in this recent scholarship.

ALGORITHMIC FAIRNESS AS AN IDEALIZATION

The first line of criticism of algorithmic fairness I consider is well expressed in Annette Zimmermann and Chad Lee-Stronach's claim that researchers aiming at formalized fairness "do not intervene in the social world, but in the algorithmic model" in a way that is problematic in the face of "a nonideal real-world social context."[28] Algorithms are too often looked at through idealizing assumptions.

One prominent instance of this involves an understanding of fairness-satisfying algorithms as technologically neutral in precisely the sense discussed earlier in the chapter. According to this understanding, algorithms that satisfy fairness metrics, and yet get deployed in systems that nevertheless produce harms, can still be presumed neutral in that the harms can be regarded as the result of bad data inputs ("garbage in") or harmful implementations ("bad actors") rather than an effect of the algorithm itself. My argument that this view relies on tech neutrality may seem unexpected. After all, the goal of algorithm fairness begins with the insight that algorithms can in fact be harmful. Yet this insight gets lost in the idealized conception of the algorithmic model as exhibiting fairness in itself outside of any actual social context. The leading insight that harms may ensue from algorithms needs to be given a wider scope—harms accrue not just from the algorithm but from across the computational system in its actual practical use in actual social situations.

Particular data technologies always demand assessment in terms of the real-world impacts of particular algorithms and formats. Such assessment requires evaluative methodologies that are prepared to interrogate real impacts. Yet, Zimmermann and Lee-Stronach argue, scholarship in support of algorithmic fairness too often forwards a "restricted" and even "obfuscatory" picture of how data technologies actually operate.[29] One way of putting this point is to say that algorithmic fairness involves idealizations that leave us unprepared to achieve precisely what this ideal claims to provide: a diagnosis of harms in data technology. Algorithmic fairness blocks certain real harms from view, insofar as it relies on idealizing assumptions about how algorithms operate in the wild.

I have mentioned idealizing assumptions a few times now, and each time disparagingly. It is important to be precise about what is being claimed in attributing idealization to algorithmic fairness, tech neutrality, or anything else. A related, and very common, argument about data technology here looms in the wings. According to this other argument, all data are abstractions and should therefore be rejected. It is one thing to critique specific ethical ideals for data technology because they presuppose idealizations. It is quite another thing to criticize data technology itself for implementing abstractions. It is crucial to not confuse critiques of the limits of idealizations with more generalized criticisms of abstraction as such.[30] This confusion has proven especially tempting to critical data studies scholars. It is true that all data are abstractions. And it is also true that all abstractions entail risks. With this much in view, many critical data studies scholars have adopted a posture of default suspicion toward all abstracting data as such.[31] Such skepticism toward data's "displacement of situated, informal, qualitative knowledges" is today so widespread that Christopher Newfield, Anna Alexandrova, and Stephen John label it "the Original Critique" in their introduction to an influential collection of interdisciplinary essays on quantitative reasoning.[32] An overly skeptical stance poses obstacles to effective inquiry. It prevents us from getting inside of data's abstractions to understand what is going well, what is going wrong, and also just what is going on. It forestalls engaging with the politics and ethics of actual practices of abstraction, modeling, and datafication. In data-saturated social configurations such as ours, the most effective counter to the real risks of abstraction is not to abandon abstracting data in hopes of mounting something else that is somehow supposedly immune from abstraction, but rather to build better abstractions. Idealization gets in the way of the crucial work of inquiring into how abstractions operate.

Similar to outright data skepticism, my concern with algorithmic fairness is that it mounts an idealization of the very technology it is meant to assess. So how exactly does algorithmic fairness idealize? One way is in operating with an idealization of equality as a purely distributive matter. This brings me to the second of the two lines of recent criticism of algorithmic fairness my argument advances.

ALGORITHMIC FAIRNESS AS A
METRIC FOR DISTRIBUTION

Models of algorithmic fairness operate with an assumption that distributive equality is the correct framework for assessing inequalities produced by algorithms. Concerns about this assumed framework are beginning to emerge in critical scholarship. Hoffmann was the first to develop this critique in detail in calling attention to "data-based discriminations beyond distribution."[33] Sina Fazelpour, Zachary Lipton, and David Danks more recently observe of "fairness-enhancing" algorithmic design that these interventions are focused "narrowly on the properties of allocation outputs" in isolation from "broader dynamics" in a way that "can result in distorted evaluations."[34] Atoosa Kasirzadeh similarly notes that "the primary focus of philosophical investigations of algorithmic fairness has been rooted, in one way or another, in accounts of distributive justice."[35]

In line with these critical observations, a central argument of this book is that when we are concerned with equality, there is more that we ought to care about than just distributions of goods. Critics of the limits of algorithmic fairness, coming as they do from different disciplines and theoretical perspectives, stand in need of a unifying idea for what can augment, extend, or even replace algorithmic fairness. The concept of data equality serves this unifying need.[36] Proponents (and even most critics) of algorithmic fairness have yet to consider—or even be fully confronted with—the distinction between distributive and relational equality.[37] The concept of data equality begins with a notion of relational equality (or democratic equality) that is both broader and deeper than the limiting assumptions of distributive equality. In the same way that theorists of relational egalitarianism have described the views of distributive egalitarians as largely correct and yet needlessly narrow, a concept of data equality helps us recognize the narrowing limits of the idea of algorithmic fairness. In this, my approach agrees with Hoffmann's observation that models of algorithmic fairness are unable to "account for the (re)production of the full range of social hierarchy."[38] Putting hierarchical inequality first, rather than starting with unequal allotments of pie slices of goods, helps us see why algorithmic fairness both is a necessary component of full-scale data equality but also on its own falls far short of robust relational data equality.

I still need to describe exactly how the limits of the distributivist framing are operative within algorithmic fairness. There are at least two ways that distributivist assumptions typically underwrite algorithmic fairness. One concerns a focus on computational bias as the problem to which fairness is a response; the other concerns a focus on algorithmic processing as the technical location where bias creeps in.

The Focus of Algorithmic Fairness: Biased Distribution

The vast majority of work on algorithmic fairness presents this ideal as a candidate solution to problems of computational bias. A familiar context for these problems is that of predictive (or otherwise classificatory) determinations made by a machine-learning (or otherwise algorithmic) system. These predictions are distributed across those subject to them in ways that benefit some and burden others. For example, credit-scoring systems make predictions about individuals in ways that tend to confer benefits associated with higher ratings. These predictions, and so the benefits or burdens they confer, can be biased. Predictive algorithms have been shown to be actually biased in numerous cases across a range of domains: credit scoring, employment, health diagnostics, parole sentencing, recidivism assessment, and education.[39] These biases are particularly concerning when they adversely impact members of historically disadvantaged groups, thereby qualifying as discriminatory bias.[40] Problems of discriminatory bias as they figure in algorithmic fairness thus involve concerns with the distribution of comparative advantages and disadvantages associated with machine-made classifications.[41] The focus for algorithmic fairness is therefore on mitigating the biased distributions of algorithmic predictions and, by proxy, the biased distributions of benefits and burdens flowing from those predictions.

It is notable that algorithmic fairness does not address why underlying biases exist or persist in the first place. Yet it is worth pausing to consider how concerns with discriminatory bias can ever emerge. Concerns with bias are at their most salient (and only qualify as discrimination) when the biases at issue adversely impact members of groups who have historically been treated as inferiors in the context of hierarchy. So while discriminatory bias often shows up as a problem of distribution, it is also conceptually rooted in the historical inheritance of relational inequality. An unequal distribution is unlikely to be discriminatory where it is not the product of unequal relations. A weather event spoiling one farmer's crops and nourishing another's produces inequality but not biased inequality. Whether the lasting effects of such a natural inequality are unjustifiably biased is an interesting question (for instance, with respect to the availability of crop insurance), but either way, the inequality itself does not qualify as biased. As such, advocates of algorithmic fairness who are concerned with discriminatory bias are both right to be concerned with unequal distributions in predictions and at the same time wrong to restrict the sphere of their concern just to distributive matters, given that such maldistributions can be taken to be problematic biases only where generated by a pattern of hierarchical inequality. Stated more positively, proponents of algorithmic fairness stand in need, by their own lights, of a fuller theory of equality for data technologies. Unfortunately, this need is often fulfilled unreflectively when implementations of algorithmic fairness are plugged in to existing classifications for the sake of compliance. This is not nothing. Nor is it enough.

The Object of Algorithmic Fairness: Algorithmic Processing

A second observation that clarifies the distributivist assumptions limning conceptions of algorithmic fairness concerns the tendency of these conceptions to take algorithmic processing as their primary object of concern. This may seem like an utterly obvious point—of course algorithmic fairness is concerned with algorithms. But the unobvious implications of this point are worth considering.

A useful starting point here is the observation that where one's normative conception of equality is restricted to concerns with distribution, then one's focus may be consistently restricted to a concern with a value of fairness as operational over procedures for distribution. Distributive equality, considered purely on its own without respect to its premises, can be satisfied by fair procedures for distribution, as is shown by John Rawls's theory of justice, and specifically his argument establishing the difference principle.[42] However, from this observation we can also begin to see that where one's normative conception of equality is concerned with more than just distribution, fair procedures may not be enough to achieve equality so conceived.

The typical way algorithmic fairness gets operationalized is through measures focused on the outputs yielded by algorithmic processes. Take again the example of algorithmic credit ratings. A ratings algorithm that yields a biased distribution is taken to be biased in its process. Algorithmic processing is sometimes so complex (indeed, even to the point of inscrutability, or opacity) that the only reliable indicator for what happens within the algorithm are its outcomes.[43] Where this is the case, outcomes are analyzed as proxies for what goes on within opaque processing. Whether a given algorithm is opaque or transparent, the center of attention is always on the algorithmic process itself. The algorithm is that which is fair or unfair.

Proponents of algorithmic fairness neglect any inequalities not fully reducible to the algorithmic processing stage of computational treatment.[44] Nina Grgić-Hlača and colleagues observe about machine-learning fairness: "To date, most works on fair learning have focused on achieving a fair distribution of decision outcomes."[45] This general observation has been echoed by research on fair machine learning in the domain of education; for instance, Ryan Baker and Aaron Hawn's note that "much of this recent work addressing algorithmic bias has focused on mitigating bias at the model evaluation and postprocessing stages of the machine learning pipeline."[46] The field is focused on how algorithms process data, with little attention given to the prior stage of formatting data for input. Baker and Hawn rightly emphasize that "fairer algorithms" are "a step towards" but not a complete account of equality in data.[47] In the face of this limitation, they advocate for "improving data collection," though they leave this unspecified beyond a call to "collect extensive demographic data."[48] This is a step in the right direction but as a generalized approach remains limited, infrequent, and theoretically underdeveloped. Subsequent chapters develop a fuller account of how to achieve better (understood as more egalitarian) data-collection, -curation, and -labeling practices. For now, what is important to register is that for the purposes of interrogating inequality, a focal range limited to algorithms is needlessly restrictive. What about biases, or other problematic forms of inequality, that are not functions of algorithmic processing? What about problems where inequalities are at least partially a function of the data that form inputs for the algorithmic processors?

Technological Neutrality and Data Hierarchy in Algorithmic Fairness

The most common response to the possibility (and even the actuality) of inequality or bias in input data is a subtle form of tech neutrality: quickly dismiss it as somebody else's problem. The algorithm is frequently taken to be the engineer's sole responsibility. When conditions of algorithmic fairness are satisfied and problems nevertheless ensue, it follows that these problems are somebody else's responsibility—typically, whoever (or whatever) is responsible for the unequal input data. Oftentimes it is assumed that the inequalities yielded by the operative system are simply mirrors of preexisting social inequalities, such that the fault lands at the feet of society itself. Wherever the blame falls, it is not on the algorithm, because this is taken to be neutral in virtue of satisfying a fairness metric. Notice, however, that neutrality can be ascribed to the algorithm only if the algorithm is abstracted from the actual operations of the computational system. By way of this subtle idealization, algorithmic fairness simultaneously invites tech neutrality through the front door and thereby leaves the back door unattended for data hierarchy to maintain its unwanted presence.

Algorithmic fairness, as theorized to date, relies on a false dilemma between correcting bias in algorithms and dismissing data-born inequalities as an unavoidable effect of existing social inequalities. There is, however, an unexplored third option. In many important cases, unequal data inputs may flow from how data are structured or formatted. A central aim of this book is to bring into view this third possibility of focusing on formats as value-laden technologies.

Getting formats in view enables us to clearly distinguish a third class of cases where current debates about algorithmic fairness proceed with an assumption that only two kinds of cases are possible. The first kind is where algorithmic modeling is demonstrably shown to yield biased predictions. For instance, in a widely circulated exposé of a criminological risk prediction tool, Julie Angwin and colleagues at *ProPublica* analyzed the tool's data outputs to show that Black data subjects were far more likely to receive higher-risk predictions than White data subjects.[49] The second kind of case is where an algorithmic system is trained on input data that are themselves unequal, or otherwise problematic, in a way that results in models that reproduce the problem. Kristian Lum and William Isaac show how criminological risk assessment tools whose models are trained on existing crime data are often still biased insofar as historical crime data was itself produced by biased policing practices.[50] Critics pointing to bias in historical data often intend to show that using assessment algorithms in criminological contexts has a much higher burden of proof to demonstrate equality or justice than previously thought. But too often, technologists (and the corporations employing them) take arguments like this as evidence that they can rightly disclaim responsibility for any bias resulting from their algorithms—for, they argue, the bias exhibited by an algorithmic model merely reflects already-existing societal bias in a way that does not implicate the algorithm. This leaves out a crucial third class of cases: those in which inequalities in a computational system are generated, or even just magnified, by problematic data formats. Consider how criminological data can be biased against certain populations not because of bias in policing or judicial practices, but due to data-collection, -curation, and -collation techniques. For example, racial bias in risk assessments can show up with anomalies that result from the merging of different databases that employ different taxonomies of race, as often happens when data sourced from criminal justice contexts is joined to a database sourced from medical or psychiatric evaluations. Such issues of what is often called *data interoperability* require data analysts to consider difficult questions that typically cannot be answered simply on the basis of existing datasets—and unfortunately, these decisions often get made pell-mell.[51]

Where this third class of cases is left out of view, we come to an impasse: computational harms are either due to the design of the algorithm (which the satisfaction of fairness conditions can then be presumed to cure) or are the uncontrollable accident of social realities that the input data merely reflect. This false dilemma not only safeguards the algorithm itself as a purportedly neutral tool (when shown to satisfy fairness conditions), it also safeguards the data formats as neutral too, insofar as they are disregarded as a potential source of values getting designed into the system.

There are countless examples of precisely this impasse in algorithmic fairness scholarship.[52] Consider the discussion of algorithmic fairness by Michael Kearns and Aaron Roth in their influential book *The Ethical Algorithm*.[53] Their chapter on algorithmic fairness describes techniques for resolving bias in algorithmic models as "one of the most exciting areas of ongoing research."[54] Following a detailed discussion, they briefly consider at the conclusion of the chapter the possibility of bias in input data: "Here the problem is not the algorithm but the mismatch between the input to the algorithm and the real world, caused by the bias already embedded in the data."[55] Having raised the problem, they have almost nothing to say about it other than to chalk it up to a classic case of "bias in, bias out"—a variation on the old computer science "garbage in, garbage out" quip about junky data.[56] The contrast in how Kearns and Roth regard the two kinds of bias is telling. Regarding bias in algorithms, they claim that "the design of fair machine learning algorithms can be made scientific and is (at least in principle) easy to implement in practice," but concerning bias in data, they insist that "these problems are as much social as algorithmic, and are accordingly more difficult," such that effective solutions are "simply impractical to implement."[57] In other words, bias in input data is not a problem that the coder or the engineer needs to concern themselves with. It is an impractical object of concern for computer science. What we see so vividly here is that the focus for advocates of algorithmic fairness has become so firmly fixated on computational solutions to bias that advocates can now just casually brush aside cases that do not admit of a computational solution. But Kearns and Roth are not only computer scientists—they are also people. Our political and ethical obligations do not stop at the doorways of the department.

Datasets, and all the formatting decisions and labor costs that go into them, are typically construed as a kind of raw resource that should be made available to the technologist, who can then freely train on them all the "compute" at their disposal. Where nobody else has built the data that are needed, technologists are rarely eager to take up the work. The first thing that will be tried is automation. But data harvesting often yields a poor crop—dirty, damaged, and deficient data that were designed for other purposes anyway. What is tried next varies. Those in the corporate sector eyeing future profits will often enter into outsourcing contracts that offshore manual data labeling tasks to impoverished workers hired at low wages who have every incentivize to confirm the expectations of their much richer employers.[58] Those in less well-funded research spaces in academia will often find themselves resorting to idiosyncratic procedures for forcing low-quality data through high-powered algorithms. An irony in all these approaches is that the implicit goal of computer science is to seek algorithmic optimization in a way that will invariably outpace the amount of insight that can be mined from extant datasets—and thus there will never ever be enough usable data. It will forever be somebody else's job to call forth more and better data.

This aversion to dealing with the difficulties of data was brought home to me at a recent AI conference. This was an international hybrid academia-industry conference with an attendee list in the thousands—3,453, to be exact.[59] A poignant moment occurred during one of those semi-informal moments in open discussion that help reveal under-documented assumptions within a scholarly field. At a small workshop session of about seventy-five attendees focused on artificial intelligence in education, a panel of scholars was asked to describe what the field needs most to make advances. There was near consensus on the panel, and no disagreement from any panelist, that the field has a striking and urgent need for better public datasets for education. After this response from the panelists, a commenter in the room chimed in, agreeing strongly. Many others nodded along. Here playing out in front of my eyes was something I had been observing in the writings and workings of data technologists for years. Yet I had never seen it in such crisp display. I was in a room filled with computer scientists, data scientists, and a handful of education scholars, most of whom were academic researchers but a substantial portion coming from industry (including from some very well-known companies) and nonprofits. Everyone in the room acknowledged that there was a need for better datasets. Yet nobody indicated that they considered it their responsibility to help construct, collect, and curate those datasets.

In the face of prevailing tendencies to downplay the work of data curation, some recent publications suggest that fault lines may be emerging on this point, even within computer science and more clearly within the fledgling field of data science.[60] We may indeed be on the cusp of a dramatic change in how technologists treat data. If so, this book is in service of that change. The change this book looks to is that of focusing more attention on how data inputs are designed (and often inadvertently) to render input data themselves, and not just the social facts these data capture, into vehicles for hierarchical inequality. If this is right, then what we need is not only fairness in algorithms, but also equality within data.

The theory of data equality can ultimately be looked at by proponents of algorithmic fairness as enriching and enlarging the central concerns that motivate a concern with values in technology. At the same time, critics of algorithmic fairness can recognize in data equality an opportunity to overcome some of the narrowing limitations of a view that seeks only fairness and only in algorithms. The proponents and the critics both have their points. We need to maintain algorithmic fairness, but also decidedly move beyond it. There are two challenges that need to be met here: expanding our concern with equality beyond fairness alone, and expanding our focus on computation beyond algorithms alone. Data equality meets both.

The first challenge requires values that reach beyond formalized fairness without abandoning altogether a respect for fairness as a necessary quality of processes of equal treatment. Data equality requires that fair algorithmic processing conditions be combined with a companion notion of equitable entry conditions without which fairness on its own is not only limited but also potentially quite harmful. I show in chapters 3 and 4 that this conception of equal treatment follows from relational equality appropriately understood. The second challenge requires an angle of technological vision that takes in more than just algorithms (or those of their proxies, such as outcome distributions). Algorithm-centered approaches to data equality have major shortcomings insofar as their target—namely, information systems and computational programs—involves not only algorithmic processors but also data formats or data structures. I show in chapters 5 and 6 that there is no good reason to attend only to the processing stage of information technology while ignoring the technical dimensions central to the input stage.

These two arguments can be combined succinctly in a formulaic statement: *equality in data = equitable entry (in formats) + fair processes (in algorithms)*. This statement, though only formulaic, expresses a richer and fuller conception of data egalitarianism than that currently held by most advocates of fair data technology. Before explicating this formula in parts 2 and 3 of the book, I turn first to offering a positive argument for data equality that pushes the needle beyond negative skepticism about algorithmic fairness.

Data Equality in Social Structure
An Opening

In the first half of the nineteenth century, Alexis de Tocqueville famously accused democracy, represented by America, of a limitless love of egalitarianism: "For equality their passion is ardent, insatiable, incessant, invincible."[1] A generation later, W. E. B. Du Bois's public and scholarly writings stood witness to his country's unrequited passion for equality with respect to race. At the same time that his essays and treatises became the voice of his nation's greatest problem of inequality, Du Bois was also quietly working on the side as one of his age's greatest innovators in informational analyses of inequalities. Du Bois the great public intellectual and race activist was also a pioneering sociologist whose contributions to both quantitative and qualitative analysis for too long went unrecognized.[2] This chapter explores Du Bois's egalitarian data work to present a motivating precedent for the concept of data equality called for in chapter 1 and developed in detail in the chapters to follow.

Why look for a precedent? Why turn to history to locate a conception for something that is needed in the present? One reason is because present-day technology, and especially today's data technology, is so often presented as wondrously outside of history. Yet we all know that data technology is historical too. By neglecting the history of present-day data technology, we fail to heed both how it has operated and how it could operate otherwise.

Du Bois's innovations in quantitative social science in the 1890s and 1900s were contemporary with Francis Galton's innovations in statistics noted in the previous chapter. The data-technological advances of both men preceded the onrushing wave of datafication that would crash over democratic nations from the 1910s to the 1930s.[3] Each was therefore prescient in sighting what the tides would soon bring in. Although Du Bois and Galton explored data techniques with very different ends in view, they nevertheless worked within the shared space of a technologically unsettled moment when a sizable data-fication apparatus was visible, but was not yet installed so widely as to become almost invisible. Theirs was a significant historical moment. Data as a structural force in our lives did not originate with information theory and cybernetics (in the 1940s), computationalism (the 1950s), digital infrastructure (the 1980s), internet culture (the 2000s), or artificial intelligence (the 2020s). It was in the early twentieth century when pathways were laid out that so much of subsequent data technology would track. Turning to a period prior to data's later consolidations gives us glimpses of unsettled moments in which early data activists and information technicians could experiment with new techniques that were far from assuming the heft they would soon come to have, and have had ever since. Where Galton's experiments were focused on how technical innovations could be harnessed to dreams of hierarchical inequality, Du Bois's work sought to show how the same could be put to work in pursuit of equality.

Yet it is crucial that Du Bois's data work not be taken as comfort for today's technologists who would like to think that their work can be used for good as much as for ill. Such comfort indulges the false promise that data technologies can be neutral in the actual context of deployment. In truth, adding that which is presumptively neutral to inequality can only ever result in reiterating inequality. Du Bois knew this quite well, and long before almost anyone else was even asking the question. He did not seek neutral data technology, but rather actively pursued equality in data.

What is most compelling in Du Bois's data designs is that he not only pursued equality *with* data, but also equality *within* the data themselves. This distinction is a fine one—much of the rest of this chapter is devoted to explicating it. To put it preliminarily, the point of this distinction is to better understand how data themselves can form a terrain upon which equality or hierarchy can be instantiated. In Du Bois's case, his data work relied on, and also amplified, the idea that unless one explicitly and fervently pursues equality within the very parameters of datafication, then inequality is almost surely bound to follow. This idea reverberates throughout his early data-centric writings, where it can be grasped in the ways he took it upon himself (almost always collaboratively with others) to produce techniques and schemas for datafication that demonstrated possibilities for, and realities of, racial equality. Du Bois's datafications exhibit a compelling strategy of pursuing equality within data as distinct from (and as presupposed by) the much more familiar work of using data as an instrument for equality. Datasets today are frequently employed as *tools for equality*—for example, in being used for statistical analyses of discriminatory disparate impacts. Far less common is the work of interrogating data as a potential *terrain for inequality* that serves to reproduce extant inequalities, exclusions, and divisions. Where data can be a tool for equality, egalitarians pursue equality *with* data. But before data can be used for that, there must first be equality *within* data.

Understanding how data form a terrain where inequalities can be meted out requires taking a structural perspective. This chapter begins by presenting the very idea of a structural perspective in a minimal form (later chapters will enrich that perspective). With this minimal structural view in place the chapter then turns to Du Bois's data work as a motivating exemplar for the theory of structural data equality (later chapters will then explicate in greater detail the two eponymous concepts of data equality defined here).

A Structural Perspective on the Informatics of Race

The idea of social structure can be provisionally conceived as referring to those elements of social order that actively configure what we can do, who we can be, and how we can relate to each other. Adopting this provisional conception, it is a crucial question for highly technological societies such as ours whether technologies are significant components of social structure so conceived. In later chapters, I develop the argument that technologies are indeed features of contemporary social structure (chapter 5) after first offering a number of crucial elaborations to the minimal idea of social structure just sketched (chapter 3). What I offer in this chapter is a first response to the crucial question of technological structure by taking it up with respect to the particular form of hierarchical racial inequality occasioned by the work of both Du Bois and Galton. This concerns the issue of how racial inequalities specifically might be reproduced through structural data technologies that constitute what I have called in previous work the *informatics of race*.[4]

A familiar distinction between structural racism (sometimes also referred to as *institutional racism*) and attitudinal racism (sometimes simply called *racial prejudice*) exemplifies and informs my structural perspective on the informatics of race.[5] This distinction demands of us that we interrogate our practices not just for overt racist attitudes, but also for covert and overt structures that reproduce racialized patterns of inequality. A concept of structural racism alerts us to the possibility that ongoing racial inequality is not just an unwanted afterimage of centuries of intentional racial domination but is more pressingly an integral part of the practical functioning of our social structures.

Considering the role of data technologies in situations pervaded by structural racism is an urgent concern in contemporary critical data studies.

Numerous scholars in this field show how recent deployments of data science risk a bevy of racial injustices, variously conceptualized as "automated inequality," "default discrimination," "algorithmic oppression," "discriminating data," and a form of technological "racism-without-racists."[6] A structural perspective underlies each of these analyses.

Structural concerns are discernible in Ruha Benjamin's description of how algorithmic decision-making—for example, that facilitated by predictive policing algorithms—is discriminatory not by intention but by design. These systems are often programmed in ways that "[build] upon already existing forms of racial domination."[7] She argues that even those who are most committed to fairness in these technologies often "still use the crime rate as the default measure of whether an algorithm is predicting fairly, when that very measure is a byproduct of ongoing regimes of selective policing."[8] The only result can be the deepening of entrenched disparities, such as disparities of unequal treatment by race. Benjamin further shows how these structural inequalities can shape even do-good high-tech projects in "technological benevolence" that often serve to reproduce already-embedded forms of discrimination despite an intention to counter it.[9]

Also with an eye toward data sciences for doing good, Virginia Eubanks discusses projects located at the intersection of social science and social welfare. Focusing on family services work, Eubanks details the construction of what she calls "the digital poorhouse."[10] Her exemplar is the Allegheny Family Screening Tool (AFST) employed by a social services agency in Rust Belt Pennsylvania. The directors of the agency, she reports, "see little downside to data collection because they understand the agency's role as primarily supportive, not punitive."[11] Theirs is a project of state-sponsored uplift. Yet similar to predictive policing algorithms, these systems are beset by the logic of self-fulfilling prophecies. In this case, "a family scored as high risk by the AFST will undergo more scrutiny than other families."[12] Higher scrutiny generates more data, and more opportunities for data-based alarms. The intention might be support, but the design promises to unequally mete out punishments.

These arguments challenge familiar assumptions that otherwise offer comfort to the idealizations that support tech neutrality. Technologists convince themselves that they can, in virtue of their own virtuous rejection of bigoted beliefs, separate today's technological implementations from yesterday's technological hierarchies insofar as technology is itself essentially neutral.[13] And with that they take their duties to be discharged. They move forward in confidence that they are deploying neutral data technologies of connection and classification without exacerbating odious hierarchies. What is stunning about this self-conception is that we know for a fact that even where racial prejudice is widely rejected, racial inequalities nevertheless persist. Given that we know this, why should we focus our scrutiny on the presence or absence of prejudicial attitudes? Given what we know, why should we not rather insist that structural forces ought to take priority in normative evaluations of inequality, injustice, and unfairness? The benefit of neutrality—at least, for those who do benefit from it—is that where the focus is on attitudes, there can be a neglect of structures, and wherever structures are not actively resisted, they are likely to remain in place, benefiting those who benefit from them.

A crucial plank in the structural view I am advancing is that hierarchies tend to hold in place unless they are actively resisted. This plank generalizes Naomi Zack's claim that "institutional racism continues through a kind of social inertia unless specific measures are taken to change it."[14] There is precision in Zack's term *inertia*; it illuminates how social structuring is a process. A generalized restatement of Zack's insight—namely, that hierarchies are inertial—implies that inequalities are not so much fixed structures as they are processes of structuring that tend to change slowly because of their immense heft. It is due to the inertia of entrenched heft that inegalitarian hierarchy can only ever be dismantled by active pursuits of equality, and never by remaining neutral. In a social setting where two groups are unequal, adding a neutral element to that setting can only leave those parties unequal. As the point can be formulaically asserted: *if $A > B$, then $A + 1 > B + 1$*.

Hierarchies are inertial and cannot be expected to dismantle themselves. If so, we ought to be able to explain how this works. How, for example, can structural racism be reproduced through data technologies designed by groups who are explicitly anti-racist in their attitudes such that they never overtly intend to exacerbate racial inequality? What is needed here is an account of a technological mechanism for the adhesion of racial hierarchy to social structure that does not rely on categories of attitudinal racial prejudice as the explanatory variable.

Consider the following description of a possible three-stage mechanism for how hierarchy may adhere or persist through technology. At the first stage, a technology is taken to be neutral. For example, statistical processing algorithms are widely believed to be neutral because usable for good or for ill. Such an assumption, where it is lodged in place, is typically bolstered by the explicitly anti-hierarchical beliefs of those deploying that technology. In virtue of their morally upright beliefs, it is often difficult for designers and users of these technologies to recognize their own complicity in inequalities. In a second stage, designers and deployers refrain from interrogating the effects of their technologies for the simple reason that these technologies are already assumed to be neutral. A firm belief in tech neutrality offers strong support for maintaining ignorance about ways in which a particular technology may not be neutral. In a third stage, these technologies are implemented with wide latitude, leaving them uninterrogated as potential linchpins for the reproduction of inequality. This happens even when the evidence piles up that inequality persists or is exacerbated in domains where these technologies are widely employed. In such cases, the familiar refrain is that it is not the technologies themselves that are furthering inequality, but rather their misuse or some other non-technological factor that explains exacerbations. This three-step mechanism offers one way of understanding how seemingly neutral technologies can function to reproduce hierarchies without anyone ever intending it. This account thus helps make sense of how hierarchy, once already in place, tends to reproduce itself as a default setting.

What, then, does the active pursuit of equality in data technology look like? Consider now Du Bois's datafications as a motivating precedent.

W. E. B. Du Bois's Pursuit of Equality within Data

In her study of the aesthetics of racializing data at the turn of the twentieth century, Autumn Womack describes Du Bois's work as expressive of a commitment to the political capacities of the early-twentieth-century genre of the social survey.[15] The social survey was particularly prominent among late-nineteenth- and early-twentieth-century social reformers.[16] As a research method, the social survey combined first-person ethnography, immersive participant observation, and data collection and visualization techniques that were often statistical in form. What Womack finds in Du Bois as a practitioner of the social survey is his commitment to what she calls "an attempt to make data move."[17] To make data move means "to realign the presumed equation between black life and data while also insisting on a data regime that might allow us to perceive and receive social life."[18] Womack's idea of moving data makes vivid Saidiya Hartman's claim that Du Bois's "figures, charts, and graphs aspired to be a moving picture of black life," a "story in motion" narrating "a changing and variable entity."[19]

A concept of moving data tracks a radical egalitarian achievement by Du Bois, which I describe below as an effort in formatting racial data.[20] The stakes of this effort are clarified in Womack's refusal of "an easy ideological distinction between documenting and experimenting" and her correlative affirmation that "in the face of black life, documenting was always already an experimental process, one that had the potential to reorder and disorder the easy bundling of data and black life."[21] Where data formats are calcified such that they are no longer available as ongoing objects for inquiry, we lose the possibility for what Womack calls "undisciplining data" through experiments in documentation.[22] And with that we lose the very possibility of equality in data. The work of making data move is thus not itself a clean solution, but is rather an effort that can be pragmatically cultivated as a condition of possibility for leveraging alternatives to the technological reproduction of inequalities.

EQUALITY WITHIN DATA

To explicate the egalitarian potential inherent in making data move, I need to parse more rigorously the contrast between two ways of establishing a connection between data and equality: one way is to pursue equality *with* data, in which data is equality's tool, while another is to pursue equality *within* data, such that data is understood as itself a terrain for equality or inequality. To explicate this distinction, I offer two clarifying cases.

The first case considers different ways Du Bois documents the social domain he calls "the problem of problems"—namely, education.[23] This statement is not a mere turn of phrase. The theoretical category of "the problem" is central to some of Du Bois's most famous and powerful statements, such as his assertion in 1903 that "the problem of the twentieth century is the problem of the color-line."[24] Du Bois's statement that "education is the problem of problems" is significant from the perspective of a pragmatist problem-centered methodology in social theory.[25] Its significance is also borne out by the fact that nearly all of Du Bois's major book-length publications include at least one full chapter dedicated to the role of education in achieving (or failing to achieve) racial equality. Two of these chapters illustrate my distinction.

The use of data as a tool for pursuing equality is exemplified in Du Bois's 1920 book *Darkwater*. In chapter 8, on the subject of education and race, Du Bois considers "the figures of the Thirteenth Census" from which he excavates a set of facts about illiteracy rates.[26] He notes that among African American children ages 10 to 14, the illiteracy rate at the time of the census was 18.9%; among the same population, 31.4% did not attend school. This figure is compared to a citation of the same-age White demographic, among whom "nearly a tenth were not in school," as well as a figure of 9% illiteracy for White Americans ages 10 to 19.[27] Du Bois means the reader to see striking inequality in levels of educational attainment in concert with disparities in access to education. These data are central to an argument whose statistical form is utterly familiar to us today, meant to demonstrate an unjust fact of the structural production of inequality. Such uses of statistical data for the exposition of undeserved inequality are surely important. But such data themselves cannot carry the argument all on their own, for such data cannot always be relied on to be there, or to be there in sufficient numbers. Du Bois's insight—truly striking, given his historical context—is that pursuits of equality making use of data need to also consider the formation of the very data apparatus enrolled in such arguments.

This brings us to Du Bois's pursuit of equality within data, which is exemplified in the chapter on education in his 1903 *The Souls of Black Folk*. Here Du Bois charts the impact of "the establishment of schools to train Negro teachers," which he had already discussed in a previous chapter on Booker T. Washington's anti-intellectual model of vocational education.[28] Du Bois mobilizes his argument by effectively citing educational statistics that do not so much prove an inequality to be rectified as they prove a more basic equality already in existence. The reader is made to acknowledge the fact of this more basic equality as well as its having been only episodically achieved. Du Bois writes, "Fifty years ago the ability of Negro students in any appreciable numbers to master a modern college course would have been difficult to prove. To-day it is proved by the fact that . . . we have, then, nearly twenty-five hundred Negro graduates."[29] Du Bois presents data that effectively counter allegations of racial hierarchies in intelligence and educability. But what is most crucial to observe is that Du Bois took it upon himself to form, and format, the data-collection apparatus through which such statistics on education and literacy could even be accumulated.

Du Bois's data here (and elsewhere) are a record of his realization that someone would have to put in the work to collect, collate, and curate data on the educational (and other) achievements of early-twentieth-century African Americans. He knew how much such data would matter. And as such, he contributed to the formatting of multitudes of data types that would affirm equality across the color line. It is too easy for us today, awash as we are in statistical data, to simply look past these efforts in datafication as a minor technical task. So it is all the more crucial to recognize that what we are awash in today are data that often simply did not exist in Du Bois's day before he (and others) helped build the techniques and schemas that would bring them into being. Du Bois's work was a constitution of data. Crucially, this work is not only laborious, but it is also a labor in which the data scientist confronts manifold choices that must be made by any curator of information. What data fields should be collected? What variables shall be permissible within those fields? What relations hold between those variables? How ought we to construct our database schema that will format information such that it can be reliably solicited, stored, processed, and disseminated? And what values get designed into those schema such that they might either foster or disallow equalities? These are among the many questions of data equality.

Consider now a second case exhibiting a contrast between equality with data and equality within data. This case looks sideways from Du Bois's data work to his contemporary Ida B. Wells. Du Bois, I argued, designed projects in data collection such that claims for equality could be evidenced within a database. Wells's use of lynching statistics in a series of publications culminating in her 1895 *A Red Record* appears at first to exemplify the more common contrasting case of pursuing equality with data. Her work leverages existing datasets toward a tactical argument for equality—specifically, an argument "that the law shall punish all alike."[30] According to a common interpretation, Wells's approach expresses a kind of positivism about data (even if little else in Wells's writings would have been positivistic).[31] On this reading, Wells's dry reproduction leaves the statistical data as they are and builds its argument around them through narration. Whatever its merits, the narrative contextualization of data is not the same maneuver as Du Bois's, who sometimes reproduced statistics already made for him, but more often and more interestingly designed new databases capable of warehousing statistics that would not otherwise have existed.

But consider a different angle on Wells's use of data. Naomi Murakawa has recently noted the striking fact that even if *A Red Record* leaves intact the quantitative statistical values Wells took from others, it nevertheless introduces nontrivial changes at the level of their presentation, the most important of which concern the arrangement or organization of the given facts. Murakawa keenly observes that Wells arranges the data by alleged crime rather than by date, as they were originally presented in a *Chicago Tribune* annual retrospective lynching calendar. Wells thus "essentially transformed a calendar into a slate of criminal charges against black people," argues Murakawa.[32] Wells's redesign forcefully demonstrates the politics of the formats inhering in a dataset. Indeed, it demonstrates this at the very level of the data themselves. The point of Wells's argument depends on designing data differently. Her argument both makes strategic use of existing data to pursue equality with data (wrapping existing data within a reinterpretation) and also redesigns an aspect of data in order to more effectively highlight an existing inequality within those data (reformatting a crucial aspect of those existing data).

We can recognize in Du Bois and Wells alike projects in data design that go beyond the mere use of data to make a case. Theirs are critical projects of challenging existing datasets with data-collection and data-redesign apparatus tailored explicitly to the possibility of tabulating (in)equality. What the work of Du Bois and Wells shows, among other things, is that achieving equality does not require us to choose between data and descriptions. The more relevant distinction is that between egalitarian data or description on the one hand, and on the other hand those data and descriptions that serve to entrench inequality (including by way of feigning neutrality). What we need is to put equality first and then harness everything else to that. Egalitarianism can avail itself of data designs alongside other toolkits and methods, including those of qualitative research, philosophical speculation, and poetic revelry. Egalitarians need not beware of abstracting data as such—data can assume forms expressive of all manner of abstractions.

EGALITARIAN DATA MOVEMENTS

Having explicated a distinction between pursuing equality with data and designing equality within data, I offer now a few exhibits of equality within data from Du Bois's wide-ranging corpus. These datafications show how Du Bois even in his earliest publications was already much more a pragmatist empiricist than the naive positivist he has sometimes been interpreted to be.[33]

Du Bois's Data Portraiture

Du Bois traveled to Paris in 1900 for the Exposition Universelle, where he curated the *American Negro Exhibit* (or *Exposition des Nègres d'Amérique*) in the Pavilion of Social Economy, a presentation that included a number of handsome hand-drawn charts and graphs expressive of Du Bois's early virtuosity in quantitative design. Recently published in book form, what stands out about Du Bois's "data portraits" is their unabashed expression of positive facts of African American progress and equality.[34] In the words of Du Bois's collaborator on the exposition, Thomas Calloway, the team's work focused on "compiling data and collecting material for an exhibit of the progress of the American negroes in education and industry."[35] In Du Bois's own words, the exhibit offered "a series of striking models of the progress of the colored people, beginning with the homeless freedman and ending with the modern brick schoolhouse and its teachers."[36] By featuring African American "development" and "progress," Du Bois and his collaborators skillfully countered the discourse of the eugenicists and hereditarians who would have been present in Paris with their own exhibits.[37]

A chart reprinted in the recent volume as plate 27 was titled by Du Bois "Occupations of Negroes and Whites in Georgia." This uniquely designed pie chart shows the share of employment of each race in various kinds of trades. Striking is the equal percentage of both races employed in "Agriculture, Fisheries, and Mining" (62% of "Negroes" and 64% of "Whites"). "Domestic and Personal Service" is shown to be clearly much more common among "Negroes" (28%) than "Whites" (5.5%). Most important, though, is the visual affirmation of "Negro" employment in "Manufacturing and Mechanical Industries" (5%), "Trade and Transportation" (4.5%), and "Professions" (0.5%). The point is made not just through numbers but also visually. As the volume editors note, "Du Bois builds dynamic tension by cascading color around the chart in opposing clockwise and counterclockwise directions, making the diagram look as if the 'Negro' wedges [placed at the top of the chart] might collapse over the 'White' wedges [placed beneath them] at any moment."[38]

Another exhibit of equality in data is offered by plate 47, "Illiteracy of the American Negroes compared with that of other nations." This is a classic bar chart with ten measures protruding from left to right, each bar labeled (in French). No exact percentages are given, and so the chart serves a purely comparative purpose. At the top of the chart are bars for "Roumanie," "Servie," and "Russie," each indicating roughly the same level of illiteracy. Just below them, showing significantly less illiteracy, is a bar labeled "Negroes, U.S.A." followed by "Hongrie," with only slightly less illiteracy. The last five bars are all Central and Western European nations with comparatively lower illiteracy, though that in Italy is not much lower than in Hungary, and Sweden (at the bottom of the chart) is shown to have remarkably higher literacy than even France (second from last). In describing the exhibition the following year, Du Bois called attention to this particular chart as a model for the series.[39] The editors of the reprint note that plate 47 serves to unambiguously "correct misconceptions about the education of black Americans," for it demonstrates visually that inequalities in education owe more to socio-historical factors than biological-racial ones.[40] It should not be overlooked that the argument made by this illustration relies on the innovative work in data production through which Du Bois and his team made data move in ways that preexisting datasets could not.

Du Bois's Data Collection

Du Bois's 1899 *The Philadelphia Negro* is based on his gargantuan efforts in compiling a huge volume of data on an urban Black population, the first such study of its kind on any demographic in any city.[41] This book offers insight into Du Bois's data-collection methods including those employed to produce the Paris exhibition data portraits. Of particular interest are the book's appendix reproductions of the questionnaires, or "schedules," Du Bois used to ascertain his data.[42]

The appendix reveals how Du Bois's formats oriented his inquiry to the many modes of development possible within a politically excluded population. One example of this that would resonate in Du Bois's presentations in Paris the next year is his study of the growth of literacy rates among Black Philadelphians.[43] One footnote includes a table with a bar graph showing that the literacy rate of a sample Black population in Philadelphia was above that in five European nations, and only slightly below that in Germany, where Du Bois had completed his graduate education.[44]

What stands out most about Du Bois's schedules is his commitment to collecting those data that would reveal not so much the influence of an individual's heredity, but the impacts of their social environment. In this, Du Bois's datafications were amenable to possibilities for equality that data designed by others had simply neglected, or in many cases even actively resisted.

Du Bois's Data Measurement

Du Bois's 1904 *Some Notes on Negro Crime, Particularly in Georgia* presents the results of comparative analyses of perceptions of the criminal justice system.[45] In one survey, Atlanta-area Black youth (ages 9 to 15) are asked about their perception of the purpose of law, courts, and policing, as well as their perception of treatment by police. In another survey, an older cohort (ages 13 to 21) of Black youth drawn from throughout the state is canvassed with similar (but not identical) questions. A third survey solicits data from Black and White state officials and private citizens from counties across Georgia. More specifically, for this third survey, "reports were requested from every chief of police in the state and from various county officials."[46]

With respect to the survey of officials, Du Bois's report breaks out the results according to respondents' race. By thus categorizing the data, Du Bois brings into view some of its more telling features. One is that "nearly all the white officials thought that Negroes were justly treated in the courts."[47] This contrasts with "the reports of Negroes," the sample of which Du Bois describes as coming from "men above the average of intelligence and reliability in their communities."[48] Asking them about "justice in the courts," the report presents 43 summary responses ranging from one sentence to multiple paragraphs each. There is some subtlety in these responses, even the shorter ones, but 37 of the 43 (86%) decidedly express the view that the courts are unfair to Blacks. The report is poignant on this point: "The persons whom I asked, seemed to think that the Negro of this county received the regulation 'Georgia justice' in the courts; that is once accused, the Negro is guilty, especially so if the controversy is with a white person."[49] Du Bois next compares these contrasting views with his surveys of Black youth. Among the first (younger) survey cohort, 459 of 1,281 respondents (36%) report perceiving the police as "unkind."[50] Among the second (young-adult) survey cohort, 408 of 646 respondents (63%) answer "No" when asked, "Have police ever helped or protected you?"

Du Bois's social survey makes data move by way of a perspectival shift that remains compelling for us today. In the midst of contemporary data-driven police and parole technologies, critics call attention to the harm of using historical crime data as a benchmark for predictive algorithms.[51] Predictive systems benchmarked to historical data will at best reproduce the racist inequalities that already pervade contemporary policing and courtroom practice. What, then, are we to do? Find better crime data by which we might benchmark threat assessment applications? Du Bois's study suggests otherwise. What he proposed was a movement of the frame of focus mobilized in data technologies. Rather than finding a way to build machine-learning predictors that more finely analyze data that themselves have a pattern of targeting racial minorities unequally, we can and should turn away from racially unequal historical crime logs in order to consider potentially equalizing assessments of the justice of policing and incarceration systems. Rather than benchmarking predictive technologies to an unequal past, why not benchmark our technologies to perceptions of the (in)justice of these technologies and the criminological apparatus of which they are a part?

These and other of Du Bois's data pursuits yield a crucial imperative: where we grasp and fasten persons through data, even when it is expressly for the sake of ameliorating social conditions, our very design of data must be actively and fervently trained on equality, for otherwise it is just too hard to not reproduce inequality. This work is crucial insofar as data-driven social projects are particularly susceptible to techno-structural hierarchy. Inequality is the default condition for data-driven social research wherever the object of social inquiry is a society deeply riven by inequality. As Eubanks observes, echoing Zack's idea of inertia, "When automated decision-making tools are not built to explicitly dismantle structural inequalities, their increased speed and vast scale intensify them dramatically."[52]

Pursuing Equality within Data

Data can and should be used to pursue equality. Though a novel approach in Du Bois's time, for us today this sentiment would hardly be contested. More significant, and more challenging, is the realization that anyone doing

anything with data (including pursuing equality) ought to be fervently attentive to how inequalities may be designed into their data formats. Critical data
studies scholars have amply documented how the use of data by morally upright agents pursuing equality can and does go awfully awry. Du Bois's work
helps us understand what to do when this happens and, better yet, what to do
so that it does not happen so much. The insight his data work offers is that the
pursuit of equality within data is a condition of the pursuit of equality with
data. Stated more generally, this is a variation on the pragmatist insight that
the means must be consistent with the ends.

Du Bois makes such a compelling model of data egalitarianism because
of his adeptness at making data move in ways hitherto unpermitted by preexisting configurations of data. He built up data inside problems in ways
it had not yet traveled, or had yet to travel well. His work shows how a
commitment to equality should and can run throughout our information
technology, all the way back to the inception of designing database formats.
His work demonstrates how data equality must involve an attentiveness to
data formats (including, for instance, the relevant fields and permissible
variables implemented in techniques of datafication), an understanding of
the dangerous derivatives of innocent-seeming proxy fields (where humdrum data correlates with socially charged categories), and an explicit in-
terrogation of measuring instruments (to determine whether data default
to the reproduction of the very social conditions they might be expected to
ameliorate).

Consider in conclusion a contemporary analogy for Du Bois's pursuit
of egalitarian data design as I have described it. In writings on equality in
education, the political theorist Danielle Allen explicates a crucial distinction
between the pursuit of education for the sake of equality and the pursuit of
equality as internal to the practice of education.[53] The first pursuit involves
regarding education from the perspective of the social goals that justify it—
for example, a justification of public education in terms of the social equality
it sustains. But Allen deftly observes that questions about whether to pursue
education for the sake of social equality (in contrast to some other goal, such
as national economic growth) remain separate from questions about how to
pursue education itself from a perspective internal to its practice. In taking
an internal perspective, we can and should recognize the need to structure
our educational practices so as to treat all students as equals; that is, so that
our educational work is itself egalitarian in practice. This is prior to, and also
not fully satisfied by, pursuing equality through education. I take Allen's argument to show that equality within education is a condition of possibility
for the use of education for the goal of social equality. This analogizes to my

argument about data: equality within data is a condition of the pursuit of equality using data.

Du Bois's data work provides analogies and models for a wide suite of contemporary efforts in data redesign already underway across numerous fields. One set of examples can be located in emerging work in education research deploying theoretical strategies explicitly critical of racism within quantitative methods—these approaches involve "thinking beyond commonly used metrics" and crafting "a new survey or measurement tool" rather than relying on ready-made datasets.[54] A different set of examples from education-data science involves mobilizing data analytics methods to build models of collaborative learning as an alternative to dominant modeling strategies concentrated on learning as a personalized, or individually separated, activity.[55] Both cases involve critical data redesigns without falling into critical opposition to data as such. And these are only a few examples of an impressive multitude of projects pursuing egalitarian data redesigns.

As impressive as this and other work is, we lack a unifying cross-domain framework that both holds it all together and provides it with a common theoretical basis. The concept of data equality is intended in part to offer such a unifying perspective. Stated in terminology I explicate in subsequent chapters, what unifies all these projects as echoes of Du Bois's egalitarian experiments is the way they manifest movements in data that actively dis-entrench the hierarchical structuring that historically precedes them.

PART 2

Equality

3

Structural Equality
A Pragmatist Account of Democratic Equality

In 1910s England, a young Eric Arthur Blair, later known as George Orwell, attended St. Cyprian's boarding school in East Sussex. Though not poor, the Blair family was by no means rich. Eric was invited to the school on scholarship because of his academic promise, the implicit trade being that he would win academic prizes and enhance the school's reputation. In the 1940s, Orwell looked back on St. Cyprian's in an essay describing the school as marking him with a brand of class inferiority. A Mrs. Wilkes in charge of the school "seemed to aim consciously at inculcating a humble outlook in the poorer boys."[1] He recounts her as saying to one student, and before the entire school, "Your people aren't rich. You must learn to be sensible. Don't get above yourself!"[2] What Orwell described at St. Cyprian's was an atmosphere of inequality: "In effect there were three castes in the school," consisting first of those of "an aristocratic or millionaire background," second those of the "ordinary suburban rich," and third those "few underlings" attending on scholarship.[3] Though these inequalities were clearly connected to the economic situation of a pupil's family, what makes Orwell's recollections so poignant is that they mark how such economic inequalities can congeal into social hierarchies of superiority and inferiority. Such social inequalities may be expressed in and through distributive inequalities, but social hierarchies extend more widely and deeply than economic disparities alone. They can also inflect ordinary social relationships such as those between peers in a school. Such hierarchical inequalities cut sharply against the grain of democratic equality in that they institute structural barriers to people relating to each other as equals in their ordinary relationships.

The central argument presented in this chapter is that equality primarily concerns the social structures that shape how we can and do relate to each other. Equal structuring of relations is not the only concern we ought to have in valuing equality, but it is primary for equality. No justifiable account of equality can dispense with it. Yet this primary aspect of equality is often occluded by other egalitarian commitments.

This chapter's centering concern with equality as a feature of social structure continues the arguments from part 1. Where chapter 2 excavated a precedent for a conception of equality in data, this chapter proposes a more general account of structural equality, within which a focal concern for data equality can be situated. Though this chapter is more general in scope, it is also more detailed, for precision is needed to bring into view a coherent conception of a value as significant as equality, and to distinguish it from proximate theories.

Pragmatism about Equality

The starting point and primary focus for my discussion in this chapter will be recent philosophical accounts of what is frequently called *relational equality* or *democratic equality*.[4] Relational equality is most often identified with Elizabeth Anderson's contributions to political philosophy, and involves egalitarian commitments for which I find important precedents in John Dewey's democratic pragmatism and in W. E. B. Du Bois's racial egalitarianism.[5] Common to all relational egalitarians is the idea that equality is first and foremost about how we relate to each other. The paradigm of equal relations, on this view, is political democracy. Hence the terms *democratic equality* and *relational equality* are often taken as synonyms—I shall use the two interchangeably, relying mostly on the more technical idiom of relational equality, invoking at times the more explanatory phrasing of democratic equality.

The idea of relating as equals is best understood at the level of social structure, and more specifically in terms of acts of equal treatment within social structure. I develop and defend a structural model of relational equality by way of extending some pragmatist themes that underwrite recent contributions to relational egalitarianism. I specifically develop pragmatist themes already discernible (though not always clearly) in Anderson's account of relational equality.

Pragmatism can first of all be seen in the substantive resonance between Anderson's "democratic equality"[6] on the one hand and Dewey's pragmatist philosophy of "democracy as a way of life"[7] on the other. David Rondel observes that equality for Dewey is concerned with "the nature and quality of social relationships," such that the focus is on "which social and political relations exhibit a certain (democratic) structure."[8] These lines could equally well describe Anderson's relational egalitarianism. Anderson also explicitly employs aspects of pragmatist methodology.[9] This is clearest in her rejection of idealizing (or "ideal theory") methods that were particularly prominent in late-twentieth-century political philosophy. Anderson's orientation is rooted instead in a nonideal or realist methodology that aims to be rigorously attentive to the conditions of social practices.[10] A related aspect of pragmatist methodology is further discernible in this focus on practice. Anderson writes of claims of unfairness that they "apply only to the practices of agents."[11] The proper object of a political or moral claim is what an agent is doing, has done, or intends to do. This implicitly endorses pragmatism's actionistic analysis. Also notable is that the other leading theorist of relational egalitarianism alongside Anderson, Samuel Scheffler, comes nowhere near endorsing pragmatism and yet nevertheless also holds that equality "is ultimately a form of practice, rather than a normative pattern of distribution."[12] That at least sounds like a theoretical commitment which could be well served by a more thoroughly pragmatist focus.

As I understand pragmatism, actionistic analysis and political realism are two of its most important methodological commitments. A third central commitment of pragmatism orients these other two and yet is not brought into clear view by Anderson: a focus on processes rather than things, or dynamic flows rather than static entities. For the pragmatist, nothing sits still—that which appears unmoving is only that which is extraordinarily slow in its motions. There is no eternal repose—only roaring flux. In an earlier book on pragmatism, I referred to this commitment as pragmatism's transitionalism.[13] Pragmatism needs transitionalism to maintain its focus on its other major methodological commitments. Political realism rejects idealizations, attending instead to actual political circumstances, which are always dynamic and therefore contrast sharply with the fixity of the ideal. Actionistic analysis also puts an emphasis on process insofar as action itself is inherently dynamic and cannot be comprehended statically (in contrast to, say, beliefs, propositions, or experiences, to mention just a few other quintessential loci of emphasis in recent philosophy that do admit of analyses as static objects).

Commitments to actionism, realism, and transitionalism do not exhaustively specify every actual iteration of pragmatism. A fourth attribute of pragmatism is particularly relevant for my efforts across this book. This involves the form that pragmatism gives to our normative commitments—that is, to our values, rules, obligations, and the like. Normativity concerns correctness. Stated actionistically, normativity concerns what we should do. Pragmatism focuses normativity around a conception of betterment or improvement as expressed by its methodological strategy of reconstruction. Yet ideas of improvement are easily misunderstood. Consider how ideals of progress have historically been exploited as cover for what is in fact regressive.[14] How can pragmatism steer clear of self-congratulatory progress? Since pragmatism regards normative contents less as ideals and more as effective rules for practice, reconstructive progress needs be understood as starting where we are by working on problems we actually face in practice. This contrasts with end-state (or teleological) notions of progress that aim at some predefined endpoint supposedly possessed of normative force regardless of its relation to present problems. Philip Kitcher captures this distinction in endorsing "possibilities of progress, conceived not as steps toward some final perfect state, but as changes that ameliorate or eliminate problematic features of the present."[15] One term for this perspective is *meliorism*—a term of art for the philosophy of hope. The meliorist holds that we may yet, through our efforts and actions, improve the situations in which we find ourselves. Pragmatism's melioristic adoption of egalitarianism holds that we can squarely face the unequal social structures we have been born into and work to reconstruct them to be more equal—all without holding to the idealization that the only thing worth achieving is perfect equality. The aim is to build out more equality than we have now and then to do the same again after that.

I have discussed each of these four elements of pragmatism in previous writings—so while there is much more to say about meliorism, transitionalism, actionism, and realism, I shall take the efficient characterizations above as sufficient.[16] What I turn to now is the specific inflection that pragmatism gives to the normative commitment that is central to my argument in this book—namely, equality. How can equality be conceptualized according to the pragmatist commitments above?

ELIZABETH ANDERSON ON RELATIONAL EQUALITY

Anderson's 1999 essay "What Is the Point of Equality?" is the most influential contribution to philosophical theories of equality in the past few decades.[17] This article managed to genuinely change the topic of conversation on equality in contemporary political philosophy. Most commonsense approaches to equality have long relied on a background idea of unequal distributions as fundamental for equality. Distributive theories of equality focus on the distribution of goods (like income, wealth, health outcomes, or health-care access). The basic idea of these theories is that equality is a feature of the pattern of distribution of the benefits and burdens that flow from the way social structures shape said distributions. A canonical formulation would, for example, call for more-equal distributions of wealth and health-care access to redress the kind of inequality that today leaves the ultra-poor living in tents mere blocks away from the mansions, yachts, and golf clubs of the super-rich. Distributive egalitarians have engaged in important debates concerning what sorts of goods ought to be distributed (resources versus outcomes) and to whom (everyone or just those suffering bad luck through no choice of their own). But they have often missed the underlying justification for and meaning of equality in the first place.

Why should having less than another be objectionable in the first place? And is that really the only, or even just the most serious, form of objectionable inequality? Anderson's major contribution in response to such questions is the view that "inequality [should be] referred not so much to distributions of goods as to relations between superior and inferior persons."[18]

According to Anderson's relational egalitarianism, equality is above all a quality of relations between persons and as such requires "a social order in which persons stand in relations of equality."[19] It is the essence of unjust inequality to relate to others as if they are beneath or below one. Theories that focus exclusively on distributive inequalities do not often, of course, contravene this point. However, neither do they assert it. Such theories therefore end up postulating justifications for equality that miss the very core of the idea of equality. Distributive theories have too little to say about, for instance, the wealthy woman whose husband effectively prevents her from pursuing her intellectual or vocational passion (where the relevant background conditions include a prenuptial agreement entitling her to fully equal shares under any eventuality). A memorable literary example is that of Lucy Honeychurch in E. M. Forster's 1908 novel *A Room with a View*, set in the same period as Orwell's boarding-school days. Returning to her native England from Italy, where "any who chooses may warm himself in equality, as in the sun," Lucy finds herself hemmed in by social barriers. Her fiancé, Cecil Vyse, fancies himself broad-minded, and in many respects truly is, yet not in relation to Lucy: "A rebel she was, but not of the kind he understood—a rebel who desired, not a wider dwelling-room, but equality beside the man she loved."[20] A central plotline involves Lucy extricating herself from Cecil.

Relational egalitarians defend equality on the grounds of what is required to achieve a society of equals. A social order in which persons can and do relate as equals does not allow inequalities to become entrenched and reproduced, nor does it put persons entering into that order (by birth, immigration, or otherwise) in positions of inferiority. As I elaborate below, the injustice of such inequalities is concerned primarily with ensuring that our social structures do not place people in positions of hierarchy, paradigmatic forms of which include exclusion, separation, polarization, and marginalization.[21] A society that provides structures supporting more-equal relations is a society that at least has a shot at being actually egalitarian in a full sense that includes not only relational equality but also forms of distributive equality that are themselves justified by relational equality.

Relational Equality: A Structural Account

To clarify what equality is about, I now turn to an analysis of relational equality. I build on ideas from Anderson and other contemporary pragmatist relational egalitarians, most importantly Danielle Allen, by contrasting a structural approach to relational equality that befits their pragmatism with another approach that has gained, I argue, too much currency. I begin with the normative question of justification, then turn to a discussion of the point of equality, and finally to a detailed discussion of the relata of relational equality.

EQUALITY'S JUSTIFICATION: POLITICAL EQUALITY

What justifies equality as a value we should pursue? I develop an answer to this question in two stages, rooting things first in a conception of political justification in general, and from there building out a fuller account of a political justification of the specific value of equality.

What is a political justification? A political approach to justification contrasts with certain more prominent justifications for equality offered by many egalitarians, including pragmatist relational egalitarians. The contrast case is morally fundamentalist. Allen's "eudaimonist democratic pragmatist" theory of equality begins with the idea that "human moral equality is the fundamental concept."[22] Anderson similarly seeks a justification for relational equality in "the fact of universal moral equality."[23] I do not disagree with the content of these claims (namely, that all persons are moral equals), yet a more stringent version of the political realism central to pragmatism accepts that an assertion of a moral ideal often does too little to resolve political disagreement or to justify political claims where such justification is needed.[24] Where a justification for equality is in question, rather than already being settled, asserting a moral fact is not often going to take us very far. By contrast, a political justification appeals to the more minimal fact of our participating in a shared political order—for instance, as citizens in a state. In other words, a political starting point assumes less than a moral starting point. This is pragmatically beneficial insofar as politics is often riddled with persisting moral disagreement. Indeed, political justification might be thought to have its beginning point precisely where moral agreement has broken down.

It is perplexing that Anderson and Allen both rely on moral appeals to equality; as I read them both, each already puts forth accounts of equality that contain nearly all the theoretical resources needed for a purely political approach to justification. Anderson's defense of democratic equality even begins with a claim for a firmer focus on "the distinctively political aims of egalitarianism."[25] I turn now to explicating a political justification for equality that borrows resources from Anderson's account, though I believe the same strategy could be built up from Allen's theory as well.[26]

What I build on from Anderson is a model of "second-person" justification she endorses.[27] On this model, a theory of justification for equality is found in the basic idea of a claim to equality made by a claimant on someone else. Anderson associates this perspective with a family of views in recent political philosophy typically labeled "contractarian" or "contractualist."[28] These views adopt the model of a social contract to help explain how citizens of a society can achieve agreement in the face of serious disputes. Anderson's version of the contractualist approach involves a second-person account of justification according to which the proper object of normative assessment is the conduct of agents who succeed in (or fail at) appropriately discharging their duties of action. This contrasts to third-person accounts of justification according to which the proper object of normative assessment is with states of affairs in the world. On the second-person account, for example, a claim that an inequality is unjust is a claim against an agent (for example, the state) who brings about or allows to exist the inequality. On the third-person account, a claim that an inequality is unjust is a claim about the world and is, as it were, addressed to the world itself (though perhaps it is better described as being addressed to nobody at all and as such is not really a claim but is a description of a state of affairs). Anderson's view of these two standpoints for justification is summarized in her assertion that "justice as an evaluation of states of affairs is entirely derivative of justice as an appraisal of the conduct of agents."[29]

I endorse such a contractualist model in its general outlines, but in some presentations—particularly those that overemphasize direct relations between two individual citizens as parties to agreement—this model has significant limitations. These limitations can be overcome by way of a revised contractualist conception of second-person justification articulated in a more resolutely pragmatist mode.[30]

To motivate my alternative model, consider first another view of moral justification that is quite similar to Anderson's and which preceded it by a century, that developed by the pragmatist philosopher William James in his 1891 essay on the point of moral philosophy.[31] James's essay describes a dynamic system of claims and counterclaims that shared participants in a social order make upon each other. The basic argument is that a claim of injustice (or of any type of wrong) needs to actually be made by someone if we are going to regard a situation as unjust (or wrong). No claim, no injustice. The world is not populated by unjust states of affairs lying around going unclaimed. The underappreciated contractarian kernel of James's view is that where a claim of injustice is made, the situation is unjust unless that claim is actually defeated or overridden. A claim against injustice just is what requires the pursuit of justice. Where there are actual objections against injustices that have not been rebutted, then we are under an obligation to address and possibly also redress those objections.

Against whom is a claim to injustice made? James's original argument presents a model in which one individual makes a claim against another individual. James's model, like Anderson's, is second-person. But his is also more self-conscious in its articulation in a way that allows us to recognize that the model is actually decidedly focused on a specific class of second-person claims. James asks the reader to imagine a universe populated by only two individuals; he proceeds to argue that this universe contains all that is needed for a properly moral claim.[32] This scene is later reflected in Anderson's contractarian concern with situations "when one person makes a moral claim on another's conduct."[33] What may have previously appeared as an innocuous feature of Anderson's account now begins to assume more weight, as an implicit endorsement of moral claims as second-person-*singular* claims.

But should we not expect that a properly political view of justification actually needs be second-person-*plural*? Political relations require a structural mechanism for the reproduction of injustice rather than mere disagreements between two individual agents. Though morality may begin between two agents, politics always requires three. A second-person-singular model of justification is perhaps a positive feature of James's view insofar as he presents it explicitly as a model of moral justification; but for a model of political justification, it is decidedly a bug.

What does a second-person-plural model of political justification involve? While second-person-singular claims addressed by one individual to another are an important aspect of our political and especially our moral relations to each other, there is much that we lose sight of when restricting our understanding of political justification to this level, whether overtly or even only implicitly by way of the metaphors and examples used to present the view. On a more realist perspective, it is manifestly the case that political claims (for example, claims against unjustified inequality), are made against broader social associations. Political claims are typically addressed to the existing social structure through its representative agents in such forms as legislatures, governmental agencies, or corporations with influence over how social relations are structured. The proper way to conceptualize the form of address in which political justification is rooted is therefore almost always in the plural. Properly political claims are made by a claimant against an association ("you all") rather than against an individual ("you").

In some of our most familiar democratic contexts, a second-person-plural claim against the state also looks like a first-person-plural claim addressed to a state that one is a member of (as in "we, the citizens of the state, ought to reform the laws so as to regulate these actions"). Noting the resonance between second-person claims ("you all") and first-person claims ("us") fits well with the spirit of Anderson's view insofar as her ultimate targets are theories of equality rooted in a conception of political justification as third-person—namely, purported claims against inequality that are the result of brute cosmic luck rather than the doing of any agent. Anderson refers to such theories as "luck egalitarian" in that they conceptualize requirements for inequality in terms of the results of misfortune.[34] These views are characteristically restricted to a focus on those unequal distributions that flow from dumb luck. What such views tend to miss, however, are those aspects of inequality that concern our relations to each other prior to any inequalities in distributed benefits and burdens (whether those distributions are the result of luck or of the choice of some agent or agents). Relational equality, in other words, shifts the vantage for equality from a third-person state of affairs, where there are no agents of equality, to first-person and second-person contexts, where we all are potential agents responsible for instituting equal relations.

The interesting resonance between second-person-plural and first-person-plural justification not only clarifies political justification in general, but also carries particular normative force for political justifications of equality. Consider that if I am asked to offer a political justification on behalf of my claim for equal standing or equal status in my political relations to others, that very request for a political justification already implies the general kind of equal standing or equal status for which a justification has been solicited. Said differently, one cannot present a political justification for inequality to a purported unequal without implicitly addressing that justification to the other as a relative equal, at least in justificatory matters. Were I to attempt to justify to you a view that you are not my equal, my very attempting to justify this to you already belies the content of my justification. You are at least my relative equal insofar as I take you to be worthy of persuasion. Expanding the scope of concern now, consider that all of us taken together as represented by the state cannot justify to some particular one of us (or some subset of us all) a standard of manifestly unequal treatment. The purported attempt at justification would already bring the recipient of unequal treatment into the orbit of political equality. Now, to be sure, the state can (and in reality does) treat some unequally. But the state cannot justify that unequal treatment to those who are subject to it—which is to say, such unequal treatment by the state of those subject to the state is unjustified (and presumably therefore also unjust).

The gap between a justification of unequal treatment and the capacity to nevertheless inflict such treatment without justification illuminates the basic distinction between persuasion and force that constitutes political legitimacy. The first question of politics is always that of order (or stability)—and the second question, already implicit in the first, is always that of legitimacy (or agreement).[35] Contractualism is the most compelling model of political legitimacy that we have, for contractualism models agreement as a matter of political justification rather than forcible coercion. Justification is what we provide to each other in the medium of persuasion as compensation for the losses we may suffer from living in one kind of political order rather than another. It is always an option to conduct oneself in some other medium, such as that of force. But where that option is taken, there can be no question of the outcome being justified (at least to the vanquished, who are subject to the imposition of force). The crucial distinction between contexts of persuasion and of force is thus constitutive of the very possibility of relating to each other as equals. We so relate when we interact in the medium of persuasion, and we fail to so relate when we impose on each other whatever force we may muster. This distinction is thus regarded by many, including the pragmatist philosopher and cultural critic Richard Rorty, as what is best in liberalism: "A liberal society is one whose ideals can be fulfilled by persuasion rather than force, by reform rather than revolution, by the free and open encounters of present linguistic and other practices with suggestions for new practices."[36] Consider also this more gnomic articulation by the (partly pragmatist) process philosopher Alfred North Whitehead: "The creation of the world . . . is the victory of persuasion over force."[37]

Consider now how the value of equality is affected simply by being located in a contractarian context of persuasion or justification. Where a question of equality's justification has been raised, it is in at least a beginning sense already answered by having entered into the space of justification. In standing to each other in relations where we demand and accept justifications from each other, we already stand in a relation of (at least rough) political equality. To be sure, a justification for fuller forms of equality does not yet flow from this rather minimal political equality of standing. But any justification for a fuller conception of equality must at least be consonant with the beginning idea of a justification for standing in relations of political equality. And that first point of equality, I have shown, follows from the very nature of political justification itself. This serves well for a minimal approach to political justification. In political theorizing, we should start with the thinnest of assumptions, and do what we can to build thereon. We can always of course serve up richer ideals by assuming more at the outset, such as widespread agreement about universal moral equality, but we will then be in the awkward position of assuming what we need to show.

Some readers will sense a tension looming in the background in light of my rejection, posed in the introduction, of deliberativist and communicativist conceptions of democracy. According to these views, democratic relations primarily concern our mutual engagement with each other in discussion, debate, and dialogue. Like Rorty, Anderson endorses such a view—for instance, when she writes, "Democracy is here understood as collective self-determination by means of open discussion among equals, in accordance with rules acceptable to all."[38] My own view is that this is an admirable statement of one feature of democratic equality, but it is incomplete when presented as a full conception of democracy. As I outlined in the introduction, democracy involves practices of collaborative interaction that include, but are by no means exhausted by, deliberation. However, this appears to lead to the following tension: in developing a political justification for equality I have here made use of an element in the deliberativist conception of democracy; namely, the idea of claims made within a medium of persuasion. It might appear as if my view both wants to help itself to, and yet also deny the importance of, deliberation.

This apparent tension can be resolved as follows. My view holds that deliberation is necessary for democracy but also insufficient for it. Indeed, deliberation is not only necessary for democracy but also specially necessary for it. Deliberation, or what I have referred to as persuasion, is surely necessary for an initial political justification of equality to get off the ground. Deliberation therefore always remains in the background as a necessary condition for the maintenance of democratic equality. However, once equality has been so justified in a context of persuasion, it must be enacted in many forms and cannot be expected to be maintained by purely deliberative means. Crucial for the ongoing renewal of democracy is not just that we deliberate as equals but also that we cocreate social structures for treating each other as equals. Structures for equal treatment often involve linguistic interaction and communicative rationality. But in nearly all cases they involve forms of collaborative conduct that cannot be restricted to the linguistic, such as forms of technological mediation. A properly pragmatist emphasis on action as the primary context for theoretical analysis enable us to bring into view the full expanse of what is required for democratic equality, including in the midst of contemporary forms of technological mediation.

POLITICAL EQUALITY'S POINT: EQUAL RELATIONS

What is the point of equality? Anderson's famous answer to this question is that the value of equality is present where "people stand in relations of equality to others."[39] Standing in relations of equality means that all can, and presumably often enough do, relate as equals. More recently, Allen develops a similar view by way of a relational idea of reciprocity, which she defines as referring to "the relational ethic that citizens have with one another; the ability to look one another in the eye; the ability to propose the need for redress of grievances and to be secure in the expectation that redress will be possible within the constraints of reasonableness and rights."[40]

Relating to each other as equals contrasts to relating to each other through hierarchies of status, identity, or class. Where relational equality prevails, nobody is the master of anyone else, because all are to be (and often enough actually are) treated as equals. No one bows and scrapes before another. No one is beneath anyone else. There is no hierarchy that places individuals or groups at the feet of another or sets them on a pedestal above the rest.

A commitment to relating as equals need not suffice on its own for a complete theory of equality but can rather serve to establish the point of equality in a way that carries with it a number of corollaries for full-scale egalitarianism. One important such corollary involves a commitment to levels of distributive equality necessary for individuals to relate as equals. Distributive equality follows from relational equality at least up to the point at which less-equal distributions would begin to undermine relational equality robustly understood, which is already a much higher standard for distributive equality than currently enjoyed in most liberal democracies.[41] Importantly, however, there is no independent political justification for distributive equality outside the justification supplied by relational equality. We need to take ourselves to be related as equals in order to even begin justifying a proposal for more-equal distributions among ourselves. Other approaches to justifying distributive equality are always going to have to eventually pick up an endorsement of relational equality on their way toward distributive equality. Without that endorsement, there is no non-question-begging way of maintaining any proposed justification for distributive equality. Where relational equality has yet to be established, an opponent to a proposal for increasing distributive equality can simply reply, "This all sounds well and good, but the bottom line is that I do not consider all of us equals because I find some of us superior to others such that we are justified in benefiting at their expense." Except for the crucial premise asserting hierarchy, the reasoning here is unimpeachable, even if unkind. Indeed, this is precisely the sort of reply many of us would give to any number of extreme proposals for more-equal distributions between (in order of increasing implausibility) humans and nonhuman animals, humans and arthropods (like insects), humans and plants, humans and robots, or innocent children and virulent bacteria.

On the relational view, distributions of benefits and burdens that unequally lower some people's access to important goods like wealth and health in order to expand access for others who already enjoy more of these benefits are wrong not because of a factual state of affairs of maldistribution, but because and insofar as they institute barriers to relational inequality. Relational equality, therefore, seeks to root our understanding of what is unjust about distributive inequalities in a fuller picture of equality of relations. For the relational egalitarian, what is ultimately unacceptable about poverty is not the brute fact that some people live without sufficient means, but rather the political fact that they are made to (or, more often, left to) live without the means for living well enough. Where distributive inequalities reign because a social structure subjects persons to unequal treatment, they express relational inequality. In democratic contexts, these social structures are constructed and maintained by us. It is we who push some of our fellow citizens into immiseration. That some are immiserated is deeply unfortunate. But the injustice of immiseration consists in maintaining a social structure that actively immiserates some—that is, in treating some as less than the equal of others. Those living in destitution are, in virtue of their persisting destitution, being treated as less than the equals of the super-rich, whose fabulous wealth is both permitted and incentivized by a social structure shared by the moneyed and the destitute. Distributive equality is therefore crucial on the relational egalitarian view, but is also justificatorily derivative of the requirement for equal relations.[42]

The foregoing discussion of how relational equality implicates distributive equality raises the question of what theory or theories of distribution are in fact justified by relational equality. This question is beyond my remit here but worth noting is that I follow Anderson in thinking that the capabilities approach as developed by Amartya Sen and Martha Nussbaum well expresses the kind of approach to distribution justified by relational equality.[43] The capabilities approach is sensitive to differences between persons, a requisite feature of any proposal for distribution to be justified by relational equality. As Sen puts it, "Human diversity is no secondary complication (to be ignored, or to be introduced 'later on'); it is a fundamental aspect of our interest in equality."[44]

Of course, relational equality justifies not only redistributive social structures, but also and more primarily, social structures that combat social separation, polarization, exclusion, marginalization, and other expressions of hierarchy. Relational equality in its strongest form requires that we are able to (and actually do) relate to each other as equals. This requires implementing social structures that function to minimize—and even mitigate, where possible—the inequalities in relations imposed and incentivized by extant social structures. There is a virtuous circle in this way of understanding equality. Relational equality requires of those of us who would relate as equals that we ourselves implement the social structures in virtue of which our equal relations are cultivated. Though it might seem paradoxical, this feedback relation is nothing more than the virtuous circle of democracy itself. Democracy requires that we democratic citizens institute and maintain the conditions for our democratic status. This illuminates why Anderson initially referred to her egalitarianism as "democratic equality" even if the "relational equality" label has come to be more prominent in later scholarship.[45] Labels aside, in light of the direct democratic provenance of relational equality, perhaps the most conceptually challenging question regarding this view concerns what it is that relational equality would have us hold together in equal relations. This is the question concerning the relata of relational equality.

RELATIONAL EQUALITY'S RELATA: PERSONS AS RELATED BY STRUCTURE

Who or what ought to relate as equals? If equality is a relation, what are the terms of that relation? Nobody, after all, would assert that all agents or entities ought to be able to relate as equals.

Paradigmatically, we who ought to relate as equals are persons.[46] This seems uncontroversial enough, but there is actually a rather complicated series of questions concerning how we conceptualize those relations as well as their relata. What is the nature of the relations between persons who are equals? To develop an answer to this crucial question, I bring into focus a major fault line that separates two prominent approaches to relational equality.[47] This fault line remains relatively neglected in the current scholarship. But I believe it deserves more attention, for it helps us gain clarity on two fundamentally different ways of conceptualizing relational equality.

Two Models of Relations: Direct or Structural

The idea of relationality has come to assume two different forms in recent discussions of relational equality. A first sense emphasizes ways people relate to each other by interacting directly with each other. Think of how people's lives are shaped by their direct interactions with family members, paradigmatically with a spouse, parent, or child. A second sense is more complicated—it emphasizes ways people are related to each other by social structures that configure possibilities for relating. How people are related by structure can be constitutive of (some of) their actions, beliefs, desires, and even life plans. Think of how classroom peers may take themselves to be related to each other in light of educational policies or pedagogical technologies that visibly differentiate some from others.

I shall emphasize in the first model its feature of direct relationality by calling it the *direct model*. By contrast, the second of these models focuses on that which structures the ways people are related to each other. Accordingly, I shall call this the *structural model*. The structural model locates the weight of relationality in *how we are related* to each other by means of the social structures that institute those relations. The direct model emphasizes *how we relate* to each other in our direct dealings with each other.

How are these two forms or senses of relationality connected? The structural model incorporates the interpersonal relations of the direct model and thus offers a way of inquiring into how our interactions are structured. The direct model therefore lacks something that the structural model offers: a way of interrogating the conditions of interpersonal relations. The structural model thus helps show why a basic intuition supporting the direct model is mistaken: there are no purely direct relations in complex social relations, only mediated relations.

A basic theoretical distinction between structural and direct models of relationality leads to a number of concomitant distinctions. One concerns where we locate relations of (in)equality. The direct model is more individualist in its bearings and so freely looks toward psychological states, paradigmatically attitudes, as indicators of (un)equal relations. The structural model is more inclined to look toward overt behavior or action—or, better yet, social practices—as the locus of (un)equal relations. Were economy of labels not a virtue, I might describe this contrast as between the structural-behavioral and the individual-attitudinal models of relationality. But stylistic economy does matter.

So too do leading metaphors. Daniel Viehoff finds in recent discussions of relational egalitarianism a similar split between two "significantly different interpretations."[48] One interpretation is focused on relational equality as exhibited by a leading metaphor of "a well-functioning *friendship* or similar relationship," such as a marriage, to take a case that recurs with surprising frequency in the literature.[49] Insofar as friendship and marriage are "quintessentially egalitarian relationships," they provide an ideal of what equality should look like.[50] The ideal they offer features equality as a function of our direct interactions with each other, in the way that two spouses directly interacting can shape their own relationship as equal (or unequal). Viehoff also describes a contrasting interpretation of relational equality focused on social hierarchy—that is, on how equality is exhibited in "a society not governed by social hierarchies."[51] He refers to this as the "anti-caste paradigm" of relational equality, with an eye toward caste as a clarifying metaphorical case expressing inegalitarian hierarchy.[52] Viehoff's metaphors clarify how two different familiar images of equal relations prime our intuition about two different theoretical models of relational equality. One kind of equal relation, as expressed in marriage or other intimate settings, gives rise to what I am calling the direct model of relational equality. Another way we can relate as equals, involving the rejection of caste relations, primes our intuition in the direction of what I am calling the structural model of relational equality. To develop a more nuanced understanding than that supplied by our intuition as primed by metaphors, I turn now to a detailed examination of the direct and structural models themselves.

Two Conceptions of Structure: Systemic or Contingent

The distinguishing feature of a structural model of relational equality is its emphasis on social structure. Structure is best understood as a methodological category for gaining epistemic grip on (that is, conducting inquiry into) how conduct is significantly configured by influences beyond the control of individual actors. These influences are always both historically evolved and presently evolving—as such, they assume a stunning variety of forms, including built environments, spiritual traditions, cultural norms, economic patterns, and technological capabilities. Given its breadth and variety, social structure can be extremely difficult to gain grip on. Indeed, it has long been one of the most conflicted methodological categories across the social sciences.

A valuable starting point for elaborating a model of social structure is provided by the work of John Rawls.[53] According to Rawls's idea of "the basic structure of society," we ought to understand structure in terms of how institutions "distribute fundamental rights and duties and determine the division of advantages from social cooperation."[54] Rawls's idea is not only a valuable starting point in its own right but is also of interest in the context of seeking a model of relational equality because of how the idea of a basic structure is connected to concerns about inequality. Rawls writes of basic structure: "The intuitive notion here is that this structure contains various social positions and that . . . the institutions of society favor certain starting places over others. These are especially deep inequalities."[55] Rawls explicitly rejects models, like the direct model, that construe political values in terms of direct relations between persons.[56] A typical Rawlsian thought is that one individual can mistreat another individual as unequal in an isolated instance, but that this rises to a serious concern of political inequality only if it is reproduced, sanctioned, or in some other way incentivized by social structures.

With these general features of Rawls's structural model in view, many questions remain. Some concern matters that lead to a basic divergence between the conception of a structural model I endorse (following a more pragmatist line) and that proposed by Rawls (and others, including Anderson).

One point on which Rawls's conception of structure is controversial is his understanding of structures as highly individuated. His view holds that social structures are in one-to-one correspondence with similarly shaped units called societies. For Rawls, each individuated society has its basic structure; hence his canonical phrase "the basic structure of society" rather than "the multiple structuring forces of social orders." By methodologically individuating social structure, Rawls conceptualizes structure as unified, and thereby *systemic*—Rawls's concept of "the structure" speaks to a politics of "the system" in a parlance reminiscent of mid-twentieth-century radicalism. A core feature of this view is that we have at our disposal a well-formed methodological category that helps us pick out the unified system in virtue of which all important structuring elements of social interaction among all relevant participants are interlocking pieces. As a methodological heuristic, such an assumption can be useful. But as a methodological category guiding empirical inquiry into actual social reality, such an idealization will often prove misleading, especially for social contexts where structuring elements do not hang together in a unified way and whose very terms may themselves be an object of social conflict.

In contrast to idealized unifying accounts of basic structure, I endorse what I will call a *contingentist* conception of social structuring, largely motivated by the pragmatism of Dewey's political theory, and borrowing as well from Bruno Latour's philosophy of socio-technical associations.[57] The specific strain in pragmatist methodology motivating this view is its transitionalist focus on social orders as ever-changing, always-transforming, processes of association. Whereas accounts of structure as systemic tend toward structural fixity, conceptions of structuring processes tend toward structural contingency. According to a contingentist conception, structure is never settled but is always in process, and is never systematically unified, since always evolving. That which is structural is always doing its work of structuring—it is never simply there. The crucial insight of the view is that social orders are never stable in virtue of the rule of necessity (be it rational or causal necessity)—association holds together or falls apart by way of an enormous complex of mobile parts.

In contrast to a systemic conception of structure, the contingentist conception appears to retain a notable degree of vagueness in just those places where a systemic approach achieves greater precision through the theoretical unity of structure. But what appears to an ideal theorist to be the vice of vagueness is actually the virtue of a methodology that takes seriously the contingency that is characteristic of actual social and political transformation. The multi-layered forces that structure our complex social orders are never settled and so never precisely individuated and unified. They are always in transition. Some of these transformations are slow and long, others are quick and sharp. But nothing in structure is ever fully frozen, locked up in the full stability of complete isolation. For methodological purposes, we can of course theoretically assume that certain elements of social structures are fixed and individuated blocks. But this will not get us very far for pragmatic purposes, where what matters are the actually evolving processes of political order as they are composed, decomposed, and recomposed. According to a contingentist conception, it is across a range of forms including technological machinery, cultural practices, communities, polities, and governments that our relations to each other are structurally mediated. Each of these forms, as well as what qualifies as such a structuring form, is always subject to transformation.

A contingentist conception of structure allows us to ask clearly whether it is not just institutions that structurally mediate our interactions, but also other elements, such as technologies. In most contemporary contexts, the conditioning role of technologies almost feels obvious—as in the case of technological infrastructure like roads, railways, telephony, and digital exchange protocols that help configure commercial and familial relations. Or think of how friendships are now mediated by the technical qualities of various social media platforms, or text messaging, or the rise of predictive text in messaging apps. Like human languages, technologies increasingly form media within which we interact. Without media through which we can relate, we remain unrelated, or better yet, unable to relate. A contingentist conception of structure can help us establish whether a particular technology operates as a structuring medium for our relations to each other.

How does the contingentist view of structure contrast to the basic presupposition of systemic social structure animating Rawls's account? Crucial here is Rawls's quite classical picture of structure as limited to "major institutions," defined in terms of "the political constitution and the principal economic and social arrangements."[58] Can this view accommodate technology as part of social structure? On the one hand, as the critical theorist Andrew Feenberg observes, Rawls "abstracts systematically from technology" by regarding "the technical sphere as a neutral background."[59] On the other hand, Rawls explicitly notes that his conception of structure "does not provide a sharp definition, or criterion, from which we can tell what social arrangements, or aspects thereof, belong to [the basic structure]," such that specification could be provided later in the analysis of actual societies.[60] Perhaps Rawls's view leaves room for a conception of technological structure that he himself happened to abstract from.

Taking up this latter option, Mathias Risse recently redescribes Rawls's view as helping to show how "technology is not neutral, as many still think, but is intensely political."[61] Risse develops this redescription by combining Rawlsian ideas with insights from Latour, Marx, and others.[62] In effect, Risse's proposal involves a contingentist reframing of Rawls's idea of structure. I am sympathetic to Risse's political theory of technology, especially insofar as my arguments for democratic equality are very much informed by the general style of the Rawlsian liberal egalitarianism that he also takes as his starting point.[63] Yet a sticky impediment to Risse's conception of structure remains in the form of Rawls's view that the basic structure of society is a unified system. When social structure is conceptualized as systemic, it proves challenging to recognize as structural those elements that impact persons outside, and also against, any established unified system of formal institutions. In the case of technological structuring, it will be difficult to recognize those technologies that configure our relations to each other by means of mechanisms external to those already countenanced in formal regulatory institutions. For these and other reasons, where Risse's view commits to reframing Rawlsian structure, my view begins with Rawls's conception of social structure in order to surpass certain of its core aspects, chiefly an understanding of social structure as highly systemic and therefore relatively fixed. Specifically, where Risse's view seeks to expand Rawlsian structure by way of theories of technology from Latour and Marx, my view goes beyond Rawlsian structure by emphasizing the centrality of contingent sociality for Dewey and Latour, and by turning to Foucault instead of Marx for insights about how structures actually operate.[64] This last distinction, between Foucault and Marx, raises the always crucial structural question of power.

A corollary of a contingentist conception of social structure is a contin-gentist conception of political power. The beginnings of such an approach can again be mined from Dewey's writings.[65] But the best source for a con-ception of power remains the French political philosopher Michel Foucault.[66] Unfortunately, much of the more analytically informed political philosophy on which I draw in this book entirely neglects Foucault's analyses of power.[67] In so doing, this work remains wedded to a model of power as always operat-ing through overt coercion, by which certain actions are required or forbid-den of subjects—this is precisely the model Foucault famously refers to as *sovereign power*.[68] The coercion or sovereign model of power often assumes what needs to be investigated—namely, how power actually operates in a given social setting. Foucault shows why we should refuse to define power as essentially sovereign. This does not mean we can neglect the analysis of sovereign power; rather, it means we must seek out whatever specific form of power is operative in our field of inquiry. The Foucauldian view is that power at its most general level refers only to "the conduct of conduct," or the ways action (both actual action and menus of possible action) is shaped.[69] By adopting this conception, political philosophy can follow power wher-ever it is exercised—that is, wherever it operates. In light of his own version of a contingentist conception of structure, Foucault empirically investigated how multiple forms of power shape our actions in significant ways including where they do not emanate from the concentrated locale of a coercive sov-ereign state. Best known are his detailed studies of the effects of *disciplinary power* and its normalizing role (as exhibited in settings of education, medi-cine, and psychology) and of the regulatory functions of what he calls *bio-power* (as exhibited by efforts to regulate sexual conduct).[70] There is nothing in Foucault's approach that limits us to only these three shapes of power. We might add to this list an analysis of the power of information technologies, or a modality of *infopower* structuring who we can be and what we can do by fastening us to detailed data formats.[71]

In considering any configuration of power we can bring into view, we might be concerned with the ways specific exercises of power threaten to (or actually do) limit our exercise of freedom. Surely Foucault was con-cerned with power as a limit on freedom. And indeed, freedom is a central political value. But like all political values, as I argued above in discussing political justification, what we are concerned with when we are concerned with freedom is really equal freedom.[72] The power exercised through and by social structure can shape our individual lives and social relations in ways that manifest deep inequalities. Structural views hold that individuals do not independently relate to each other, but are always related to each other through and by shared social structure. It is precisely in virtue of how we are related by structure that contingent structuring forces carry crucial implications for equality.

The Structural Model: The Primary (or Structural) Level

We are now in a position to grasp the significance of a structural view as a model of relational equality. As I conceive it, the structural model situates the equality of relations at two levels.[73] First and primary is the level of the equal treatment of all individuals subject to the social structure by its agents (the paradigmatic agent of social structure being the state). Second, and crucial though not primary, is the level of equal treatment of individuals by each other in their interactions with each other within the medium of social structure. First comes *being related to each other as equals*. Second comes *relating to each other as equals*. I consider each level in turn, offering an extended contrast to the direct model along the way.

The primary level of equality concerns how we are related to each other by a structure. Individuals are related as equals when a structure subjects individuals to treatment as equals. Where a structure treats individuals subject to it as unequal to each other, those individuals are related as unequals. They are, as it were, confined to interacting in a medium of inequality. This is relational inequality in its primary form. By contrast, relational equality in its primary form, or primary-level relational equality, consists in being related as equals by a significant social structure.

The first level is primary because it is conditional for the second, which focuses on equality in how individuals treat each other. The possibility of our relating to each other as individual equals is conditional upon our being related to each other as equals. Consider as an example the way students may be treated in a classroom. We expect classmates to relate to each other as equals, that is, to treat each other as equals and consider each other as having equal status in important respects. So that students might have a chance at this, we typically expect teachers to treat students as one another's equals and in a way that the students can recognize each other as being so treated. Were a teacher to regularly and openly play favorites with one student at the expense of others, it would be unrealistic to expect the students to be able to effectively relate to each other as equals, at least within the context of the classroom.

A crucial feature of primary-level relational equality is that it involves no conditions on the structuring of equal relations beyond actual observable acts of equal treatment. There is no additional condition of attitudinal regard. This aspect of the structural view stands in contrast to models of relational equality in which it is criterial for persons relating as equals that they hold attitudes of regarding each other as equals. Before turning to the secondary level of relational equality on the structural model, I consider these two-condition accounts in some detail. These accounts are central for the direct model of relational equality. I describe how two leading features (which in my view are two chief defects) of the direct model go hand in hand: an account of individuals as directly relating to each other, and an account of their relations as equal only when those individuals hold attitudes regarding each other as equals. I will call these the *individual-centered* and *attitude-dependent* features of the direct model. By contrast, the structural model is *structure-centered* in its methodological focus and *behavior-dependent* in its approach to normative assessment.

The Direct Model: Individuals

The direct model's methodological individualism renders its analyses of relations strikingly incomplete. The problem is not so much that an emphasis on individual interaction is present in the direct model, but rather that it is present there in a way that requires the absence of a fuller picture of how we are related as individuals. It is of course the case that we relate to each other as individuals and that our interactions with each other matter greatly for an assessment of whether we can and do relate as equals. Equal relations within individual interactions constitute a second level of equality for the structural model and are therefore necessary for equality on that model. Equal interpersonal relations are crucial, yet nevertheless insufficient, for equality.

What exactly is the problem with considering the level of individual interaction by itself? One issue is that we just do not interact or relate with each other directly or immediately, without any support of shared social structure. We always interact through a medium of interaction: convention, expectation, language, law, physical infrastructure, technological infrastructure, and much more form the structural context within which we can relate to each other. Take away all that setting and we have nothing within which to interact, or even to act. Another issue is that even if we were to concede the point and accept that individuals do relate to each other directly without the mediation of social structures, it would nevertheless remain true that individuals do not always relate to each other directly. Not even the most ardent adherent to the direct model will deny the fact that mediating structures shape at least some of our interactions. Even if a methodological focus on individual interactions were to hold, it could not pertain to all cases. We would still need to gain grip on social structure, and the methodological individualism of the direct model interferes.

To more fully explore individualist approaches to relational equality, consider Scheffler's prominent statements of relational egalitarianism as a leading exhibit. Scheffler's individual-centered approach contrasts sharply to the more structural view I adopt here myself and discern in certain aspects of Anderson's presentation.[74] His view also offers an instructive point of contrast in that he and Anderson are typically regarded as the two leading theorists of relational equality.[75]

Scheffler explicitly positions equality as primarily an interpersonal relation between individuals when he writes, "Relating to others as equals is best thought of as a complex interpersonal practice."[76] His view is not so much that relational equality only holds between individuals as it is the view that we best understand relational equality by first looking at equality between individuals: "One of the advantages of the relational conception is that it represents equality as a value that applies to human relationships of many kinds, and we may learn things by looking at its nonpolitical applications that will help us to understand how it applies to the political case."[77] Scheffler proposes to analyze egalitarian personal relationships such as marriage to extrapolate features of these relations to more properly social and political relationships.

This method of analysis leads to emaciated conceptions of social and political relations.[78] This is so in two senses. First, we cannot generalize from relations between individual agents to relationality under the influence of group agents (such as states and corporations). The cases are simply too dissimilar. Second, once one has analyzed direct relations between individuals, it will be difficult if not impossible to inflect the terms of that analysis with the social patterns of influence that mediate individual action. On this point, it appears as if Scheffler wants to treat interactions between individuals first as immediate, and then as mediated. But interactions cannot be both immediate and mediated. By contrast, an analysis moving in the other direction (such as that which I adopt) can effectively begin with the mediating influence of social structure and then incorporate individual relations as mediated by social structure. In light of these two problems, Scheffler's view never manages to offer a truly social and political view of relationality, and instead remains mired in decidedly individualist formulations of relational equality. Consider a few examples.

The shortcomings of starting with interpersonal relations are most explicit in Scheffler's attempts to analogize public relational equality to the model of equality in private interpersonal relationships like marriage.[79] Marriage is a unique kind of relationship. Part of its uniqueness is that those who ought to relate as equals are (almost always) simultaneously the primary agents of their so relating (or failing to). In this respect, at least, marriage makes a poor analogy for politics—even a democratic politics of mutual consent. Where we ought to expect relations of equality between all persons in a democratic polity, we are rarely in a good position to regard any individual person (ourselves included) as a primary agent of so relating. The tension between the people who are the equal subjects of a democracy and the administrative complexity of the impersonal agencies of democratic equality form a juxtaposition that is, to say the least, quite interesting. (I briefly return to this curious combination near the end of the chapter.)

Individualist features are elsewhere in the background of Scheffler's strong criticisms of an analogy for social equality offered by Ronald Dworkin.[80] Dworkin describes a situation in which a parent is devising their estate to their children in a way that treats each child as an equal. Scheffler's objection is that Dworkin's vignette is a significant disanalogy for social equality because were we to adopt it, we would find that "citizens are represented, again asymmetrically, as objects of treatment by some kind of centralized subject."[81] Yet this picture of equal treatment is exactly what my structural model proposes as the primary level of relational equality. In light of the plausibility of such structural models, it might be asked if Scheffler is here arguing for equality or arguing against a centralized state apparatus. Protestations against "an autocratic parent" vaguely reminiscent of "an autocratic government" are misleading.[82] Relational equality requires equality of treatment in the sense of equal consideration of all those who are to be treated as equals—but it does not require equality between the agent of treatment and the subjects of treatment when that agent is, say, the state. Dworkin's testator does in fact treat their legatees as equals. The state, in familiar forms such as a criminal court or a parliamentary assembly, does (or at least can) treat its subjects as equals where it expresses equal concern for each subject. A state official or a corporate agent can achieve equal treatment perfectly well without having to somehow make themselves equal to those whom they treat. Indeed, in many (but not all) contexts, an agent of social structure can achieve equal treatment only if they do not position themselves as equal to the subjects of equality. Equal treatment often requires a rule-bound, highly impersonal, and bureaucratic administrative authority that establishes a practical framework for, but is not itself a direct subject of, egalitarian social relations. Crucial to such practical frameworks is a distinction between authority and hierarchy, where an authority is justifiably not positioned as equal to its subjects of treatment while a hierarchy involves unjustifiable statuses of superiority and inferiority.[83] A distinction affirming that authority can be legitimate is of course perfectly consistent with an understanding that state power should be regularly and reliably subject to the episodic rebalancing achieved by democratic elections, oversight, and accountability.

To put a pin in all of this, consider how Scheffler seems to sneer a bit when he refers to Dworkin's view as an "administrative conception of equality."[84] By contrast, I find quite intriguing a suggestion of Anderson's about "the egalitarian potential of bureaucratic modes of authority."[85] It is a cliché of contemporary culture to be a critic of bureaucracy—but this critical posture is a simplification relying on the pretense that in place of the slow bureaucracy there would be, well, nothing at all. But of course there would be. And would it be worse? Anderson offers a clear contrast between bureaucracy and historically prior forms of administration by "patrimonial domination."[86] Scheffler's argument serves up a different kind of contrast between bureaucratic equality and the achievement of equality through direct personal relations. If endorsing patrimonial domination is an unnecessary concession to power politics, then a wishful reliance on personal relationships as a backstop for equality seems to epitomize the idealizing perspective that all too often gets assumed where moral philosophy plays at politics.

The Direct Model: Attitudes

With the individualism of the direct model of relational equality in view, I turn now to its other central feature: a requirement for attitudinal regard as a condition of equal relations between individuals. Scheffler's view here again affords an exemplary contrast to the structural approach. "Relating to others as equals," he says, "is a practice that makes substantial demands on the attitudes, motives, dispositions, and deliberative capacities of the participants."[87] On his view, the "primary concern" of "participants in egalitarian relationships" should be "with their attitudes toward one another and with how seriously each takes the interests of the other in contexts of deliberation and decision."[88] Scheffler is by no means alone in endorsing an attitudinal criterion for relational equality; others include Kasper Lippert-Rasmussen (endorsing an "attitudinal" requirement of "regarding as equals" for equal treatment) and Niko Kolodny (analyzing a form of hierarchy he calls "disparity of regard" that can sometimes be expressed in "disparities of esteem" which "need not have any further practical upshot" beyond "mere detached appraisal").[89] Requirements for attitudes of equal regard have even been endorsed by proponents of distributive equality.[90]

Such two-condition analyses requiring attitudes of equal regard above and beyond actions of equal treatment contrast sharply with a pragmatist conception of a structural model of equality. Both kinds of approaches agree that actual acts of equal treatment are a necessary condition for relating as equals. But the structural model rejects the proposal for an additional attitudinal criterion as both unnecessary and confounding for the purposes of assessing relations as equal or unequal. There are two primary objections to the idea that equal regard is a necessary component of relational equality that stands independent of equal treatment.

The first objection is rooted in the familiar pragmatist point that the only differences that make a difference are those that show up in practice. Does an attitude of "equality of regard" make any difference in practice that does not already show up as a difference in actual actions of equal treatment? If not, a requirement for attitudinal regard is a redundancy. This pragmatist objection can be levied in each of two ways: epistemic and normative.

The epistemic form of the pragmatist objection holds that it is difficult to see what might count as a non-behavioral test for an attitudinal requirement. This way of putting the point is epistemic in its concern with the status of evidence for attitudes. How could we detect the presence of an attitude that does not manifest in behavior?

The normative form of the pragmatist objection is even stronger. Consider someone with specific attitudinal mental states (or brain states) that do not show up in the way they act. Of what normative significance are those attitudes if they do not resolve into actual practices (or behaviors) of equal treatment? Lippert-Rasmussen endorses the view targeted by the normative pragmatist objection in asserting that "relational egalitarians object to belief sets . . . at least in part because of how those who subscribe to such belief sets regard others, independently of how their subscription to the relevant belief set manifests itself in the way in which they treat others."[91] But why should relational egalitarians require assessments of instances of regard that do not show up in actual action? If there is no manifestation of a belief in actual acts of treatment, what is the normative force of the concern? Relational egalitarians ought to be concerned with actual practices perpetrating inequality. A requirement that attitudes figure in normative assessment makes too much of possibilities. It is of course possible that a harbored attitude of unequal regard may manifest in practice, but until it does so, all we have is a mere possibility. Possibilities are cheap, for they are endless. Meanwhile, actualities are the stuff of which our political, social, and moral lives are made.

Pushing this objection a bit further clarifies why an attitudinal requirement is not only misguided, but also potentially harmful. Insisting on attitudes of equal regard as a criterion for equality evinces a willingness to flaunt liberalism's central commitment to freedom of conscience or thought. Liberal tolerance cautions us against the idea that egalitarian ends can be achieved only if all citizens exhibit certain attitudes (regardless of their actual actions). Liberalism and pragmatism both hold that we should leave people's thoughts alone where those thoughts do not manifest in actual harmful action (including harmful speech). I might abhor some of your beliefs, but if you constrain yourself from acting on those beliefs in ways that harm others, then I have little to object to from a political point of view. I relate to you politically as an equal by respecting your freedom to hold beliefs that you limit yourself from inflicting on others through your actions (including your speech).

Actions taking the form of speech deserve further consideration. One response to the pragmatist objections above might begin with the observation that actual practices of unequal treatment sometimes take the form of demeaning (or otherwise inequality-displaying) linguistic utterances. Beneath these utterances, a defender of attitudinal requirements for equality might claim, are attitudes we can impute to their speakers.[92] Yet this hardly counts as a defense against my objections. An assertion by one person that someone else is of lesser worth or value is already a paradigm case of relationally unequal treatment before we even bring imputed attitudes under scrutiny. Such a case counts as actual treatment just insofar as such speech is actual action. What is at issue in the pragmatist objections are not attitudes as such, but only attitudes additional to acts of treatment. What the pragmatist denies is that we need concern ourselves with attitudes that fail to manifest in action, inclusive of overt linguistic behavior.

Having marshaled the first pragmatist objection to equality of regard as a necessary component of equal relations, consider now a second objection. This one ties in with the individualist feature of the direct model as discussed above. Taking equality of regard as an independently necessary condition of equality requires attributing an attitude to the agent of (in)equality. Such attributions of course have implications concerning who we take the agents and subjects of relational equality to be. According to the structural model, relational equality requires that people mutually subject to a social structure (for example, fellow citizens of a state) can and often enough do relate as equals. For people to relate as equals, a fundamental requirement is that their shared political structures treat all as equals. In modern democracies, citizens relating as equals involves their treating each other equally not only in their direct interpersonal dealings, but also—and much more importantly—in their shared political project of setting up administrative agencies that subject all to treatment as equals. As I argued above, in most of the important political settings in which some agent treats subjects equally (or unequally), the agent is not an individual but a complicated social structure to which it does

not make sense to attribute attitudes. However, it is individuals who have attitudes, not institutions (the Ministry of Treatment cannot be said to possess
an attitude of equal regard, though we sometimes impute such attitudes to
such institutions, and when we do so it is solely on the basis of their actions).
In this respect, there is a decidedly individualist cast to the requirement that
equal relations exhibit attitudes of equal regard. Taking attitudes as a condition of equality doubles down on the individualism of the direct model—it
thereby focuses attention on instances of inequality perpetrated by individual
agents where what really matters are the inequalities produced and propa-
gated by social structures. Structural inequality just is more important.

Having posed two independent objections to attitudinal accounts of equal
relations, consider now an objection in turn against my treatment-only egalitarianism. A seemingly plausible objection to my view is that the removal of
an independent condition of regard invites the possibility that equality could
be achieved only on the basis of merely accidental equal treatment, such that
any equality achieved is an unstable equality. Concerns about stability are
certainly reasonable; however, this objection can be discharged in two steps.

First, we should recognize that equality is an attribute of rules of treatment (or patterns of treatment, if not explicitly stated as rules) rather than
single isolated instances of treatment. An isolated incident might matter for
one individual, but our focus regarding a concern with equality should always be the broader political probabilities. Attitudes may seem useful insofar
as they promise to keep singular incidents of inequality from coming to frui-
tion. Even so, what matters are broader patterns of actual practices of relating
as equals as expressed in patterns of actual equal treatment. In considering
such patterns, we should be prepared to admit that attitudes may never show
up in practice, and especially where practices follow well-designed rules for
treatment. I take it that this is part of what Anderson is pointing to in her
underappreciated argument for the importance of bureaucracy for equality.[93] I will take the impeccable rule-following bureaucrat at the Ministry of
Treatment any day over the unpredictability of the well-intentioned but in-
competent clerk at the Ministry of Kindness who regards me as equal to all
their other clients else but fails to actually treat me as such. Equality is robust
where we manifest equal concern for all by actually treating all as equals.
This ought to be the primary focus of equality in contexts where inequality
is already running rampant. Further conditions concerning inner states that
affect our regard for each other may seem preferable, but if they matter for
equality at all, it is only in a derivative sense.

This brings me to a second step of my reply to the objection. It might be
argued that equal regard is itself a necessary condition for equal treatment.

For instance, one might hold equal regard to be motivationally requisite for the stable maintenance of equal treatment. I do not object to this possibility, but neither do I assert it. Were empirical psychology to demonstrate that attitudes of equal regard are motivationally requisite for persons to actually treat each other as equals, then we would have compelling reason to be concerned with attitudes. Yet this reason would warrant only a derivative interest in attitudes insofar as they bear on behavior. This would not impinge the arguments I have presented. The target of my criticism is only the claim that equal regard is, independent of actual equal treatment, necessary for equality. In objecting to that claim, what I object to is the idea that equality itself requires something above and beyond actual practices of equal treatment. As to what is instrumentally required to realize equal treatment in different settings, this is an altogether different question that involves a much larger inquiry.

The foregoing discussion points to some fairly deep problems with attitudinal criteria for relational equality—at least, where such criteria put equality beyond the grip of observable practical tests and set up requirements concerning metaphysically murky inner states of individuals. Anderson emphasizes that relational equality "supports the use of objective tests of unjust disadvantage" wherever such tests are available.[94] I take one of the signal benefits of pragmatism to be its methodological focus on actual practices such that equality can (with much hard work, of course) be clearly identified where it is present.

The Structural Model: The Secondary (or Interpersonal) Level

Having presented arguments against the two defining features of the direct model, I turn finally to the second level of the structural model: its concern with equality in interactions between persons. Whereas the direct model is concerned exclusively with equality in interpersonal interactions, the structural model takes up the interpersonal as conditioned by structuring elements. Recall that the primary level of equality on the structural model requires equal treatment such that those related through structure can relate as equals. The second level of equality concerns whether those who are related as equals actually do relate to each other as equals. The structural model is concerned with equal treatment within both interpersonal interactions and the structuring activity of states, corporations, communities, and the manifold technological apparatus wielded within each of these. The structural model always holds in view how our interpersonal interactions are always already structured by the mediating apparatus of social structure.

How does the structural model incorporate a concern with persons relating as equals in their interactions? The basic idea has already been canvassed above in discussion of the direct model. The direct model is focused on direct or immediate relations between individuals, and the quality of those relations as exhibiting equality (in such forms as equal treatment and equal regard). The structural model in its secondary concern with interpersonal relations is focused on how individuals can and do relate to each other given how those relations are already mediated by social structure. An important question to ask when taking this focus is whether in fact two individuals do relate as equals to each other in ways typically understood in the practice that forms the setting for their relating.

An explicit focus on individuality at this level is important. Contrary to a hostility to individuality common in certain strains of egalitarianism, especially those rooted in critical theory, it is important to affirm that individuality matters a great deal for relational equality. Individuality is not inconsistent with equality—only that which separates individuals is. Individuality itself is actually a condition of equality, for without the integrity of individuality, there is no way persons would ever be able to treat each other as equals.[95] A structural model ought to be able to affirm this. On the structural view I am advocating, normative assessment is focused on whether individuals are able to exhibit equality in their dealings with each other by treating each other as equals.

Since the structural model treats the interpersonal level of equality as secondary to, and shaped by, the presence or absence of equality in the primary structural level, normative assessment of relations on the interpersonal level should proceed in light of the ways that people in their dealing with each other have been related by social structure. The structural model enables us to recognize that individuals who are put into unequal relations with one another by some significant aspect of shared social structure are not in a good position to interact as equals. Normative assessment should take this into account. In doing so, of course, we should assume that the influence of social structure is never fully determining but always probabilistic.

There are two central advantages of the structural model over the direct model in its construal of interpersonal interactions. The first is that the structural model better acknowledges that we all relate to each other through the mediating influence of shared social structure. The direct model's methodological hypothesizing of immediate relations is unfounded. None of us ever relate wholly directly or in pure immediacy. The second advantage is that the structural model affords a clearer view of the kinds of mechanisms at play in the vast majority of our social relations, especially those that are relatively impersonal but nevertheless interpersonal. Think, for instance, of the multitude of ways you are impersonally related, as an individual, to a fellow citizen you will never meet who boxes goods you regularly purchase. With such relations in view, the structural model replaces the direct model's psychological mechanism of attitudinal regard with the properly political mechanism of structural treatment. The majority of our political relations do not hang on attitudes and other psychological statuses so much as they hang on the ways we are structurally related to each other, even across vast (and even unbridgeable) distances, times, and contexts. And even in those closer-knit interpersonal relations of domesticity, employment, and neighborhood where we do hold attitudes about those with whom we relate, these attitudes taken on their own are never a sufficient explanatory mechanism for how we relate insofar as our attitudes are themselves always inflected by social structure.

An Interesting Juxtaposition in Democratic Equality

Relational equality is simultaneously structural and interpersonal. A curious juxtaposition hides within this simultaneity. With respect to the two levels of equality composing the structural model, the relata of relational equality are individual persons. On one level, individuals are related to each other by way of their own agency in their interpersonal dealings. And on a more primary level, persons are related by social structure such that the relevant agents of relationality are elements or aspects of social structure. That the relata of relational equality are not always the same entities as the agents of relational equality may seem undemocratic. But it is not. In actually existing democracies, people relate as equals, but not often directly because almost always through the means of impersonal institutions (paradigmatically, but not only, the bureaucracies of the administrative state).

Relational equality in a democracy involves political relationships that foster the kind of social, economic, and cultural complexity in virtue of which it is both unlikely that any individual citizen will function as a primary agent of inequality and also highly likely that structural apparatus (such as state agencies and capitalist corporations, as well as technological ensembles like computational systems) do regularly function as a primary agent of inequality or equality. This illuminates again the intimate connection between democratic politics and bureaucratic administration. In a democracy, we recognize that we ought to relate as equals, but the relational equality that matters most is not often (and certainly not only) a function of how we treat each other individually. In a democracy we relate as equals not primarily by way of virtuous communitarian interaction with civic neighbors, but by way of effectively operating democratic institutions in which all who come before them are treated as equals in such a way that they can continue to relate to each other (both interpersonally and impersonally) as equals. This is why the form of equality that matters at the primary level concerns how those subject to social structure are treated, and why there can be no egalitarian aspiration to, for instance, individual citizens being themselves equal to the state.

Citizens relate as equals not by each one being equal to the state, but by all establishing a state that treats each as the equal of all others. Only in that way can, for example, the judge on the bench be possessed of the unequal authority to require of a defendant such as a state agency or a business firm that it subject all those with whom it deals to equal treatment. This does not make the state, or the individual who occupies the role of judge, a master.[96] But it does make the authority of the state, as well as such of its offices as that of judge, a facility for equality or inequality. Where equality is achieved, this is the form of democratic equality we have come to expect, and ought to continue to demand more stringently, from the courtrooms, corporations, classrooms, credit agencies, and computational systems that form the structural apparatus of contemporary democratic society.

SUMMARIZING THE TWO DIMENSIONS OF STRUCTURAL RELATIONAL EQUALITY

Relational equality consists in the connection between two kinds of equality: first is equality in persons being related to each other as equals by relevant agents that shape social structure (such as the state), and second is equality between persons who are so related being prepared to and then also actually relating to each other as equals. Each of these aspects of relational equality is crucial. So too is their order. The primary level brings into focus how our practices, institutions, and customs structure the relations between persons such that they are related to each other as equals. The secondary level brings into focus whether people actually can and do relate to each other as equals. Equality in interpersonal interaction is necessary for relational equality, but actions on this level are always structurally (and so too causally) conditioned. How I treat a friend is in large part a function of what I do, which is itself in large part a function of the social structure that conditions both my doings and my relations. It is just insofar as the direct model neglects such conditioning that it is inadequate as a model of political inequality (and probably much else besides).

One way to think about the two-level structural model I have presented is by comparison to a two-dimensional theory of equality developed by Rondel, who like me takes a pragmatist perspective on equality.[97] Rondel describes equality as coordinating between a vertical dimension of our mutual subjection to the state (or some other form of social structure) and a horizontal dimension of interpersonal relations.[98] He associates the vertical dimension with the distributive obligations of the state and the horizontal dimension with requirements for relational equality.[99] On the contrasting view I have presented, relational equality is as much a feature of our vertical subjection to social structure as is distributive equality. Setting my view in Rondel's terms, I adopt a broader view of verticality, such that it encompasses all forms of equal treatment (not just distributive forms, but certainly including them too) that social structure (paradigmatically, the state) ought to deliver to those subject to it. Further in these terms, the horizontal dimension of equality involves interpersonal relations between persons as equals, which relations are already significantly structured along a vertical dimension of more top-down structuring where conditions of relational equality between all those subject to the structure should obtain.

I have referred to my structural view as pragmatist because it puts practice first—prioritizing practice involves assessing egalitarian aspirations, ideals, and principles with respect to how they actually manifest (or fail to) in practice. What we find whenever we look at human practices are interpersonal interactions (on the horizontal dimension) that are deeply conditioned by processes of structuration (on the vertical dimension). Assessments of equality, accordingly, ought to be dual-dimensional or two-level. On both levels, what matters for satisfying the requirement of equal relations is how people are treated. Regarding the primary level, or the vertical dimension, we ask: are people treated as equals to each other by structuring agents such that they are able to relate as equals? Regarding the secondary level, or horizontal dimension, we ask: can and do people who are related to each other as equals by their shared social structures also treat each other as equals in their actual interactions? This structural and behavioral model of relational equality finds its philosophical coherence in a pragmatism according to which actions can be seen to be distinct from merely physical events in virtue of being structured by practices that are themselves structured by wider networks or associations of social elements.

Although I have offered a generalized defense of a pragmatist prioritization of structure and behavior as a requisite feature of a general theory of equality, it is also worth noting that these two features also possess unique advantages in the specific context of analyses of equality in data technology. Technologies are not individuals to whom we relate, nor are they attitude-bearing entities. First, technology is decidedly not just another individual to whom we relate. We do not expect the computer to treat us as an equal to it. What would this even mean? Rather, technology is relevant to questions of equality only insofar as it contributes to the social structures that shape our relations to each other. So we do, or at least should, expect a computational process to treat those subject to its processes as equal to each other. Second, technologies cannot be properly said to bear attitudes. Though some of the furthest edges of posthumanist theories may wish to attribute attitudes to machines, the evidence for these attitudes will always only ever be overt behavior on the part of the machine. Machines display behaviors (or, on a more physicalist account, they play a causal role in the genesis of events). But they do not therefore harbor attitudes. When it comes to data technology, what matters to assessments of equality are, for both structural and behavioral reasons, processes of treatment.

A conception of equal treatment referring to the structural model of relational equality presented in this chapter offers an effective critical vantage for many of our most familiar concerns about data technology. There is increasing concern about how our abilities to relate to others are being reconfigured by data technologies in ways that are unexpectedly, and often even unintentionally, hierarchical. Consider again problems of political polarization.[100] What is it that makes polarization a problem? According to typical liberty-based perspectives, it is difficult to see a clear problem here. Polarization can easily look like people interacting with just whom they please. According to another typical perspective, that of distributive equality, it is also difficult to see the problem. Increased polarization is not obviously correlated with increased inequalities in distributive outcomes. But seen through the lens of relational inequality, the problem of polarization comes into clear view. Technologies that separate us—as social media so thoroughly and efficiently do—leave us largely indisposed to relate to each other as equals. We do not see in each other someone who might be our worthy interlocutor or mutual collaborator, but rather only an avatar or a username or an almost indistinct sea of text. This involves a profound loss of capacities for relational equality.

In these and other cases, what we are experiencing in the face of data deployments is the loss of democratic social structures that help shape our interactions into more-equal forms. These egalitarian relations are what we feel to be under threat when we are forced to confront our social and individual vulnerabilities to many of the most widely perceived threats of data technology. It cannot merely be an accident that we are witnessing such stark democratic decay at precisely the moment where data technology has fully saturated so many domains of our lives. Data prospers, yet democracy totters.

4

Equal Treatment
Equitable Entry + Fair Processing

Amartya Sen observed more than a quarter century ago that "equal concern, in some form or other, provides a shared background to all the major ethical and political proposals . . . that continue to receive argued support and reasoned defense."[1] Even the most ardent opponent of economic equality who praises freedom as nonnegotiable presumably justifies that praise as focused on a conception of equal freedom. Nobody pretends to justify freedom as valuable only to themselves, though some may surreptitiously seek just that.

What specifically do we affirm in endorsing the value of equal concern for all? The answer advanced in the previous chapter was that equal concern is a concern for democratic equality in our relations. I presented and extended Elizabeth Anderson's relational egalitarian theory that "to be an egalitarian is to commend and promote a society in which its members interact as equals."[2] Building out Anderson's view, I developed a structural account of relational or democratic equality. According to this view, the distinctively political concern we have for equality is a concern for equal relations between people insofar as their relations are configured and conditioned by social structures. In endorsing equality, what we care about is whether people can relate as equals as influenced by whether social structure relates them as equals.

What are the criteria for equality in relations such that we can know whether relations are equal or unequal? In practice, equal treatment is the primary pragmatic criterion and behavioral test of equality. What matters for actually enacting, and hence enjoying, equality are acts of equal treatment. This view requires working out an idea of equal treatment, or more precisely, an idea of treating people as equals.

What, then, does equal treatment involve? How do we know when people have been treated as equals? To answer these questions, this chapter develops a conceptual analysis of equal treatment. Partly with an eye to my broader argument for equality in data technology, this analysis emphasizes the fact that equal treatment is a quality of a process—specifically, a process of treating people. In virtue of this fact, a treatment-centered account of equality is particularly suitable for equality in computational programs and other data technologies, for computational programs are essentially processes too. As processes, both equal treatment and computational programs have three stages: entry, processing, and exit. In some systems, these stages may recursively reiterate or even overlap synchronically. But they can always be analytically distinguished with respect to operational roles. An insight advanced in this chapter, then, is that we can correlate the inputs, processes, and outputs of information-processing technology with the requirements for a process of equal treatment at each stage. The argument I develop is that equal treatment occurs when systems both establish entry conditions for those subject to treatment in a way that enables them to relate as equals and institute fair processes of treatment for those subjects. This can be stated in a formulaic slogan: *equal treatment = equitable entry + fair processes*.

Procedures of Treatment

Equality consists in equal treatment. Equal treatment connotes a quality of an activity, or a process, of treating. Treatment is itself procedural, implying a beginning and an end (including cases where both are only vaguely defined). Treatment is also directional in that it flows from an agent to a subject—from a treater to a treatee. This holds even where the agent and the subject coincide, as in cases where a formalized group is the subject of its own treatment through instruments like recursive policies of governance.

In the previous chapter, I presented a two-level account of relational equality. At the primary level, equal treatment flows from some element of social structure to those subject to its treatment—canonically, people, but possibly also groups of people, such as informal social groups or formalized organizations. At the secondary level, which I referred to as the interpersonal level, equal treatment is a quality of interactions between two or more persons. While there are many interesting questions to ask about interpersonal equal treatment, I argued in the previous chapter that relational equality and equal treatment need to begin at primary-level or structure-level considerations concerning how structural agents treat those subject to a structure. Accordingly, I focus in this chapter almost exclusively on equal treatment at the structural level, acknowledging that extrapolation to cases of interpersonal equal treatment cannot be merely formulaic.

Equal treatment is particularly pertinent to equality within data technology. Treatment procedures and computational technology are both processes; both are essentially procedural. Equal treatment is a quality of actions—namely, actions of treating. Computational information technology has its purpose and point in what it operationally does—namely, the process of dealing with data, or, somewhat redundantly, the process of data processing.

One way to understand this parallel between equal treatment and information technology is in terms of a model specification of both processes in terms that enable us to superimpose each on the other. As noted above, any process taken in its generality can be specified in terms of three stages: initiation, processing, and conclusion. This general model applies well to both treatment procedures and computational technology. The parallels such a model brings into view provide terms for potential value alignment. This can be shown by unpacking the terms on each side of the parallel.

Take computational programs first. According to the widely employed IPO model, information technology is operationally defined by a three-stage process: receiving information as an *input*, information *processing*, and sending or storing information as an *output*. At the input stage, a computational system receives information or data.[3] Crucial at this stage are the informational formats, or data structures, in virtue of which the system can receive data. Any systems receiving data must be designed for that receiving. For instance, a computer cannot receive visual data from an environment unless it has a camera. Structured entry inputs form conditions for entry and thereby for every downstream stage in a procedure. Though there are many forms of processing, the most commonly discussed and perhaps even the most commonly employed are those stepwise processors known as algorithms. Algorithms process data that have been structured such that algorithms can read, redesign, and rewrite those data. Once data have been sufficiently processed according to the designs of the algorithm, information technology concludes at the third stage, outputting its processed data. According to the most coherent versions of the IPO model, the output stage is a pure function of the processing and input stages, such that output consists only in passing processed data to another program or routine—for instance, programs for storage or for hard-copy printing.

Next, take procedures of treatment, construed in their generality such that they can result in either equal or unequal treatment. A model isomorphic with the IPO schematization can be defined here. Call the EPD model a schematization of treatment whose three stages are *entry, processing,* and *determination.* Any process of treatment begins with entry. Those subject to the treatment enter into it by way of protocols for entry. Exemplary are legal procedures of entry in a court—any formal courtroom setting operates by protocols for the intake or entry of those being treated by a judicial procedure, such as a defendant in a criminal trial. (There are also numerous other subprotocols for the entry of others relevant to the trial, such as the selection of the jurors or the admission of witnesses.) Once those subject to treatment are entered into the system, the second stage of processing or dealing with those entered can begin. Here again there are protocols binding on processing. Courts, to continue with that example, operate with protocols regulating evidence, testimony, and relevance of arguments. Finally, at the third stage there is a conclusion or determination. In formal settings, the decision stage is purely a function of processing and entry conditions, such that the determination adds no new content but is instead designed to pass a result to some further process of treatment. Though hard cases requiring judicial discretion are inevitable, the vast majority of decisions in a court of law should accord with what prevailing rules prescribe for the facts of the case. Only in this way can a trial have a chance of being objective rather than only ever a collation of the subjective opinions of jurors or a judge. Jurors, for instance, are meant to weigh the evidence and facts of the case against the requirements of the law and are not meant to pell-mell introduce into the decision their own opinions that fall beyond the scope of governing law and admitted evidence. If they do, the procedure of the court has not been followed, and their intended decision is void. Said differently, where actions contrary to defined protocols are introduced, then the determination is void because arrived at through some other procedure than that of the formalized procedure of law that the court is meant to operationalize.

This brings us to a crucial observation about processes of treatment and the possibility of equal treatment. Protocols for entry, processing, and exit in a courtroom do not apply only to single cases. If they did, the law would be unpredictable and unjust. Rather, these protocols apply to all cases in all courts in a jurisdiction with respect to all defendants. Only in this way is there a chance of equal treatment—that is, different defendants being treated as equals with each other. Anticipating the discussion of the next section, it is crucial to recognize that trial proceedings should (and in most democratic jurisdictions actually do) contain protocols that enable courts to treat differently situated individuals differently rather than identically. For instance, rules of treatment are different for adults and minors, as well as for adults who are recognized (by formal entry protocols) as unable to take responsibility for their actions due to mental incapacity.

Compare now the two abstracted kinds of processes I have presented. The three stages of the IPO model parallel the three stages of the EPD model. Their parallelism can be schematized as follows:

Computational program	Treatment procedure
Data inputs	Entry conditions
Data processing	Processing conditions
Data outputs	Determination conditions

This parallel between computational programs and treatment procedures offers a way of thinking about how we can, and should, achieve equality in technologies for data computation. We already have rich bodies of thought concerning what equality looks like in procedures of treatment. Exploring such ideas of equal treatment should shine parallel light on how we might understand data equality.

A Conceptual Anatomy of Equal Treatment

What does equal treatment involve? A beginning insight for considering this question is that equal treatment is a quality of a procedure of treatment in which all those subject to the procedure are treated as equals. This way of stating the requirements for equal treatment has the advantage of clearly specifying the relevant relations to which equality primarily applies. Equality of treatment refers to equality among those who are treated by a procedure, rather than, for instance, equality between an agent of a procedure and a subject of that procedure.

This insight can be stated in terms of my distinction from the previous chapter between primary-level (structural) equal treatment and secondary-level (interpersonal) equal treatment. In a matter of equal treatment by the paradigmatically structuring force of the state, there is no question of equality between the agent (the state that does the treating) and the subject (the individual citizen it treats). A claim that equality should apply between the state and the citizen would be a category mistake. It may be a forgivable category mistake when rooted in conceptions of equal treatment focused on the secondary level of interpersonal interactions, for at the secondary level, equality of treatment appears to coincide with the idea of equality between the agent and subject of treatment. In two-person cases of mutual equal treatment at this level, both persons are at once agent and subject of treatment. Unfortunately, though, this category mistake obscures equal treatment at the primary or structural level. What is requisite for equal treatment at the primary level is a form of treatment that establishes equality among those subject to treatment. Recall that the central idea of equality is that of equal relations rather than equal distributions. With respect to people subject to a procedure, equality requires that they be treated by the procedure as standing in relations of equality with each other that those subject to the procedure can express in their interactions. What form should this take?

EQUAL TREATMENT IS TAILORED TREATMENT

One common misconception of equal treatment is that it requires identical treatment. Treating persons as equals cannot possibly involve treating them in exactly the same way, unless of course they are all already identically situated. But this is almost never the case. What we endorse when we endorse equal treatment is not mathematical identity, but equality of relations with each other. What we want from equality is to be related to each other as equals even and especially where our differences come into view. Treatment as an equal, accordingly, requires what I will call *difference-sensitive treatment*, or *tailored treatment*.

An understanding of equality as requiring tailoring has a long pedigree going at least as far back as Aristotle in 350 BCE.[4] Looking just within the last century or so of pragmatist egalitarianism, John Dewey and W. E. B. Du Bois both argued explicitly that equality does not imply sameness. Here is Du Bois in 1915: "The equality in political, industrial and social life which modern men must have in order to live, is not to be confounded with sameness. On the contrary, in our case, it is rather insistence upon the right of diversity;— upon the right of a human being to be a man even if he does not wear the same cut of vest, the same curl of hair or the same color of skin."[5] And here is Dewey in 1932: "[Equality] does not mean sameness; it is not to be understood quantitatively, an interpretation which always ends in ideas of external and mechanical equality."[6]

These philosophical arguments concerning equality eventually found their echo in United States law. Supreme Court Justice William Douglas's majority opinion in the 1974 *Lau v. Nichols* case concerning English-only instruction for non-English-speaking students in San Francisco public schools held that "there is no equality of treatment merely by providing students with the same facilities, textbooks, teachers, and curriculum, for students who do not understand English are effectively foreclosed from any meaningful education."[7] Nine months later, Congress passed the Equal Educational Opportunities Act, requiring schools to proactively "overcome language barriers that impede equal participation."[8]

On the heels of these and other legal implementations of equality, the philosopher of law Ronald Dworkin solidified a crucial formulation according to which we should understand equal treatment not as identical treatment but in terms of "treatment as an equal."[9] Equal treatment requires treating as equals all those treated by a procedure or rule. Insofar as those treated by a procedure are always in some respects different from each other, treatment as equals always requires difference-sensitive treatment and often requires nonidentical difference-sensitive treatment. Dworkin offers an example of a parent treating their children as equals by way of treating them quite differently with respect to their different health conditions.[10] Sen concisely captures the general point of such cases in his pithy formulation that "equal consideration for all may demand very unequal treatment in favour of the disadvantaged."[11] That may sound paradoxical at first blush, but once given due consideration, this emphasis on differential tailoring turns out to be a very clear-eyed conception of equal treatment.

What, then, of relational equality? The central purpose of tailored equal treatment within a framework of relational equality is twofold: to block procedures that structurally incentivize unequal relations between people and to cultivate procedures that structure their relations in more-equal terms. Unequal relations can take many forms, including social exclusion, stigmatization, marginalization, blatant maldistribution (large disparities in income, health, or life opportunities), or outright domination and oppression. Being each other's equal in all the senses brought into view by relational equality typically requires tailored, or nonidentical, treatment.

What exactly does tailored treatment involve? What are the criterial elements of difference-sensitive treatment as equals? To answer these questions, I shall borrow the egalitarian philosopher T. M. Scanlon's metaphor of a "moral anatomy" of equality.[12] Crucial to the metaphor of anatomy as I shall employ it is the idea of making visible different operational components of a system. A biological anatomy makes visible the components that compose organs and tissues. An anatomy in any form involves conceptualizing and visibilizing operational units and their subunits.

According to the anatomy of equal treatment, there are two operational components involved in treatment as an equal. One of these concerns processing conditions for treatment. Equality here requires fairness such that processing neither generates new relational inequalities nor magnifies existing relational inequalities between people. This can be referred to as *fair processing*. The second operational component, discussed far less often, is both conceptually and sequentially prior to the notion of procedural fairness. This component is operative at the first stages of a procedure where entry conditions are in force. Equality here requires that people be entered into treatment in ways that situate them as equals to each other rather than as superiors and inferiors, or in any other way as so separate from each other that they cannot relate as equals. I refer to this component of equal treatment as *equitable entry*. Mapping each of these components to the three-stage model explicated earlier, these two egalitarian values can be schematized as follows.

Computational program	Equal treatment	Treatment procedure
Data inputs	Equitable entry (*ee*)	Entry conditions
Data processing	Fair processing (*fp*)	Processing conditions
Data outputs	Equality (= *ee* + *fp*)	Determination conditions

According to this schema, fully equal treatment consists in coordinating two independently necessary and jointly sufficient conditions: equitable-entry conditions plus fair-processing conditions. The idea is that at each stage, we can test procedures for stage-appropriate aspects of equality. At the entry stage, we test for equity in a way that establishes equality as difference-sensitive rather than difference-insensitive. At the processing stage, we test for fairness in a way that establishes equality as unbiased. Where equality is achieved at both stages, a process arriving at a determination will have enacted equal treatment.

I turn now to describing in detail these two criteria for equal treatment. The purpose of the anatomy to follow is to make visible and intelligible the two parts of equal treatment where such treatment satisfies requirements for relational equality. The focus will be on the entry and processing stages of procedures of treatment with an eye toward what relational equality distinctively requires at each of these stages. I begin with fairness, since that notion will already be more familiar for most readers (for instance, as it features in the ideal of algorithmic fairness). In this way, I start with what is already widely assumed in order to show why the content of this assumption is insufficient for inequality.

FAIR PROCESSING WITHIN EQUAL TREATMENT

The basic idea of fairness in processing is that a procedure ought not arbitrarily institute inequalities between people who are similarly situated in being subject to the procedure. Unfair processes are those that arbitrarily differentiate among those subject to a procedure in such a way as to result in their being made more unequal.

Two grades of procedural fairness, or fair processing, can be distinguished. What I call *modest fair processing* sets a standard according to which procedures ought not generate new or additional inequalities among those subject to the procedure. By contrast, *robust fair processing* is a standard according to which procedures ought to both refrain from generating new inequalities and also go the further step of actively and actually decreasing (or even going so far as minimizing) the reproduction of existing inequalities. On the more robust grade, processes are unfair not only where they create new inequalities, but also where they manage to prevent new inequalities yet nevertheless reproduce existing inequalities.

Procedural fairness in contexts aiming to achieve distributive equality has been widely discussed. What about procedural fairness that aims to achieve relational equality? This involves procedures that do not generate additional relational inequalities (on the modest condition) and that even inhibit the reproduction of extant relational equality (on the robust condition). The idea is that those subject to treatment by some agent facilitating the operation of some element of social structure are not subject to procedures that institute (or reproduce) among them any hierarchies of exclusion, separation, and the like.

Consider a case where the agent of treatment is the state in the context of public education. In the aforementioned 1974 *Lau v. Nichols* ruling, the Supreme Court held it unfair to institute a procedure in which students are instructed in skills by use of curricula that incidentally require linguistic competencies that some students possess and others do not.[13] The unfairness at issue here is perhaps more intuitive with respect to matters of distributive inequalities that are likely to flow from such a procedure. Those receiving instruction that matches their existing linguistic competencies will tend to accrue not only more educational benefits but also more education itself. Yet the unfairness here has a relational aspect too. A procedure that needlessly divides a class into students who can understand classroom proceedings and those who cannot thereby separates the students into two distinct groups—in this case, on the basis of existing linguistic competencies. From such divisions flow tendencies to not easily relate as equals to those in other groups. This is a form of relational inequality. The ruling in *Lau* cannot be fully explained without reference to the uniqueness of relational, in contrast to distributive, equality.

Clearly, procedural fairness matters much for both distributive and relational equality alike. But is it sufficient for each? Familiar arguments about the role of procedural fairness in distributive equality suggest that it may be in that case; one idea here is that rigorously fair procedures are capable of instituting sufficiently stringent requirements on the patterns that can be taken to express equality in distributions.[14] Given this, one idea would be to attempt a kind of conceptual expansion of procedural fairness such that it could similarly be shown to be sufficient for relational equality as well. I would not rule out such attempts as unachievable. Yet it is hard to see how procedural fairness could suffice for relational equality, since relational equality is not as clearly patterned in the way that distributive equality is. Rather than attempting to gather the multiple values of equality under the single heading of fairness, I pursue an alternative approach.

The approach I take is motivated by a number of recent interventions in relational egalitarianism we might refer to as *fairness-plus arguments*. According to these views, fairness on its own cannot suffice for equality. What other values have been described as necessary for realizing equality?

One candidate, defended by Jonathan Wolff, is respect.[15] Wolff's argument is that equality requires not just an idea of fairness, but also an idea of respect. The claim is that fairness taken on its own can often be seen to be, or at least felt to be, undermining of respect for persons. On Wolff's view, "There are, in fact, at least two ideas which are equally central to egalitarianism, and the heart of my case in this article is that there can be a degree of tension between them."[16] Squaring fairness and respect is, it turns out, not easy. But it is crucial for equality that we make every effort to try. Simply going with fairness alone can lead to, well, disrespect. And where this happens, we fall short of equality.

Another familiar value that we might take to be coordinate with fairness is that of equality in opportunities. Scanlon's anatomy of equality of economic opportunity presents this idea as consisting in three components, of institutional justification, procedural fairness, and substantive opportunity.[17] Of particular interest is Scanlon's requirement for substantive opportunity as coordinate with, yet clearly irreducible to, procedural fairness. This argument is meant to help us see why it is one thing to have one's employment application scrutinized fairly, but quite another thing to have a substantive opportunity to be selected for a position in the first place. Scanlon's argument is that attempts to implement fairness on its own without also satisfying substantive opportunity will yield something, but whatever that is will fall short of full equality. We might envision it as a kind of fairness among those subject to a selection process, except that many would-be selectees are unable to effectively enter into the process.

The two views just canvassed are fairness-plus views. The question prompting both is the same: fairness plus what? Plus respect? Plus opportunity? In light of arguments advanced in the previous chapter against attitude-dependent conceptions of equality, the answer I pursue is one that builds out a norm of substantive opportunity rather than one of attitudinal requirements for respectful regard. I argue that treatment as an equal requires coordinating a notion of fair procedures with the value of equitable entry conditions—an idea conceptually quite proximate to substantive equal opportunity.[18]

EQUITABLE ENTRY INTO EQUAL TREATMENT

When it is the case that people are on unequal footing, and it almost always is, a form of treatment that passes along preexisting inequalities does not qualify as fully equal treatment, but is better described as treatment that leaves those who are unequal in a state of inequality. A concern with how people are made more or less equal by entry conditions for processes of treatment can help address such persisting inequalities.

The idea of equitable entry expresses a concern with equality within a procedure of treatment at its initial stage—that is, at its input, or entry, stage. The concern here is with how equal persons are upon entry into a procedure. A question about "how equal" persons are can be taken in two senses. One sense refers to the extent of equality such as when we ask how wide open conditions for entry are. To take an analogy, we might ask how wide open a door is so we will know how many people can fit through it at once. A second sense of "how equal" refers to specific profiles for entry that impact individuals differentially. Here the analogy is with different ways a door admits entry, since doors can be closed, ajar, unlocked but too difficult for some to open (such as young children who cannot use a handle), or ajar but built in a way that imposes difficulties of use for some (such as a doorway that requires those entering to take a step up). An idea of equitable entry conditions includes both of these features of extent (or breadth) and profile (or shape) of entry. Entry conditions institute requirements for entry into procedures of treatment that concern how and whether persons can be processed at the second stage of processing. Entry conditions for a procedure of treatment yield inequality in the specifically relational sense of equality where they separate entrants according to any of a number of mechanisms of hierarchical inequality: exclusion, marginalization, or even outright segregation.

Consider a companion example to the above-discussed legal ruling about unfair processing in the delivery of instruction in public education. A Supreme Court ruling that forms an analogue with respect to entry conditions is that in *Brown v. Board of Education of Topeka* from 1954. This case is particularly informative insofar as the central inequality recognized in the ruling concerns relational, and not just distributive, inequality. Its assertion that "separate educational facilities are inherently unequal" unambiguously distinguishes the court's unanimous opinion from the view that separate facilities may be equal despite the separateness they induce.[19] One legal scholar observes that, given its own earlier rulings, the court "could easily have held that all the African American facilities before it were unequal to the parallel white institutions" in the sense of provisioning worse educational outcomes along visibly racial lines.[20] Instead, the court held that facilities were unequal precisely because of their status as segregating, and therefore would be unequal even if equal educational outcomes were provisioned. This is a statement about relational inequality. The court's reasoning even explicitly expresses this concern with relational equalities—for instance, in asserting that "to separate [some students] from others of similar age and qualifications solely because of their race generates a feeling of inferiority as to their status in the community."[21] While *Brown* was thus clearly focused on relational equality, what of its focus with respect to the three stages of a procedure of treatment? Whereas the *Lau* decision focuses on processes for delivering equal instruction in public education, the *Brown* decision (preceding *Lau* by twenty years) focuses on the prior stage of entry into public education facilities. The question in *Brown* primarily concerns whether there shall be relational equality (rather than segregation) at the front doors of the schoolhouse, whereas the question in *Lau* primarily concerns whether there shall be relational equality in the contents of instructional processes. The two rulings together articulate the two necessary elements of equal treatment for relational equality: equity at the gates of entry and fairness in such standard processes as delivery, assessment, or selection.

The idea of equitable entry can, like that of procedural fairness, be distinguished into two grades: what I will call *robust equitable entry* and *minimal equitable entry*. Minimal equitable entry stipulates a standard according to which persons ought not be barred from entering into a process because of some quality they possess that is actually irrelevant to the process. Equitable entry in even a minimal form bars, for instance, discrimination against protected classes. That said, equitable entry allows that some qualities of persons are relevant to some processes. For instance, a position at a law firm that requires advanced legal expertise may justifiably stipulate that applicants must have a law degree from an accredited institution, have passed a bar examination, and so forth. It is not inequitable to close entry in this way, but it would be if instead of requiring direct certifications some assumed proxy for them was used, especially if the proxy is actually irrelevant to the nature of the conditions (such as barring applicants who are blind or deaf because of discriminatory misconceptions about requisite abilities for passing the bar or even for practicing law). A minimal level of equitable entry can be an extremely powerful notion; in particular, in contexts where it is not widely affirmed.

Yet minimal equitable entry often does not go far enough when our concern is with treating all those subject to a procedure as equal to each other. Robust equitable entry goes further—indeed, much further. It involves the idea that all persons (or more precisely, all relevant persons) are permitted to enter into a procedure and are also sufficiently enabled to enter on terms that position them as equals to others also entering. Scanlon writes of the neighboring notion of substantive opportunity that it "is fulfilled if no one has a valid complaint that they were not able to compete for positions of advantage because they did not have sufficient access to conditions" relevant for the position and in particular "conditions that are necessary to become a good candidate for selection" in a fair process.[22] If you and I intend to apply for the same job, robust equitable entry is lacking if you are allowed to apply but unequally encumbered in applying (say, by having to submit additional evidence of a qualification that I am simply assumed to have) or set on a separate track in applying (say, by having your application vetted for lower-status positions) in ways that are not justified by requirements of the position.[23] Though categorizing or bucketing applicants (based on, say, skill sets) can sometimes be justified, the point of requiring an actual justification for such categorization is not to provide an excuse for bucketing. For equitable entry to truly be robust, the burden of justification for bucketing needs be quite high. To justify bucketing applicants it may not always suffice to merely claim that a higher-status position requires a particular skill set. Such justifications should also require showing that the position itself could not have been reconfigured to include training in that skill set as part of initial employment training. As Scanlon observes, "An institution is open to objection if it disadvantages poorer applicants by presupposing a skill that it could provide training in without great sacrifice of efficiency."[24] Such an institution, in my terms, fails to achieve robust equitable entry.

Of course, that a process fails to meet robust equitable entry does not mean that it fails to meet minimal equitable entry. And for some processes, that is all that can be pragmatically achieved. Why go further than the minimal condition and implement robust equity? One reason is that equitable entry is subject to some of the same criticisms that have been levied against equal opportunity, which is in some respects a much-maligned notion in recent political thought. Most of equal opportunity's perceived vices apply only to minimalist understandings of its requirements. If you are far less likely than someone born into an ultra-rich family to achieve some goal that we all agree should be available to all, then this should be seen as not only unequal but also, presuming that social policy could redress or cure the inequality, objectionably unequal. Why this is objectionable can be seen by way of some observations about equal opportunity presented by Bernard Williams.

Williams's argument is that the key to an effective, or what I am calling robust, practice of equal opportunity is the idea of considering persons in abstraction from the unequal conditioning structures that have played a causal role in their (in)ability to pursue and achieve opportunities. Elaborating a case concerning a hypothetical Smith and Jones, Williams maintains that "to give Smith and Jones equality of opportunity involves regarding their conditions, where curable, as themselves part of what is done to Smith and Jones, and not part of Smith and Jones themselves."[25] For example, socioeconomic status is not part of who Smith and Jones are, but is rather part of how social structure situates them. Equality requires abstracting people from their unequal conditions such that we do not simply retrench unequal structuring forces. Treating people as equals means affirming the equality of each despite the inequalities in condition that presently and contingently attach to them. Williams thus says that "individuals whose opportunities are to be equal should be abstracted from . . . features of social and family background."[26] It is an enormously difficult question, he observes, where this should stop—at social conditions, at familial influences, at hereditary genetic differences, or even further. But we need not settle this difficult question for all possible cases (including mostly hypothetical ones, as in genetic engineering) to affirm that it is a question that deserves an answer.

Williams's argument can be adapted from the idea of equal opportunity to that of equitable entry by recognizing that entry conditions are themselves part of procedures for treatment, rather than regarding entry as a merely factual matter that preexists the entire treatment procedure in a way that must be simply accepted as given. The key formulation I take from Williams is that "curable" conditions are "part of what is done" to persons but not "part of [the persons] themselves."[27] Restated in my terms, the idea is that how persons are entered into a procedure (for example, how their data are formatted as inputs) is part of what that procedure does to them and not simply just a part of those persons themselves. Of course, figuring out how entry conditions shape people entering into a procedure often involves some very hard questions. But it has always been the case that questions of value, including questions of equality, are very hard. This does not mean that we get to set them to the side in unbridled pursuit of easier questions. Doing so would be unjustifiable and, in the case of equality, might even be cruel.

Discussions of equitable opportunity are easily misled into being solely concerned with comparative levels of disadvantage flowing from characteristics of individuals. But what really matters, according to my relational egalitarian perspective, is how individuals are related to each other. Where equality is focused only on distributions, equity gets construed as a comparative notion for measuring relative qualities of individuals like incomes and assets or markers of social position and identity. However, the proper object of scrutiny for equitable treatment is first and foremost relational rather than comparative. What takes priority is whether differences in income or identity stand in the way of persons relating as equals. From this may flow downstream consequences for matters of distribution. But relational equity is also concerned with matters that are not easily understood as distributive at all. Social segregation in public education is relationally inequitable, and so objectionable, regardless of whether educational outcomes in segregated conditions are roughly equal. Political polarization as amplified by technologies of separation is also a relational inequity even where it is not correlated to items on a standard list of distributive burdens and benefits. Cases like these involve relational inequity, and not just unfairness in processing, where the social structures under survey introduce or reproduce inequalities by separating people at the entry gates of treatment. As the decision in *Brown* illustrates, it matters much who is let in and who is kept out by the entry doors of a social structure quite independent of whether all are treated identically after being sent through doors that separate them at the start of treatment.

In light of the preceding discussion, it may seem puzzling that equal opportunity is subject to such widespread criticism, and not only from conservatives but from professed egalitarians too. The typical egalitarian objection to opportunity equalities (and by extension to entry equity more generally) rests on an analytical truth: that entry conditions are not identical to obtained outcomes. But this objection relies on the fact that opponents of equality—including those who claim to endorse equality but neglect to seek it in actual action—too often exploit this difference between opportunity and outcome. I have offered terminology that enables us to see that this exploitation is possible only if equal opportunity is not taken seriously enough in the first place. To take equality seriously, to affirm robust equitable entry including robust equal opportunity, would require us to do what we can to detect and mitigate any patterned probabilities of differential starting conditions that situate people as unequal to each other within whatever process of treatment they are being subject to. This involves interrogating entry conditions for how they situate, shape, and profile people in their relations to each other. In sum, it requires instituting entry conditions that foster relations of equality among those entering into a process of treatment. Taking equality seriously thus requires equalizing upstream conditions for entry alongside making fair those downstream procedures that depend on these entry conditions.

The Priority of Entry to Processing

Equity in entry and fairness in processing are both requisite for achieving equality in procedures treatment. Though relational equality is expressed through both conditions, equitable entry is not only sequentially prior to fair processing in any procedure of treatment, it is also conceptually prior to it. Similar to the logic by which *Brown v. Board of Education* is both conceptually and chronologically prior to *Lau v. Nichols*, equity in entry is a presupposition of effective fairness in processing. Without equitable entry, fair processing is likely to lead to procedures that reproduce initial relational inequalities. Fair processing without equity entry might root out blatant cases of playing favorites, for example, but it will eliminate little else. Even standard anti-discrimination conceptions of fairness assume some prior operative sense of entry equity—for instance, by helping themselves to predefined categories of protected classes (a point I return to below, in chapter 6, discussing algorithmic auditing).

The priority of entry conditions to processing conditions points to a way of connecting the conceptual anatomy of equal treatment to cases of computational treatment. Observe that the reasons for entry-condition priority in equal treatment also apply to the other half of the three-stage schema elaborated above. What takes sequential priority in computational programs are data inputs as presupposed by algorithmic processing. The stakes of this come into view when we consider how attributes of persons become features of algorithm-generated models of persons. It is widely recognized that computational systems algorithmically process the data streams that form their inputs. Less widely acknowledged is that computational systems also, and also must, design or format data in a way that makes inputs possible in the first place. Computation relies on data being structured in stable and readable form such that it can be usable by an algorithmic process.

Data are not just lying around in well-formed shapes already usable by computational algorithms. Data first have to be made in order to be taken as givens by a machine. Making data usable involves the work of formatting or structuring data, paradigmatically in the form of designing and curating a database. Making data is the primary way in which features of people (such as bodily or behavioral measures) get loaded into computer models such that a person can become subject to the treatment procedures that some computer programs are. I refer to this initializing work of making data or forming information as *formatting*. I have argued in this chapter for including alongside the dominant discussions of fairness a clearer articulation of the primary importance of equitable relations at that entry stage into procedures of treatment, including computational procedures of treatment. It is now time to argue for including alongside the dominant discussions of algorithms a clearer articulation of the priority of formatting input data as a condition for algorithmic data processing.

PART 3

Data

Structural Data
Formats + Algorithms

Too often, what we can clearly see, we also find opaque to understand. Our inherited vocabularies do not help us grasp what is going on right before our eyes and right beneath our typing fingertips. While our received theoretical tools remain broadly relevant to contemporary social and political life, most are also increasingly inapplicable to the particular politics of the social structures emerging through our data technologies. What conceptual repertoire would be adequate to data such that we could both understand the structuring conditions they propagate and evaluate the political effects of that propagation? What forms of power do these data constitute, and what kinds of political subjects do they implicate? Where such questions come into view, it is clear we lack a political theory of data despite the increasingly widespread sense that there is a politics at play where all these utterly ordinary data are being deployed.

Some of these theoretical gaps have been explored in recent work marking the first steps toward a theory of the structural and political effects of data.[1] These emergent theories of data politics extend (even if not always fully consciously) an earlier volley of scholarship developing a broader political theory of technology.[2] This chapter aims to enrich this body of theory by furnishing it with a set of conceptual and methodological expansions that illuminate how data technology can be, and actually is for us today, an important aspect of social and political structure. I develop these expansions by way of an exposition that moves from more obvious to less obvious instances of social and political structure.

I begin with what I take to be the most obvious aspect of social structure according to both the conception of structure developed in earlier chapters as well as any number of more classical conceptions of structure. Anyone who accepts the premise that there exist structuring forces that condition our social and political orders surely accepts that institutions are among such forces. I agree that institutions are crucially important for understanding the politics of our data. But, I shall argue, an analysis of institutions is insufficient for these purposes. We need to also take seriously the question of whether there are technological dimensions of structure independent of their effects on institutions. To consider this question, I begin with technology in general and move from there to the specific dynamics of data or information technologies. In considering the political role of data technology, it is immediately striking that nearly all contemporary scholarship on these topics is focused on algorithmic technologies, or the processing operations internal to computational uses of data. The recent spate of attention to algorithmic politics is both compelling and insightful, yet it is also strikingly incomplete. Excepting the most trivial of counterexamples, no computational program runs on algorithms alone. Programs require data as material for algorithms to process. This suggests that there are crucial operations of the structuring force of data in the work of what I call *formats*, or what are often referred to in computer science as *data structures*. My argument thus ultimately concerns how data structures contribute to social structure—or how the data structures we design and deploy end up structuring us.

The concept of formatting picks out the technical-and-conceptual apparatus that constitutively organize data such that they can be recorded, processed, stored, and retrieved. Formats are deeply involved in forming our data. They therefore matter much wherever we act through our data. We are today deeply structured by formats that constrain, channel, and configure what we can (or cannot) do and how we can (or cannot) interact. These formats are widely visible in our everyday interactions but are also almost always overlooked. Formats for behavior, learning, cognition, health, employment, credit, and identity specify the shapes of our data, be it via high-performance machine-learning systems or legacy paper machines like intake forms affixed to a clipboard. These formats structure our actions and interactions not only in the way they function as political prostheses for traditional political operations of coercion, but more significantly in the way they perform the work of what I call *fastening* subjects to all manner of databases and systems. Fastening both pins us down and speeds us up. Such canalizing and quickening is often deeply unequal.

This chapter's exposition of the fastening instituted by formats is offered as a generalizable theory of the structuring politics enacted through data formats of all kinds. When bringing generality into view, specificity is often illuminating. I therefore thread my analysis in each section through examples drawn from a single domain: education. I trace the way that education is politically and socially structured by a multiplicity of elements. I begin with standard accounts of how institutional activities like policymaking work to structure education, then turn to a focus on how technologies like computer tablets can do the same, and finally descend to two particular elements of education-data technology: algorithms (such as those that model students for the sake of prediction) and formats that structure data about students (such as those data that make students more predictable). Examples showing how education practices, and the learners at the center of them, are structured in multiple ways both illustrate the potential of a structural approach to equality and also expand the purview of such a structural analysis beyond its focal, and often exclusive, concern with institutions.

Institutional Structure

Institutional forms like legislative bodies and executive agencies, along with their standard instruments of policy and law, remain the preeminent referent in contemporary thinking about how social structures condition our actions and interactions. Institutions clearly contribute to the structuring and restructuring of our practices and relations. The very idea of an account of the structuring politics of data might thus seem to refer in the first place to data's impacts on more-formal political institutions, extending therefrom to more-informal institutional groupings like social movements, interest groups, and political culture.

Traditional analyses of this type are clearly valuable. But they are also quite limited. This approach involves taking data technology as only derivatively political, that is, as political only insofar as data figure in the exercise of political power in traditional institutions. Data technology, on this perspective, can only ever be prosthetically political, that is, as an extension or instrument wielded by the institutional forms that are taken to be truly political.

What if there are cases for which we need a theoretical perspective that interrogates technology itself as political? Deepening polarization on social media indeed carries effects for democratic elections. But social media polarization is also political in the way that platforms configure how we see ourselves and each other irrespective of participation in political institutions. Social media sharing might help turn a voting bloc to extremist paranoia. It might also encourage hundreds of millions of users globally to understand their own lives (and their relations to the lives of others) in terms of brief and episodic status updates. We need an expanded theoretical repertoire capable of comprehending the structuring that inheres in both kinds of dynamics.

Such an expansion of methods of political inquiry beyond a focal concern with traditional political institutions is also needed with respect to theories of democratic, or relational, equality. While I have thus far largely followed Elizabeth Anderson's work in developing a conception of democratic equality, there are notable limits to her approach when it comes to conceptualizing an explicitly structural model of democratic equality. The most poignant such limit is that her view tends to neglect structuring factors beyond traditional institutions, laws, and policies. In the context of an argument for a democratic egalitarian approach to data technology, to take just one kind of example, such institutionalist approaches do not offer guidance on how to understand and evaluate the structuring role played by technologies themselves.

My argument for enriching democratic equality by focusing it on non-institutional structural factors implies a criticism of the institutionalism characteristic of leading views. Anderson's work, to the extent that it is also guilty of such institutionalism, should be seen as merely replicating dominant methodological tendencies of the last few decades of political philosophy. These tendencies are dominant largely through the influence of John Rawls, who was not only Anderson's mentor but also a preeminent theorist of social structure in twentieth-century political philosophy in its analytic variants. Rawls showed political philosophy how it could leave to the side the serious consideration of non-institutional structuring factors.[3] On the Rawlsian view, such factors are best addressed after philosophy has done its work, at that point when policy experts pick up philosophical ideals and carry them out into the real world.

Yet not all Rawlsian theory has fallen into line with strict institutionalism. As noted previously, Mathias Risse departs from strict adherence to institutionalism in order to elaborate a Rawlsian approach to digital technologies as effectively structural.[4] Also in contrast to the letter of Rawls—in particular, his explicit commitment to a method of ideal theory in political philosophy that neglects questions not directly pertinent to articulating perfected principles of justice—Anderson explicitly presents her work as an effort in nonideal theory that aims "to cope with the injustices in our current world, and to move us to something better."[5] Any nonideal or realist theory ought to be impatient with the assumption that we can leave for later the work of empirically scrutinizing what counts as social structure. A nonideal or realist theory of structure therefore ought to be prepared to address how structuring operates within particular sites and through particular means.

I turn now to such particulars by showing how a pair of Anderson's articles on racial inequality in education exhibit the dominant institutionalist focus (though also worth noting is that her well-known 2010 book on racial segregation, *The Imperative of Integration*, is similarly institutionalist).[6] When we are concerned with the structural forces that render certain educational practices inegalitarian in specifiable ways, what do we take the range of our concern to be? Are we only concerned with the impact of institutional conditions such as funding mandates issued by Congress and policy requirements enacted by the Department of Education? Or are we also concerned with other kinds of impacts such as how specific technologies help entrench unequal educational landscapes?

In a 2007 article applying a relational egalitarian perspective to issues of equal opportunity in education, Anderson offers an argument for "comprehensive group integration in all of a country's institutions and hence for integration of schools at all levels."[7] The end goal here is integration within institutions. The means toward these ends are clearly focused on institutional reforms. These ends and means match Anderson's diagnosis of the problem itself in terms of institutional deficits, such as "class-exclusionary zoning laws" that often function as a proxy for racial segregation.[8] In a 2012 article focused on the causes of racially disparate outcomes in education (in the US context), Anderson challenges those "cultural explanations" of acquired racial differences that historically replaced biological accounts of innate racial difference.[9] Anderson's alternative account is impressively subtle in her descriptions of what schools do to inadvertently perpetuate unequal outcomes. It is also focused throughout on educational institutions: "Educational outcomes are the iterated product of institutional responses to student and parent conduct, which is itself shaped in part by prior institutional responses."[10]

Anderson clearly sees schools as vectors for formalized policies concerning curricular design, student assessment, behavior management, and other aspects of educational practice. Nowhere does she deny that schools are sites where extra-institutional factors deeply shape students and their relations to each other. Yet nowhere in her work does she explicitly take up such factors—like technological conditions—for analysis (at least not yet, to my knowledge). This will appear puzzling to anyone who recognizes educational assessment, curriculum, and discipline as all eminently technological. This speaks to the need to methodologically expand institution-centric analyses so that they may also interrogate technologies as structuring factors.

It is not a surprise that political philosophers have tended to follow Rawls and other institutionalists in focusing their analyses on classical forms of social structure like governmental agencies, legislative statutes, court rulings, and policy activism. The clear advantage of such an approach is that it provides unambiguous arguments with straightforward normative implications. Ascribing culpability to governing institutions yields a powerful argument, because the state, even if only indirectly, impugns us all in any injustice it metes out. And yet the clear argumentative force of this approach sometimes gets in the way of understanding the complex and contingent political dynamics involved in the structuring of our relations beyond just those forms of structuring formally enacted by the state. This complexity is better affirmed by another theorist of social and political structure influential for both Anderson and myself, namely John Dewey. Dewey's idea that "democracy is a way of life" entails that democracy is "more than a form of government" and "cannot now depend upon or be expressed in political institutions alone."[11] The Deweyan approach affirms that we need to go looking for social structure not just where we have stipulated in advance that structuring is operative, but everywhere that the configuring and disposing forces of structure are actually operative.

Technological Structure

Although political inquiry in our so-called information age remains overwhelmingly focused on institutions (as well as other classical politically categories, such as social movements and interest groups), there is now a robust and growing body of work that attends to the structuring operations of technologies in fields such as science and technology studies, the history of science and technology, and the philosophy of technology.[12] One insight common across this work is that technologies often operate to structure our social and political relations. Across a range of political problems and social sites in modernity, technology has increasingly configured more and more of what we do and how we interact. Technologies are much more than the mere instruments of other elements in social structure that wield them as a kind of prosthesis. They structure in their own right.

The very idea of technological structuring immediately raises a challenging methodological question. If technology is structural, how is it structural? In contexts where a political value such as equality or liberty is at stake such that technology is structurally political, how is it political? The philosophy of technology provides three basic lines of response to these questions: determinism, instrumentalism, and a less widely considered view I shall call associationism.

On the first view, technologies are political because of the sheer force they exert. On most prominent versions of this view, technologies are possessed of an inner solidity, essence, or rationality from which flows significant effects on human (and nonhuman) lives. Consider the toxic byproducts inherent to the process of nuclear fission. From this ineliminable material feature of a technological process flow enormous social impacts. These consequences determine a range of possible actions for those subject to them. This view is accordingly frequently labeled *technological determinism*.[13]

While technological determinism gets something right, most scholars rightly regard it as deeply flawed.[14] One irredeemable defect of this view is its assumption that technologies operate in an almost inevitable manner without the willful support of massive social infrastructures sustaining them. That nuclear fission takes place, as well as the way it takes place, is already a thoroughly socio-technical process. No technology, and certainly no network of technologies, effectively sustains itself or autonomously dictates its own destiny. Maintenance is a necessary condition of all technology. Contingencies of breakdown are highly unpredictable; eventualities of breakdown are highly probable. As such, we help sustain all our technologies, even those that appear most autonomous from us and hence most in control of us.

A second view of technology foregrounds the crucial work of human agents in composing, operating, and sustaining technology. In foregrounding the human scaffolding for technology, this view construes technologies as tools and utensils at the behest of the humans using them. This position is often called *technological instrumentalism*. Instrumentalism takes up technology in relation to the social contexts in which it operates and thereby refuses to attribute to technology a self-sufficient solidity. There is much to recommend this view, especially in contrast to the flaws of technological determinism.

Yet instrumentalism easily risks inverting the erroneous assumptions of the determinist, for instrumentalism tends to locate the political and social salience of technology wholly within the hands of the humans who operate it. This means the instrumentalist can never get into a position of seeing technology itself as structuring our political orders. Tools can only ever be a conduit for the political intentions of their human users. One way to grasp this point is in terms of instrumentalism's teleological bearings: instrumentalism treats technologies as directed toward their ends. A technology is always for something, says the instrumentalist. That which it is for is the end that its designer or user holds in view when wielding it. Thereby does instrumentalism conceive of technology as a tool—a mere prosthesis of its operator. Once that conception is in place, the tool cannot be understood as itself exerting structuring, but only as extending the structuring reach aimed for by its bearers. Wherever technologies exceed their purposes, however, instrumentalism is incapable of interrogating how technologies structure our actions.

This and other defects of instrumentalism complicate my account of technological structuring considerably, for instrumentalism is the main view of

technology associated with pragmatism. Indeed, pragmatism is widely regarded as the primary source for philosophical iterations of the instrumentalist conception of technology. The writings of pragmatists are rife with
references to technologies as an instrumentarium that waits at the behest of
human purposes. Dewey himself is a chief source of instrumentalist prag-
matisms because of his frequent assertions to the effect that "by its nature
technology is concerned with things and acts in their instrumentalities . . .
in behalf of other things of which they are means and predictive signs."[15] He
writes elsewhere: "The telephone, telegraph, radio, steam locomotive, electric
light, dynamo, internal combustion engine, automobile, and airplane are, for
example, so many exhibits testifying to the reality, already effected, of knowledge as instrumentality of action."[16] As this passage suggests, Dewey's instrumentalism about technology derives from his more primary instrumentalism
about knowledge.[17] Instrumentalist epistemology holds that knowledge always has a purpose, which for most pragmatists is understood in terms of
problem-solving, or what the neopragmatist Richard Rorty refers to as "cop-
ing" with obstacles in our natural and social environment.[18] Similarly endorsing Dewey's instrumentalism, the contemporary pragmatist philosopher of
technology Larry Hickman writes that "technology in its most robust sense,
then, involves the invention, development, and cognitive deployment of tools
and other artifacts . . . with a view to the resolution of perceived problems."[19]
This is a quintessentially teleological view defining technology as being for
something else—namely, solving problems. Stated as such, pragmatist instrumentalism appears all but ready to move over into techno-optimism.

Despite my concerns with the limits of instrumentalist optimism, some
degree of instrumentalism about technology is already presupposed by my
broader argument in this book insofar as I propose a normative reconstruction of data technology. Any argument about what we should do to meliorate
the problems instituted by technologies must assume that we can reconstruc-
tively intervene in the design or operation of those technologies. This pulls me
in two directions with respect to instrumentalism. The normative approach
to data technology that I advocate presupposes that we can do much to reconstruct the problematic socio-technical milieux in which we find ourselves. Yet
my methodology also requires resolute attentiveness to the depth of the challenges that our technologies have mounted around us wherever they exceed
our purposes. For this reason, the kind of instrumentalism that my normative
approach requires can be adopted only if situated against the broader background of a more complicated philosophy of technological structuring.

What is needed is the idea that technologies form milieux that condition
our actions by channeling and configuring what we can (and cannot) do. On

this view, technological milieux or associations dispose our action, but only ever with assistance from us in that we are in every instance ourselves a part of the associations that dispose us. I will refer to this perspective as *techno-logical associationism* (or sometimes as the *milieu theory of technology*).

Consider a machinic example of associationism. Modern electrified refrigeration conditions vast swaths of what we can and cannot do. It makes possible (and seemingly impossible) entire arenas of human action. This conditioning, or disposing, dimension of a technology is in and of itself structuring. It is also, for that reason, often eminently political. Technologies for refrigeration impact our freedoms to do or not to do, as well as our equalities and inequalities therein (just consider how the actions that refrigeration shelters are differently available to different persons and groups). Refrigeration, moreover, does none of this by itself; it operates only insofar as it is part of multiple kinds of associations, including not only machinic associations that network refrigeration devices to electrical grids, but also, much more importantly, a series of techno-social associations in virtue of which a stunningly wide set of humans work to maintain operative refrigeration across many pockets of the planet.

What philosophical resources motivate and support this associationist view of technology? Though pragmatism has typically been aligned with a more instrumentalist approach to technology, instrumentalism is not the exclusive interest of pragmatist philosophies of technology, for there are also aspects of technological associationism in pragmatism. This is true even of Dewey's pragmatism, despite his being the leading envoy of pragmatist instrumentalism.[20] When we turn from Dewey's epistemological and metaphysical writings to his books on politics, we find frequent invocations of specific technologies in service of the broader point that the tools we wield can reverberate back on us. In his 1927 *The Public and Its Problems*, a book that frequently references media technologies, he writes of how "the physical and external means of collecting information in regard to what is happening in the world have far outrun the intellectual phase of inquiry and organization of its results" in ways that pose challenges for political regulation.[21] Dewey is here not so much marking the instrumental power of technology to serve our goals as he is describing how technologies often outrun our purposes in unanticipated ways.[22] That said, the associationist or milieu model of technology remains at best episodic in Dewey.

Associationism is more fully developed in the contemporary pragmatist-inspired philosophy of technology developed by Barry Allen.[23] In considering the role of technology in human knowledge, Allen claims that "the most important thing about tools . . . is that they are already artifacts when we

pick them up, already products of others' artifice with other tools, recipro-
cally linked to other tools and other people in an economy of actions, agents,
and artifacts."[24] This is a view of tools as essentially interrelated: there is no
such thing as a tool by itself without its artifactual milieu, which of course
includes the agents who wield it. "A single tool," Allen says, "is as improb-
able as a single word."[25] This interrelation reverberates in every direction. The
agent wielding a tool is not a master who makes it their instrument, but is
themselves capable of effective tool use only because of broader artifactual
associations that sustain tool and agent alike.[26]

Allen's approach to the philosophy of technology points to a way of making certain pragmatist commitments resonant with what I regard as the
fullest and best source of the associationist philosophy of technology. This
is a lineage in French philosophy that includes Gilbert Simondon, Michel
Foucault, and Bruno Latour.[27] The most recent iteration of this lineage is
presented in Latour's theoretical reconceptualization of social inquiry as
the "tracing of associations" in the form of inquiry closely following the
"movement[s] of re-association and reassembling" taking place between
humans, technologies, and other objects and actors.[28] But it is Simondon's
work that offers the most compelling theory of the associative conditioning
of artifacts in relation to humans—for his theory best shows how technology
forms an associated milieu for humanity in such a way that we too are parts
of the association.

Simondon's theory of technology as presented in his 1958 *On the Mode of
Existence of Technical Objects* is meticulously precise yet frighteningly dense
in its reliance on a dizzying throng of neologisms: "technical element," "technical individual," "technical ensemble," and "associated milieu," to name just
a few. I focus here on one of his concepts: the underappreciated notion of
"coupling." Simondon introduces this idea in a compact sentence that at once
distances his view from both determinism and instrumentalism: "Man can be
coupled to the machine as an equal, and not merely as a being who directs or
utilizes it through the incorporation of ensembles, or as a being who serves it
by supplying matter and elements."[29]

Simondon's most crucial insight is that the connectedness of coupling
must be understood non-dyadically, or more precisely, non-dialectically.[30]
Coupling involves multiplicitous connections that yield metastability among
all participating elements. The coupling of humans and machines is not the
aggregation of two prior entities; nor is it the resolution of a tension between
two entities in opposition. Coupling is, rather, the outcome of a process of
iterated interactions whose increasing density eventually holds all interacting
terms together as coupled.

The most significant implication of Simondon's concept of coupling is that coupling becomes requisite for that which is coupled. Associates become dependent on their association. That a coupling establishes a dependency illuminates how technologies are, and could have become, practically obligatory for us. Think again of refrigeration—surely a technology that you and I cannot go without. We can imagine ourselves without our particular refrigerators, but what would our lives be without any refrigeration at all? Would we, living over there in that imaginary world, really be the same people who unthinkingly rely on refrigeration over here for storage and transport of items as diverse as pasteurized dairy, cut flowers, and ultracold vaccines? Now take this one step further. Simondon's concept is most compelling when considered not with respect to individual technological forms, but rather in light of vibrant technological ensembles. Our coupling to refrigeration already implicates a flock of other couplings, including electrification, industrialization, and pasteurization. Couplings of human and machine proliferate throughout socio-technical orders.

The radical implication of technological associationism is that humans as we exist today do not predate machines in such a way that the contemporary human can be comprehended additively as a pre-machinic essence plus whatever the machine appends to that essence. Rather, contemporary humans and machines are the hybridized product of the genesis of a dense assembly of relations. Inextricability can be the outcome of a genetic process that did not presuppose it at the beginning. To understand technology, think not of one man and his hammer. A more illuminating starting point is the way in which vast numbers of human lives today are woven into databases. You can take the hammer from the man and each remains (more or less) intact. But try to imagine detaching all of us from all our databases and consider what of us, as well as what of our databases, would remain.

Associationism conceives technology as exerting structuring force over what we do even as part of what we do is restructure our technological carapace. There is a reciprocity to coupling. Our efforts to reconstruct our technologies are not processes of command wherein we wield technologies as instruments. Instead, our tools bear us along while we cultivate their every operation. As the political and media theorist Davide Panagia describes Simondon's philosophy of technology, "The human and technical do not stand apart from one another but partake and participate with one another" in dynamics of "pluri-participation," such that there can be no sensible question of "the hierarchical domination of form onto matter."[31]

With the associationist theory of technology in view, I can now articulate a dual-aspect philosophy of technological structuring. My dual-aspect view combines the associationist theory of technological structuring with a modest version of the instrumentalist theory. In one of its aspects, this view affirms that instrumentalist orientations are crucial for any viable political project of reconstructing, redesigning, and recomposing our technologies. In its other aspect, this view recognizes that this very viability depends on humbling the instrumentalist impulse by diminishing its teleological tendencies in light of two central features of the associationist view: first, a recognition of the multitude of ways that actual technological operations exceed the intents of their designers, deployers, and users; and second, a commitment to understanding how we are inextricably coupled to our technologies such that they form a carapace for our every action while we form a custodianship for their ongoing operation.

A concern emerges at this point with respect to my combination of associationism and instrumentalism. Some critics might regard this combination as unviable. Does associationism not destabilize our traditional conceits about human agency? How can we (any of us individually or some set of us taken together) exert the agency to gain critical purchase if each of us is actually already associatively distributed across a thousand databases? This objection is important insofar as my combination of associationism and instrumentalism is a central premise for the main arguments of this book—the very idea of data equality both acknowledges that we have become irrevocably coupled to our data and commits to addressing the inegalitarian effects of this coupling by way of strategies already internal to our inherited democratic structures. But, the objection goes, if we humans are essentially parts of associations whose other parts are data technologies, do we not thereby lack the capacity for reflective critique as it is currently expressed in inherited structures of liberal egalitarian democracy such as citizenship and representation?[32]

This objection to pragmatist instrumentalism's endorsement of a capacity for critical agency both takes associationism too far and also not far enough. It takes it too far in making associationism into a metaphysics or an ontology. But all that is really needed is a methodology, or epistemological analytic, for understanding our socio-technical situations. Associationist methodology does not undermine self-reflexive critique—indeed, it exhibits it. The objection also, however, fails to take associationism far enough in that the metaphysical articulation of associationism loses sight of the historical, or genetic, quality of all associations. Seen historically, there is no automatic impediment to affirming that the associated milieu we are presently in is one that has accumulated historical trajectories of critical agency in such forms as democratic representation, liberal citizenship, and reconstructive experimentation. These complex ensembles are historical contingencies, to be sure, and so they will one day dissipate. However, when they do, it will not be because of violation of a metaphysical principle. It will be for causes that need to be studied empirically—for example, the ascendance of anti-democratic and anti-liberal hierarchies.

To further explicate my dual-aspect commitments to instrumentalism and associationism, and to make complete the case that technologies can operate as structuring factors, consider this view in light of another example drawn through my thread line of education technology. The needed idea here is of technology that exhibits structuring force not fully reducible to institutional policies nor yet fully insulated from instrumental reconstruction. Of course, institutional questions of policy are likely to be relevant in any domain where we find political structure operative. So the issue concerns whether there is a politics that inheres in the way an education technology operates that precedes and prompts questions of policy at the institutional level.

Consider differential impacts on students that flow from different education technologies that can be formative of the basic milieu in which education takes place.[33] Two clear examples of such technological differences are, first, online education versus classroom education and, second, digital curricula versus print (or otherwise physical) curricula. Physical versus digital classroom technologies (be they curricula or the classroom itself) configure the actions and interactions of learners differently. Such differentia clearly impact different populations of learners differently—for instance, some learn better from printed curricula, while digital curricula afford accessibility to others. That is as clear evidence of technological structuring as anyone could hope for.

In considering such cases, we may eventually find ourselves confronted with a policy choice to be carried out in formal institutional settings. But that there even is such a choice is a feature in part of the differing affordances of technologies themselves, not just a feature of institutional will.[34] Consider another example. Contrast a school district policy that forbids students below a certain level of academic achievement from enrolling in certain advanced courses with a hypothetical district setting in which any student may enroll in a particular advanced course, yet the curriculum for that class requires afterschool online access. The first is a case of institutional policy enacting exclusion (of students not meeting the achievement threshold). The second is a case of the technological enactment of exclusion (of students without afterschool internet access). In cases like the latter, technological differences may prompt reconsideration of institutional policies, but they might also prompt technological redesign independent of policy. For cases like these, we need to be able to scrutinize technologies for their structuring influence even where formal institutional channels for policy consideration do not yet exist. What is needed is just to recognize that, in the words of the education theorists Neil Selwyn and Keri Facer, "the design and use of digital technology in education is a profoundly *political* concern."[35]

Informational Structure

Technologies shape, or structure, our individual lives and social relations. But different families of technology structure us in different ways. I turn now to structuring in the specific case of information or data technology.[36] It is within the more limited range of information systems specifically (a range that is truly enormous in our current moment) that this book seeks to excavate structuring tendencies that carry significant political consequences for, among other things, our ability to relate to each other as equals.

Recent years have seen an increasing number of scholars seriously considering information technology as structure. Yet contemporary accounts of the impacts of information technology, as paradigmatically represented by work in the two fields of critical data studies and data ethics, tend to be highly concentrated on a single technical element factoring in data-driven structuring: algorithms. I argue below that we need equal (and probably even greater) attention on another necessary element for data technology: formats. Before turning to formats, I want to first survey some recent work on algorithms that is both crucially important, yet also very much incomplete on its own.

ALGORITHMS IN DATA TECHNOLOGY

An impressive roster of work on the politics of algorithms has emerged across the past decade and more in disciplines as diverse as science and technology studies, communications, literary studies, geography, anthropology, law, political science, and just about every other field.[37] There has also been a surge of analyses of algorithms within the subfields most central to the perspective I adopt in this book: namely, political theory and political philosophy.[38] Indeed, new work on algorithms is sure to rush out between the day this book is printed and the day it arrives in your hand. Accordingly, I shall focus my discussion of this scholarly tendency on a singularly insightful contribution to the political theory of algorithms that resonates well with my associationist conception of technological structuring. I appealed above to Panagia's explication of Simondon's philosophy of technology; I turn now to considering how Panagia trains the associationist perspective on our algorithmic moment.

Panagia describes how algorithms exercise political power by disposing us as subjects of their data (which, of course, are our data).[39] The algorithm is politically salient, he argues, precisely because of its technical capacity "to predict future outcomes and to coordinate action" such that we become disposed to be predictable and coordinated.[40] Algorithms, on this analysis, are effective technologies for producing a political order of things oriented toward predictability.[41] As Bernard Harcourt and Bonnie Sheehey similarly show in their work on predictive policing systems, the temporality of prediction is one in which the present is rushed toward its own anticipated future.[42] What is so often involved in such algorithmic deployments, Sheehey argues, is a politics of paranoia in which a fantasized fear of the future is invoked as a strategic justification for preemptive action in the present.[43]

Panagia's formulations well capture how algorithms predispose their subjects to act in ways that the algorithms help configure. On this view, an algorithm is a structuring political technology, "not because it constrains freedom through various forms of domination, but because it proliferates controls on variability and, in this way, governs the movement of bodies and energies."[44] The concept of algorithmic disposition can be understood in terms of the associationist model of technological structuring presented above. According to this model, algorithms dispose us by enveloping us in a certain range of possibilities (and impossibilities). Algorithms do not determinatively dictate what we must do. They dispose us toward certain tendencies and against certain others. In this disposition, they structure our actions and relations or, in Panagia's vocabulary, govern our movements.

One way of understanding Panagia's account of data as dispositional is through Ian Hacking's concept of "looping effects."[45] This concept captures how categories, once ascribed to persons, are often taken up in ways that reconfigure the possible actions of those who have been categorized according to the terms of their categorization. Just as patients often cultivate a special relationship to their anxious behaviors after a psychologist diagnoses them with an anxiety disorder, subjects of data often cultivate a closeness to labels ascribed to them by an algorithm: financially trustworthy (credit reporting), potential perpetrator (predictive policing), or unlikely to succeed in graduate school (standardized testing). The idea of a looping effect helps us see that Panagia's point is not that algorithms covertly coerce us, but that algorithms are a danger because they efficiently proliferate dispositional probabilities in plain sight.

On this view, algorithmic dispositioning is not strictly bound to the aims of the institutions or individuals deploying algorithms. Indeed, algorithms are highly portable technologies that travel easily across institutional domains.

As Louise Amoore puts it in her work on algorithms that bridge finance and the military: "At the level of the algorithm, there is a profound indifference to the context of whether these norms and anomalies pertain to financial trades or the movement of insurgent forces."[46] The mobility of algorithms across familiar institutional contexts suggests that their structuring work is not just a function of their institutions. The sorts of dispositions, and forms of subjectivation, instilled in us by algorithms involve effects extending well beyond institutional influence.

With a theoretical case for algorithmic structuring now in view, I turn again to an example. I shall draw from an information-intensive field of education technology research known as learning analytics, which will also be the primary area in education technology I take up at greater length below, in my final chapters.

The critical education technology scholars Carlo Perrotta and Ben Williamson offer an instructive example of algorithmic disposition in their discussion of uses of cluster analysis algorithms in learning analytics.[47] To briefly describe this family of algorithmic techniques, cluster analyses work by partitioning data in order to establish clusters of similarity in which all the data points within a cluster are more like each other than they are like data points in other clusters. Cluster algorithms are usable only where researchers can determine the relevance of the features, or measures of likeness, constituting a cluster of data points. Relevance can assume one of two forms: either researchers provide a system with a set of predefined features (perhaps contained in a labeled field in a dataset), or they analyze clusters produced by an algorithm that they then take as relevant (almost always by establishing natural-language labels for what are really unlabeled statistical groupings).

Perrotta and Williamson analyze two empirical studies that employ clustering in developing analytics for course participation in online courses. One study clusters student data from a large online platform using algorithms that yield four categories ("completing, auditing, disengaging, and sampling") while the other clusters student data using algorithms that result in five ("strong starters, mid-way dropouts, nearly there, late completers, and keen completers").[48] Algorithmic calibrations leading to four-category versus five-category clustering can have implications for how students are treated. One well-documented way in which such algorithmic differences manifest is in predictive biases. A cluster analysis using only four buckets might be biased against some subset of student models where a similar analysis whose thresholds are set in a way that generates five buckets might not be. In such cases, algorithms exert structuring not only in functioning as surrogate instruments for institutions of different scales, but they can also be understood as enacting, on a scale of their own, a series of disposing looping effects that constitute the terms of our relations to each other and even to ourselves. Algorithms can establish dispositional differences that can come to be structurally salient. Cluster-analysis algorithms of online course performance can establish such dispositional looping effects when an algorithm determines that a student is "disengaging" versus being a "late completer." It is unlikely that in such systems these labels would automatically loop back directly to the subject of analysis (that is, the student). Yet such looping effects are likely to be instigated and expanded by other algorithms working in concert to leverage the results of clustering; for instance, by personalizing learner curricula to deliver only certain types of content to certain clusters of students. A different example is that of algorithmic decision-making through "school choice algorithms" used by school districts to place students in particular schools with open-enrollment options—once placed at a school site, students often form conceptions of themselves in light of the composition of the student body at their school, the patterns of which were selected by the algorithm.[49]

Of course, not every instance of dispositional looping enacted by computing technology is a factor of algorithmic processing. In a recent meta-review of forty-nine empirical articles documenting predictive bias in machine-learning applications in education, Lin Li and colleagues found numerous articles ascribing computational bias to pre-processing factors that exert their effects prior to algorithmic processing.[50] I now turn to matters of pre-processing and other aspects of formatting.

FORMATS IN DATA TECHNOLOGY

A 1976 computer science textbook offers as its title the instruction that *algorithms + data structures = programs*.[51] Insofar as this conceptualization is adequate to describe today's data systems, formats (the term I use to refer to data structures) are the missing piece of the equation in recent critical and ethical scholarship on data technology, a scholarship that focuses almost exclusively on algorithms.

How can the formats that constitute data have gone missing in scholarly fields that define themselves in terms of data? Consider a few prominent examples. Amoore, whose analyses of algorithms I endorsed above, rightly notes in a more recent book that "the architecture of the cloud is defined spatially by the relations between algorithms and data," yet then neglects without explanation the work of data structures.[52] Taina Bucher cites the same textbook noted above in *If . . . Then: Algorithmic Power and Politics*, but then immediately states that her focus "will almost exclusively be on algorithms."[53] Paul Dourish's paper "Algorithms and Their Others" almost makes an exception to the rule when he cites the same textbook, then explicitly laments that discussions of "data structures . . . have been less prominent" in comparison to scholarship on algorithms, and yet finally turns his own analysis almost exclusively to algorithms.[54] Why does researcher after researcher adopt such avowedly narrowing strategies for a recognizably complicated technology?

The near silence about formats is striking in a research field that has been almost as rowdy about algorithms as the tech-industry marketing apparatus promoting them. That said, if one squints hard enough, a few exceptions can be found.[55] The clearest exception to the trend, and also the one closest to my proposal for format anatomies presented in the following chapter, is Lindsay Poirier's model for "reading datasets."[56] Poirier's approach involves inquiry that takes place recursively across three levels to examine data's literal meanings (as expressed in data dictionaries), cultural contexts (as expressed in the genealogies of datasets), and politicized processes of signification (as exhibited by representational limits and absences in datasets).[57] At each level, Poirier's model focuses on how data gets invested with meanings and values. This model disproves the all-too-common wish that data can be scrubbed of its harmful implications by mere "technocratic fixes" exalting "the neutrality ideal."[58] In particular with its attention to how values are coded into data dictionaries, Poirier's approach runs in parallel with my argument for greater attention to data formats.

Analyses of algorithmic structure are necessary, but attending exclusively to the algorithm as the only structurally significant element in data technology is not. Indeed, such exclusive attention to algorithms (whether on the part of software engineers, tech-firm marketing executives, or critical data scholars) might be more than a missed opportunity; it may also be conceptually and computationally inoperable. All but the most trivial of algorithms can be run only conditionally on some prior formatting of data. As Niklaus Wirth, author of the 1976 textbook, states, "The structure and choice of algorithms often strongly depend on the structure of the underlying data," such that the two are "inseparably intertwined."[59] Understanding how data technologies operate as social structures therefore ought to require reading and studying both the algorithms and the formats intertwined within data computation—for formats, just like algorithms, uniquely contribute to the social structures enacted by data.

So what is a format? As I employ the term, *format* does not explicitly refer to a file type (such as HTML or PDF), but much more broadly to those techno-conceptual specifications that organize forms, registers, records, dossiers, databases, fields, variables, and other files of all kinds. Formats define, in a manner simultaneously conceptual and technical, how data are to be constituted—how information is to be formed. In specifying what data must be, formats configure the specific shapes that are allowable for any data point. These configurations are instantiated at multiple scales, thereby pointing to the multiple sites within which and across which data-driven technologies operate.

The concept of the format overlaps, without reducing to, other familiar concepts in information technology: categories, conventions, standards, dictionaries, and more. One proximate concept that makes for a particularly instructive contrast is that of measure. Measures matter much for how information gets structured.[60] Formats matter in much the same way. But formats have a wider scope than measures, in that they concern not just quantitative structuring (for example, scales on a mental test), but also taxonomical structuring (for example, racial categorization schema) and even purely conventional structuring (for example, rules for human names). It is that wider assembly of structuring that I refer to with the concept of the format. This broader range is part of why formats can so efficiently, even if often only aspirationally, ensemble across sites in ways that cannot fail to structurally dispose their subjects.

Studying ensembles of formats—for instance, through methodologies like the anatomy of formats or the reading of datasets—helps us understand what formats actually do, including most importantly what they do to us and what we do others with them. Studying formats in operation helps us understand what we are doing when we implement data technologies that then quickly spin beyond what we anticipated of them. To show why, I discuss now a number of technical and conceptual considerations concerning formats.

Technical Features of Formats and Data

One reason the widespread oversight of data structures is puzzling concerns the technical priority of formatting to algorithmic processing. Formats make data possible such that there can be computable data rather than an incomputable nothing. The very idea of "raw data" (according to which there could be information without formatting) is nonsensical—as if chaos could be computable or disorder could be data. Recent discussions of machine learning often rely on a misleading distinction between unstructured data and structured information. The more appropriate distinction for computer science and machine learning is one between relatively less-structured and relatively more-structured data. As Lisa Gitelman puts it, following Geoffrey

Bowker's iconic formulation, "'Raw data' is an oxymoron."[61] Or, in more technical terms, all data are already-structured data.

To see why, we need to consider in some detail certain aspects of the technical underpinnings of the relation between data and formats (that is, between data points and data structures). Information theory taught us at its inception that all data are necessarily structured in some way, yet this lesson is often lost today. This insight appears in what is generally regarded as the founding statement of information theory, Claude Shannon's 1948 paper "A Mathematical Theory of Communication."[62]

Shannon defines the concept of "information" quantitatively as the measure of choice in a communication system.[63] My concept of the format reflects Shannon's technical specification. Consider Shannon's idea as exemplified by the drop-down list format. The possible amount of information in a drop-down is determined by the number of options in a predefined list. If the drop-down is formatted with two options, the amount of information provided by a user of that drop-down is (by Shannon's measure) less than the amount of information given by a user of a drop-down with three options, which is less in turn than that provided by a user of a thirty-option drop-down. For Shannon, quantity of information equals measure of choice. My related claim about formats is that they specify the minimal structuring whereby choice—that is, information itself—is made possible. In the example of the drop-down, the formatting is that which defines the number of options, the specific options available, the logic of option selection, and the operationalizability of those options in a user interface. Information exists only where such formatting first establishes choice, or what is also known as the possibility of information.

Why do such technical details of information theory matter for assessing data technology as socially and politically structural? Consider a few examples. Census categories for racial classification have been much discussed in recent years.[64] Competing racial categorization schemas can be seen as structuring in that they establish formats that technically and conceptually delimit not only ways individuals can be represented but also ways they can be treated. Another example are those deceptively simple selectors for "gender" we regularly encounter in user-profile forms. Clicking on the label populates a list of options, often two, sometimes more. A gender drop-down enacts a very precise formatting of a user as a subject of data. Certain options are possible. Others simply do not matter (regardless of whether they matter to the user) because they cannot be formatted by that system as storable data. The form formats what can count as gender information. A user's "gender" on the form may or may not be their gender, but it is crucial to recognize that for their gender to be any kind of data at all, it must be formatted in some way. Add to this the fact that for most such forms, "gender" is a required field such that one's gender must be made to be data.[65]

Examples like these provide an intuitive case for understanding formats as technical components contributing to our technological structuring. I turn now from intuitive examples to two related arguments making the case that formats structurally dispose us. The first argument shows that anyone who cares about the structuring role of algorithms already has reason to care about the structuring role of formats. The second argument directly shows that formats, and more especially ensembles of formats leveraged in coordination with each other, function as structuring technologies by disposing or configuring our activity.

The Dependent Argument: Algorithm Relevance
Presupposes Format Relevance

Formats are functional preconditions for algorithms. Formats set the terms according to which any algorithm might operate. Only after information already exists, constituted by a format, can algorithms then do their work. This point is also observed in Wirth's 1976 textbook: "The choice of structure for the underlying data profoundly influences the algorithms that perform a given task."[66] Wirth's example is of how the choice of a numeric sorting algorithm often depends on whether the data to be sorted are formatted for storage in sequential files on disks or in a computing machine's random-access memory.[67]

It follows that wherever the social conditioning of the algorithm is operative, it is necessarily continuous with the social conditioning of the format, and for specifiable technical reasons. Since algorithms and formats are designed to operate together within any nontrivial data system, a political theory of the algorithm already solicits a political theory of the format.

Why, then, are data formats so visibly neglected in a moment when the critical and ethical study of algorithms has begun to emanate so brightly? One reason surely has to do with the hypervisibility of algorithms in our contemporary cultural moment. Over the past decade or so, our techno-fetishizing culture (and an impressive corporate marketing apparatus propelling it forward) has reconceived algorithms as possessed of an unapproachable mystery that makes them almost seem sexy. In contrast to the impressive allure of the algorithm, formats feel a bit boring. Perhaps this is because the format seems much more basic, maybe even rudimentary, in contrast to the algorithmic hypercomplexity of machine learning and artificial intelligence.[68]

The format's seeming simplicity, however, is actually an advantage for gaining grip on how data technologies serve to structure what we can do and how we can relate, for formats are not simple so much as they are approachable. Formats present us with sites of tractable leverage precisely where algorithms are unapproachable. Consider someone who readily understands that data technologies operate as parts of our social structure that carry political influence. Someone in this position may believe that they themselves cannot meaningfully intervene in this structure if they do not know how to read code or rewrite computational algorithms. But that same person is much more likely to rightly recognize numerous ways of intervening in the operations of the conceptual-technical formats that also carry political consequences. Formats are legible in contrast to the inscrutability of algorithms. They not only deserve our attention. They can have it much more easily.

In summary, the first argument for the social weight of the format holds that if algorithms function as social structures, and if algorithms depend on formats, then any structuring internal to algorithms is a structuring already reliant on the formats that constitute data. This is a dependent argument: the attention due formats is dependent upon that attention already accorded to algorithms. I turn now to an independent argument: this involves showing that there is structuring internal to formatting itself independent of downstream uses of data by algorithms, other technologies, formal institutions, or anything else.

The Independent Argument: Formats Operate as Social Structure

Formats specify how data get defined. This work of specification is salient insofar as the data points we accumulate around us are formatted in specific ways such that different formats dispose different subjects of data toward different effects. Formats of all kinds shape us in all manner of ways. Some of these shapes appear, and in fact are, innocent. Others seem innocent but actually serve as sites for the reproduction of relational inequalities and other social harms. Still others cannot even begin to appear as neutral in their manifest hierarchy. In this respect, formats are structural in the same way that guns or nuclear reactors are: not because they themselves kill or pollute, but rather because they are such effective instrumentalities for killing or polluting and so massively useless for doing so many other things (you would not use a pistol as a doorstop, or a nuclear plant as a hospital). A binary drop-down gender list on an account-registration form does not automatically affiliate a user with a predefined gender identity, but it also clearly affords few uses other than that.

Formats not only configure information, they also configure us. Consider how some social media platforms allow users to choose any username they like, whereas others require that users represent themselves through the fixed identifier that is their official legal name. Social media platforms thereby make visible how even our names—which might otherwise feel so natural and obvious to us—are in fact highly formatted pieces of data technology. You need only think of the remarkable variety of possible names people have but which fail to fit the formatting requirements of most social media platforms (as well as most legal registration procedures): a name containing multiple last names (not the familiar technology of hyphenation but actually having two different last names), a name without a last name (be it familial or any other kind of second datum), a name that changes depending on social context, an extremely long name, or a name written with certain characters not included in the predefined character-set library implemented by the platform. My point is not that the formatting of names is a coercive harm, as if there is some political good in the freedom to have any kind of name at all. Rather, the point is that names are precisely formatted, and their formatting cannot but dispose some of our actions and as well dispose us in ways that dole out unequal burdens and benefits to different people. Run this simple algorithm to validate my claim: sum together all the hours of work that women have put into changing their legal names across dozens of bureaucracies upon marriage (or divorce) and subtract from that number the hours of work that men have put into doing the same upon marriage (or divorce).

The independent argument that formats enact structuring really takes hold when we observe that formats rarely operate in isolation, but in most instances function within networked ensembles of formats. Consider how the formatting of a name in a database intersects with innumerable other formats that also database us. In many cases, the name format functions as a technical condition for the collection, processing, storage, and distribution of other individualizing data points. If we already grant that there may be structural conditioning within the format of the name itself, then even more palpable is the structuring that is spread across entire ensembles of formats within which the name operates as an identifying node.

The ensembles of ground-level formats through which data get constituted are, alongside the algorithms through which they often operate, socio-technical structures. It is true that formats and algorithms are often implemented in the context of institutions to produce political effects. In many such cases, formats are leveraged in ways that produce political harms, like inequality. But both kinds of data technology can also produce these effects on their own outside of institutional dynamics. They can also be operationalized in ways that produce political harms even where nobody in-tended those harms, and even in cases where those involved explicitly aimed to avoid harm. A format can have a profound impact when burned into the operation of a gadget, a website, or a printed blank. And that impact can exceed its being merely a conduit for the intentions of individual and insti-tutional actors.

The Structuring Infopolitics of Formatting

I have made frequent reference to techniques of formatting as not just struc-turing but as politically structuring. My implicit argument in referring to the politics of formats has been that formats are technologies through which political power operates. In earlier chapters, as well as at greater length in a previous book, I referred to what I call *infopolitics*, in virtue of which forms of political organization get enacted by informational structure. At the risk of rehearsing an argument I have presented at length before, this idea deserves some clarification here.[69]

Infopolitics refers to a mode of political power that is wholly distinctive from that classical model of power as sovereign coercion that has reigned so dominant in modern political theory, from its advent with Thomas Hobbes in the seventeenth century down through its consolidation in the early-twentieth-century political theory of Max Weber (and numerous others).[70] In specifying a form of power that operates outside the model of sovereign coercion, my conceptualization of the infopolitics of formats can be seen as analogous to Foucault's famous arguments that power admits of more forms than that comprehended in the classical model of a sovereign coercing its subjects.[71] Foucault showed how power is also enacted in the way subjects are disciplined by agents who are anything but sovereign masters.[72] The prisoner is disciplined by the psychiatrist, the patient by the clinician, the student by the teacher. The exercise of disciplinary power shapes its subjects not by the physical force of coercion but by the surveillance and classification of conduct.

Since my concept of infopolitics also departs from the sovereign model, it might be thought that my idea replicates Foucault's prior analyses of disci-plinary power (or anatomopolitics) and regulatory biopower (or biopolitics). Such continuities are important, but the politics of formats is not merely one more instance of these historically prior models of power.[73] Infopolitics offers an analogy to, not an identity with, Foucauldian biopolitics and anatomo-politics. The infopolitics of formats consists in the ways they imprint us, and dispose us—specifically, as the information or data through which we have come to conduct ourselves across so many aspects of our lives.

The grip that formats enact involves a distinctive operation of power: fastening. I employ this word because it holds in view two meanings. The work of fastening is a double operation of formatting through which the subject of data is pinned down to the format's delimitations at the same time that the subject is hustled up by the efficiencies afforded by a common formatting. Canalizing and accelerating, entrenching and quickening, the conceptual-technical hybrid that is the format bores into us with remarkable celerity. We are pinned down to the prefab formats of our favored social media platforms, and then in virtue of this pinning our communicative interaction is quickened. We are tied down to the racial categorization presented on the census form, which in turn fastens us further when the form is loaded into database upon database that are used to generate a volley of community analyses. Information, since it is choice, yields precision in a way that always affords an acceleration that tends toward, but will never fully achieve, automation.[74]

Though the grip of fastening is tight, and gets wound tighter over time, the work of fastening is neither inevitable nor incontestable. As is evident in the case of gender drop-downs and census race schema, formats can also be (and can always become) sites of contestation and transformability. We need an analytical category to better understand how contestation operates in contexts where we are pinned down and sped up. The analytical categories I have proposed for these purposes are those of formatting and fastening.

To further clarify the structuring work and political salience of the fastening enacted by formatting, I turn now to a final example in my thread line of education technology. One of the most popular classroom-facing education technology platforms today is ClassDojo, a form of educational social media that links teachers, students, and parents. According to its parent company, ClassDojo is used in 95% of K–8 schools in the United States as well as in 180 countries.[75]

Even with its lightning growth in use as a communications platform, ClassDojo retains at its core a behavioral management system. According to one team of critical education scholars assessing the platform, it fosters "a view of behaviour as emerging in isolation and unaffected by external influences" in a way that "situate[s] responsibility for behaviour entirely with the student."[76] This is a complex claim, but one way to consider it is in light of ClassDojo's "codified set of behaviors" through which the software "provides the digital framework on which to overlay the behaviour code."[77] What Jamie Manolev and colleagues here refer to as the overlay of a technical "framework" and a categorial "code" are brought together in my singular concept of the format.

Their case can be confirmed by examining the specific formats ClassDojo uses to collect and curate student data. The focus is on behaviors labeled either "positive" or "needs work" (an all-too-familiar euphemism for "negative"), differentiated into unique categories in which students accumulate points. Default categories include "listening" and "quiet" (in the "school points" category) or "ready for bed" and "family time" (in the "home points" category).[78] The formats embedded in the application both accelerate and entrench the perception of students in the terms established by the format. Teachers allocating points have cause to think of their students not only in terms of fixed behavioral categories but also as loci of points in a way that ultimately also invites students to see themselves through precisely these formats.

The platform offers no easy way of storing data about what Manolev and colleagues call "structural and contextual barriers to success" alongside its main classes of metrics.[79] Although the labeling for ClassDojo's point categories are highly configurable, the formatting remains a point accumulator. Consider in that light how little sense it would make for teachers to allocate points to their students on familiar metrics of socioeconomic status, housing conditions, nutritional status, or familial illness. A teacher, parent, and student may all be aware of such mitigating conditions, and yet the platform structures student data in such a way that these conditions cannot be easily stored and analyzed. In short, ClassDojo institutes a formatting of student data in psycho-behavioral terms that sideline well-known socio-structural conditions of behaviors. This prioritization of psycho-behavioral formats is by no means unique to this program; it represents a broader trajectory frequently found wherever datafication takes hold—for example, in contexts as otherwise different as education and health.[80] It is not my argument that this wider tendency, or ClassDojo's exemplification of it, is always unjustified. My claim is rather that such underlying data formats can function to structurally dispose classroom practices in ways that bear on the political values of classroom education.

Dissecting the Structuring in Formatting

Once data have pinned people down, those data can travel in two ways: they can spiral outward centrifugally in ways that quicken numerous other processes concerning these subjects of data. And those same data can also loop back to their subjects with the velocity of a centripetal feedback that quickly alters what a user takes themselves to be capable of. The fastening enacted by formats involves an exercise of power that travels widely, deeply, and in all kinds of ways that can be enrolled in processes of institutional policy, technological purpose, and even algorithmic processing.

In their sprawling work of fastening, data technologies are relatively unique among technologies in that they operate simultaneously technically and conceptually. Unlike technologies as small as a hammer or as gargantuan as a hydroelectric dam, data technologies operate through and help make operable conceptual categories. A powerful combination of the conceptual and the technical inheres in whatever is data-driven. That power, in its full political sense, comes into view only if we interrogate the structuring work of data in light of the formats that, alongside algorithms, enable data technology to operate at all. Without dissecting data's formats, we risk misunderstanding data themselves (not to mention the technologies built atop them) as inexorable, inevitable, and automatic.

Absent a more fulsome attention to the structuring work of formats, today's data technologies will continue to dispose and divide us in ways that we are failing to come to terms with. Wherever social structure exerts its influence, our refusal to look more deeply into what is going on right in front of us either visibly makes things worse or faintly lets them go that way. The need to look more deeply into data, to dissect our data, raises a number of pressing questions: how can we, and how ought we, study up on the structuring conditions of data formats? With what methodologies can we effectively inquire into the structuring work enacted by data structures? These questions motivate the methodology for data dissection proposed in the next chapter.

Format Anatomies
A Methodology for Dissecting Data

If data technologies generate and reproduce inequalities, then we need methods for better inquiring into these technologies and their operations. Since computational data technology relies on both algorithmic techniques and formatting techniques, we need methods for inquiry into both algorithms and formats. Accordingly, this chapter develops a methodology for mobilizing the theory of data equality with respect to often-neglected techniques of formatting. Methodology is crucial for the work of mobilization, or implementation, because what methodology offers (according to the classical Greek *methodos*) is a way of proceeding, and even more specifically, a way of proceeding within an investigation or inquiry.

The methodology I propose in this chapter is one I call an *anatomy of formats*. This methodology can be understood as a project in dissective examination. Anatomies seek to make visible and intelligible that which is obscure. What a format anatomy specifically seeks to make visible and intelligible are the values designed into those data with which a given computational system operates. Following an anatomy, the values that have been exposed can then be more rigorously evaluated against the values that the system under survey ought to exhibit. Such anatomies and evaluations are usable in many different kinds of contexts. Recall the metaphor from the introduction of the three-legged stool on which democratic reform balances: legal regulation, technological design, and human education. An anatomy of formats can profitably be implemented in any of these contexts, including policy change, technological redesign, skill building, and more.

Following this chapter, I offer in the final two chapters of the book an illustrative case of a format anatomy of personalized-learning projects in education technology that prepares the way for evaluating those formats that increasingly configure the educational experiences of students across a wide variety of sites. Before turning to this illustration, I first present the outlines of the methodology itself in this chapter.

From Algorithmic Audits to Format Anatomies

The concept of data equality consists in two parts: a normative component involving a structural account of relational equality (or democratic equality) and a technological component emphasizing data formats (or data structures) as significant for social structuring. An abundance of reasonable options are available for realizing both components. There is no benefit in postulating a neat one-to-one correspondence between the methodology of format anatomies I propose here and the value of democratic relational equality I presented in earlier chapters. The methodology of the anatomy of formats can be used to excavate values designed into databases with an eye toward evaluation in terms other than that of relational equality. A format anatomy could be used to excavate tendencies toward data deanonymization that are then measured against a value of privacy (and, moreover, a specific valuation of privacy rooted in concerns with liberty rather than equality). And just as format anatomies can be mobilized for evaluation across multiple values, so too can the value of relational equality be examined and evaluated in data technology in different ways.

Such theoretical possibilities affirmed, there are nevertheless important elective affinities between format anatomies and a fully egalitarian assessment. These affinities suggest a way of contrasting the format anatomy to (but without opposing) the methodological strategy of the algorithmic audit—arguably the most prominent methodological tool brandished in data ethics today. The overwhelming focus for the initial design and continued implementation of algorithmic auditing has been on discriminatory bias as defined by the consensus concept of algorithmic fairness. In short, algorithmic audits tend to be framed through the kind of distributivist concerns that are typically assumed as the background for aspirational algorithmic fairness (as described in chapter 1). Taking data equality seriously (as also argued in chapter 1) involves shifting our attention with respect to both our normative commitments (from narrowed conceptions of fairness to fuller conceptions of equality) as well as our technological foci (from narrowed algorithmic inquiry to fuller data inquiry) and therefore also with respect to the methodologies employed to realize this commitment and focus. To see why, consider algorithmic auditing in a little more detail.

The enormous attention on algorithms that is characteristic of the existing literature in data ethics and critical data studies has led to the good result of a set of methodologies for the critical study of algorithms. A leading, if not the leading, approach within this space is algorithmic auditing.[1] According to one prominent statement, algorithmic auditing is "a method of repeatedly and systematically querying an algorithm with inputs and observing the corresponding outputs in order to draw inferences about its opaque inner workings."[2] Some of the most common strategies include direct code audits, data scraping via web queries, and "sock puppet" methods whereby researchers pose as regular users to solicit and receive data from an algorithm.[3]

The motivating cause for algorithmic audits is typically the problem of the maldistribution of discriminatory bias. According to Christian Sandvig and colleagues in the first influential article documenting these approaches, certain "normative concerns that have been raised involving algorithmic discrimination" have reached a pitch at which these concerns "demand an audit of online platforms."[4] While algorithmic auditing in recent years has expanded to target other problems including personalization, disinformation, and user exploitation, the central focus for many employments of this family of methods remains the problem of algorithmic discrimination.[5]

The goal of algorithmic audits, as stated by Sandvig and colleagues, is to achieve "public interest scrutiny of algorithms."[6] In this respect, advocates of algorithmic auditing correctly trace this approach back to social science methods from the 1960s and 1970s of "audit studies" in which researchers sought to detect racial discrimination in housing, lending, and employment practices.[7] Since being introduced just over a decade ago on the basis of these previous methods, multiple forms of algorithmic auditing are now in wide circulation across numerous domains in which algorithms are used regularly.

Although public interest goals continue to motivate much work in algorithmic auditing, the methodology has in recent years migrated into the tech industry, where algorithmic audits are now routinely run as internal company processes strategically deployed in the interests of self-regulation. Numerous technology consulting firms (including many of the largest names you already know) currently advertise the value of boutique algorithmic audits to potential clients—a simple web search for "algorithmic auditing" will quickly lead you to their marketing materials. Many of the university students who are today being trained in algorithmic auditing will go on to deploy those skills at research nonprofits and regulatory agencies serving public interests. Many other students being trained in the same methods in the same classes will be hired, at sizable salary multiples, by corporations that will instruct them to conduct closed internal audits that help them avoid public scrutiny.

Partly in response to the corporate capture of algorithmic audits, a related research methodology commonly referred to as "algorithmic impact assessments" has emerged.[8] Originally constructed on the model of social science impact assessments in other domains, including environmental and human rights assessments, this approach is similar to algorithmic auditing in its emphasis on making algorithms and their outputs more transparent. These assessments have much to offer, and yet this approach has also quickly migrated to the tech industry as a strategy for self-regulation.[9]

Both algorithmic audits and algorithmic impact statements can be excellent tools for exposing how algorithms work. But on both approaches there is a lack of attention given to what precedes algorithmic processing in data technology. There is, in short, an inattention to formats within the extant methodological space of auditing and assessment itself insofar as these methods are trained primarily on algorithms. That said, audits and assessments need not ignore formats. In many cases, in fact, audits and assessments are inattentive to formats only because they operate with uninterrogated formatting schema as their presupposition. In such cases, the format anatomy is a valuable tool for looking more patiently at what has already been merely presupposed.

Consider the presence of the unreflective presupposition of formats in audits that function as post-processing detectors for differential outcomes with respect to a predefined set of group membership variables. A common example is the compliance audit specifically targeting discriminatory bias. A typical approach involves post-processing statistical analysis of differential outcomes of an algorithm tracked across known membership in protected versus nonprotected groups as defined by prevailing discrimination law. In an approach like this, the audit's categorization schema of protected versus nonprotected attributes is itself a presupposed format. But instead of being an internal object of study in a review process, auditing merely helps itself to a formatting schema by way of pulling off-the-shelf categorizations from prevailing legal requirements. Such approaches invoke a formatting schema, but in a rudimentary way that involves only post-processing analyses of differential outcomes rather than pre-processing and database-structure analyses of how those subject to the algorithm are in the first place formatted at the moment of system entry into input data.

Algorithmic audits that unreflectively presuppose a formatting will be highly preferred in contexts where the rationale for auditing is organizational or legal compliance. We should not undervalue the importance of such analyses, especially from the perspective of regulatory enforcement. Yet one concern is that existing regulations are woefully inadequate. Another is that compliance and enforcement are by no means the only important aspects of effective legal and administrative regulation. A third is that regulation is by no means the only important aspect of the effective reconstruction of data technologies—it is just one of the legs of a tripod whose other two supports are technological design and educational engagement. Taking this broader perspective enables us to better see the limitations of audits that unreflectively deploy existing formatting schemas. In part to overcome these and other limitations, this chapter proposes and develops a methodology for the anatomy of formats that is intended to complement algorithmic audits and assessments.

The Anatomy of Formats

A format anatomy involves the patient work of dissecting the formats through which data can be collected, constructed, and concocted. Rather than dismissing the data themselves by being indifferent about them (an attitude that is common among both technologists who develop algorithms and many of the critical scholars who study them), a format anatomy is concerned with how data are constituted. The object of interest for a format anatomy, what it is designed to make visible and intelligible, is how information is formatted. There are always multiple choices in the design of any database, even the simplest ones. A format anatomy brings these choices, both those made and those declined, into clearer view.

Like algorithmic audits and assessments, format anatomies admit of multiple variants. Distinguishing some of the dimensions along which format anatomies can vary will be of value, though I do not take the distinctions below to be exhaustive or unrevisable. Four methodological dimensions warrant discussion: those concerning the multiple *levels of granularity* at which formats can be objects of inquiry (the "what" of format anatomies), *research strategies* for conducting an anatomy of formats (the "how"), the *moments of operation* at which formats are particularly prone to encode and implement values (the "when"), and finally the justificatory warrant for scrutinizing formats with respect to the particular kinds of *problems* or *harms* that formats can occasion (the "why").

WHAT TO STUDY IN A FORMAT ANATOMY (WHAT TO LOOK AT)

What does a format anatomy look at? The short answer to this question is: formats, or data structures. A longer answer begins with the fact that we can always distinguish different *levels of granularity* of formats. Having this variety of levels in view better positions any given format anatomy to focus on the range of formats under its survey in distinction from other levels of formats also present. Wherever data technology is operative, we should be able to distinguish three levels of formats. Stated concretely, these are the levels of data system architectures, data models, and data inputs. Stated abstractly, these three levels can be referred to as macro, meso, and micro.[10] Or, following my metaphor of anatomy, these can be referred to as the system, organ, and cellular levels.[11] A format anatomy can and often should be conducted across multiple levels or layers of data formatting. Such an anatomy can show, among other things, how different levels of formatting in a model hang together. For instance, system-level architectures often embed domain assumptions that will pervade input-level formats.

Anatomies of System-Level Format Architectures

At the macro level, we look at data formats in terms of their systemic operation. Here we ask: what are the systematizing concepts that organize the basic workings of a dataset? What needs to be brought into view at this level are the orienting operational assumptions in virtue of which something can even count as data about whatever is being modeled. What are the basic conceptual assumptions about that which constitutes a viable model of an economy, a genome, or a learner? How are these assumptions embedded in the system-wide technical architectures where these models are operating? This level is often expressed in data standards for scientific research or industry interoperability. Of course, in many technological contexts, standards have yet to be established, or are established but routinely neglected by practitioners.

Anatomies of Model-Level (and Model-Feature or Model-Construct) Formats

A next stage is the meso level of organization, or the metaphorical level of the organ. Here we ask questions like: how are economies, genomes, or learners functionally defined in models? This involves examining the data variables specifying the features or constructs composing a model. To contrast the meso level with the macro level, the meso is more focused on the technical designs of models and their features, whereas the macro is more focused on wider architectural requirements expressive of axiomatized conceptual assumptions.

Anatomies of Input-Level Formats

The finest resolution is available at the micro level, akin to the cellular level for anatomy. A format anatomy conducted on this level involves looking at the data points that are used to compose model features, how those data points are structed or defined, and therefore how features can and cannot be composed from granular data points. For example, most models of learners in learning-analytics research define their objects (learners) in terms of features representing their knowledge of some domain. Such variables are constructed by processing data inputs like learner answers to quiz questions in a course management system or past learner performance in related courses. Establishing reliable relationships between modeled features and data inputs has been described as "making reliable links from 'clicks to constructs'—the new version of making inferences from behavior to constructs."[12] It is often crucial to observe input-level formats insofar as reliable links strongly depend on stable data inputs that have been, if they are truly stable, precisely formatted. An example of a kind of input-level formatting that is almost ubiquitous in data systems is that of defining (or typing) variables for the collection and conservation of data—familiar forms of variable types include numerical versus text (or string), array versus stack (versus instance or token), or discrete versus continuous quantities. Studying the definitions of empty variables that will host data points helps us reconsider the many choices that get made where formats configure the very possibility of input data—for, as one critical quantitative education researcher notes, "variables encompass what has been included *and* omitted from the statistical model."[13]

HOW TO IMPLEMENT FORMAT ANATOMIES (HOW TO LOOK)

The idea of a *research strategy* refers to the ways a methodology is mobilized according to accepted (and perhaps also experimental) practices and styles of research implementation. Along this dimension, there are countless ways a format anatomy might proceed. A handful of potential strategies stand out as precedents. I consider five in turn, sorting my list alphabetically (with one exception of a potential outlier, which I describe last): analytical, genealogical, interpretive, sociological, and documentational. My list does not distill exclusive strategies, but rather describes independent strategies that may overlap.

Analytical Format Anatomies of Conceptual-Technical Categories

An analytical format anatomy involves the work of explicating the categories present in a dataset. This approach can be seen as a particular way of pursuing the more general philosophical project of conceptual analysis. What is conceptual analysis? To attempt to state in a single sentence what is surely one of the most influential and diversified methodological strategies of the past century of anglophone philosophy, a conceptual analysis works by taking a concept and explicating its relations. At its best, conceptual analysis involves two kinds of explication. One kind involves exploring a concept's internal relations or subcomponents—this is atomistic analysis in the classical sense of breaking down a concept.[14] Another kind of analysis involves explicating a concept's external relations—this second kind of explication most prominently considers inferential connections between concepts that are frequently employed together.[15] Less common in the longer history of philosophical conceptual analysis, but more prominent in recent decades, is the work of documenting external conceptual relations in terms of locating the relations between concepts and other aspects of the practices that form the sites where concepts are used.[16] The work of the philosopher of science Ian Hacking affords some of the best models for this third kind of approach to conceptual analysis. On Hacking's view, "A concept is nothing other than a word in its sites."[17] The sites where concepts are wielded involve a multiplicity of kinds of elements: not just other concepts, but also active behaviors, sensory perceptions, historical processes, causal events, and technological operations.[18] Attending to how concepts are related to other concepts as well as to other aspects of their sites is one way of conducting conceptual analysis without falling into the idealistic temptation of proceeding as if all that exists are concepts, ideas, or reasons. With respect to the anatomy of formats, this third form of conceptual analysis underscores how categories in a data structure are possessed at once of conceptual-inferential structure and also technical-functional structure. Although conceptual analysis in some form or other has been a dominant methodological approach in anglophone philosophy for almost a century, there is precious little work that brings this approach to bear on data formats. Of course, every rule has its exceptions, and the most important one in this case are the studies of data in the biological sciences by Sabina Leonelli, whose methods are also partially influenced by Hacking (as well as by John Dewey's pragmatism).[19] Where Leonelli tends to be more focused on the philosophical analysis of data-centric natural sciences, I find myself more drawn to the analysis of data-driven human sciences (as well as the quasi-sciences and even non-sciences through which humans often become subjects of datafying formats). This minor difference is noted only as an indicator of plurality, not incompatibility.

Genealogical Format Anatomies of Genesis or Emergence

The central idea of a genealogical anatomy of formats is that we can learn about how formats function today by studying the various forms of historical inertia they contain within them. It matters where a format came from and how it was composed. Such genealogies are not focused on first origins or first cases—they are not primarily attempts to trace a format back to its very first usage, though they may arrive there. Much more important is tracing backward from the present the various contingencies through which formats have been perturbed and pushed in light of strategic oppositions and opportunities. By attending to such contingencies, a genealogy of formats can excavate both how a format has been designed as well as the relations of this design to other aspects of the sites in which it functions. This approach is underutilized in contemporary research on data technology. The under-explored value of such an approach can be clarified in part by distinguishing the genealogical anatomy of formats from more prevalent efforts in the history of data—the former is focused on tracking the conceptual and technical conditions of formatting, while the latter tends toward histories of the social conditions or social impacts of certain kinds of data.[20] That said, precedents for data genealogy can be found. Among them are my own prior efforts in data genealogy focused on formats, such as a collaborative study of how clinical medical records were first formalized only after insurance providers had already instituted requirements that clinicians report standardized medical data for their billing purposes.[21] A different kind of genealogical approach to datasets is offered by Emily Denton and colleagues in a genealogy of the popular ImageNet machine-learning dataset describing the conflictual discursive conditions through which a dataset gets stabilized rather than connecting these conditions to the technical formats structuring the dataset's functionality (but such connections could clearly be made in future research).[22]

Interpretive Format Anatomies of Context

The interpretivist approach to format anatomies is best exemplified by the model of "reading datasets" developed by the anthropologist of data Lindsay Poirier.[23] I find Poirier's approach the clearest effort to date of developing a critical-analytical mode of inquiry into the data work I have been describing as formatting. As described in the previous chapter, Poirier's approach involves three levels of inquiry that recursively shuttle between data's literal meanings (as expressed in metadata documentation like data dictionaries), cultural contexts (as explicated by historical and genealogical analyses), and politicized processes of signification (as exhibited by, for example, a dataset's gaps in representation).

Poirier offers as an example a reading of a City of New York Police Department public dataset documenting stops by police officers.[24] Her discussion of this dataset both documents the values encoded in the dataset's columns (including analyses of permissible variables for the police stops recorded in each row) and analyzes discourse about policing practices (from news articles, press releases, and legal decisions) that reveals institutional incentives for police officers to record certain kinds of police activities in ways that favor desired statistical outcomes in the data. What Poirier's reading shows, among other things, is how "the numbers are wrapped in institutional systems that exploit certain bodies and over-surveil certain communities, while erasing the crimes of others."[25] Though this conclusion might have been reached otherwise (such as by way of a historical analysis of police racism), a clear virtue of Poirier's approach is that it makes its case on the basis of available public data. Another virtue is in how Poirier's multilevel model situates what otherwise looks like unimpeachable data in social contexts of conflict that enable us to recognize how data can be the strategic outcome of contested interactions. In this and other respects, the structure of Poirier's interpretivist approach to reading datasets is highly complementary to the methodology of format anatomies I am calling for.

Sociological Format Anatomies of Experience and Use

Another way to develop an anatomy of formats involves studying how formats are both used and experienced. Relevant here are perspectives of those who are subjected to categories as well as those agents who participate in the circulation of categories to which others are subject. Work in the sociology of categories and categorization offers instructive precedents in this vein; so too does work by legal scholars on categories in the law, perhaps most notably categories of persons in discrimination law.[26] Just as I distinguish genealogical format anatomies from histories of the social effects of data, it is helpful to here bear in mind a distinction between sociologies of formats themselves and research on the social impacts of particular formats and their platforms. One widely cited work in the sociology of categories that effectively straddles this distinction is Geoffrey Bowker and Susan Leigh Star's 1999 book *Sorting Things Out: Classification and Its Consequences*.[27] This book presents meticulous accounts of how categories are both experienced (by those subject to them) and used (by those tasked with the subjecting). These accounts are sometimes more historical (in which case they shade into the genealogical approach just noted), sometimes more documentational (in which case they begin to look like the final approach discussed below), and sometimes more ethnographic (which makes them rather more distinctively sociological). This variety as exhibited in a single work attests to the multiple ways that anatomies of formats can be implemented.

Documentational Format Anatomies

A final precedent I consider is in important respects aligned with the methodology of format anatomies, but perhaps not as clearly as the others listed
here—I thus consider it a bit of an outlier. The body of work I place under this
heading includes efforts developed under a variety of labels such as datasheets
for datasets, nutrition data labels, and data documentation.[28] The central
strategy linking these efforts involves taking an existing dataset and looking
into its structure, variables, and encoding in order to produce a thorough
metadata accounting. On the one hand, this approach clearly anticipates the
format anatomy methodology: it involves patiently looking into the technical
features a dataset. On the other hand, this approach differs from format anatomies in that it tends to remain sealed up within the technical specifications
of the dataset. Whereas the analytical strategy for format anatomies described
above perhaps risks remaining too much inside the conceptual categories of
databases without connecting those categories to other aspects of practical
implementation, the documentational approach to format anatomies carries
a contrary risk of getting stuck inside the technical specificity of databases
without connecting technical specifications to the ways that databases actually operate in their sites. I note this difference, but I also note it as theoretically minimal—for it is easy to envision a documentational approach specific
to format anatomies built atop the precedents cited here.

WHEN TO CONDUCT FORMAT
ANATOMIES (WHEN TO LOOK)

Another axis along which format anatomies can be distinguished concerns
the *moments*, which might also be thought of in terms of the *operational activities*, at which data systems are prone to express problematic values. The
distinguishing question here is: at what moments along a chain or flow of
formatting operations ought we to inquire when searching for values that
have been designed into formats?

Moments of Repurposing (or Secondary Use)

Repurposing involves the reuse (or secondary use) of data that originates
in one context within another context that is in some ways significantly different. Where this happens, formats can pull forward assumptions about
or features of their originating context into new situations where these assumptions or features may not hold. This can take many forms, including

significant social, cultural, geographical, and historical differences in context. Repurposing is quite common—indeed almost startlingly so in recent computational implementations that leverage artificial intelligence, or machine learning. One cause of this is the tendency of researchers, both in corporate and academic settings, to marvel at the algorithm and discount the data. As the authors of the ImageNet genealogy cited above note, "Despite the foundational role data plays, data work is rarely considered foundational," evidenced by the fact that "guidance or advice on how to construct ML [machine-learning] datasets occupy little to no space in ML textbooks and curriculum."[29] Researchers are strongly incentivized to locate the cheapest and easiest sources for data inputs. For instance, it is quite common for researchers employing machine-learning methods to leverage a freely available dataset on which to train their models, despite knowing full well that the dataset was originally composed for rather different purposes than that posed by their own research.

Moments of Entrenchment (or Standardization)

If repurposing involves the reuse of formats in contexts that differ significantly from those in which they originated, *entrenchment* refers to the tendency of formats to persist in contexts to which they do not readily apply. This can sometimes take the form of formats predetermining data technology in certain contexts or for certain purposes despite not being a strong fit for those contexts or purposes. At its most general level, entrenchment can be thought of as context creep: it occurs where formats curated for one context predetermine aspects of research questions, methodologies, or findings in another context with significant differences from the originating context. Formats may be problematically entrenched wherever significant contextual variations are present but where formats persist. Repurposing and entrenchment are clearly related, but they are not identical. They seem alike because in some situations these concepts refer to the same moment looked at from different directions: entrenchment looks upstream to prior data, digging in deeper, while repurposing looks downstream to present data being diverted to unplanned uses. But data can be repurposed toward unplanned uses in ways that do not serve entrenchment: a research project may make secondary use of data for a very narrow purpose that is so idiosyncratic as to not have wider implications for other purposes. To clarify the difference, it helps to think of entrenchment as increasing along a gradient that runs from one-off cases of secondary use at one end, to cases of established benchmark datasets near the other end, with full-scale standardization as the extreme case. As

Kathleen Creel and Deborah Hellman write, "The supply-side availability of readily accessible databases may lead companies to choose them rather than gathering their own data, thus pushing them towards standardization."[30] This is true, too, of well too much data science research in academia where similar incentives in favor of cost-cutting and against database curation are in place. Creel and Hellman describe one study of how deep-learning algorithms in clinical medicine draw disproportionately on datasets sourced from hospitals in just three states (California, Massachusetts, and New York). They attribute this circumstance to the probability that "the rich hospitals in those states are the hospitals most capable of running studies using deep learning and of producing the kind and scale of data appropriate for deep learning."[31] The problem of entrenchment in this case is that the findings of the algorithms trained on this dataset have a lower likelihood of generalizing to clinical patients in the other forty-seven states, especially members of subpopulations in those states not well represented in the three states from which data are sourced. This would be even more problematic if the data formats from the three-state dataset were to be officially standardized (as a matter of policy, either by law, or by fiat within the context of a certain medical research community). But even short of full-scale *de jure* standardization, problems can already arise in situations of *de facto* entrenchment.

Moments of Interoperability (or Merging)

Interoperability occurs where datasets implemented in two or more different systems need to be integrated, joined, or merged in some third system (whether that third system replaces the originating systems or is built atop them).[32] Outside of situations where established data standards strictly govern the formats implemented in datasets subject to a merge, questions will arise as to how two different sets of formats can be made compatible. Interoperability is typically achieved by way of custom or boutique solutions for one-off data-exchange problems. In such cases, questions typically arise about how to merge disparate data. Some of these questions will have easy answers; in most cases, though, difficult challenges will arise. How are two incompatible category taxonomies to be rendered compatible? How are data from a finer-grained taxonomy to be translated into a rougher-grained schema? Or moving in the other direction, how are lumpier categories to be translated into more precise categories? How are data missing from one taxonomy to be imputed into the other? Must they be imputed? In some instances, technologists have looked to develop algorithms to answer these questions. But given that these data will often be the basis for downstream statistical inferences,

significant consequences can follow from choosing an algorithm for interpo-
lating missing data or from randomly allocating data stored in coarse formats
across finer formats.

Moments of Production (or Specification)

Chronologically upstream from all the moments of data conveyance just discussed are the originating founts where data structures are first implemented.
At these moments of production, numerous decisions are made about how
a given dataset is to be formatted. Once made, and once systems are implemented, these decisions quickly become irrevocable (or, at least, too costly to
revoke easily). Three kinds of features at moments of production can make
them especially prone to the production of formats that lead to downstream
problems. First, those producing data formats may be inattentive to, or otherwise uncareful about, downstream consequences of the conceptual categories
and technical functionality they are implementing. Given that, as observed
above, data curation is typically second-class work in corporate and academic
spaces of data-driven research, this kind of problem is remarkably common.
Second, those producing data may be socially positioned in such a way that
they will tend to be ignorant of how conceptual or technical implications
could have adverse consequences for members of other social groups. This
problem could be partly remedied by ensuring that teams establishing data
formats are more diverse, but this remedy is often not implemented because
it is regarded as too costly given the relatively high fiscal costs of human collaborators in comparison to cheap technological solutions. Third, since data
curation and data management are usually second-class concerns where data
systems are implemented, they are also frequently mere afterthoughts. This
often results in hurried production of category taxonomies and other elements of formatting. Buried deeply away in so many server farms are the lin-
gering artifacts of formatting decisions made just before a launch deadline
by a coder without any domain knowledge whose decision procedure was no
better than a coin flip.

WHY FORMAT ANATOMIES ARE
NEEDED (WHY TO LOOK)

Another relevant methodological dimension that is especially important for
methodologies for normative political or ethical inquiry concerns the *harms*
or *problems* that a format anatomy can bring into view. A list of familiar
problems that have been diagnosed in different domains of data technology

includes: political polarization, social separation, discriminatory bias, violations of privacy, lack of trustworthiness, lack of explainability, undermining the autonomy of persons, and outright informational coercion. Like any such list, this one remains necessarily incomplete both in its range and its depth.[33] With respect to range, surely there exist other harms engendered or amplified by data formats; and even more surely, other such new harms shall emerge in the future. With respect to depth, it is crucial to recognize that each class of problems admits of multiple subclasses. Discriminatory bias in data can be further decomposed following taxonomies such as that proposed by Harini Suresh and John Guttag (distinguishing sampling bias, aggregation bias, evaluation bias, and more), or by the education analytics researchers Ryan Baker and Aaron Hawn, who present five different taxonomies of bias in machine learning.[34] Privacy harms have similarly been decomposed by means of mappings of the multiplicity of dimensions out of which any given privacy violation is composed.[35] Similar mappings and taxonomies would surely show other formatting harms to be similarly complex.

THE MULTIPLE MODALITIES OF FORMAT ANATOMIES

The methodological dimensions of format anatomies just canvassed give rise to multiple possible permutations. The differing approaches along each dimension can be combined with multiple options along the other dimensions to yield a rich array of basic orientations guiding a given anatomical investigation. One example is a historical genealogy showing how health insurance standards for billing data led to the entrenchment of data-input formats in clinical medical care databases.[36] Another example is a historical genealogy of education-data formats used to specify and operationalize conceptions of familial and socioeconomic backgrounds.[37] A third, presented in the next chapter, is a technical-conceptual analysis of how student-data formats operative in personalized-learning platforms rely on and effectively reproduce student learning as an isolated, rather than collaborative, activity. The purpose of the foregoing explication of methodology is not to seal up any one particular approach to format anatomies. It is, rather, to clarify a range of choices that the serious inquirer must confront in conducting an analysis of the formats of a data system.

Of course, there are numerous other dimensions along which format anatomies admit of variance. One obvious dimension I have not discussed is that of the *sites* where we look at data in conducting a format anatomy. I have left this dimension to the side because the potential sites for data are as dizzyingly multitudinous as data themselves are. Data are often universalizable—they can frequently be made to move almost anywhere, though it may take much work and effort to do so. In considering data's uncountably many sites, then, it probably matters less to draw up an inventory of potential locales in advance, and matters more to find ways of following data wherever it flows or travels. What matters, as Jo Bates and colleagues document, is being methodologically prepared to follow datasets on their "journey through inter-related sites of data practice."[38]

Other dimensions of analysis relevant to conducting format anatomies concern typical methodological issues facing any form of rigorous social inquiry. A full discussion could therefore easily balloon into an entire book. The goal of my explication here is not an exhaustive typology, but rather an initiating clarification of those dimensions of inquiry that perhaps require particular comment in the context of an anatomy of formats.

With a working typology of format anatomies now in hand, I turn in the final part of the book to an implementation of the theory of data equality in the context of personalized learning in education technology. This will be a two-step effort, the first step of which is a format anatomy of learning-analytics methods in personalized education, with the second step being an evaluation of the findings of that anatomy. The design of the format anatomy conducted in the next chapter is anticipated by the methodological dimensions canvassed above. What I will present can be described as a *conceptual-technical analysis* of *problems of relational inequality* reproduced at the moments of *data entrenchment and production* as made visible by examining formats across multiple levels of granularity as they constitute *learner models and their input data.*

Democratic Equality in Education Data

7

Artificial Intelligence for Personalized Learning
An Anatomy of Learner-Model Formats

Across numerous domains of contemporary life, our data systems are increasingly operating as technologies of separation. From commerce to health care to education, new innovations wrought by social media, data analytics, machine learning, and artificial intelligence tend to drive us apart. In so doing, they fail to fulfill that halcyon promise of the internet age encapsulated in Facebook's longtime motto of "making the world more open and connected." The slogans persist, yet the cracks that separate us widen. Data technologies drive disconnection, not relation; hierarchy, not equality. As Tim Berners-Lee, the founding architect of the internet protocols underlying the World Wide Web, observes, "The web has evolved into an engine of inequity and division."[1]

One astonishing feature of this situation is just how frequently tech elites admit to it. A scandal breaks, apologies are rolled out, and then the tech class (along with everyone else who accepts their way of doing things) hits "refresh" the next morning and resumes their faith in the mega-promises of high-tech connection. Recall when shortly after the 2016 US presidential election, Mark Zuckerberg delivered another in a long line of empty apologies. This one stood out for its candid admission of Facebook's failure to live up to its own stated mission: "For the ways my work was used to divide people rather than bring us together, I ask for forgiveness and I will work to do better."[2] But Facebook (and its parent corporation, Meta) is not doing better—Zuckerberg's companies continue to silo, segment, and separate their users. Since his 2016 confession, not only has Zuckerberg pleaded publicly for forgiveness time and again, but he has aimed his ambitions ever higher and wider.

Through the arm of his for-profit philanthropic foundation, the Chan Zuckerberg Initiative, the Facebook founder has even targeted what is perhaps the central democratic institution of liberal societies: public education. The Chan Zuckerberg Initiative's involvement in remaking rather than simply reinvesting in education is (like that of other prominent philanthropic organizations, including the Bill and Melinda Gates Foundation) both wide in its reach and deep in its pockets. Its website has for years described initiatives that will transform education on the basis of the same techniques and technologies Facebook employed to transform the way people relate to each other (or fail to do so) as friends and acquaintances. Facebook personalized our relationship to friendship at the same time that Google personalized search and advertising, Amazon personalized shopping, and Twitter (alongside Facebook) personalized news. Now Chan Zuckerberg, Gates Foundation, Google Education, and others promise to personalize learning.

Personalization is a strategic vision being implemented across a wide variety of deployments of data technology.[3] Personalization promises a better internet, better social media, better searches—pages, feeds, and results will be tailored to your particular interests. Broader than online life, personalization is rolling out in domain after domain of social interaction: financial planning, medical care, consumer marketing, voter targeting, and democratic participation. But personalization is especially disorienting, at least for democratic and egalitarian aspirations, in education.

For a sense of just what personalized education is, consider the familiar language-learning application Duolingo, iconized in its cheerful little green owl and tutoring coach, Duo. Described on its website as "the world's most downloaded education app," Duolingo currently offers instruction in forty-three languages (thirty-nine of them for English-speaking learners) ranging from Arabic to Zulu, including offerings in Esperanto and Klingon (the artificial language from *Star Trek*).[4] Duolingo works by harvesting enormous amounts of data from its users and then analyzing those data to deliver more tailored, more precise, and (presumably) more educative experiences. This business strategy has impressed investors to the tune of a $10 billion market capitalization. In a *New Yorker* profile of company cofounder Luis von Ahn, previously a MacArthur genius grant recipient for his work on artificial intelligence and cryptography, interviewer Carina Chocano asked him whether he enjoys running the company. His reply: "For me, this is very fun. Except for the people problems. Those are no fun."[5] Pressed on this by Chocano, von Ahn admitted that in his view, human beings in general "are just hard to deal with."[6] Predictably, he also aimed this skepticism at his company's chief competitors in education—that is, educators. As he told Chocano, "Some teachers are good, but the vast majority are not all that great."[7] She also reported that "von Ahn told me that artificial intelligence would eventually make computers better teachers than people."[8] Perhaps it will in some ways. But will artificial intelligence make computers better than teachers at the work of dealing with people? What about the work of dealing with people seen as causing problems? The very promise of data-driven and scaled-up personalized learning is premised on taking out of the equation both the way students relate to their teachers as well as the way they relate to each other. What Duolingo leaves out of its platform, and by explicit design, are collaborative partners in learning—and it presumes they are readily replaceable by avatars like Duo.

For the better part of a decade, such projects in personalized learning have been heralded as crucial tools for furthering educational equality by numerous government education agencies,[9] technology corporations,[10] and nonprofit philanthropy spokespersons,[11] as well as by many in the academic research community.[12] Any purportedly egalitarian aspiration with strong support from government, industry, and academia is of course highly interesting.[13]

Personalized learning is interesting not only in light of its broad support, but also because what the rush for data-driven personalization in education is actually producing are democratic deficits of relational inequality. But this is by no means obvious. This chapter and the next detail the unequalizing effects of personalized learning. I first develop an anatomy of formats for learner data in personalized learning in this chapter, followed by an evaluation of the implications of those formats in the next. I also turn in the next chapter to alternatives to personalization as currently being developed through data-centric projects in collaborative-learning analytics.

Why Education Matters to Democratic Equality

The effects being wrought by personalizing data technology in education need to be aired in their own right. But I also have an additional purpose here: in the context of the broader arguments of this book, the following analyses of education technology serve to mobilize methodologies and conceptions developed in earlier chapters. Education technology offers a paradigm case of how to conduct an anatomy of formats with an eye to the value of data equality. But why take education and its data technology as a paradigm? To answer this question at the outset, I begin with a brief explication of the internal relationship between education and equality. This relationship suggests why education ought to be a primary field of concern for any relational egalitarian, which is to say, for anyone committed to democratic equality.

In considering the relationship between education and democracy, there is no better starting point than the pragmatist philosopher and education theorist John Dewey, and his view that "faith in democracy is all one with faith in experience and education."[14] Throughout his life, Dewey wrote about and participated in education reform. His most influential contribution was his 1916 book *Democracy and Education*.[15] As one should expect of a book with that title, part of what Dewey develops there is an account of why education is central to democratic equality, as well as a specification of what democratic equality requires of education. Dewey discusses the "familiar fact" of the "devotion of democracy to education."[16] Seeking a fuller understanding of this connection, Dewey rejects as "superficial" those explanations focusing on the utility of education for securing an informed electorate.[17] Asserting a signature formulation recurring across many of his books, Dewey argues that "a democracy is more than a form of government; it is primarily a mode of associated living, of conjoint communicated experience."[18] What Dewey's formulation brings into view are forms of social interaction in which "each has to refer his own action to that of others" such that all can relate with each other as equals by way of "the breaking down of those barriers of class, race, and national territory which [keep] men from perceiving the full import of their activity."[19]

Throughout *Democracy and Education*, Dewey refers to experiences of technological development, commercial globalization, and mass immigration as forming challenges to democratic modes of living together. The unifying thread running through these challenges is that they transform societies and polities into associations "composed of a combination of different groups."[20] Dewey thereby anticipates later democratic theory's conception of pluralism—for instance, in his observation that "a modern society is many societies more or less loosely connected."[21] The challenge set by pluralism, Dewey argues, needs to be met by, among other things, egalitarian democratic structures in which "intellectual opportunities are accessible to all on equable and easy terms."[22] If we ask where such structures can be effectively stood up, one answer is in infrastructures for public education. On Dewey's conception of democracy, education stands out above all other aspects of social structuring for its potentiality to function both as an active obstacle to entrenched inequalities and as a facility for upbuilding equality in the midst of plurality. Dewey's view thus refers to the internal connection between democracy and education—the one involving forms of social interaction exhibiting equality of relations, the other functioning to cultivate such equal relations within and across generations.

Dewey's argument is of course not framed in terms of Elizabeth Anderson's later relational egalitarianism.[23] Yet he anticipates something of this later idea in his discussions of democratic equality. Throughout *Democracy and Education*, Dewey emphasizes the unique function of education (in contrast to what he calls mere "training") in situating the learner as "a partner in a shared activity" and a "copartner [in] conjoint activity."[24] Another good term for Dewey's vision that I shall make much use of is "collaboration," understood as naming endeavors that take place between learners as well as between those learners and their teachers. Collaboration is not achieved where an instructor trains a student directly or where an individual learns entirely on their own without others. What is essential for collaboration is that it involves relational continuities among those who are learning. This, for Dewey, is what makes education so preeminently important to democratic equality. Democracy too is essentially collaborative.

Consider now a few of the ways in which what we continue to expect from education today connects it to democratic equality. One widespread expectation is that education unleashes social mobility, which is the correlate of disrupting social hierarchies. Another common expectation of education is as a public project, where learners from different walks of life work together in common without distinctions of status serving as causes for segregation. A third expectation is well articulated in two recent books on education by pragmatists of somewhat different stripes. Danielle Allen's *Education and Equality* shows how "intrinsic to the practice" of education there is a cultivation of skills for "participatory readiness" that lead indirectly to strong egalitarian tendencies.[25] Philip Kitcher's *The Main Enterprise of the World* similarly shows how "humanistic education" prepares the way for "deeper mutual engagement when citizens need to deliberate together."[26] Each of these three common expectations of education reaches beyond the familiar thought (regarded by Dewey as true yet superficial) that learning prepares informed citizens. More important is how education prepares us to act together as citizens—that is, as democratic collaborators who can and do relate to each other as equals.

There is a strong case for taking education seriously as a domain from which we ought to, and reasonably can, expect increasing equality. We ought to expect equality in just about every other domain too. But we should also acknowledge realistically that there are numerous domains where making an internal argument for equality faces steeper slopes. Even in contexts where public goods are widely affirmed, such as biomedicine, it is not always clear inside the domain (for example, within for-profit pharma giants) why or even how we should pursue equality. Education, by contrast, is a domain where equality is widely wanted, and in particular where what is aspired to is democratic relational equality. This is not to deny that there is today ample cynicism about the egalitarian effects of education—a cynicism easily fueled by quick observations of inegalitarian correlations between educational attainment and family income.[27] Yet recent research by the education sociologist Douglas Downey shows why such cynical accounts are largely ill informed—those disappointing correlations between learning outcomes and family incomes are shown to largely dissipate in research designs focused not just on one-off measures of education but on longitudinal measures of learning gains whose periodization takes into account learning loss suffered during summer months, when few students are actually in school.[28]

For these and other reasons, education not only makes a good paradigm case for my broader argument about data equality, but it is also already internal to that argument insofar as my focus is on democratic equality in data. With respect to being a paradigm case: surely if data egalitarianism can get off the ground anywhere, then it ought to be in education. And with respect to education being internal to my argument: if data equality does not help reshape the education technologies currently reorganizing education, then there is a real threat of the loss of the internal connection between education and democracy, and thereby the threat of losing democracy itself.

Personalized Learning and Its Techniques

If equality in education matters, then equality in education data matters too. Rebecca Eynon observes that "data is becoming a defining feature of the education system."[29] Education is by no means unique in the intensiveness of its datafication. Numerous other contemporary domains are given to similar tendencies, and equally long histories, of data saturation; these include biomedicine, psychometrics, and accounting, to name just three other domains I have written about elsewhere.[30] Though not unique as a site of datafication, education is as much a site of datafication as any other major domain of democratic societies, and what we ought to expect of educational datafication is that it not only not undermine the democratic effects of education but that it help enrich democracy too.

How is education being datafied? To provide some bearings for the analysis that follows, I begin with a brief survey of four related families of education-data technology: education technology (or EdTech, in industry parlance), artificial intelligence in EdTech (AIEd), and two particular EdTech and AIEd projects at the center of my discussion: learning analytics and personalized learning.

EdTech refers to technologies that are employed to assist, transform, and in some cases disrupt education—the term typically, though not exclusively, refers to the use of data technology in education.[31] Among the many now-standard EdTech projects are teacher training and credentialing, data-assisted administrative decision-making, and data analytics for student learning. Projects fitting into this third class of data analytics for learning are typically conducted under the auspices of two increasingly interrelated research programs: learning analytics and educational-data mining.[32] The last decade especially has seen explosive growth in these fields. Though both preceded the recent boom in artificial intelligence, a good share of the recent growth of interest in learning analytics and educational data mining is due to the even more explosive recent growth of AIEd. Though the idea of artificial intelligence is ultimately more of a marketing term than a scientific concept, a wide range of EdTech research is migrating toward computationally expensive methods that promise new ways of getting at old problems in education. Such projects in AIEd typically involve building data models (usually of learners or learning processes) on the basis of both vast stores of data (usually student data and education software-user data) and machine-learning approaches (such as artificial neural networks or generative pre-trained transformers).

Learning analytics is a field in want of a common definition.[33] One widely cited conceptualization was offered at the field's first international conference in 2012: "The measurement, collection, analysis and reporting of data about learners and their contexts, for purposes of understanding and optimizing learning and the environments in which it occurs."[34] The authors associated with this definition soon after described learning analytics as "a bricolage field drawing on research, methods, and techniques from numerous disciplines such as learning sciences, data mining, information visualization, and psychology."[35] On almost any definition, learning analytics refers to projects with at least the following three major steps: collection and pre-processing of data about learners, analysis of those data with an eye to action, and postprocessing of data that serves as a feedback mechanism for the pursuit of ever-refined analytics.[36] Each of these three steps can take a multitude of different forms.

A diversity of data-processing methods are employed in learning analytics. The most prominent include: predictive classification, cluster analysis (and related forms of structure discovery such as factor analysis), relationship mining, and visualization (and other ways of distilling data), as well as more complex approaches that plug results from one of these methods into another.[37] More recently, with the rise of AIEd (beginning around 2012 and taking off considerably around 2017), there has been increasing focus on machine-learning techniques for pattern discovery in learner data.[38]

What specific purposes do learning-analytics researchers hold in view when they are focused on understanding and improving learning? Here is where personalized learning enters the picture.[39] Personalized learning has gained increasing prominence over the past decade within learning analytics as well as across the broader fields of AIEd and EdTech. As two leading AIEd academics state in a white paper titled *Intelligence Unleashed: An Argument for AI in Education*, "AIEd offers the possibility of learning that is more personalised, flexible, inclusive, and engaging."[40] Though numerous EdTech approaches have been geared toward personalized learning, Ben Williamson observes that "learning analytics is perhaps the most prominent application of education-data science for personalized learning."[41]

What is personalization in education? The main idea involves using data technology to differentiate educational delivery for differentiated students. Personalized learning serves as a kind of umbrella under which fits a variety of associated projects in adaptive learning, intelligent tutoring, personalized assessment, and learning prediction.[42] Among the variety of educational elements subject to personalization are: instructional content, sequencing and scheduling of different instructional modules or smaller-scale elements of instruction, modes and media of representation of content (audio versus textual presentation of the same content), instructional or pedagogical methodologies, assessments of student work and learning, structured supports for learning, real-time recommendations and feedback, human–machine dialogue, pre-learning and post-learning interventions, as well as various forms of predictive modeling.[43] The leading edge of interest in the research community at present, according to one recent literature review, is the personalization of instructional contents.[44]

Personalization in education is conceptually quite proximate to other forms of personalization already widely familiar through consumer recommender systems—think of content streaming and online shopping. This conceptual affinity is widely acknowledged in the literature.[45] In some cases, there have even been direct links.[46] Personalization as a technique is thus not particularly unique within education. But it is unique here in its motivating purpose of enhancing learning outcomes. The research literature frequently cites the famous two-sigma finding published by the education psychologist Benjamin Bloom in 1984: students receiving one-on-one tutoring surpassed their classroom peers by two standard deviations of performance.[47] Personalized-learning advocates have high hopes that virtual personalized tutors can replicate the results of Bloom's study of the effects of human tutors.

I noted above that learning analytics is widely affirmed by its proponents as still wanting unifying definition. This is also a familiar refrain in the literature on personalized learning.[48] One perspective is afforded by implementations of the 2015 Every Student Succeeds Act (ESSA), which required state-level personalized-learning policies yet without strictly defining the term. In an article reviewing ESSA implementation, Ling Zhang and colleagues document multiple competing definitions of personalized learning among states implementing its policies.[49] They also track a multiplicity of definitions offered by institutional heavyweights, including the United States Department of Education, the Center on Online Learning and Students with Disabilities, and the International Association for K–12 Online Learning.[50]

All the definitions cited in the Zhang study explicitly describe personalization as a way of serving "each" student or learner by tailoring, adapting, or customizing some aspect of instruction. This emphasis is also featured in numerous other definitions of personalized learning across institutional white papers, policy statements, and research articles. A typical formulation, as presented in a white paper authored by the RAND Corporation for the Gates Foundation, defines personalized learning as seeking a "clear understanding of the needs and goals of each individual student and the tailoring of instruction to address those needs and goals."[51] A journalist in *Education Week* summarizing the field writes that "the idea is to customize the learning experience for each student according to his or her unique skills, abilities, preferences, background, and experiences."[52]

These formulations all index a common currency that circulates across nearly all operative conceptualizations of personalized learning: a focus on what we could call the *each-ness* of learners. This term offers an important clue about the conceptual underpinnings of personalized learning. What *each-ness* connotes is a consideration of all members of a set taken separately as discrete entities. According to this formulation, the emphasis in personalized learning is on conceiving of learners as separate from each other. By implication, personalization does not emphasize understanding learners as continuous with, or related to, each other in important ways. This inattention to relational continuities between learners is not just an implication of how personalized learning is conceptualized. It is more fundamentally a result of how learning-analytics techniques are implemented across the data-centric designs over which they operate. These techniques are operationalized over data formats that represent learners only in their separateness from each other. I refer to this emphasis on separated learners as learner *discreteness*, a concept I explain in due course.

LEARNING ANALYTICS AND LEARNER
MODELS FOR PERSONALIZED LEARNING

Over the past decade, learning analytics and personalized learning "have become highly interrelated."[53] This has involved leveraging learning analytics for personalized learning. What are the technical guts of these projects? To find out, we need to open up the main technical component enabling this combination.

The central technical mechanism connecting learning analytics to personalized learning are the data streams and data blocks that constitute what are commonly called *learner models* or *student models*. Models of learning and learners have long been central to education practice.[54] What distinguishes the current wave of personalized learning is the idea of building its learner models by way of the kinds of data analytics strategies leveraged in learning analytics.

A learner model is "a computational representation of a student which stores information and, in some cases, simulates student behaviour."[55] Such models are typically implemented in coordination with at least two other kinds of data models: models of learning content (for example, domain knowledge) and models of expertise (for example, the role played by a tutor in intelligent tutoring systems, or an instructor in a classroom).[56] Where learning analytics is implemented for the purposes of personalized learning, the learner models are central. They have been described as the "heart," "pillar," "base," "core component," "core," "first step," and "key element" of personalized learning.[57] Learner models are that in virtue of which, and also that for which, learning is personalized.

It is reasonable to assume that learner models are models of persons, and more precisely, persons in their role as learners. What learning analytics has access to, both in its data capture and its data targeting sequences, is of course not a physical person but rather data traces of behavior. This abstraction inherent in learning analytics serves as a critical wedge for some commentators.[58] Yet there is little reason to be critical of the very idea of constructing abstract models of persons (as I argued above, at the end of chapter 1). In the case of learning analytics, the behavioral data on which its learner models are based are no less real than the physical persons whose actions are being datafied. Education, like so much else in life, is in fact largely an affair of actions, conducts, or behaviors. We should train our critical capacities not against modeling in general (as purportedly reductive), but only against particular models that entrench and exacerbate inequality (or other ills we are concerned with). Only in this way can we both locate the limits of some data systems and also be prepared to acknowledge that other systems may overcome these limits. For example, the limits of personalized learning may be effectively surmounted by alternative forms of datafication central to projects in collaborative-learning analytics.

An effective analysis of learning analytics begins with the observation that learner models can be constructed out of a wide range of differing data. Which data are brought into focus in a particular implementation involves a complex process of selecting for particular learner features (also often referred to as constructs or variables) in light of desired outcomes, educational theories, ethical and political values, and of course pragmatic conditions such as feasibility, efficiency, and data availability.

Learner-model feature selection ought to fulfill at least three conditions: relevance of each feature to intended learning outcomes, adequate learner variability on each feature (a feature or variable that is coded "high" for every learner is not useful if "low" and "medium" labels exist but are not applied), and theoretical understanding of how each feature or feature set can be adapted to produce intended outcomes.[59] Concerning the third criterion, it has been widely observed that personalized-learning projects often implement strategies that lack any kind of grounding in existing learning theories.[60] Put crudely, these observations suggest that personalization interventions have in some cases been selected on the basis of what is at best common sense or intuitive guesswork. A prominent example of this recorded by Matthew Bernacki and colleagues in their review of 376 personalized-learning publications is that "the fourth most common learner characteristic" employed in personalized-learning designs was "an individual user's 'learning style,'" even though "the existence of 'learning styles' or any such implications for learning have been largely debunked through empirical testing" by education researchers.[61]

The data that constitute learner models require scrutiny; such scrutiny is part and parcel of what makes learner modeling scientific rather than haphazard. Yet there is a crucial but too often neglected aspect of this scrutiny, concerning how values get designed into learner models. Scrutinizing learner-model data for the extent to which they realize or facilitate certain values requires inquiry into the data-formats operative in any particular learner model. Such an inquiry can be facilitated by the methodological approach of a format anatomy. In addition to conducting an anatomy of formats, we might also examine other aspects of these systems too, such as their algorithms. The range of algorithmic techniques involved in building and deploying learner models is wide, ranging from the AI-based approaches (such as predictive machine learning or neural-network clustering) and probabilistic Bayesian modeling (such as Bayesian knowledge tracing) common today to classical modeling techniques dating back five decades, where learner knowledge is conceptualized as a subset of domain knowledge (such as in overlay models). Given the variety of algorithmic techniques available, the selection of technique surely matters much to how learners are modeled and what are done with these models. That said, in all computational programs, even the most complex algorithms are ultimately dependent on the range of data inputs that can be fed into the processing engine. This is why we often learn more about a system by scrutinizing its formats than by examining its algorithms.

A FORMAT ANATOMY OF LEARNER MODELS

An anatomy of learner-model formats reveals important characteristics of the learner data that funds these models. The anatomy conducted below focuses on one specific characteristic. There is a strong tendency in learner data toward what I noted above as an emphasis on "each-ness" in which each learner is datafied as separate from all others. I shall refer to this as *discretization* at the level of the learner. As I use this term, it refers to how learners are formatted as discrete or separate entities. The operative contrast I seek with this term is separation versus continuity.

The late-nineteenth-century philosopher and metrologist Charles Sanders Peirce coined numerous neologisms, including "pragmaticism" to protect his own earlier concept of "pragmatism" from would-be "kidnappers" of his philosophy.[62] A more brilliant coinage is his term *synechism* for entities or processes exhibiting continuity.[63] Employing Peirce's term, synechistic learner data refers to data points that bridge between learners. For example, data generated by interactions between learners working in a group where these data are realizable only on the basis of these interactions are synechistic. Discrete learner-data points, by contrast, are defined as assignable only to separate learners. Consider a hypothetical learner database designed as purely discrete at the level of the learner (as most actual learner databases are). In this database, each data point would be assigned to one and only one discrete learner. This pattern of assignment would not be a contingent matter of chance but would be dictated by the formatting that determines what can even count as a data point in this database. If this hypothetical database were revised to incorporate formats that permitted the assignment of single data points to groups of learners (such as overall time spent on a project or percentage contribution toward a project), the revised database would be more synechistic. It would, at the level of data, supply some connective tissue linking or relating learners to each other.

It might be thought that the technical separation I am referring to would be better described as *individualization* rather than discretization.[64] While this label is not wholly inappropriate for my purposes, individualization carries certain connotations that the most precise formulations of my argument need not invoke. First, consider a technical aspect of learner-model data. Discreteness in these data may or may not correspond to individuality at the level of the persons to which such discrete data are attached. From a technical perspective, learner data are often not actually individual, since the data themselves are a way of dividing up an individual learner on whom data are being kept.[65] Second, it matters much for my overall argument that from an egalitarian perspective, individuality as such is not inconsistent with equality. Rather, what constitutes inequality are only those separations between individuals that strain and undermine their ability to relate as equals. Putting my point in terms of a critique of individualization, rather than discretization, thus invites misunderstanding in light of common political criticisms of individualization that I would not endorse.

With this explanation of a little piece of terminological jargon in hand, I turn now to a descriptive anatomy of learner models. What this anatomy will show is that the formats prevalent in learner models serve to discretize students—most learner models are constituted by features and data that are indexed to discrete learners rather than to collaborative learners working together. Per the description of the methodology of format anatomies in the previous chapter, I consider multiple levels of data granularity. The discussion focuses primarily on the meso level of learner-model features and the micro level of learner-data inputs, but I begin with brief comments on macro-level data architectures.

Macro-Level Format Anatomy: Data Architectures

Research in learning analytics, and other fields making use of learner models, is on the whole too variable and recent to have settled into standardized system-level architectures. Standards packages for learner data do exist.[66] Yet, to my knowledge, these standards are not widely employed in learner models.

Where they are employed in learning analytics, it is worth noting that existing standards exhibit strong tendencies toward learner discreteness.[67] That said, many of these standards do at least accommodate the possibility of learning at the group level rather than learning as only an affair for discrete individuals. One way they accommodate this is by way of data-dictionary definitions that are explicitly agnostic about whether unique learner identifiers need to refer to individual learners.[68] So while discreteness is clearly involved in architecture-level formatting of learners and learning, it is not a required technical feature. Perhaps the best way to state this is to say that these architectures technically accommodate, but do not conceptually invite, synechistic formats establishing data about continuities between learners. This architectural tendency toward discreteness exhibited by learner-data standards is reproduced in the finer-resolution formats of learning analytics.

Meso-Level Format Anatomy: Feature Variables

In their review of scholarship on features for learner models, Bernacki and colleagues conclude that "the list of learner characteristics that inform PL [personalized learning] designs is staggeringly large."[69] Some of the most common features in learner models include variables for cognitive factors, motivational factors, social and cultural factors, and emotional-affective factors.[70] These are of course only generic classifications of features. Examples of more fine-grained cognitive factors that might be implemented as a feature variable in a learner model are: content knowledge, reasoning ability, developmental level, cognitive abilities, knowledge of learning strategies, ability to self-regulate, language proficiency, and reading ability.[71] For example, a learning-analytics research project might involve modeling learners with respect to their content knowledge of a particular domain for learning—say, algebra. In such a case, the research team would attempt to train an engine to automatically model any individual learner's content knowledge of algebra so that this model might be used as a basis for personalized online instruction in algebra. One standard way of doing this is by way of machine-learning classifiers that rate an individual learner according to different gradations of their knowledge of the domain.

In light of the wide range of feature variables that have been employed in learner modeling, it is somewhat surprising that "current adaptive learning environments are responsive to a very limited number of variables, often only to one."[72] The overwhelming majority of learner models is designed to model learners with respect to variables representing what they know (knowledge attributes, also sometimes referred to as mastery attributes) or how they know what they know (cognitive attributes).[73] This is likely to change in the near future as learning-analytics research more fully incorporates artificial intelligence methods that are widely taken to be more successful at predicting affective states and other learner attributes that have historically been quite difficult to validate.[74] There is today a growing spate of research on "emotion AI," "affect modeling," "emotion detection," and other data-based derivations of feeling.[75] An exemplar is the Microsoft Azure Face API for emotion recognition, an off-the-shelf plug-in service to enterprises licensing Microsoft Azure cloud computing.[76]

Across all the most common learner features modeled in learning analytics implementations geared for personalized learning, learners are discretized. Consider that the standard lists of learner features canvassed above include features that are most easily understood as modeled qualities of individuated learners. Cognitive factors such as content knowledge or reasoning ability are widely assumed to be features of discrete learners. Rare is the learner model with features designed for collaborative skills, qualities, or achievements. Surveying the range of learner variables, one research team remarks that "almost all learner modeling is designed to represent and draw inferences about students learning 'solo,'" such that "our understanding of how to model collaboration phenomena is highly underdeveloped compared to conventional learner modeling."[77] They observe that the all-too-common idea that we can simply port extant models of discretized learners to more synechistic models of group learning (for instance, by creating discretized-learner models for each of a pair of learners working together) "would fail to capture the dynamics of collaborative learning."[78] This is a general point that holds across nearly all learner features commonly selected for in learner models.

Another way to understand the tendency toward discreteness in learner modeling is via the outcomes that learner features are selected to improve. A typical learner model will build in a learner feature only if it is taken to be relevant to a learning outcome. The learning outcomes these models are designed for are also often implemented as learner-discrete. Evidence of this is documented in, for instance, a review by Bernacki and colleagues identifying thirteen commonly targeted learning outcomes, none of which directly involve measures of learner collaboration behavior or collaborative skills.[79]

The discretization of learner features is by no means a necessary attribute of learning-analytics research. There is nothing in principle forbidding researchers from building learner models that aim to enhance collaboration and relational engagement among students. But in technical matters as much as in social ones, inertia is a real force. While there are no strict technical impediments preventing learning analytics for collaborative learning, the weight of a hefty technological precedent incentivizes gearing learning analytics toward personalized learning. In domain after domain, the story of data-driven inertia is the same: wherever multitudes of data are already cut to a certain shape, it is easier to build analytics suited to those data than to whomp up new models atop newer data structures that would require collecting new data. This is certainly true of learning analytics, as can be seen by an anatomy of the most granular level of formatting—that of the data points forming the data inputs for learner models.

Micro-Level Format Anatomy: Data Inputs

Learner models are based on huge piles of fine-grained data points. An anatomy of learner-model formats thus requires looking at the formats that structure the data inputs used to form the features of learners constituting a learner model. In the context of an anatomy of learner-model formats, this is akin to moving from the organ level (the features or constructs defining learners) to the cellular level (the data out of which features are composed).

There are many ways of categorizing the input data that are used to compose learner models. One common categorization schema focuses on the provenance of these data, and distinguishes accordingly two kinds of data sources.[80]

The first general class of learner-model data are externally sourced. These data are assembled from extant datasets such as education records that include not only academic performance but also often demographic and socio-economic characteristics, as well as behavioral data. These are often referred to as *student information system data*. A typical set of such data would be the student records stored by a school registrar. Other data types employed here might be derived from psychometric instruments testing students on various capacities from cognitive abilities to personality traits.

The second general class of data used to constitute learner models involves internal usage data generated as byproducts of user engagements with digital learning environments. These are often referred to as *internal log data* or *trace data*. Digital learning systems, ranging from intelligent tutoring systems to learning-management systems (such as the Canvas platform or Google Classroom) often generate vast troves of transactional byproduct data. This usage data of "logged behaviors and actions" can be summarized as data capturing "what the user did during his interaction with the system."[81]

Capacities for internal data generation have been referred to as "the datafication of learning."[82] The datafication of learning is like any effort in datafication in that it depends on defined variables that simultaneously omit and include—or neglect and embrace. Digital learning environments subject an impressive multiplicity of events and objects to datafication. The most obvious are those ordinary data points such as in-platform tests that register and collect assessment data of individual students. Yet much more is subject to datafication than what appears most obvious. In a study of data usage in a set of nine learning-management-system–supported courses, Dragan Gašević and colleagues assembled a summary list of trace data that included assignments, book downloads, chats, course logins, feedback access, forum participation, quiz scores, plagiarism detection, and use of other resources and modules.[83] Each of these can be recorded at various levels of granularity, ranging from simple binary conditions (whether a user has ever accessed a resource) to more fine-grained-count data (how many times a user has accessed a resource, durations of access on each occasion, and behavioral data such as page turns or video pauses captured during access).[84] Even more granularly, systems can also capture byproduct data generated by mouse clicks, cursor location (including measures of smooth versus erratic motion), typing speed, and number of times the backspace or delete key was depressed, as well as data generated by digital sensors. A camera might be used to generate facial recognition and eye-gaze saccade data that can be used to model engagement and attention. Other systems have experimented with external devices tracking heart rate, electroencephalograms (EEGs) measuring brain activity, and skin-conductance bracelets quantifying stress levels and emotional intensity. Bror Saxberg, a former vice president of learning sciences at the Chan Zuckerberg Initiative, succinctly encapsulates the multitudinous internal data drawn on for learner modeling: "The evidence can accumulate at multiple levels, from clickstreams, motion position data, speech streams, gaze data, biometric and brain sensing, to more abstracted feature sets from all this evidence."[85]

In the face of such bewildering lists of learner-data inputs, it would be remiss not to remark on the genuine privacy concerns that accrue around all this dataveillance. There are entire armadas of researchers (as well as educational administrators, unwitting instructors, and obliged students) signing on to such laundry lists of student-data collection without even the slightest humility. It is beyond the scope of the present discussion to explore this problem here.[86] But given my wider arguments about data equality, it is worth noting in passing that these privacy issues, though often presented as matters of individual liberty, can also be understood as concerns about democratic equality.[87] Without downplaying the significance of intrusions upon individual liberty, data-privacy violations can also be seen to disrupt our ability to openly and equally relate to each other in light of the chilling effects of data collection. In the case of learning analytics, intrusive levels of dataveillance are a countervailing force against learners interacting with each other collaboratively and sharing their learning experiences.

Prior to any sustained discussion of ethical or political concern around data inputs (be it privacy or equality or anything else), what needs to be considered first are the technical features of the data themselves. What do these warehouses of input data look like? How are these data kept and stored? What variable types delimit what these data can and cannot be? In short, what characteristics do the data themselves thereby exhibit? Like all sizable stores of data, learner data have numerous characteristics; indeed, often uncountably many. Which of these characteristics matter most? One property that makes a difference is their historical quality—all data are almost by definition imprints of past performance, and this certainly holds in the case-learner data. Other properties that often matter refer to demographic distinctions among learners (such as race, nationality, or even just geographic locations of home and school).

Another particularly interesting, and important, characteristic of much, indeed nearly all, extant learner data is that of learner discretization. How is discretization a property of learner-data inputs? In a typical system, all such data, from mouse clickstreams to learner assessments to longer-term student-records data, are deeply and in many cases purely learner-discrete. Platforms may vary in exactly what data they collect for feature modeling or in how they combine external student-records data with internal log data. But almost all these systems rely entirely on learner-discrete data for models— that is, on data that are specifically indexed to each learner taken as an independent entity.

These data can be visualized on a spreadsheet as cellular data points stored in series of columns organized according to a unique identifier in the first column that represents each unique learner on a separate row. All data across each row are indexed to that unique learner. Each row will typically consist of all the data that can be collected around a unique learner behavior or a unique learning event indexed to a unique learner. The spreadsheet thus constitutes a repository of data that are all indexed to discrete learners. Consider a few examples.

Two commonly referenced learner datasets provenanced from internally sourced log data exhibit exactly this formatting. One is the HarvardX Person-Course Academic Year 2013 De-identified dataset, version 3.0, gathered during the first year of HarvardX courses on the edX platform. Its second column heading is "userid_DI," specifying a unique user identifier that is repeated across many rows of the dataset as a trace of multiple system interactions by a single registered user.[88] Another is the ASSISTments dataset, whose first column heading is "user_id," which is defined as "the ID of the student doing the problem."[89]

Data of an external provenance will typically exhibit the same kind of discretization. A look at your own education transcripts will attest to this.

The highlight of your high school career may have been that team project in physics class for the science fair—however, in all but the most atypical of cases, your transcripts contain only data referring to you as a discrete learner with no data points that imprint how well (and even if) you learned with others. Taking a longer view, we can observe discretization as a tendency in student-records data going back at least one hundred years to some of the first attempts to standardize education records.

Consider now a timely objection to my attribution of discretization to all these input data. Has the functionality I discern in discretized data not been rendered irrelevant by recent machine-learning techniques? These techniques are capable of analyzing multiple data inputs to form a learner model as a holistic composite rather than as an aggregate of discrete bits of data. So, the objection concludes, it is irrelevant whether most (or even all) of the learner-input data discretize learners. Two responses quickly discharge this objection. First, we need to ask whether a given machine-learning technique can actually be shown to analyze holistically in this way. If this question is empirically unanswerable, because the machine-learning implementation is impossible to see inside of, then there is no basis for assuming that the implementation really does analyze holistically rather than proceeding datum by datum. To the extent that most machine-learning approaches are probabilistic (in relying heavily on statistical forms of inference), the more reasonable conjecture is actually that their internal logic is inductive (built out of an accumulation of data) rather than composite (or abductive in form). Second, even if it were shown that a machine-learning implementation analyzes its learner features as a kind of abductive composite, the specific formatting of those individual data that compose that composite still very much matter. You cannot pull together a composite exhibiting continuity on the basis of discretely formatted data.

From Anatomizing Technical Formats
to Evaluating Technological Values

One major factor in the recent explosive growth of personalized learning is the wide availability of precisely those kinds of data for which personalization-aiming learner models are so hungry. Learning analytics works best with large stores of data. If one were to go hunting for massive-size data stores in the domain of education, pretty much all the datasets of sufficient size one would find consist of already-discretized past-performance learner data. There is an elective affinity between the already-entrenched data apparatus of student-learning data and efforts in learning personalization.

Is this perhaps more than an elective affinity? Since the entrenched-data apparatus (or, at least, a large share of it) preceded personalized-learning implementations, there is also a sense in which learning analytics was set to work in contexts already significantly conditioned in favor of personalization. This conditioning was largely an effect of preceding regimes of data capture that can now be understood as having prepared the way for personalization. Extant student data—as well as older predigital learner models and standards based on those data—have long been largely learner-discrete and performance-focused, thereby preparing an efficient technological pathway leading toward personalization.

In considering all those troves of discretizing data that long preceded personalized learning, it might be thought that the ills of discretization are not the fault of personalized learning but are due to much older assumptions guiding education systems. This objection surely has it right that learner-discrete data have existed in education for at least a century. Yet the objection wrongly draws an inference from the existence of this class of data to the quite separate idea that these data should so thoroughly drive so many aspects of education (rather than, say, teacher-driven or collaboration-centered). Data was never so central to education as it is today and as proponents in EdTech want it to be. A more accurate account would be the following: data technology came along, found a domain where huge data stores were widely available as a cheap incidental resource, and then drafted those stores into service for an agenda that to date had not really been all that prominent within that domain. This is an exceedingly common story—domain after domain has been incorporated by its own incidental data to such an extent that those data are now the center of the domain. This is the story of becoming data-driven.

What one observes in data technology as it roams into domain after domain are strong incentives for employing hypercomplex algorithmic processes and high-performance computing machinery on existing data sources that are comparatively cheap. Time and again, the data that are simply already there are the data that get used. This is one of the deepest ironies of the information age. Huge amounts of time, money, and talent are invested in improving algorithmic processing and computing machinery—yet comparatively minimal effort is invested in generating quality datasets and guiding formats. This is partially because of the enormous expense of the sheer labor required to build good datasets. Good data can be extremely costly in terms of both the labor required for initial labeling as well as the iterative testing required to ongoingly refresh conceptual-technical formats. Faced with high costs of designing new data, most tech projects prefer the more efficient route of building fast applications on the basis of whatever data are already given. That is just the business model of data tech today—if it needs doing, then write code to do it, and never hire a team to do with precision what running code can automate with good-enough accuracy. Those data that already exist may be faulty in all kinds of ways, but their huge advantage is that they are a cheap resource that can be efficiently leveraged for plausible goals. In at least one way, the common comparison of data to oil is apt: both are relatively cheap resources carrying high costs in terms of unplanned externalities.

Collaboration versus Personalization in Democratic Education
Evaluating Equality in Learner Data

Data-driven education projects leveraging learning analytics toward personalization manifest as what I call *technologies of separation*. Common datasets for learner modeling, analyzed in the anatomy of personalized-learning formats in the previous chapter, strongly evidence discretization at the level of learners. The evaluation undertaken in this chapter shows how such learner-discrete data exhibit the egalitarian deficit of separating learners.

Yet these are not the only projects made possible by training artificial intelligence on education data. What might more-egalitarian education technology look like? One answer is evidenced in work in which data analytics are implemented for the sake of collaborative (rather than personalized) education. Accordingly, a main goal of this chapter is to develop an evaluative contrast between personalization and collaboration in education technology. Before presenting this contrast, I begin with a brief review of why a focus on democratic equality (and its companion commitment to collaboration in place of separation) is important in contexts of data technology.

Current Assessments of Personalized-Learning Technology

How does my focus on equality—and specifically, democratic or relational equality—square with other recent scholarship assessing the political and ethical ramifications of personalized learning? The first thing to note is that there appears to be a dearth of reflection on the ethical and political ramifications of learning analytics and personalized learning (as well as AIEd more broadly). This is especially true of surveys of published research focused on building and validating tools. A recent review of AIEd research in higher education finds that of 146 relevant articles, just two reflected critically on ethical challenges of artificial intelligence, prompting the authors to claim that "a stunning result of this review is the dramatic lack of critical reflection of the pedagogical and ethical implications as well as risks of implementing AI applications in higher education."[1] Nathalie Smuha similarly observes, "Tailored ethical guidance for the development and use of AIED remains sparse."[2] In the fields of learning analytics and personalized learning, the situation is not all that different, despite the fact that personalization in education is widely championed precisely for its promise of increased equality.[3] Even in the field of computer-supported collaborative learning, to which I turn below as a positive exemplar for how learning analytics can be used to achieve more-equal relations in education, it is noted that "sociopolitical issues remain at the periphery of the field and require further theorization."[4]

Against the background of what is almost a vacuum of rigorous research on the ethics of learning analytics and personalized learning within these fields, there have emerged critical voices from positions that are adjacent to these research communities, and most notably by critical education scholars. It is worth comparing the egalitarian approach I adopt to this critical literature for two reasons. One is to highlight aspects of this critical literature that are complementary to my efforts. Another is to highlight how the particular approach I take remains strikingly absent even across this critical literature.

Most of the critical work on EdTech (and especially on learning analytics and personalized learning) can be bucketed into two categories. First are epistemic criticisms focused on issues of what is knowable, what evidence can be amassed for conclusions, and the scientific methodologies capable of building arguments. One common criticism along these lines concerns the abstractionism inherent in learner modeling, which many critics regard as unjustifiably reductive.[5] Another common such criticism points to the lack of evidence backing the rather sizable promises issued by advocates of personalized learning.[6] This criticism echoes misgivings already internal to the field itself, as indicated by research teams who recognize that "the evidence of impact remains one of the greatest challenges that learning analytics researchers must address."[7] These concerns are certainly important. But I believe we should ultimately trust the community of science to get its epistemic affairs in order; perhaps not right away, but certainly over time. There are just too many incentive structures in place in the practice of science (including data science) for it to be likely that entire research communities are going to contravene basic epistemic norms of warrant, evidence, and justifiability. Much more likely—and certainly much more concerning, from my perspective—is that science will sometimes get things right at an epistemic level but in a way that unintentionally propagates ethical and political values that we ought not to be forwarding.

This brings me to the second category of criticisms on offer in extant critical literatures on personalized learning and learning analytics. These are criticisms focused on the values instantiated by these and other education technologies. Some criticize personalized learning for undermining learner agency and autonomy.[8] Others criticize these systems for extracting profit from the work of harvesting or mining data from their users, who are often children.[9] A related but distinct critique concerns the value of privacy and how learning-analytics methods risk violating data-privacy principles.[10]

The particular focus on democratic, or again relational, equality that is central to my evaluation has yet to be voiced in any serious way in the extant critical literature concerned with the values underlying education technology. Indeed, it is striking just how little of the critical literature on personalized learning and learning analytics raises concerns about inequality in any form at all. All the other criticisms I have cited loom larger in the scholarship. Consider Sharon Slade and Paul Prinsloo's 2013 survey article on the ethics of learning analytics, which appears to be the most-cited article on ethics in learning analytics to date (with over one thousand citations). The article proposes an "integrated, sociocritical ethical framework and principles for learning analytics."[11] Yet none of the six principles enumerated therein are focused on fairness, let alone equality. Similarly, a 2016 special issue of the *Journal of Learning Analytics* on the topic of "ethics and privacy" in learning analytics was devoted almost exclusively to privacy, with only a few cursory nods to distributive equality (in the form of a concern over digital divides) in the editors' introduction.[12]

Yet it may be that the field right now is on the cusp of a pivot. A 2023 special issue of the *Journal of Learning Analytics* takes as its focus fairness, equity, and responsibility in learning analytics.[13] The issue includes numerous discussions of various aspects of equality, equity, and fairness in learning analytics. A 2023 volume titled *The Ethics of Artificial Intelligence in Education* includes three chapters focused primarily on issues of fairness and equity.[14] At least two other papers published independently in 2023 are devoted to the same topics.[15] This recent increased interest in equality in learning analytics is certainly welcome.[16] And yet this work still relies on narrow fairness-only conceptions of equality like the prominent ideal of algorithmic fairness. Suraj Uttamchandani and Joshua Quick observe about learning analytics that this body of research "has approached issues of equity . . . through the notions of algorithmic fairness and absence of bias," while Ryan Baker and Aaron Hawn find that data ethics in education exhibits "an intense focus on fairness."[17] A major concern is that the singular attention to fairness and distribution on the part of critical scholars too conveniently replicates assumptions that enable learning analytics and personalized learning to avoid more transformational change.[18]

I adopt a rather different approach that is relatively novel in this space, yet not entirely without precedent. Neil Selwyn raises concerns with how personalization in education nourishes an individualistic view of learners.[19] I take arguments such as this to be invitations to focus on technologies of separation, for what I think Selwyn is probably targeting with his concern over individualism in personalized learning is actually better understood as a tendency toward what I called in the previous chapter *discretization*. On my account, discretization entrenches separations between learners in a way that can only be properly grasped through a framework of relational, rather than distributive, inequality. Discretization in learning analytics for personalized learning tends to generate relational inequality even in those very instances where it is being pursued for the sake of more-equal distributions, as for instance in projects in "equity analytics," which exemplify the clean-conscience self-image of research that puts data in service of equality, yet without serious attention to whether the data themselves are already containers for inequality.[20]

Personalized Learning and Its Values

I turn now to presenting two evaluative arguments about personalization in learning. Both arguments show that data technologies aiming at personalizing learning exhibit relational inequality. The first argument shows that relational inequality flows directly from discretized data in learner modeling. I call this *the argument from discretizing data*. It shows that personalized learning often functions as a technology of separation. The second argument shows how relational inequality flows from learner modeling by way of the intermediary stage of compounding distributive inequalities. According to this argument, relational inequality forms a feedback loop with patterns of distributive inequality that get entrenched by relying on prior performance data in learner modeling. I call this *the argument from prior performance data*. This argument shows that personalized learning tends to function as a technology for the reproduction of entrenched patterns of inequality. Neither argument is logically dependent on the other. A particular technological system could exhibit either of these forms of inequality without exhibiting the other. Personalized learning happens to exhibit both.

Both arguments as I present them are concerned with relational inequality. The data discretization argument focuses directly on how we are related to each other, while the prior performance argument is indirectly concerned with how the intermediary of socioeconomic maldistribution reinforces relational inequality. Both aspects of personalized learning are concerning in their own right. Taken together, they paint a rather bleak picture for the much-touted egalitarian aspirations of personalized learning, for they show that personalized learning functions as an educational structure which directly undermines relational inequality (as a technology of separation) and also deepens existing distributive inequalities (as a technology of reproduction) in ways that indirectly reinforce relational inequalities.

EVALUATING DISCRETIZED-LEARNER DATA:
TECHNOLOGIES OF SEPARATION

The argument from discretization holds that personalized learning functions as a technology of separation. This argument consists in two claims. The first is a technical claim developed in the anatomy of learner-model formats presented above: learner models built atop learner-discrete student data dispose the learners they model toward isolated and separated learning practices rather than collaborative ones. The second is a claim concerning the value of equality, or lack thereof, in models of learners and the personalization they support. This is the claim that these technologies of separation exhibit a tendency toward structural inequality insofar as they position students in ways that fail to augment (at best) and even actively inhibit (at worst) students' abilities to relate to each other as equals. The first and more technical claim having been already shown in the previous chapter, the focus here is on the second, more evaluative claim—that discretization renders personalization an inegalitarian technology of separation. I shall consider the second claim in two passes. At an initial pass, I will consider this claim from a more intuitive perspective, mostly with an eye toward elucidating the meaning of the claim. Then, in another pass, I shall consider the claim more analytically and normatively by way of the model of structural relational equality detailed in previous chapters.

An Intuitive Evaluation of Discretization

Picture a classroom full of students, each silently fidgeting at their desk as they stare into the screen of a learning device. These students are not all engaging the same instructional content but are immersed in their personalized materials. While it may transpire by chance that some of them are learning the same lessons in the same way, they may never know it, their teacher may never know it, and in any event, they are not engaging it together. This is a rather dour picture of learning as fully discretized at the level of learners. I doubt even the most ardent EdTech enthusiasts would endorse it.

In other more humdrum situations, personalized learning may look more lively. It may look like a classroom of elementary-school kids during free-choice time: some roam over to the bookshelf to read their favorite story, some crowd at the drawing table excited to create new kinds of animals, some work at a station with math blocks, and yet others grab their tablets off the cart and log in to a virtual learning environment to complete a gamified learning scenario they had left unfinished the day before. Those with books may be reading alone, or reading to each other, or gathering at the feet of a classroom helper reading the next chapter. Those at the art table might work in isolation, but they might also work together to see who can draw the wildest beast, or even as a coordinated team, with each member drawing a different animal part on a large sheet of paper. Those working with the math cubes might collaborate on basic arithmetic. But those working on digital tablets are in a different position. Each learner must begin by logging in to their own account. The learning exercise itself is not designed for collaborative teamwork. It is a personalized experience. A student working on a digital puzzle might nod to a friend looking over their shoulder, but only one of them can control the device. According to the designs of the software, they are not even supposed to be taking turns.

This image illustrates differences in technological affordances.[21] Books, art supplies, and math blocks afford interaction, collaboration, and relation in ways that handheld computers loaded with software requiring individual student licenses and logins simply do not. In the realm of logical possibility, it might be the books that are licensed to isolated readers and the tablets that afford cooperative interaction with classmates connected by the cloud. But in the realm of actuality, those conditions do not obtain in today's classrooms.

The humdrum scenario just sketched is today exceedingly common. But even variants of the more dour scenario are not as far from reality as we might like to think.[22] Some form of it was widely witnessed by parents (and of course students and teachers) in the course of the massive experiment in remote education conducted during the first six to eighteen months of the Covid pandemic. The calculus that resulted in widespread school closures was a complicated call involving many factors, among them certainly the boastful promises of EdTech companies that they could deliver quality remote learning to students staying at home.

Public health is always a complicated balance. As early outbreaks developed into a full-blown pandemic, that balance was already tilted by a decade of promises trumpeted by leaders in EdTech. I am not suggesting that different public health regulations should have been implemented (one alternative would have been to divert larger federal stimulus packages toward more emergency teacher hires instead of the bipartisan idea of funneling sizable payments to upper-middle-class taxpayers whose investment portfolios subsequently swelled the speculative interest in financial instruments like cryptocurrencies, non-fungible tokens, and meme-leveraged stocks of failing media corporations). I am observing how concerning it is that gargantuan decisions were made on the basis of big promises about data tech that were presumably well intentioned but also, as it turned out, not well informed.

What is disturbing is just how familiar this story is in Big Tech. Big promises are made, frothy market valuations are achieved, and while some of the boasts occasionally succeed, the reality is that most data technology never works as planned. This is exactly what happened to EdTech in the pandemic: students failed to learn at the levels that were promised. This is now widely acknowledged.[23] Less widely acknowledged, and perhaps more important, is this: students failed to be supported in relating to each other as equals in their learning. Learning technologies of separation kept them apart. The problem was not really that public health officials kept students from physically relating to each other. The real problem was that EdTech was marketed to public health officials and their political counterparts (city mayors, county supervisors, state governors, and their staffs) with the promise that learners could just as well learn without physically relating to each other. Not only did this turn out to be unsupported as a theory of learning, but it also happens to be a perilous political project for democracy. While Big Tech was largely wrong in its promise about learning, its boosters seem to have never even considered its potential damage to democracy.

The argument just sketched captures some intuitive concerns about personalized learning. But intuition is ultimately insufficient for argumentation. I turn now to a more analytical approach to showing how personalized learning operates as a technology of separation.

An Analytical Evaluation of Discretization

Equality is a value that pertains not only to our interpersonal relations, but also and more primarily to how our relations to each other are structured. Social structures that establish, encourage, and enable persons to relate as equals are equalizing structures. Social structures that impose burdens disincentivizing people from relating as equals are inegalitarian. The structures that are more or less equal can range from large-scale institutions (like governments) to more granular technologies (like learner models in software), which in turn can also be implemented at a range of scales.

When considering whether social structures are equal or unequal, the focus of assessment ought to be, as argued above (in chapter 3), on how structures relate people—specifically, on processes of treatment that structure how people relate to each other. A structural analysis of equality in terms of processes of equal treatment is particularly fitting for the assessment of computational technologies, which are themselves essentially procedural as well. As detailed above (in chapter 4), the three steps of a process of equal treatment (entry, processing, and determination) correspond to the three steps of computational processing (formatting inputs, algorithmic processing, and outputting results).

To conduct an evaluation of equality in a computational system, we subject the treatment it involves to a two-part assessment of its conditions for equitable entry in input formatting and fairness in algorithmic processing. A schema for this assessment consists of two questions. First, how are the entry conditions at the starting gates of the procedure formatted with respect to those subject to the procedure? Can those entering into the procedure, given their differences, nonetheless relate to each other as equals? Second, how fair is the algorithmic processing through which these input data are run? Are those subject to the procedure algorithmically treated in ways that enable them to continue to relate as equals?

The operative sense of equality in these questions is that of relational equality, rather than purely distributive equality. The central normative question for democratic or relational equality is: how well can persons relate as equals? Thus the question pertinent to evaluating a treatment procedure for equality is: are those subject to this treatment better able or less able to relate as equals as a result of the treatment? To be sure, distributive inequalities such as achievement gaps in education or income gaps in employment can and frequently do engender relational inequalities. Yet one reason for emphasizing the primacy of relational equality is to maintain vigilance about forms of inequality that are not reducible to distributive inequalities of resources or opportunities. In an educational context, for example, a procedure of treatment might structure students' relations with each other in ways that make it more difficult for them to relate as equals without thereby also generating achievement gaps.

Recall that equal treatment requires treatment as an equal rather than identical treatment. My argument, therefore, is decidedly not that personalization is problematic because it treats different learners differently. Tailored treatment does not in and of itself generate objectionable inequality. Yet tailored treatment can generate objectionable inequality when the tailoring produces relational inequality by structuring relations between those subject to the procedure in ways that burden their ability to relate as equals.

In light of both the format anatomy of learner models conducted above and the schema for the evaluation of equal computational treatment just rehearsed, my primary focus for this argument will be on the first question, concerning entry conditions. The issue raised by the second question about procedural fairness is not unimportant. Critics are rightly concerned that personalization often exhibits algorithmic bias. Yet some research suggests that this can in certain circumstances be largely (though certainly never entirely) mitigated by more carefully designed algorithms incorporating more types of student data.[24] I thus assume, and merely for the sake of argument, the plausibility of personalization achieving sufficiently fair processing. With this hypothetical assumption in place, we are in a good position to consider the value of scrutinizing data systems at their first step of entry conditions, where the central egalitarian value to be met is that of equitable entry.

The operative question about equity entry in personalized learning is this: do the entry gates of personalized learning situate learners in relation to each other in ways that increase their separation from each other or in ways that support their ability to relate as equals?

The technical concept needed to answer this question was detailed in the previous chapter's format anatomy of personalizing learner models: discretization. Personalized learning is a process of differentiating learners as discrete, fully separable entities. In most implementations, personalization exhibits few or no opportunities for establishing relational continuities between learners. The discretization that is requisite for personalization occurs in the data formats structuring learner models; in particular, in the conceptualization and training of the learner features at the core of these models, and in the formats that shape the data inputs that are the basis for initial model training and ongoing model operation. With a particular focus on data formats at the input stage, we can recognize discretization as an attribute of how learners get situated by entry conditions as they enter the gates of a personalized-learning environment. Consider, for example, the external student data loaded into many learner models by way of student-information systems. These data situate learners at the entry gates as highly discrete entities—that is, learners are discretized by these data insofar as these data define entry into personalized-learning environments in terms that define learners as acting separately from each other.

It is important to be clear about the technical specificities of what counts as an entry gate into personalized learning; otherwise, it might be thought that my analysis holds only for personalized-learning systems that employ learner models derived from historical student information system data, but not for similar systems whose learner models are wholly derived from internally generated data (like log data from learning-management or intelligent-tutoring platforms). This conjecture involves a confusion about what constitutes entry conditions for personalized learning. Consider a hypothetical personalized-learning platform that relies on a cold start when a new user first logs in—no data have been collected or imported except for a username. This platform would quickly accumulate significant user-indexed log data for use in building learner models. At each recursive step where the platform personalizes some aspect of a learning process, the learner model on which that personalization is based constitutes at that point the entry condition for the user. Different systems will iterate recursively at different junctures—some will personalize each question posed to a learner or every page displayed to them, while others will adapt to users only at the end of larger segments like modules. The point is just that recursive processing of learner models is part of the very point of personalized system.

Whether learner models are built purely from log data or from logs in concert with student-record data, there will be a deep drift in those models toward the discretization of learners, for both kinds of data sources out of which learner models are constituted tend to be discretized. At the level of learner data and therefore also at the level of the learner models in virtue of which personalization is enacted, personalized learning is designed (albeit not often intentionally) to reproduce and sometimes even multiply inequalities of separation. From a relational equality perspective, the discretization made visible by a format anatomy helps us see how personalized learning not only functions as, but in a way almost has to function as, a technology of separation. In short, the aim of personalization in education technology serves to discretize and therefore separate learners.

Therefore separate? How? What is the connection between discretization in learning and the separation of learners? Two tendencies of discretizing personalization bring into view the way it invests and enhances relational inequalities of separation.

One aspect of personalization in virtue of which it induces separation is its strong tendency to construct the learning process as conducted by a learner in isolation without significant relationships to fellow learners and often even to teachers. This lack of relational continuity within the learning process renders education an isolated activity. A ramification of this is that learners are effectively structured in ways that undermine their ability to relate to each other as equals. Learners operating in personalized environments are, quite simply, afforded little practice and instruction in engaging fellow learners as equals. Shunting various aspects of the learning process into isolation leads to deskilling in collaboration, teamwork, and other such practices of relating as equals.

A second aspect of personalization that contributes to hierarchical separation is its tendency to propagate a comparative spirit through which learners are primed to recognize when they have learned something a fellow learner has not (or vice versa). It is not accidental that most learning platforms implement extensive gamification techniques that rely on comparative, often even downright competitive, ways of engaging with others. Learners subject to gamifying personalization are incentivized to make social comparisons through visual cues like leader boards, user rankings, and progress bars. These gamifying designs enact a socio-technical structure of comparison and competition that is inimical to collaboration. The comparative orientation to which personalization disposes its users, be it in learning systems or on social media (where social comparison is especially rampant), tends toward hierarchy rather than equality. Users faced with technological designs for comparison—like course completion rankings or prominent displays of social status markers like counters of friends or followers—tend to slide into regarding each other in terms of status differentiators, which cannot but connote superiority and inferiority. Techniques of personalization therefore not only negatively induce a lack of connection in education practices, but also generate effects that are themselves positive indicators of hierarchical inequality. Personalization produces education that is both separate and unequal.

The central activity of education is learning. It matters much whether we engage in that activity together or separately, collaboratively or comparatively. Collaboration in learning upbuilds habits that last learners' lifetimes. So too does separation in education. The question is this: which of these two kinds of habits helps cultivate better lives? Are learners capable of continuing to learn together as part of teams, communities, and societies? Or are they unable to relate to others as equals, learning only by themselves, being informed only by themselves, and taking whatever content shows up on the screen as trustworthy despite what their classmate or neighbor would say if they would only go and talk to them?

EVALUATING PRIOR PERFORMANCE RELIANCE:
TECHNOLOGIES OF REPRODUCTION

Personalization might be seen as participating in a broader assembly of technologies, techniques, and practices that serve as a driving wedge for separation and inequality in contemporary education. One such vector for inequality in education has surely been the trend toward increased accountability and assessment over the past few decades, emblematized by what some describe as a culture of testing.[25] Another prominent vehicle for inequality in education in recent decades has been curricular tracking.[26] In perhaps unexpected ways, personalization is much more like tracking than its proponents want to admit. This connection is at the center of a second argument demonstrating the potential harms, and already real limits, of personalization.

Tracking has been widely derided because of how it results in the reproduction of distributive inequalities. But tracking also exhibits tendencies toward the separatism of relational inequality. If personalization is much more like tracking than is commonly understood, then personalized learning too ought to be evaluated with respect to mechanisms of reproducing inequality. Were it to exhibit the same kinds of tendencies as tracking, this would be concerning in light of the high potential for amplifying feedback between relational and distributive inequalities.

Consider an abstracted three-step model of the feedback that can form between relational and distributive equality. In a first step, modest forms of social hierarchy become intensified (sometimes intended, sometimes not) and take shape as substantive relational inequalities. In a second step, these relational inequalities form background conditions that are causative of distributive inequalities (such as unequal distributions of educational goods). In a third step, this maldistribution is so solidified as to become the basis not only for its own reproduction but also for the intensification of those originating relational inequalities on which the maldistribution is based. Such feedback mechanisms are particularly concerning insofar as it is above all the reproduction of inequalities that makes them objectionable. An episodic and unintended inequality that arises between two groups may or may not be objectionable. Inequalities that are reproduced from one generation to the next are paradigmatically unjust. The argument from discretization developed in the previous section concentrated on insidious forms of inequality that serve as the first-step background conditions in this cycle. The argument in this section is focused on the reproduction of extant distributive inequalities and so concerns the third step in the cycle.

Learning analytics, because of its heavy reliance on historical data, tends to reproduce those extant distributive inequalities reflected in the historical data it incorporates into its analytics. Though only briefly mentioned in the anatomy of learner-model formats conducted in the previous chapter, these systems are primarily and often exclusively responsive to data derived from prior learner performance—that is, most learner modeling input data are formatted as records of past performances. This is true of student information system and other externally sourced data, which are often composed of records of grades, scores, certifications, achievements, and past decisions about a learner as well as standard (and sometimes even standardized) demographic data. It is also common for internally sourced learning-platform data to be records of past performance, ranging from data on student assessments to computed data on average platform-usage time to just about everything else these platforms can keep track of.

Reliance on prior performance is concerning because, as Kenneth Holstein and Shayan Doroudi have observed, "machine learning algorithms will tend towards further propagating, or even exacerbating, existing biases present in historical datasets."[27] They explain that when operating on a dataset with fewer records for members of minority groups than members of majority groups (which is the typical pattern to be expected from any sufficiently representative dataset), "most machine learning algorithms will be *inherently biased* against minority groups" insofar as they are designed to optimize for the majority of cases.[28] What their argument shows is that data systems built atop past performance data will, all else being the same, tend to reproduce extant inequalities.

This suggests that educational programs will tend to reproduce extant achievement gaps wherever they differentiate students on the basis of models derived from prior performance. Why is this concerning? Because, as the education researchers Helen Ladd and Susanna Loeb argue, students deserve to be treated according to a conception of equality for which "social disadvantage would not be an excuse for differential outcomes."[29] Inegalitarian excuses are not the sole province of education-data technology, but are broadly at work in all manner of educational projects that differentiate students on the basis of prior performance. One such widely practiced project is curricular tracking.[30] Tracking is not only inegalitarian in its assumptions but also happens to be a mistaken educational strategy. Contrary to the intuitive common sense that would seem to support tracking, research has shown that schools offering higher-track curricula to all students with appropriate educational supports in place lead to higher curricular mastery even for students who would have been, or formerly were, lower-tracked.[31] That said, tracking in curriculum is one thing, personalization in learning another. Or so it is commonly said.

Once you seriously consider the possibility, it is hard to shake the thought that personalization is really just tracking taken to the extreme. Students subject to personalized learning may not be tracked into separate classroom spaces with differentiated curriculum, but they are being tracked into highly separated educational spaces inside apps on devices that they work on in isolation from their classmates and schoolmates, all of whom are together enjoying a purportedly non-tracked environment. This point, of course, relies on my earlier assessment of personalization as a technology of separation. To this assessment I have now added another: even if the inequality problems of relational separation engendered by personalization could somehow be avoided, personalization's necessary reliance on prior performance data tends to reproduce extant distributive inequalities like achievement gaps in exactly the way curricular tracking does. These compounded distributive inequalities inevitably feed back into inequalities at the relational level. Compounding achievement gaps structure learners in ways that over time undermine their ability to relate to each other as equals too.

More-Equal Data Analytics in Education

Some critics advocate that we should just not do data. This is decidedly not my argument. Indeed, I find the very idea incomprehensible. A premise for my view is that we truly have no idea of what it would even mean to somehow slough off the entirety of that data apparatus within which our lives are now so tightly ensconced.[32] Data technology is an unavoidable prior of the world that has been built for us. This is why it constitutes such a fraught space. It is precisely because data technologies are obligatory that they can function as effective technologies of inequality. If we could simply opt out of data, then the inequalities they institute could not be significant—those feeling the burden would simply walk away.

My claim is not that we should wish to get rid of data technology, but that we urgently need to do data differently. Specifically, I have been arguing that we need to make data more equal. I turn now to describing an exemplary form of more-equal data in education. Just as persons and learners can be abstracted into data points that situate them as discretized individuals, it is also quite possible to fashion formats that abstractly situate persons and learners in more-equal relation to each other—for example, as collaborators. In the foregoing pages I have described some of the shapes assumed by technologies of separation in service of inequality. But what about technologies of collaboration that further equality? How do, or how might, data structure persons such that they can better relate as equals?

As a frame for this more-egalitarian alternative for data, recall the motivating exemplar of data equality I excavated from the data work of W. E. B. Du Bois (in chapter 2 above). According to my argument, Du Bois models how to transform the foci of regimes of data surveillance (or dataveillance). His work deftly swaps out traditional collections of data for different datasets that more clearly convey the equalities and inequalities of race. Autumn Womack's idea of "making data move" well captures how Du Bois's styles of datafication both destabilize extant patterns of racial data and mobilize innovations in data accumulation and analytics.[33] A conception of moving data frames the value of, as well as the need for, refusing to confine our data technology to entrenched structures such that we might allow ourselves to take wider views of the kinds of data that we experimentally employ across our many data pursuits.

RECONSTRUCTING EDTECH FOR EQUALITY: LEARNING
ANALYTICS FOR COLLABORATIVE LEARNING

What would making data move look like in the context of education technology? To begin to answer this question, it is important to recognize that data analytics—and even more specifically, methodologies like artificial intelligence approaches that are increasingly internal to learning analytics—can be deployed for purposes other than the production of personalized learning and other such technologies of separation. As long ago as 2006, in a contribution to an early OECD report on education technology, Sanna Järvelä contrasted "social-focused analyses of learning" with the "individual-focused studies" of personalization, pointing explicitly to technology-assisted collaborative learning as exemplifying the more social aspects of education.[34] Yet this and other calls for education technology to serve more collaborative conceptions of education have largely gone unanswered. What we have witnessed instead is EdTech doubling down on the idea that learners are discrete actors whose learning activities are fully disconnected from each other.

Even so, at least one clear alternative to AIEd-powered personalized learning has grown in prominence in recent education research: AIEd-powered, computer-supported collaborative learning.[35] This alternative offers a promising way of moving the subject of data at work in EdTech.

The field of computer-supported collaborative learning is focused on using computational methods and tools to better support the work of learners who learn together. The challenges facing any such effort are many, especially in view of assumptions about learners that have become entrenched across much of EdTech. Learner data is, as shown in detail in the anatomy presented in the previous chapter, overwhelmingly structured as discretized data that separates learners from one another. In the face of the weight of this tendency of current data systems, it would be easy for pursuits of data-informed collaborative learning to be co-opted back into the service of personalization for discrete learners.[36] Though we envision data as light and vapory, it is possessed of a tremendous weight once locked into large databases. Yet the formidable inertia of data technology does not make alternative configurations impossible. Indeed, there exist not just possibilities for, but also actual projects of, building educational environments that facilitate relational equality among collaborative learners.

To bring these projects into view, I begin with a useful orienting distinction proposed by the collaborative education researchers Alyssa Wise, Simon Knight, and Simon Buckingham Shum in a piece on learning analytics for computer-supported collaborative learning. What they call the *analytics of collaborative learning* involves using learning analytics as a tool for mining data for knowledge about collaborative learning, whereas what they call *collaborative-learning analytics* involves using learning analytics to directly facilitate, support, and improve projects in collaborative learning.[37] Following this distinction, we can recognize the latter project of collaborative-learning analytics as a kind of collaborative counterpoint to personalized-learning analytics.

Yet the contrast between collaborative-learning analytics and personalized-learning analytics cannot be effective if it is merely a function of the intentions of its designers. What is also needed are different datasets that can serve as the focal inputs for systems oriented by different goals. Such differences at the level of data inputs refer to what Wise, Knight, and Buckingham Shum call "a long-standing area of consideration" for collaborative computing in education—namely, the question of levels of analysis. As they put it, "different work" is involved in "taking individual learners, small groups, and large collectives as the unit-of-analysis."[38]

According to the methodology of format anatomies, this question of levels of analytical units is a question about data inputs in relation to model features. Which data inputs will be warehoused to form the basis for which learning features that will be modeled by learning analytics? This is the classic question concerning what Wise and Järvelä, in a piece jointly authored with Carolyn Rosé, call "the chain of inference" in virtue of which a system moves from clicks to constructs.[39] What clicks to collect in light of the constructs that need to be modeled? All too often this question is glossed over when researchers elect to simply use already-available datasets as the primary inputs for computationally expensive algorithms. Systems that rely only on extant data inputs tend to entrench data in a way that fails to consider whether different data would do better. Wise, Rosé, and Järvelä raise the crucial issue of "how the metrics themselves might be developed differently."[40] How, said otherwise, do we make the data move so that we can do data differently?

In the case of collaborative learning, systems resourcing extant datasets are unlikely to successfully model collaboration. For the data already in circulation in so much of education technology are largely indexed to individually discretized activity. Those data often contain little or no records of actual interactions between learners, including between learners whose learning has been designed to be collaborative. As Wise, Rosé, and Järvelä observe, "The majority of attention [in the field of learning analytics] has focused on modeling individual learning, often through a series of snapshot views."[41] Gerry Stahl similarly notes that the vast majority of work in this context is rooted in "sciences of the individual or of the society, not of the collaborative group."[42]

These observations point to the philosophical backdrop for pursuits of collaborative learning. Stahl writes of group processes as "not necessarily reducible to processes of individual minds," in that they "may take place through the weaving of semantic and indexical references within a group discourse."[43] These ideas are reminiscent of collaborative conceptions of cognition and action that have been articulated through philosophical pragmatism.[44] According to this view (which is also endorsed from numerous other twentieth-century philosophical perspectives), the most important instances of human thought and action are essentially social in both genesis and enactment. Much of our thought and our conduct depend deeply on thinking and doing in concert with others. Take away our continuities with each other and you take away much of what we can think and do. The pragmatist insight that cognition and action are socially synechistic, to invoke again Charles Sanders Peirce's neologism for continuity, forms a guiding philosophical thread for research in computer-supported collaborative learning.[45]

In drilling down from these broader philosophical ideas to specific issues at stake in learning analytics, we are confronted with the crucial matter of operationalization. What exactly is involved in building data analytics that can better capture learning data usable for modeling and facilitating collaborative learning? The central issue here concerns what types of collaborative-learning features or constructs need to be modeled, and what types of data inputs are needed to build these models, such that neither are fully reducible to discretized-learner features and the discretized data inputs out of which they are formed. As Carmel Kent and Mutlu Cukurova argue, we must "question whether the cognitive ecosystem of the learning group can be modelled as a linear additive function of its individual cognitive ecosystems."[46] According to their research, there are important cases in which "the collaborative cognitive act could not be reduced to and discussed in terms of individual cognition."[47] This point is made even more forcefully by Lanqin Zheng and colleagues: "Group learning engagement is not simply equal to the sum of the learning engagement measures of individuals since collaborative learning is a complex system that is not merely the sum of its parts but is often distinct from those parts."[48] And yet, her team observes, "previous studies have mainly focused on individual learning engagement" even in the context of research on computer-supported collaborative learning.[49]

Consider a few alternatives exhibiting collaborative data inputs. Roberto Martinez-Maldonado and colleagues describe work developing a learner construct meant to model "the extent to which a group of learners is collaborative" as being built on the basis of two sub-constructs labeled "transactivity" (derived from the learning sciences) and "symmetry of action" (derived from computer-supported collaborative-learning research).[50] The sub-construct of transactivity is described as modeled from input data that are distinctively collaborative. It is the type of construct that simply could not be modeled on the basis of learner-discrete data inputs. The second sub-construct of symmetry of action is described as a comparative function of two streams of individual log data. The construct of "collaboration" formed out of these two sub-constructs thus illustrates an ongoing tension in collaborative-learning research between employing irreducibly collaborative constructs and additive approaches that derive collaboration constructs from flows of learner-discrete data.

Other types of irreducibly collaborative constructs are discussed by Kent and Cukurova, who describe "reciprocity of interactions in a network" as a kind of proxy for "mutuality" and measures of "group cohesion" such as network "density."[51] In describing such model features, they emphasize the need to "analyze the process of collaboration rather than just its outcomes," such that "the unit of analysis should reflect on the whole group, aiming to reflect on the interdependencies between participants."[52] Another account of collaboration in learning–model features has been developed by Zheng and her team in what is to date the most in-depth research on collaboration-focused learning analytics. The six central features that Zheng describes in a chapter on learning analytics in her book *Data-Driven Design for Computer-Supported Collaborative Learning* are cognition, metacognition, behavior, emotion, social network, and alignment (of design and execution).[53] Each of these features, according to Zheng's analysis, can include individual or discretized elements. But for most of these constructs (specifically, cognition, metacognition, behavior, and social network), Zheng holds that usable models require collaboration-focused constructs that are more than products of additive functions of individual-centered constructs and learner-discrete data.

A crucial insight we should take from this recent research in computer-supported collaborative learning concerns the potential of training AIEd toward collaborative endeavors. While cheap sources of discrete data abound, datasets of irreducibly collaborative data are more expensive to build and maintain. The potential for more collaborative AIEd is being neglected for the sake of efficiency. But quality datasets on learning collaboration can be constructed.[54] And if efficient education cultivates significant inequality, how efficient is it in the longer term?

The importance of collaboration consists above all in the equality that it furthers, not just in the benefits in knowledge outcomes that collaboration also carries.[55] It is said often by critics that artificially intelligent systems cannot perform as well as a skilled professional such as a teacher with respect to standard measures like learning outcomes. This may be true. But the focus of my concern about these systems is quite different. Even if it could be shown that artificial intelligence could outperform teachers with respect to student-learning outcomes, those artificial instructors still need to be evaluated for how well they perform with respect to structuring equality among the students they teach. Here the central issue cannot be the question that first springs to mind for so many parents: "How much will my kid be learning?" The question we all need to focus on, rather, concerns equality: "How are all these kids being structured by this educational environment with respect to their ability to relate to each other as equals?" Anyone who has spent any amount of time around children will lean rather heavily toward the view that kids who are taught by artificially intelligent robots are far less likely to be well prepared to relate to each other as equals than are kids who are taught by human beings.

Robot teachers with artificial intelligence? Really? You could be forgiven if, in reading the last few lines, you find yourself wanting to dismiss all this as either idle speculation or science fiction. Consider, however, that the robot teachers being dreamt of today are not futuristic androids made in our image—they are the apps that our children already hold in their hands. What are those animated avatars populating popular learning platforms if not little robots already endowed with artificial intelligence? Even if it could be shown that these apps, or any other kind of robot, on average outperform classroom instructors on learning-outcome metrics, we should still refrain from adopting them if significant inequalities flow from installing these technological teachers in our classrooms. What such educational technology is most likely to produce are beneficial learning outcomes for learners who will struggle mightily to enact the many forms of relational equality requisite for democracy.

Conclusion
Becoming Data Equals

Equality within data is needed wherever data technology drives the configurations of what we can do and who we can be. The foregoing chapters provision, explain, and justify the concept of data equality. This concept speaks to a range of considerations from early-twentieth-century quantitative analysis to later-twentieth-century theories of democratic equality to twenty-first-century research thrusts delivering artificial intelligence into the educational practices with which we entrust our yearnings for the furtherance of human intelligence. The work of describing and warranting data equality raises issues of implementation that concern how we bring equality into the orbit of our inquiries about technology to implement it where data technologies play a significant role.

Matters of implementation matter much. Since any implementation always begins with inquiry, methods for inquiry matter much too. We must first comprehend a matter to have an informed sense of both what to change and how to change it. Methodologies for inquiry into data technology, like the method of format anatomy, prepare the way for implementing data equality in actual practical sites, such as situations where education technology poses threats to educational equality. What might that next step of implementation on the basis of sustained inquiry look like?

The democratic practices of reform requisite for implementing data equality cannot be restricted to a single mode of intervention. The motions of democratic reform are always balanced on at least three legs at once: legal regulation, technological design, and human education. Since a complete account of this tripartite conception of reform would require at least another full book, a brief overview follows, after which I discuss in more detail the third, and I believe most crucial, leg of education.

With respect to regulating data technology, there is today increasing support across the political spectrum for more active regulatory involvement in this space. The basic operative model for regulation in liberal democracies is that of the administrative state. The Food and Drug Administration was instituted in the United States during the Progressive Era to protect citizens against consuming milk preserved with formaldehyde and meats preserved with borax.[1] Today's innovative data technologies require their own regulatory agencies. This requirement not only should, but also can, be met—contrary to the techno-libertarian insistence that data tech breaks the model of administrative regulation. Regulatory agencies for data can help guard against the technological toxicities produced by computational programs.[2] One clear justification for strengthening regulation is that these firms have accrued the excessive power they currently wield on the basis of regulatory protocols already in force. The familiar refrain that internet firms operate in an unregulated frontier, while clearly partially true, unfortunately obscures this justification.[3] The fact is that today's biggest data tech firms have become the most capitalized corporations in human history by leveraging (some say exploiting) existing regulatory regimes—perhaps most notably trade-secret law for amassing data, contract law for excluding competition, and Section 230 of the 1996 Communications Decency Act for immunities against being held responsible for distributing false and harmful content.[4] More accurate is that these firms are both under-regulated (for instance, with respect to the mental health safety of their products) and at the same time reliant on overprotective regulation (for instance, with respect to granted immunities). One way of improving regulation over data technology firms would be to cease the unnecessary regulatory advantages already extended to these firms; for example, by sunsetting immunities enjoyed by internet platforms not also granted to traditional publication platforms. Of further importance is to more vigorously extend existing areas of traditional law, such as anti-trust and consumer safety rules, so that they more fully reach new technologies; for example, by pursuing anti-monopoly cases against the exclusionary practices of the largest internet firms or by instituting basic requirements for safety testing of social media products.[5]

The second reformist leg of technical redesign is most important where it involves reconstructing the values that get designed into technologies in ways that reconfigure the kinds of activities that technologies afford.[6] One common misconception that often serves up obstacles to effective values-in-technology redesign is that of technologies as neutral, or value-free. But no technology operates without values. All technological operations take place in situations already pervaded by valuational statuses—for instance, those of rampant hierarchy. Equality in data design counters data hierarchy.

The third leg of democratic reform is education. Education is the primary site wherein are cultivated the virtues and dispositions through which we are prepared to engage in projects of regulatory reform and technological redesign.[7] The dispositions and understandings that education cultivates, of course, apply to more of us than just the lawyers implementing regulations and the technologists redesigning interfaces. Users of data technology also need education about how they are being used by their data, as well as how they unwittingly use others through theirs. Beyond its instrumental values, there is a further aspect of education that especially matters for democratic reform. This has to do with the internal connections between the work of education and the maintenance of democracy.

For a better appreciation of the tight relationship between education and democracy, I return in conclusion to the philosophical pragmatism of John Dewey, with whose thoughts about thinking this book began. More than any thinker past or present, Dewey's particular iteration of pragmatism helps tighten the connection between the three central egalitarian themes of this book: data equality, democratic equality, and educational equality. Yet Dewey's presentation of these ideas stands in need of both clarification and, on some important points, reconstructive revision.

Dewey describes democracy as inclusive of, but also wider than, the standard menu of governmental institutions; his is a conception of democracy as a way of life in which we associate with each other as relative equals.[8] This conception implies that education is internal to democracy—for education, especially education as conjoint activity, instantiates the very equality expressed by democratic interaction.[9] Fully comprehending this connection requires understanding the social and political problematics to which Dewey was responding.

Dewey's conception of democracy was formed against the background of a sweeping set of social and political transformations that took hold in liberal democratic states in the early twentieth century. Prominent across almost all these transformations was a tsunami of datafication that increasingly submerged people's everyday actions and interactions. One effect of these onrushing technologies of datafication was the emergence of what I have called the informational person.[10] Living on the other side of this tidal shift, we are today all obligated to our data; we act frequently and fervently through dossiers, records, analytics, statistics, and other informational accoutrement. Contemporary with the emergence of a datafied form of subjectivity was the creation of an impressive array of governmental agencies forming the first iterations of the administrative state.[11] Some of these major new administrative agencies included the Food and Drug Administration (established in 1906), the Federal Trade Commission (1914), and the Federal Radio Commission (1927, which soon became the Federal Communications Commission, 1934). A major challenge to liberal democracy began to well up within these emerging contexts of the administrative state, the informational person, and other structural behemoths of the early twentieth century that remain with us today.[12]

This challenge received its first pointed expression in Walter Lippmann's 1922 masterpiece, *Public Opinion*.[13] Lippmann's book poignantly articulates the presence of a vast new personnel of "statisticians, accountants, auditors, industrial counsellors, engineers of many species, scientific managers, personnel administrators, [and] research men," all of them equipped with "filing cabinets, card catalogues, graphs, loose-leaf contraptions, and above all the perfectly sound ideal of an executive who sits before a flat-top desk."[14] In the rise of so many information managers and information technologies is an undeniable confirmation of the demise of an earlier democratic ideal— "the omnicompetent citizen," who could do all their governing themselves.[15] Omnicompetence is nowhere to be found, and thus no longer to be hoped for, under new conditions of simultaneous informational abundance and epistemic uncertainty. Affairs have grown too complicated. So how can democracy persist amid such complexity? Though Lippmann's book pinpoints the question with precision, it nevertheless fails to develop a convincing response. Lippmann's reply to the problem of information overload feels redundant: more information, more expertise, and the "coordination, not of decision and action, but of information research."[16] What Lippmann never really gained sight of was the particular qualities in virtue of which technocracy could nourish democracy—or how to do things with data that diminish hierarchy.

If Lippmann's *Public Opinion* sets the question, then Dewey's 1927 book *The Public and Its Problems* seeks to settle the answer, or at least the beginnings of a few different answers. Dewey's direct response to Lippmann's poignant observation of hypercomplexity is itself interestingly complex. It reveals Dewey's own conception of democracy as woven together from three notably different strands of political thought: communicative deliberation, communitarian nostalgia, and collaborative equality.[17] But Dewey's book does not always separate these strands clearly enough and so fails to state which one ought to assume priority as a guide to the other two. The result is that in different moments, different strands come to the fore. On some pages of *The Public and Its Problems*, Dewey bangs the drum of communication—he celebrates "free and systematic communication" as well as "full and moving communication."[18] Yet even though communication is clearly necessary for democratic collaboration, it is a deep mistake to think it sufficient (a point I argued in the introduction).[19] Perhaps glimpsing this himself, other pages of Dewey's book emphasize local community life—"Democracy must begin at home, and its home is the neighborly community."[20] Yet such localism seems sentimental and sweet in the face of the horrifying political conflicts attendant to mass globalization and technologization.[21] In some moments of Dewey's book, he even brings these two answers together, as in his insistence on "immediate intercourse" and "face-to-face relationships" taking place with "the local community as its medium."[22]

In seeking communicative and communitarian responses to problems of democratic organization in this and other writings from the 1920s, Dewey neglects the better insights of his own earlier and later writings on democratic education, the most important of which remains his 1916 book *Democracy and Education*.[23] Dewey there argues that what matters most for democratic education is how learners can and do interact with each other as equals (not just how they communicate, or where and with whom they interact). He affirms that among the conditions for such democratic interaction in education are the ways learner actions are undertaken with and through technologies. He would later state this with particular clarity in a book on education from 1938: "[Education] includes what is done by the educator and the way in which it is done, not only words spoken but the tone of voice in which they are spoken. It includes equipment, books, apparatus, toys, games played. It includes the materials with which an individual interacts, and, most important of all, the total *social* set-up of the situations in which a person is engaged."[24] More contemporary examples that Dewey could not have comprehended, but which I hope are clear enough at the conclusion of this book, are the datasets used to train learner models, the algorithms employed to build those models, and the formats that constitute the possibility of the data that the algorithms process. Such data technology matters much to what learners can do, and what can be done to them, in educational settings. Surely any list of education infrastructure today would include such education-data technologies. Reconstructing these technologies requires attention to elements of database formatting and algorithm selection that are best thought of as forms of technological action. Structuring a database variable so that a user is required to select a category (such as gender or race) is not in any straightforward sense establishing communication or community with them. It is better understood as interactively disposing the user as they are entered into the database.

To make sense of technological disposition as a major part of the politics of democratic education (or any other aspect of democratic practice, for that matter), we cannot rely on ideas of communication and community alone. Pragmatism's actionistic perspective offers a way of expanding its conception of democracy beyond the limits of communicativist and communitarian approaches, but while also retaining the important insights that deliberation and locality are often necessary conditions for democratic achievement.[25] The actionistic perspective goes beyond what is necessary by orienting a fuller conception of democracy as an active practice of collaborative equality—this conception in turn helps steer communicative exchange and communal experience toward more-egalitarian forms than they might otherwise take.

Consider this knotted triad in a little more detail. Communication connotes interacting with each other linguistically. The actionistic analogue of communication refers to acting with each other—participating in joint, though not centrally coordinated, activities. Collaborative interaction thus includes, but is not limited to, communicative interaction. For its part, community in its standard senses connotes ways of being together, though not necessarily ways of acting together. This explains why calls for community can appear nostalgically localistic in a world where we can and often do effectively act together at a distance. Community's more actionistic analogue is also collaborative interaction, which also includes community but is not limited to it.

Where Dewey wrote of democratic "communication" (as echoed by contemporary democratic theorists of deliberation) and of "community" (whose echo today is found in communitarian arguments), we should substitute for those notions a wider conception of democratic "collaboration" that expresses the fuller breadth of our practical engagements with, and relations to, each other. Taking such an approach, what does Dewey's idea of the public becomes when translated out of his terminology of communicative communities and into a vocabulary of collaborative publics? It becomes the basis for a conception of democracy as a mode of egalitarian interaction between those whose actions directly and indirectly impact each other.

An understanding of democracy as consisting in publics of collaborative action illuminates why collaborative education is not just one more case of what democracy might hope to achieve but is also paradigmatically expressive of the practice of democracy at scale. This does not make collaborative education, or the technologies facilitating it, a panacea for democratic deficits. Rather, it means that collaborative education exemplifies the democratic egalitarianism of acting together as equals.

Educational equality exhibits the mission of democracy in modest ways. This is fitting. Democracy ought to be made of modest stuff. Dramatic ideals of forceful heroism and violent revolution well suit the glorious. Meanwhile, the maintenance of democracy is bureaucratic, often even boring, but also by and large decisively advantaged in that it is far less bloody and far more reliable. Those who seek their excitement from politics too often find themselves romping in passionate pursuits that require giving themselves allowances whenever those passions visit unintended harm on others. Instead of putting ourselves in a position to make exceptions in our own interest (which is on one prominent account the very essence of immorality), we ought to be willing to regard our pursuits of bliss as largely private aesthetic affairs so that we are less likely to inflict collateral cruelty on others and more likely to secure reliable regulations concerning public matters.[26] Democracy is made of the hard grind, but also the simple joy, of working together on long projects aiming at the fulfillment of our egalitarian aspirations. Collaborative learning is not only a preparation for such democratic associations, but it is also an exhibit of it. If it is true that democratic societies must find ways of renewing and reiterating themselves by democratic means, then the democratic education of the young (as well as the ongoing education of the mature) must itself be a democratic process in the main.

Consider in this light the contrast drawn in earlier chapters between technologies of separation and technologies of collaboration. The democratic idea of collaborative equality in education helps us better understand this contrast. My distinction between two kinds of technologies recapitulates a more general contrast between hierarchical authoritarianism and democratic egalitarianism. Understanding this brings into view how the formats we employ for defining data are either expressive of equal relations between persons (as in datafying connective continuities between learners) or are unable to facilitate any meaningful form of relational inequality (as in datafications that thoroughly discretize users). Where our data are defined in ways that render them unusable for pursuing equality in our relations with each other, it does not matter how sophisticated the analytics get, how many computational cycles they can be run over, or how many more layers the development team throws on the neural network. Such data simply cannot be tortured into achieving equality and will over time only serve to compound existing hierarchical inequalities. Yet there are always alternatives that provision ways of exhibiting equality across the cryptic cells in which variables get populated with numbers or words that will form the basis for models we only ever witness through a glass darkly.

None of this should be expected to be easy. Even where we attain some level of equality within data formats, this feature by itself cannot be presumed sufficient for solving inequality, if only because inequality is not the kind of problem that admits of a solution. It is only with vigilant attention and considerable effort that we can turn more-equal data toward actually achieving those aspirations of equality we so often proclaim. But where those aspirations go unfunded by more-equal data, where professed progressives at the helms of data-tech corporations and data-science research labs casually neglect to collect and curate more-equal data, there we actually have no chance of becoming egalitarian. At best, what the technological faithful will achieve in such scenarios are forms of data fairness that will reproduce and eventually magnify a very unequal status quo.

The egalitarian aspiration pulsing within data-intensive democracies requires affirmative implementations of data equality. An egalitarian reconstruction of data technology must be oriented toward our being equals to each other with respect to our data—our being equals *in our data*. The force of, and need for, data equality today begins with the observation that we now live our lives through our data to such a profound extent that we have actually become our data. Whatever else we have always been, we are now also our data. Any such transformation in who we are, and who we can be, carries crucial consequences for our democratic orders. At the center of democratic courage is the confidence that a people can govern themselves without obedience to any greater authority than their collaboration with each other as equals. Where we have become our data, the very viability of the daring hope that is our democracy now depends on our becoming data equals.

Acknowledgments

I first presented the full sweep of this book in Rome at a seminar at Sapienza Università di Roma. I am grateful to my host and friend Sarin Marchetti for organizing the occasion, as well as for the inspiration of conversations about pragmatism that now span many years. I am also grateful for many challenging questions I received from those in attendance. I subsequently presented the full project at a seminar series at the University of California at Irvine, where I was again challenged in ways that improved the final work. I am grateful to the organizers and attendees, particularly Kevin Olson for conversations about our mutual experiments in philosophical genealogy that very much form part of the background for this book even if the foreground is decidedly that of pragmatism. And though our scheduled times in Irvine could not align, I thank Catherine Malabou for discussions of pragmatism and geneaology across many years.

I presented selections from what later became the book, usually in the form of drafts of individual chapters, at annual meetings of the American Philosophical Association (Pacific Division Main Program), the International Association for Computing and Philosophy, the Western Political Science Association, and as a keynote at the Radical Philosophy Association. I also presented individual chapters at the "Omnes et Singulatim": Algorithmic Governmentality conference (cohosted by Warwick University, with thanks to Daniele Lorenzini), the Sovereignty in the Age of Data conference (hosted at the University of British Columbia, with thanks to Wendy Wong and Stefan Kehlenbach), and a meeting of the Summer Institute in American Philosophy (on my home campus). Individual chapters were presented at the following institutions, in some cases remotely: UCLA (in the Political Science Department, with thanks to organizer Davide Panagia), New York University (at the Digital Theory Lab, with thanks to Joe Lemelin and Lisa Gitelman),

Fordham University (in the Department of Philosophy, with thanks to Samir Haddad), the New School for Social Research (in the Department of Philosophy, with thanks to Daniel Rodriguez-Navas), Eastern Michigan University (Department of History and Philosophy, with thanks to Laura McMahon), the University of Memphis (Department of Philosophy, with many thanks as always to Mary Beth Mader), King's University College at Western University in Canada (at the Centre for Social Concern, with thanks to Antonio Calcagno, Allyson Larkin, and Russell Duvernoy), and Karlstad University in Sweden (Department of Political, Historical, Religious and Cultural Studies, with thanks to Michaela Padden). I am grateful to all these hosts and audiences for engaging the ideas herein, and thereby improving them.

I am also grateful to many other colleagues, interlocutors, and friends from a variety of intellectual and institutional spaces who generously gave of their time in reading draft material, confirming intuitions, offering a suggestion (or many), and in some cases engaging in extended discussion of these matters.

I am especially grateful for the insightful comments and criticisms I received from three colleagues who read an earlier version of the full manuscript: thank you, Carlos Montemayor, Davide Panagia, and David Rondel. Carlos and Dave deserve additional thanks for their time in traveling to the University of Oregon for a manuscript workshop and spending a day carefully poring over arguments (and also edifying me at night with truly great conversation on so many topics beyond data and equality). Caroline Koopford later read the penultimate version and found a few stray thoughts—more importantly, she discussed many of these ideas with me on many occasions and always in ways that helped me be a better thinker and writer. I am also grateful for responses to individual chapters (in some cases on much earlier versions) from Verena Erlenbusch-Anderson, Joanne McNeil, Lindsay Poirier, Nick Schuster, Bonnie Sheehey, and Naomi Zack.

For supporting the project at a crucial moment, I remain very much indebted to both Bernard Harcourt and Shannon Vallor—it is no small joy to be able to thank two writers whose contributions on these topics have (as noted in the introduction) for a long time now helped me shape the very questions I find important to try to answer.

Any academic worth their salt can come up with plenty of things to nitpick about local conditions at their home institution. But nearly every day I am reminded of how grateful I am to teach and write at a public institution that bathes me in the brilliance of bright colleagues all across campus.

Some of these brilliant colleagues at the University of Oregon generously read chapters and discussed them with me. I am grateful to Michael Allan (who deserves all kinds of other thanks too for so many kicks that keep me moving forward), Gerald Berk (whose responses to my chapters on pragmatism were customarily perfect in articulating what I really wanted to be saying), Bryce Newell (whose suggestions of other ideas to explore were always on the mark), and Whitney Phillips (who also deserves thanks for keeping my mind on its toes during great walks). I am also grateful to have had the chance to discuss the topics central to this book with a number of graduate students (some having since completed their degrees) who engaged my ideas on these topics, and in some cases read the entire manuscript. My thanks to Brooke Burns, Gonzalo Bustamante Moya, Asher Caplan, Shiloh Deitz, Sarah T. Hamid, Patrick Jones, Mare McLevey, Paul Showler, and Valérie Simon.

In addition, the material in this book was informed (and I believe quite improved) by discussions over the past few years about the philosophy of data as well as related issues in the philosophy and history of science with my colleagues Ramón Alvarado, Vera Keller, Nicolae Morar (who deserves additional thanks for discussions of so many other aspects of philosophy), and Jacob Neal. Numerous other colleagues from across campus engaged various parts of the book with me in the context of semiformal seminars or presentations at the UO Data Science Seminar Series, the UO Libraries Data Services discussion group, and the UO Science and Technology Studies reading group. A few other local research groups informed the thinking that went into this book. One was an interdisciplinary reading group on QuantCrit in the School of Education (with thanks to Jerry Rosiek for the invitation). Another was an interdisciplinary group spanning philosophy, biology, and educational psychology discussing statistical techniques in genetics and psychometrics (with thanks again to Nicolae Morar for organizing the opportunity). Both of these venues greatly expanded my thinking about how to understand quantitative measure. Another local occasion informing this work was a graduate seminar on pragmatist philosophy and cognitive science taught by my departmental colleague Mark Johnson, which I was fortunate to attend just as I was pulling into view this book's main lines of argument.

A different kind of local source of sustenance also deserves mention. I completed some of the earliest iterations of parts of the book while serving a term as head of the Philosophy Department. The work of a head or chair is famously challenging, according to common lore in academia. I learned much in this role and perhaps because of that also found myself even enjoying it at times. For making the position feel mostly manageable, I thank my faculty colleagues, my administrative dream team of Pat Martin and the late T. K. Landázuri (and then later on Emily Ellis); and for their steadying wisdom in crucial moments, both Harry Wonham and Karen Ford in the College of Arts and Sciences. Because of you all, I found a way to serve in administration and still kindle hope for writing another book once the position would rotate. I am also grateful to the staff at the University of Oregon Libraries. Individuals often unknown to me chased down countless articles and books borrowed from other institutions, and all the while, one of the library buildings afforded what I always found to be a rather luxurious environment in which to read and write.

I am grateful for the opportunity to entrust another manuscript to the thoughtful and professional staff at the University of Chicago Press. My thanks especially to Elizabeth Branch Dyson for taking time to offer detailed advice in the earlier stages and to Kyle Wagner for generously supporting the project as soon I sent the full thing over and for then expertly shepherding it through. Beth Ina kept the manuscript on track through production while also giving me some very desirable breathing time when a deadline coincided almost precisely with a late opportunity for public presentation of the manu-script. Finally, I am grateful to again be typing these words on the heels of the humbling experience of working with a very sharp copyeditor, Johanna Rosenbohm, whose facility with the written word well exceeds my own—I am grateful for the experience of rereading pages that were already rewritten dozens of times only to find jotted down on the margin some elegant writerly solution that says it all so much better.

Sections of a few of the chapters were previously published as journal ar-ticles. In all cases that material has been extensively revised here; addition-ally, the articles in each case include material not incorporated into chapters here. A few pages in the introduction on Dewey and Malabou expanded upon a single page in "Artificing Intelligence: From Isolating IQ to Amoral AI," *AI & Society* (2024). A portion of the material in chapter 2 on Du Bois as well as a more extended discussion of Galton was previously published as "From Galton's Pride to Du Bois's Pursuit: The Formats of Data-Driven Inequality," *Theory, Culture, & Society* 41, no. 1 (2024): 59–78, https://doi.org /10.1177/02632764231162251, © 2023 by Colin Koopman. A much earlier ver-sion of portions of chapter 5 about algorithms and formats appeared as "The Political Theory of Data: Institutions, Algorithms, and Formats in Racial Redlining," *Political Theory* 50, no. 2 (2022): 337–61, https://doi.org/10.1177 /00905917211027835, © 2021 by Colin Koopman. The discussion of Simon-don in chapter 5 is based on material prepared for publication as "Human-Data Coupling: Informational Personhood & Artificial Intelligence through

Gilbert Simondon's Philosophy of Technology," *Social Epistemology* (forth-coming, 2025).

I received funding that directly supported the development and completion of this book from the National Endowment for the Humanities in the form of an NEH Fellowship. I am immeasurably proud to have been supported by the main public and governmental stream of funding for humanities research in the United States. I hope that the book that is now in your hands lives up to such an important structure of public support for the humanities.

I also received support through a number of local funding streams at the University of Oregon. These funds in each case provided me with that most precious resource for the writer and researcher: time. I am grateful to ac-knowledge funding from a Presidential Fellowship in Arts and Humanities from the Office of the President, a Faculty Research Award from the Office of the Vice President for Research and Innovation, and a Humanities Summer Stipend from the College of Arts and Sciences and Office of the Provost.

Writing a book takes its toll on other pursuits. This includes home life. I hope with this one I found more of a balance. Everything I think and write about is made much more interesting by sharing words with my wife—thank you. And thank you to all three of you for your insatiable curiosity across so many meals and trails—and as well as for your persisting patience as I worked on this book away from home during long nights at the library and at other times when I was physically present yet mentally distracted by some straying sen-tence. In just a few further months, these pages will be at their completion, and so we will be . . . once more to the lake!

Agate St. and 15th Ave.
Eugene, Oregon
November 2024

Notes

Introduction

1. Arendt 1968 (orig. pub. 1951), 478. Arendt describes loneliness as the experience of finding oneself "deserted by all human companionship" (474); she distinguishes this from both isolation of action (connoting impotence concerning public matters) and solitude of thought (which is often needed to think well), such that loneliness can be understood as an organized—that is, structural—condition that threatens even individuality or "the loss of one's own self" (477).

2. For two examples of such academic scholarship, see Turkle's (2011) now-classic work from a media studies perspective; and Haidt's (2024) more recent offering from a social psychology perspective. For two narrative (and non-academic) perspectives on today's technological loneliness see McNeil's (2023) novel *Wrong Way*, immersing the reader in the life of a lonely and lowly worker at a corrupt tech firm; and Jonze's (2013) film *Her*, anticipating the organized loneliness of generative artificial intelligence.

3. See Koopman 2019. *Data Equals* presents a companion argument to that developed in *How We Became Our Data*, though each book also stands on its own. The earlier book mobilized philosophical methods I sourced from Foucauldian genealogy in order to develop a diagnostic account of the problems of our data present (see also my related and much-abbreviated website, Our Data, Our Selves, https://ourdataourselves.uoregon.edu/). This book begins with that diagnosis and mobilizes philosophical pragmatism to present a normative conception of democratic equality as reconstructed for our technological present. On the relation between genealogy as methodologically diagnostic (or "problematizing") and pragmatism as methodologically reconstructive (or "problem-responding"), see the final chapters of my earlier books on pragmatism and genealogy in Koopman 2009, 2013.

4. On alignment from a fairness perspective, see Gabriel 2020. On a human-rights view, see Montemayor 2023.

5. See, for example, OpenAI CEO Sam Altman's innocent presumption that a universal moral consensus can inform alignment for generative pretrained transformers (GPTs), as I discuss the view in Koopman 2024b.

6. On pluralistic value conflict, see James 1977 (orig. pub. 1891); Berlin 1969 (orig. pub. 1958); and Hampshire 1983.

7. For a leading research statement, see Barocas, Hardt, and Narayanan 2023. For a government statement of support citing influential academic research, see the "Algorithmic Discrimination Protections" section of the "Blueprint for an AI Bill of Rights" (US White House 2022). For one example of corporate uptake, see the "Fairness Goals" articulated in the Microsoft Responsible AI Standard in Microsoft Corporation 2022, as well as further discussion below in light of the exposition in Ochigame 2019.

8. An increasingly common distinction positions equality and equity as opposed. Unfortunately, this distinction usually involves rather cartoonish pictures of equality as aiming at something like mathematical identity. The view I defend in this book is that equity is one dimension of equality, if the latter is appropriately (and non-cartoonishly) understood.

9. On relational egalitarianism, see Anderson 1999.

10. Ochigame 2019.

11. Ochigame 2019 (italics removed). Since Ochigame's publication, there has been rotation in leadership at these centers.

12. Ochigame 2019.

13. Levine 2022; McNeil 2022, 2023.

14. McNeil 2022. See also details assembled by the former Crisis Text Line volunteer Tim Reierson at https://reformcrisistextline.com/.

15. Following a script established by Meta's Mark Zuckerberg, Data & Society founder danah boyd (whose name is not capitalized) offered a public apology-cum-explanation of her role as director of the board at Crisis Text Line during the time when the board brokered the data-sharing deal and after when employees and volunteers began raising concerns. A number of months after this apology, boyd stepped down from leadership roles at both Data & Society and Crisis Text Line, and she soon after took up an academic appointment at Georgetown University while maintaining a position as a partner researcher at Microsoft Research in New England.

16. See, for example, the personnel associated with the Sociotechnical Systems and Fairness, Accountability, and Transparency in Ethics groups at Microsoft Research, many of whom are widely regarded as leading scholars in data ethics and/or critical data studies; lists are maintained at https://www.microsoft.com/en-us/research/theme/sociotechnical-systems/people/ and https://www.microsoft.com/en-us/research/theme/fate/people/.

17. Ochigame 2020.

18. Ochigame 2020.

19. For partial precedents for my approach, see works cited below in the main portions of chapter 6, pp. 156–60.

20. On pragmatism's emphasis on action, see Koopman 2014; and on process, Koopman 2009.

21. On reconstruction in pragmatism, see Koopman 2009, chap. 7; for an exemplar, see Dewey 1982 (orig. pub. 1920).

22. The category of "the ordinary" in this specification of reconstruction, as well as its usage throughout the book, is shorthand for the pragmatist insight that inquiry should be trained on what goes on in our actual practices, and in particular on aspects of our practices that are so familiar as to almost go unnoticed. For exemplars of this aspect of pragmatism, see Dewey 1983 (orig. pub. 1922) on habit; and Wittgenstein 2001 (orig. pub. 1953) on use.

23. On transhumanism, see Bostrom 2005.

24. Malabou 2019 (orig. pub. 2017), 9.

25. Malabou 2019 (orig. pub. 2017), 40.

26. Malabou 2019 (orig. pub. 2017), 56.

27. Malabou's engagement with Dewey may come as a surprise to some, since his name rarely appears in the so-called Continental canon within which Malabou is typically placed. But the surprise should really be at the persistence of parochial tendencies that still dominate the discipline today (visible above all in the persisting animus between Continental and analytic philosophy).

28. Malabou 2019 (orig. pub. 2017), 100, 102, 100.

29. For an account of epistemic agency that dispenses with phenomenal consciousness in favor of a conception of attention that is taken to be relevant to possibilities for genuine artificial intelligence, see Montemayor 2023. In the background of my own view of these matters is the pragmatist conception of mind presented in Rorty 1979.

30. Dewey 1981 (orig. pub. 1925), 215.

31. Dewey 1981 (orig. pub. 1925), 300, 215. On the transitional character of pragmatism, see Koopman 2009.

32. Dewey 1981 (orig. pub. 1925), 238.

33. Malabou 2019 (orig. pub. 2017), 109.

34. Malabou 2019 (orig. pub. 2017), 111.

35. See Dewey 1980 (orig. pub. 1916). On Deweyan education, see Malabou 2019 (orig. pub. 2017), 110–13; and more fully the recent perspective developed in Kitcher 2021.

36. Malabou 2019 (orig. pub. 2017), 110.

37. Malabou 2019 (orig. pub. 2017), 154 (from the postscript published with the English translation). On communicative democracy, see Dewey 1984b (orig. pub. 1927), 325–50.

38. On Dewey as a theorist of deliberative democracy, see Westbrook 1998; Bohman 1999; McAfee 2004; and Knight and Johnson 2011. For an overview and critique of this position in favor of emphasizing the value of "equality beyond debate" in Deweyan democracy, see Jackson 2015, 2018.

39. See Koopman 2019, 173–95. For two recent examples of the communication-centric view of digital technologies—views that I argue are incapable of addressing important pre-communicative concerns—see Lazar 2023; and O'Neill 2022.

40. Arendt 2006 (orig. pub. 1967), 231.

41. See Du Bois 1996 (orig. pub. 1903). On pragmatism as inflecting (but not fully defining) Du Bois's early work, see my argument in Koopman 2017 that Du Bois's methodology bears sufficient proximity to pragmatism to warrant considering his work as enriching pragmatism but without limiting his theoretical vision to pragmatism alone.

42. See Anderson 1999. Some might contest my calling Anderson a pragmatist, a claim I discuss below, in chapter 3, pp. 70–71.

43. See D. Allen 2023; Kitcher 2021; Hacking 2002b; and B. Allen 2004.

44. A handful of exceptions have recently emerged in work applying Deweyan pragmatism to data technology. For Deweyan approaches applying democratic equality to digital platforms and data technology, see Forestal 2022 (esp. chap. 4) and D. Allen and Weyl 2024. For broader discussions of epistemological and ontological aspects of data technology from Deweyan perspectives, see Tschaepe 2021b; and Flowers 2023. For Deweyan responses to educational data technology (also my focus in chapters 7 and 8 below), see Tschaepe 2021a, 2023; Berg 2023; Hildebrand 2024; and numerous papers collected in Flowers and Taylor 2021/2022. In what follows, I do not extensively cite these (and other) recent contributions to the pragmatist philosophy of data, but I am broadly sympathetic to the basic approach of most of this work.

45. See Williams 2005a (orig. pub. 1962); Scanlon 2018; and Kolodny 2023.

46. See Foucault 1995 (orig. pub. 1975); and Simondon 2017 (orig. pub. 1958).

47. See Vallor 2024, 2016; Risse 2023; Montemayor 2023; Floridi 2023, 2013; Coeckelbergh 2022; Panagia 2021; and Harcourt 2015.

48. See Risse 2023, 137–59; and Montemayor 2023, 223–41.

49. See Iliadis and Russo 2016.

50. See Chun 2021, 2006; Benjamin 2019; Eubanks 2018a; Amoore 2013; and Galloway 2004.

51. See Selwyn 2016; and Williamson 2017.

Chapter One

1. For a recent philosophical analysis of hierarchy, see Kolodny 2023.

2. Kolodny 2023, 97–101, 125–27.

3. For arguments motivating this distinction, see Anderson 1999.

4. On authoritarianism in its absolute form of totalitarianism, see Arendt 1968 (orig. pub. 1951). Given the pragmatist perspective orienting this book, it might be thought that my notion of authoritarianism derives from Richard Rorty's anti-authoritarianism. However, Rorty's (1999a, 14) target is "the view that human beings needed to measure themselves against something non-human," and so his concern is with the idea of human obedience to a nonhuman authority like God or Reality (for discussion, see Rondel 2021.) My concern is different, targeting a quality of interactions that always takes place between humans—that is, my concern with authoritarianism is explicitly political, whereas Rorty's is only derivatively a democratic view.

5. On epistemological fallibilism as an ingredient in egalitarian pragmatist visions of democracy, see Kloppenberg 1986; on a similar epistemic humility as a rationale for market-centric visions of capitalist democracy, see Hayek 2011 (orig. pub. 1960).

6. Koopman 2019.

7. On social media polarization, see Pariser 2011; and Sunstein 2018. For a more recent general social science perspective, see Levy 2021. For a meta-analysis of the social research literature, see Kubin and von Sikorski 2021. For more theoretical perspectives, see the media studies analysis Phillips and Milner 2021; and the philosophical analysis C. Nguyen 2020 of two distinct forms of social media separation in echo chambers and epistemic bubbles.

8. Vallor 2024, 57.

9. For a more detailed discussion of Galton's technological hierarchism, see my prior work in Koopman 2024a, which builds on Rabinow 1996 (orig. pub. 1992); Porter 1986; and Gould 1996 (orig. pub. 1981).

10. Galton 1892 (orig. pub. 1869), 12.

11. Galton 1888.

12. For a recent argument about Galtonian statistical reasoning that holds its complexity in view, see Chun 2021, 52.

13. For a canonical argument against tech neutrality, see Winner 1980.

14. Although I reject neutrality in this form, I would maintain a distinction between affirming that the aim of a practice need not involve normative determination, on the one hand, and evaluating a practice for its normative consequences irrespective of its purposes, on the other. As I have previously argued, normative modesty in the first sense is possible even where normative implication in the second sense holds; see Koopman 2013, 87–98.

15. See work cited in the introduction above (note 7).

16. See Ochigame 2019.

17. Stark, Greene, and Hoffmann 2020, 260. For a similar perspective, see work by the education technology scholars Madaio et al. (2023, 206), observing that "academic approaches arising

from the nascent fields of fairness, accountability, transparency, and ethics in AI and machine learning (FAccT) have primarily centered on evaluating the *fairness* of algorithmic decision-making systems."

18. For overviews on bias and fairness in data technology, see Mehrabi et al. 2021; Fazelpour and Danks 2021; and Barocas, Hardt, and Narayanan 2023.

19. Hellman 2020, 811.

20. Verma and Rubin 2018, 2, table 1.

21. For taxonomies of algorithmic fairness, see Verma and Rubin 2018; Caton and Haas 2024; and Chouldechova and Roth 2022. For a concise overview in line with my three-part classification, see Fazelpour and Danks 2021, 9.

22. See Mulligan, Kroll, et al. 2019, building on a related methodological approach to privacy pluralism developed in Mulligan, Koopman, and Doty 2016.

23. For the impossibility findings, see Kleinberg, Mullainathan, and Raghavan 2016; and Chouldechova 2017. For recent discussion, see Hsu et al. 2022.

24. Cooper et al. 2023.

25. Cooper et al. 2023, 2.

26. For a recognition of concerns about justice that extend beyond the purview of fairness benchmarks, see Barocas, Hardt, and Narayanan 2023, 20–22. It needs be noted that the discussion is limited to only a few summary pages in a nearly three-hundred-page book whose major focus is accurately conveyed by its title, *Fairness and Machine Learning*.

27. For a forceful recent criticism internal to ACM FaCCT (which is the academic computer science community in which the ideal of algorithmic fairness has been most fully defended), see Gansky and McDonald 2022. In addition to the critics cited below, see a genealogical analysis of algorithmic fairness in Valdivia and Tazzioli 2023.

28. Zimmerman and Lee-Stronach 2022, 14.

29. Zimmerman and Lee-Stronach 2022, 23.

30. On the distinction between abstractions that omit truths and idealizations that add falsehoods, see O'Neill 1987, 56.

31. For canonical arguments against data abstraction, see Hayles 1999, 12, on "the leap from embodied reality to abstract information"; and Peters 1999, 169. For classical forceful criticisms of quantifying measure in general, see Heidegger 1977 (orig. pub. 1954); and Arendt 1998 (orig. pub. 1958), 248–68. Such anti-abstractionist arguments are widespread today; for just one recent example from a scholar whose work I otherwise find deeply informative, see Amoore 2011.

32. Newfield, Alexandrova, and John 2022, 5. In this collection, see the political philosophy perspective by Badano (2022, 169), pushing back "against this overwhelmingly negative assessment of the simplifying power of numbers in political decision-making."

33. Hoffmann 2019, 907.

34. Fazelpour, Lipton, and Danks 2022, 45.

35. Kasirzadeh 2022, 349.

36. My argument involves a straightforwardly egalitarian alternative to algorithmic fairness, whereas other critics of this notion are primarily concerned with other values. For "structural injustice" approaches, see Kasirzadeh 2022, 353; Vredenburgh 2022, 138; Madaio et al. 2023, 211; and Edenberg n.d., §5. For a "moral sense" approach, see Grgić-Hlača et al. 2018, 52. For an "egalitarian" approach that locates equality as one dimension of fairness rather than the other way around (as I argue below, in part 2), see Holm 2023, 9.

37. As more scholars in political philosophy turn their attention to issues of data politics, there is bound to be increasing discussion of relational inequalities in algorithms and

computational systems more broadly. For recent contributions evidencing the beginnings of this shift, see Zhang 2022; Schuster and Davis 2024, 5–6; and Edenberg n.d., §4.2.2.

38. Hoffmann 2019, 910.

39. For a survey of scholarship on algorithmic discrimination, see Bandy 2021, 9–13.

40. On discriminatory bias in data technology, see Barocas and Selbst 2016; and Hellman 2020. For a theoretical account of discrimination as a matter of law, see Khaitan 2015.

41. Nearly all the literature on algorithmic fairness neglects a distinction common in political philosophy between problems of "distribution" and "allocation" as distinguished by Rawls ([1971] 1999, 77 [§14]). An allocation problem concerns how a bundle of goods is to be allotted among those eligible to receive it. A distribution problem concerns how a society should be organized such that the goods produced in virtue of its form of social organization flow to different members of that society. According to this distinction, most of the scholarship on algorithmic fairness and algorithmic bias is actually conceptually framed as an allocation problem. I use the term *distribution* throughout this book in order to be consistent with the scholarship on algorithmic fairness.

42. Rawls 1999 (orig. pub. 1971). This is not to claim that Rawls's own view is purely or even primarily distributivist. My point is only that the distributivist components of Rawls's theory (arguably its most influential aspects) are shown by him to be fully satisfied by way of procedural fairness. I agree with Anderson (2010b, 1) that Rawls's view on the whole is better understood as a form of relational egalitarianism because of conceptions he considers prior to distribution, such as that of "free and equal persons" (1999 [orig. pub. 1971], 12 [§3], 131 [§26]).

43. On the epistemic inscrutability of some algorithms, frequently referred to as *algorithmic opacity*, see Burrell 2016; and on epistemic injustices potentially stemming therefrom, see Symons and Alvarado 2022.

44. On discussions of algorithmic bias as focused on algorithms, see Fazelpour and Danks 2021, 2.

45. Grgić-Hlača et al. 2018, 51.

46. Baker and Hawn 2022, 1061.

47. Baker and Hawn 2022, 1075; their term is *equity* rather than *equality*, but the concept matches my usage.

48. Baker and Hawn 2022, 1078.

49. Angwin et al. 2016. These findings were disputed by researchers at the firm that developed the tool, but as documented in detail by Hellman (2020), this rebuttal measured bias by way of a different metric.

50. Lum and Isaac 2016.

51. On such challenges of data interoperability, see Caplan and Koopman, forthcoming.

52. For a prominent exchange that exemplifies this impasse, see that between Yann LeCun and Timnit Gebru, described in K. Johnson 2020.

53. Kearns and Roth 2020. See also Mitchell et al. distinguishing statistical bias and social bias, where the latter "may not have technical solutions at all" (2021, 146); and in education technology, similar views by Kizilcec and Lee (2023, 185).

54. Kearns and Roth 2020, 90.

55. Kearns and Roth 2020, 91.

56. Kearns and Roth 2020, 91.

57. Kearns and Roth 2020, 93.

58. On the politics of offshore data labeling contracts, see Miceli and Posada 2022.

59. The number of registrants in attendance was reported to me by registration staff on the last day of the AAAI annual conference held in Vancouver, British Columbia, in February 2024.

60. See a discussion aligned with a focus on formats or data structures by Barocas, Hardt, and Narayanan (2023, 271–74); a brief survey of work in data pre-processing techniques by Caton and Haas (2024, 12, figure 2); a statement of the importance of improvements in dealing with data prior to processing by Wing (2020, §§3–5; though note the customary call for "automating front-end stages of the data life cycle" in §8); and the small but growing body of scholarship cited below, in chapter 6, pp. 156–60, as companions to my proposed methodology of format anatomies.

Chapter Two

1. Tocqueville 1990 (orig. pub. 1835/1840), 97 (book 2, chap. 1).

2. On Du Bois's early training in what would later be understood as quantitative sociology, see Morris 2020, 20–21.

3. For an argument in support of this periodization, see my prior work in Koopman 2019.

4. See my previous discussion in Koopman 2019, 109–14, building on Muhammad 2010; Browne 2015; and Thompson 2016.

5. On the distinction between structural and attitudinal racism, see Carmichael and Hamilton 1967, 4; Zack 1998, 38–45; and Bonilla-Silva 2014, 2.

6. Eubanks 2018a, 190; Benjamin 2019, 77; Noble 2018, 4; Chun 2021, 22; and Brock 2020.

7. Benjamin 2019, 81.

8. Benjamin 2019, 82. See also Lum and Isaac 2016, noted in chapter 1, p. 47.

9. Benjamin 2019, 137–59.

10. Eubanks 2018a, 12.

11. Eubanks 2018a, 165.

12. Eubanks 2018a, 169.

13. It is not my affirmative claim that all or even most technologists today are in fact pleasantly virtuous in this sense; my argument is that it would not matter so much for structural equality if they were. That many are likely not so virtuous is documented in reporting on Silicon Valley by Chang (2018).

14. Zack 1998, 44.

15. Womack 2022, 37.

16. Womack 2022, 38.

17. Womack 2022, 49; cf. 8.

18. Womack 2022, 49.

19. Hartman 2019, 110.

20. Given widely divergent interpretations of Du Bois's politics, I note that my presentation of his early work is in the line of characterizations of him by Michael Dawson (2001, 15) as a "liberal radical egalitarian" and by Charles Mills (2018, 19–56) as a "black radical liberal." My account also emphasizes the pragmatist dimensions of Du Bois's thought, as presented previously in Koopman 2017, and without diminishing Afro-modern and Germanic influences.

21. Womack 2022, 8.

22. Womack 2022, 9.

23. Du Bois 1999 (orig. pub. 1920), 114.

24. Du Bois 1996 (orig. pub. 1903), 1, 3.

25. On problem-centered methodology as evidence of Du Bois's pragmatism, see my discussion in Koopman 2017, 192–93.

26. Du Bois 1999 (orig. pub. 1920), 123.

27. Du Bois 1999 (orig. pub. 1920), 124.

28. Du Bois 1996 (orig. pub. 1903), 81.

29. Du Bois 1996 (orig. pub. 1903), 84.

30. Wells 1997 (orig. pub. 1895), 154.

31. This attribution of positivism would seem to be contested by readers, including Goldsby (2006, 80–88), who interpret Wells's work as expressing a parodic performance of sociological statistics. Yet Goldsby's (87) reading locates Wells's subversive parody not in the statistical tables, but rather in the narrative chapters that plot a contextualizing penumbra around the statistics. This reading leaves intact a presumption about the positivism of data themselves within Wells's work.

32. Murakawa 2021, 217.

33. For the sources of my terminology here, see studies of Du Bois by Taylor (2021, 255–56, and 2011, 438–39). Taylor endorses the standard conversion narrative according to which Du Bois's pragmatic empiricism appears only in a later post-positivistic phase of his work—this narrative originates with Du Bois (1944, 47) himself. By contrast, I decline the view that writers are transparent to themselves and find instead in Du Bois's earliest data designs ample evidence of a sophisticated relationship to empiricism qualifying as a more pragmatist empiricism, or, as Taylor (2011, 438) calls it, following Du Bois's mentor William James, a more "radical" empiricism.

34. Battle-Baptiste and Rusert 2018. For online images from the exhibit, see the Library of Congress (LOT 11931, no. 47 (M) [P&P]).

35. Calloway 1901, 463.

36. Du Bois 1900, 576.

37. For direct criticisms of Galton later in life, see Du Bois 1955 (circa), ms. p. 3 (labeled "14" in top-left corner); no records show Galton in Paris in 1900.

38. Battle-Baptiste and Rusert 2018, plate 27.

39. Du Bois 1900, 577.

40. See Battle-Baptiste and Rusert 2018, caption to plate 47.

41. See Du Bois 2007 (orig. pub. 1899).

42. See Du Bois 2007 (orig. pub. 1899), 276–86.

43. See questions 8 and 9 on the "Individual Schedule," Du Bois 2007 (orig. pub. 1899), 280 (page 404 in the original 1899 edition by the University of Pennsylvania Press); see discussion of these data in Du Bois 2007 (orig. pub. 1899), 64.

44. Du Bois 2007 (orig. pub. 1899), 68n8.

45. See Du Bois 1904. I am indebted to prior scholarship on this publication by Gabbidon (2000).

46. Du Bois 1904, 35.

47. Du Bois 1904, 40.

48. Du Bois 1904, 40.

49. Du Bois 1904, 43.

50. Du Bois 1904, 54.

51. See Benjamin 2019, 82; and Lum and Isaac 2016.

52. Eubanks 2018b, para. 17.

53. See D. Allen 2016, 26. Allen draws on Rawls's "Two Concepts of Rules" (1999 [orig. pub. 1955), which offers a distinction (also relevant to my argument here) between equality *using or employing* a practice and equality *within* a practice.

54. Castillo and Babb 2024, 13. For another overview of critical quantitative approaches in education, see Gillborn, Warmington, and Demack 2018.

55. See Wise, Rosé, and Järvelä 2023. For a fuller discussion, see my analysis below, in chapter 8.

Chapter Three

1. Orwell 1981 (orig. pub. 1947), 11.

2. Orwell 1981 (orig. pub. 1947), 12.

3. Orwell 1981 (orig. pub. 1947), 11.

4. For a summary of recent literature on relational equality, see Nath 2020. Relational egalitarianism overlaps significantly with other perspectives in contemporary political philosophy, including most notably theories of recognition and of nondomination. For articulations of these theoretical approaches from a pragmatist perspective resonating with my own, see Fraser 1995 on recognition justice; and Rahman 2017 on democracy against domination.

5. Anderson 1999; Dewey 1980 (orig. pub. 1916); Du Bois 1996 (orig. pub. 1903).

6. Anderson 1999 mostly employs the phrase *democratic equality*, while Anderson 2010b employs *relational equality*.

7. Dewey 1988a (orig. pub. 1939), 226. See also Dewey 1980 (orig. pub. 1916), 93.

8. Rondel 2018, 93.

9. See Anderson 2021, 2018, 2015, 2010b, 3n4, and 2010a, 3–7, fn12, fn17, fn18.

10. On nonideal theory, see Anderson 2010a, 3–7.

11. Anderson 2010b, 10.

12. Scheffler 2015, 31.

13. See Koopman 2009.

14. See A. Allen 2016.

15. Kitcher 2021, 92. For the distinction between "teleological" and "pragmatist" progress, see Kitcher 2015.

16. On pragmatist meliorism, see Koopman 2006; on pragmatist transitionalism, Koopman 2009; on actionistic or conduct pragmatism, Koopman 2014; and on political realism and nonideal theory in pragmatism, Koopman 2016.

17. See Anderson 1999.

18. Anderson 1999, 312.

19. Anderson 1999, 313.

20. Forster 1986 (orig. pub. 1908), 127, 128.

21. My presentation locates hierarchy as the central contrast concept to relational equality, whereas Anderson more often emphasizes oppression as the contrast concept—see, for example, Anderson 1999, 313. I depart from Anderson on this point in that her concept of oppression follows Young's (1990, 48–63) multiform exposition of oppression as indexing five distinctive harms: exploitation, marginalization, powerlessness, cultural imperialism, and arbitrary violence. Rather than seeking an all-purpose conception of harm, my focus on hierarchy is meant to point to a more precise class of harms of inequality that are all clearly relational in form (whereas some forms of oppression on Young's list are not easily understood as relational).

22. D. Allen 2023, 7, 32.

23. Anderson 1999, 313. See also Kolodny (2014, 300) emphasizing "moral equals" for relational equality; and Motchoulski (2021, 637) endorsing a "shared moral criterion" underwriting it.

24. My strategy appears to concur with that of Bengston and Lippert-Rasmussen's (2023) argument that "our commitment to relational, social, and political equality" need not be "hostage" to debates about "whether all people are moral equals" (4). But whereas they aim to "detach the view that we should relate as moral equals from the view that all people are in fact moral equals" (21), I aim to detach the political justification for relational equality from a fundamental moral claim for relational equality.

25. Anderson 1999, 288.

26. An argument for compatibility in Allen's case could focus on her five-faceted conception of political equality (D. Allen 2023, 36); in particular, this conception's fourth facet of "reciprocity" as establishing a basis for the justification of democracy.

27. See Anderson 2010b, 4.

28. Paradigmatic views in recent contract theory include those of Rawls 1999 (orig. pub. 1971); and Scanlon 1998; while another recent contract approach to hierarchy and equality is presented in Kolodny 2023. According to Anderson 2010b, her contractarianism is based largely on Darwall 2006.

29. Anderson 2010b, 5.

30. Anderson (2010b, 3n4) also cites pragmatism as a companion approach where she adumbrates her contractualism, though she takes pragmatism to be a distinctive alternative to contractualism.

31. See James 1977 (orig. pub. 1891). My discussion of James's essay is based in part on my account in Koopman 2016.

32. James 1977 (orig. pub. 1891), 615.

33. Anderson 2010b, 4.

34. Anderson 2010b, 5.

35. On order and legitimacy as first questions of politics, see Williams 2005b, 3.

36. Rorty 1989, 60.

37. Whitehead 1955 (orig. pub. 1933), 90.

38. Anderson 1999, 313. Anderson further states that "democratic equality regards two people as equal when each accepts the obligation to justify their actions by principles acceptable to the other" (ibid.) in a way that foregrounds justification as more important than action. For a more recent argument exhibiting the same priority of linguistic interaction, see Anderson 2022.

39. Anderson 1999, 289.

40. D. Allen 2023, 36.

41. For the best account to date of why views like relational egalitarianism require significant levels of economic-distributive equality in such forms as supports for labor mobility, workplace democracy, and dignified jobs, see D. Allen 2023, 158–95. Allen's argument refutes the misconception that relational concepts of equality require lower sufficiency-based (or adequacy-based) standards for the distribution of resources and opportunities. For an endorsement of a sufficiency standard in education, see Anderson 2007; for an argument that Anderson's relational egalitarianism actually requires a higher egalitarian standard of distribution for education, see Macfarlane 2018; and for a related argument applying to relational equalitarianism more generally, see Heilinger 2024.

42. A looming issue in the background here is a variant of Parfit's "leveling-down objection" (2000 [orig. pub. 1995], 98) concerning cases where redistribution lowering everyone's access to a good like income would increase relational status equality. The force of the leveling-down objection has always depended on assuming a simplistic metric for the distribuendum (that which

gets distributed). Relational equality might be permissive with some amount of leveling down with respect to a simple good like income treated in the abstract. But it can be nonpermissive with respect to more-complex measures of goods like capabilities-style metrics, discussed in the next paragraph.

43. See Anderson 1999, 316–21; Sen 1992; and Nussbaum 2013.

44. Sen 1992, xi.

45. See Anderson 1999, 2010b.

46. I have no brief against the general idea of extra-personal equal relations, such as, for instance, arguments seeking to establish equality of relations between humans and certain classes of other animals. However, where such arguments begin to cast doubt upon equality between humans, they are often very seriously misleading. My view is that extra-personal equality is normally acceptable and often desirable, but always lexically secondary to the primary desideratum of equal relations between (human) persons.

47. Not only does this fault line run through Anderson's and Allen's work cited above, but it also separates those aspects of their views I here seek to justify from the views of other prominent relational egalitarians, including Scheffler 2003, 2015; and Lippert-Rasmussen 2018. The fault line is straddled, too, by different aspects of Viehoff 2014, 2019; Scanlon 2018; and Kolodny 2023.

48. Viehoff 2019, 9.

49. Viehoff 2019, 9; attributing this view to Scheffler 2015; and Viehoff 2014. For a related distinction between "friendship" and "status" accounts of relational equality, see Motchoulski 2021, 623.

50. Viehoff 2019, 9.

51. Viehoff 2019, 9; attributing this view to Miller 1997; and to Kolodny in writings subsequently featured in Koldony 2023.

52. Viehoff 2019, 11.

53. Beyond its internal merits, a secondary reason to start with Rawls's view is its influence on Anderson's (1999, 289, 314, 326) conception of social conditions for equality; Rawls's broader influence on Anderson's egalitarianism is further evidenced by the fact that he was her doctoral supervisor.

54. Rawls 1999 (orig. pub. 1971), 6 (§2).

55. Rawls 1999 (orig. pub. 1971), 7 (§2).

56. See also Rawls 1999 (orig. pub. 1971), 6 (§2).

57. See Dewey 1984b (orig. pub. 1927); and Latour 2005. For two recent statements of pragmatist recomposition influencing my account, see Berk and Galvan 2009; and Jabko and Sheingate 2018.

58. Rawls 1999 (orig. pub. 1971), 6 (§2), and 2001, 10 (§4.2).

59. Feenberg 2006, 176.

60. Rawls 2001, 12 (§4.3).

61. Risse 2023, xviii.

62. See Risse 2023, 37–46.

63. See Risse 2023, xi.

64. In the way that my view combines aspects of a Rawlsian (and Andersonian) concern for structural inequality with aspects of a Foucauldian conception of structure and structuring power it may seem unusual, but see a precedent for this atypical combination in Patton 2010, 2014.

65. On power in Dewey's political theory, see Rogers 2009; and Hildreth 2009.

66. For my prior exposition of Foucault's political philosophy, see Koopman 2013.

67. Analytical political philosophy's widespread neglect of Foucault's analyses of power extends to recent work in this vein on data politics, as exemplified in Lazar 2022, titled "Power and AI." This article presents in its first half a theorization of power without referencing Foucault. The second half of the article describes numerous ways that computational technology exercises power; here there is a reference to Foucault's concept of "governmentality" (203) that is brief (a single sentence), unexpected (not motivated by the theoretical half of the paper), and puzzling (with respect to the presumptive interpretation of this concept). Additionally, despite being an overview piece prepared for a handbook, the article neglects a large and growing literature mobilizing Foucauldian concepts and methods to specify how political power operates in data technologies like artificial intelligence.

68. Foucault 1978 (orig. pub. 1976), 88–91, 135–38.

69. Foucault 2000 (orig. pub. 1982), 341.

70. On disciplinary power, see Foucault 1995 (orig. pub. 1975); and on biopower, Foucault 1978 (orig. pub. 1976).

71. On infopower, see my prior work in Koopman 2019.

72. Readers aware of my prior work on Foucault might wonder why I find his genealogical methodology deficient for normative purposes and in need of conceptions like those offered by Rawls, Anderson, and Dewey. An answer to this question specific to the normative intent of this book is that Foucault's major political writings (Foucault 1995 [orig. pub. 1975], 1978 [orig. pub. 1976]) contribute very little to our understanding of equality. If Foucault offers any kind of normative thrust, it is on behalf of arguments for liberty, not equality. But for a dissenting view, see Tiisala 2021, arguing for a potential egalitarian seed in Foucault—indeed, one that is explicitly linked to Anderson's relational egalitarianism. I do not go nearly as far as Tiisala, but I do find bracing his thought that whatever egalitarianism we can find in Foucault would point us toward relational equality.

73. I do not find an explicit distinction between the primary and secondary levels of equality in the scholarship on relational equality, but I do believe an implicit approximation of this distinction is present in Allen's (D. Allen 2023) recent theory of equality, in particular in her distinction between two kinds of "reciprocity" (42) and perhaps even more clearly in her discussion of two principles for "social connectedness," one concerning the organization of "institutions" and the other the way individuals express "cultural habits" (103).

74. See also Lippert-Rasmussen's (2018, 144) assessment that Anderson tends to locate equality as a feature of "institutional" arrangements, while Scheffler locates it within "individual" interactions.

75. On Anderson and Scheffler as "the two main proponents of relational egalitarianism," see Lippert-Rasmussen 2018, 80.

76. Scheffler 2015, 30.

77. Scheffler 2015, 24.

78. For a related critique of Scheffler on this point, see Viehoff 2019, 33.

79. See Scheffler 2015, 24–35, and 2003, 33.

80. Dworkin is typically taken as a paradigm of the distributive approach to equality, but I agree with Lippert-Rasmussen that his view is actually grounded "in a normative conception of human relations" (2018, 228).

81. Scheffler 2003, 35. The example is from Dworkin 2000, 13 (republishing earlier work).

82. Scheffler 2003, 35.

83. For this distinction, see above, chapter 1, p. 28.

84. Scheffler 2003, 37.

85. Anderson 2008, 158.

86. Anderson 2008, 152.

87. Scheffler 2015, 30.

88. Scheffler 2015, 34. In other passages, Scheffler emphasizes dispositions rather than attitudes, but I agree with Lippert-Rasmussen (2018, 76) that even these dispositional characterizations mean to impute attitudes.

89. Lippert-Rasmussen 2018, 71; Kolodny 2023, 103, 106, 107, 113. On "attitudes" as expressing hierarchy, see van Wietmarschen 2022, 924.

90. On equal regard as rationally requisite for equal treatment, see an interesting argument in G. A. Cohen 2013, 197.

91. Lippert-Rasmussen 2018, 73.

92. See, for instance, Lippert-Rasmussen's (2018, 86) discussion of merely "implicit" beliefs.

93. See Anderson 2008.

94. Anderson 1999, 334.

95. On the importance of individuality for equality on a pragmatist perspective, see recent work by Rondel (2018, 113–35) and the earlier precedent set by Dewey (1984b [orig. pub. 1927], 355, 1984a [orig. pub. 1930], 48).

96. Crucial here is the distinction between an office and a person discharging its duties; on why an office "is not the sort of entity to which relations of inferiority (or superiority or equality) are possible," see Kolodny 2023, 134.

97. Rondel 2018, 61–70.

98. For a similar presentation of vertical and horizontal relations, see Kolodny 2023, 122.

99. On the basis of this model, Rondel (2018, 186) argues that prioritizing either distributive or relational equality over the other is unnecessary insofar as we can be pluralists about equality. I agree with Rondel's pluralistic approach with respect to questions concerning the site of equality (or where equality applies). But I do not think we can risk courting pluralism's relativistic tendencies with respect to questions of normative justification. My view is that distributive and relational equality are ultimately compatible, as Rondel too claims (74), but only because relational equality is what politically justifies distributive equality.

100. See Pariser 2011; and Sunstein 2018.

Chapter Four

1. Sen 1992, 18–19.

2. Anderson 2017, 3.

3. I use the terms *data* and *information* more or less interchangeably. In so doing I dissent from the well-known general definition of information (GDI) distinction between the two; see, for example, Floridi 2011, 83–84. I find this standard distinction untenable in its supposition of data as unstructured. Against this standard view, I focus on the truism that all data must be at least minimally structured to be computable. Rather than a binary distinction between raw data and meaningful information, more pertinent is a continuum between relatively less-structured and relatively more-structured data (where meaningfulness, a typical criterion for information in contrast to data, is one more kind of structure).

4. On numerical versus proportional equality, see Aristotle 1985 (orig. appeared circa 350 BCE), 1131a–b.

5. Du Bois 1915, 310.

6. Dewey and Tufts 1985 (orig. pub. 1932), 346. Rondel (2018, 94) observes that Dewey's egalitarianism "is committed to treating people not equally, but *as equals.*"

7. *Lau v. Nichols*, 414 U.S., 1974, 563–72, at 566.

8. Equal Educational Opportunities Act, 20 U.S.C. §1703(f), 1974. On the gains of the 1970s egalitarian legal achievements in education, as well as how these were eventually undermined by the adequacy (or sufficientarian) standards implemented by the 2001 No Child Left Behind Act, see Superfine 2013, 191–95.

9. Dworkin 1977, 227.

10. Dworkin 1977, 227.

11. Sen 1992, 1.

12. Scanlon 2018, 40.

13. *Lau v. Nichols*, 414 U.S., 1974, 563–72.

14. On procedures for selecting principles for just patterns of distributive equality, see Rawls 1999 (orig. pub. 1971). Although Rawls's view might be taken to imply that procedural fairness suffices for distributive equality, his argument relies on a prior affirmation of relational equality among those subject to the basic structure of society.

15. See Wolff 1998.

16. Wolff 1998, 106.

17. Scanlon 2018, 40–73. For earlier seeds of this idea, see Scanlon 2000 (orig. pub. 1996).

18. For a much earlier conception of difference-sensitive equal opportunity that also anticipates my conception of difference-sensitive entry equity, see the idea in Dewey and Tufts 1985 (orig. pub. 1932) that "one person is morally equal to others when he has the same opportunity for developing his capacities and playing his part that others have, although his capacities are quite unlike theirs" (LW 7:346).

19. *Brown v. Board of Education of Topeka*, 347 U.S., 1954, 483–96, at 495.

20. Seidman 2003, 135.

21. *Brown v. Board of Education*, 347 U.S., 1954, at 494.

22. Scanlon 2018, 53.

23. On this last clause, see Scanlon's (2018, 57, 65) idea of institutional justification for equal opportunity.

24. Scanlon 2018, 68.

25. Williams 2005a (orig. pub. 1962), 111 (italics removed).

26. Williams 2005a (orig. pub. 1962), 112.

27. Williams 2005a (orig. pub. 1962), 111.

Chapter Five

1. For theoretical approaches to the political structuring of data influential on my approach, see Chun 2006; Galloway and Thacker 2007; Amoore 2013; and Harcourt 2015.

2. For canonical statements of the politics internal to technologies, see Winner 1980; Kittler 1999 (orig. pub. 1986); and Feenberg 1991.

3. On this feature of Rawls's view, see the discussion above, chapter 3, p. 87.

4. Risse 2023. See also my discussion of Risse above, chapter 3, p. 87.

5. Anderson 2010a, 3.

6. Anderson's (2010a) argument in *The Imperative of Integration* for racial integration as a requirement of justice in the face of persisting injustices of segregation explicitly depends on establishing a prior claim that "the state's role in constructing segregation has been large" (68). In describing the "state's role" in redlining, Anderson focuses on how the actions of the Federal Housing Administration "promoted racial redlining" by "denying mortgage guarantees in black and integrated neighborhoods" (68). For discussion of the institutionalist and extra-institutionalist politics of redlining, both within and beyond Anderson's political theory, see an earlier version of a portion of this chapter appearing as Koopman 2022.

7. Anderson 2007, 598.

8. Anderson 2007, 619.

9. Anderson 2012, 108.

10. Anderson 2012, 121. One subtlety in Anderson's view is her appreciation of "interactions between educational institutions and the communities they serve" (111) or what she also calls "structural" and "cultural" concerns (108). If Anderson is willing to expand her analysis to include cultural forces alongside institutional forms, then my argument simply builds this out further to include other extra-institutional elements—namely, technologies. It is in part because of this potential for enrichment that I have chosen Anderson's theory as my example, in contrast to other instances of institutionalist political analysis that remain fully closed to the analysis of extra-institutional technological structure.

11. Dewey 1988a (orig. pub. 1939), 226, 1980 (orig. pub. 1916), 93, 1988c (orig. pub. 1939), 151.

12. On technologies as structuring, see above, notes 1 and 2 to this chapter.

13. For the most complicated, and most compelling, version of this view, see the techno-pessimism of Heidegger 1977 (orig. pub. 1954).

14. For a pragmatist critique of technological determinism, see Hickman 1992 (orig. pub. 1990), 140–65.

15. Dewey 1981 (orig. pub. 1925), 101.

16. Dewey 1986b (orig. pub. 1933), 94.

17. On instrumentalist epistemology, see Dewey 1981 (orig. pub. 1925), 112–18.

18. See Rorty's (1999b) endorsement of "a Darwinian account of human beings as animals doing their best to cope with the environment—doing their best to develop tools which will enable them to enjoy more pleasure and less pain" (xxiii).

19. Hickman 2001, 12 (phrasal italics removed). Hickman is explicit that "this definition is a gloss on John Dewey's instrumentalism" (187n9).

20. For a more complicating account of Dewey's instrumentalism, see Henne 2023. For a discussion of Dewey's pragmatist philosophy of technology in terms that are more associationist (in my sense) than classically instrumentalist, see Tschaepe 2021b.

21. Dewey 1984b (orig. pub. 1927), 347.

22. See also, for instance, Dewey 1986a (orig. pub. 1934), 310.

23. See B. Allen 2008, 2004. Though aspects of Allen's views press against the label of "pragmatist," there are also clear alignments with the empiricist programs of James and Dewey, as evidenced in spades in B. Allen 2020.

24. B. Allen 2008, 3.

25. B. Allen 2004, 204.

26. For his critique of instrumentalism—at least as it appears in Dewey—see B. Allen 2004, 54.

27. See Latour 2005; Foucault 1995 (orig. pub. 1975); and Simondon 2017 (orig. pub. 1958). Foucault's work is not often read as offering a philosophy of technology, but on why it should

be, see Behrent 2013; Gerrie 2003; and Simon 2023, chap. 2. For other sources relevant to the associationist model, see Kittler 1999 (orig. pub. 1986); and Arendt 1998 (orig. pub. 1958), though in both cases my suggested interpretation requires reading them against the influence of a common mentor, namely Heidegger.

28. Latour 2005, 5, 7.

29. Simondon 2017 (orig. pub. 1958), 135. For his criticisms of instrumentalism specifically, see 20, xvi.

30. Simondon 2017 (orig. pub. 1958), 173. For discussion of Simondon's distance from the logic of dialectical negation, see Panagia 2024, 164, 212.

31. Panagia 2024, 164, 160.

32. For such an objection to liberalism, specifically stemming from an associationist philosophy of technology similar to my own, see recent arguments by Panagia (2024, 15–17).

33. For further background, see Selwyn 2016, 26–53; Holstein and Doroudi 2023, 153–56; and the literature on universal design for learning summarized in Rose 2001.

34. On affordances, see Davis 2020; affordance theory is broadly compatible with, and a potential further source for, associationist philosophies of technology.

35. Selwyn and Facer 2013, 5.

36. On why I use *data* and *information* as rough synonyms, see the discussion above, in chapter 4, note 3.

37. For an example in science and technological studies, see Gillespie 2014; in communications, Bucher 2018; in literary studies, Finn 2017; in geography, Amoore 2013; in anthropology, Seaver 2018; in law, Ebers and Navas 2020; and in political science, Eubanks 2018a.

38. See Sheehey 2019; Panagia 2021; DuBrin and Gorham 2021; Kehlenbach 2022; and Benn and Lazar 2022. See also my own earlier discussion of the politics of algorithms in Koopman 2019, 66–107.

39. Panagia 2021. This piece develops an argument that builds on a broader theory of political disposition articulated by way of Foucault's analytic of the *dispositif* in Panagia 2019.

40. Panagia 2017.

41. Panagia 2021, 126.

42. Harcourt 2007, 16; Sheehey 2019, 50.

43. Sheehey 2019. For a related argument about techno-paranoia, see Chun 2006, 247–97.

44. Panagia 2021, 128.

45. Hacking 1995. In drawing on Hacking's epistemic account of looping, I depart from Panagia's ontological (2021, 14) rather than epistemic (2021, 13) approach to disposition, a difference likely reflective of our differing ontological versus methodological interpretations of an otherwise shared technological associationism.

46. Amoore 2020, 43. See also Amoore 2013, 39–45.

47. Perrotta and Williamson 2018, 9–12.

48. Perrotta and Williamson 2018, 12.

49. On school choice algorithms, see Swist and Gulson 2023.

50. Li et al. 2023, 505. Worth noting is that the particular concept of "pre-processing" employed by the authors conforms to the tendency discussed above (in chapter 1, pp. 47–49) to focus on historical biases embedded in data rather than on biases due to data formatting.

51. See Wirth 1976.

52. Amoore 2020, 33.

53. Bucher 2018, 22, 23.

54. Dourish 2016, 2, 8.

55. See, in addition to Poirier's work discussed here, my catalog in chapter 6 (pp. 156–60) of a small number of other proximate efforts for mobilizing empirical inquiry into data formats. Two possible analogues that I do not include there (because they are more akin to theoretical analogues than parallel methodological models for empirical inquiry) are Tenen 2017; and Vismann 2008 (orig. publ. 2000), the latter being deeply influential on the development of my own theoretical approach with respect to a discussion of "file plans" (142) and even a one-off reference to "formats" (7). Another apparent analogue is Sterne 2012, but this work is different in that its focus is not really on formatting data so much as on the standardization of formats, as already theorized, for instance, in Kittler 2010 (orig. pub. 2002), 37.

56. Poirier 2021.

57. Poirier 2021, 3.

58. Poirier 2021, 3.

59. Wirth 1976, xiii. The book is also explicit that computer science was at the time overly focused on algorithms to the exclusion of data structures (xii), a point made in 1976, well before algorithms were cool.

60. On measure, see Mader 2011; Beer 2016; and Brighenti 2018. On measurement in education-data technology, see Kizilcec and Lee 2023, 180–82.

61. Gitelman 2013; Bowker 2005, 184.

62. Shannon 1949 (orig. pub. 1948).

63. Shannon 1949 (orig. pub. 1948), 3, 18. See commentary by Weaver in the same volume (100).

64. On US census race categories, see Prewitt 2018 (authored by a former US Census Bureau director).

65. For an empirical analysis of gender selectors, see Bivens and Haimson 2016. For a wider theoretical perspective on policies enacting gender, see Currah 2022.

66. Wirth 1976, 56.

67. Wirth 1976, 57.

68. An alternative account of the silence about formats I am diagnosing holds that the scholarship on algorithmic politics positions the very idea of the algorithm itself as ambiguous between two possible meanings. In some of its uses, the term functions as a synecdoche such that "algorithm" stands in for the entirety of "data technology" (or "data science" or "big data"); see Gillespie 2016, 22, articulating this view. Insofar as critical attention to algorithms is part of an attempt to attend to the technical specificity of data systems, we should be more precise by carefully separating out techniques by which data is formatted from those by which it is processed. Work that respects this distinction moves toward a second and more precise meaning of "algorithm." Here the term refers to information "processing"—procedures coded into programmable machines that calculate over informational inputs. It should, however, be observed that the restricted sense of algorithms as serialized procedures is itself a historical contingency; see Yu 2021.

69. On infopolitics, see Koopman 2019 and 2018.

70. For canonical sources of the sovereign theory of power, see Hobbes 1968 (orig. pub. 1651), II.XVII/227, II.XVIII/238; and Weber 2004 (orig. pub. 1919), 33.

71. See Foucault 1978 (orig. pub. 1976), 88–91.

72. See Foucault 1995 (orig. pub. 1975).

73. See my prior discussion in Koopman 2019, 161–68, of how my concept of infopolitical fastening differs from Foucault's occasional accounts of the data-related elements of disciplinary registration and biopolitical statistics.

74. For similar observations, see McLuhan 1994 (orig. pub. 1964), 199.

75. The company has removed this claim from recent versions of its website; see, for example, its "About" from April 2020, available at the *Internet Archive*, accessed October 14, 2024, https://web.archive.org/web/20200407162713/https://www.classdojo.com/about/.

76. Manolev, Sullivan, and Slee 2018, 2.

77. Manolev, Sullivan, and Slee 2018, 9.

78. As appearing on the ClassDojo app, accessed February 5, 2023.

79. Manolev, Sullivan, and Slee 2018, 11.

80. For a historical perspective on this tendency in mental health recordkeeping, describing "a path of progressive diminution of the social determinants of mental health" in favor of "a strong emphasis on heredity and bodily phenomena" amenable to quantification, see Handerer et al. (2021, 49, 44).

Chapter Six

1. On algorithmic auditing, see Sandvig et al. 2014; and Metaxa et al. 2021.

2. Metaxa et al. 2021, 288.

3. For a description of five sub-methods of algorithmic auditing, see Sandvig et al. 2014, 9–14.

4. Sandvig et al. 2014, 6.

5. For a survey of the range of deployments of algorithmic auditing, see Bandy 2021, 9. For an example of the central focus of algorithmic audits, see Metaxa et al. 2021, which lists "discrimination and bias" as the first "research topic" pertinent to algorithmic audits (302).

6. Sandvig et al. 2014, 3.

7. See Sandvig et al. 2014, 6; and Metaxa et al. 2021, 282.

8. For an overview, see Reisman et al. 2018.

9. For concerns about accountability mechanisms in algorithmic impact assessments, see Metcalf et al. 2021.

10. I do not conceptualize these three levels according to a logic of successive containment. Rather, I conceptualize the micro level as filtered through the meso level, which organizes possible realizations of the order instituted at the macro level. The micro level is always a modality of macro level order as filtered or apprehended through an aspect of meso-level operation. For those for whom it is meaningful, my conceptualization for this schema follows the ontology of Spinoza's (1994 [orig. pub. 1677]) metaphysics of substance, attribute, and mode—important to my view are Spinoza's substance monism and attribute infinitism.

11. I intentionally leave out of my metaphor other levels of organization in anatomy, such as that of tissues, for reasons related to avoiding the logic of successive containment described in the previous note.

12. Buckingham Shum and Crick 2016, 16.

13. Frisby 2024, 5.

14. This is typical of empiricist programs in conceptual analysis.

15. This is typical of rationalistic, or idealistic, conceptual analysis.

16. This approach combines rationalist inferentialism with empiricist externalism—as such, it is methodologically the most demanding, the hardest to achieve, and therefore by far the most interesting.

17. Hacking 2002b, 17. For his initial statement, see Hacking 2002a (orig. pub. 1984), 35.

18. Hacking 2002b, 17.

19. Leonelli 2016. For other recent work in an analytical vein proximate to my approach, see the discussion of the "technological seduction" of category structures by Alfano, Carter, and Cheong (2018); and the argument for better data ontologies in light of the philosophy of induction by Li (2023).

20. For two excellent examples of the latter more historical approach to data, see Bouk 2015; and Pearson 2021.

21. Koopman, Jones, et al. 2022.

22. Denton et al. 2021. For a related approach, see Miceli and Posada 2022.

23. See Poirier 2021 and the discussion in chapter 5 (p. 140). On an emerging field of "critical dataset studies," see Thylstrup 2022; and Ciston, Ananny, and Crawford 2025.

24. Poirier 2021, 11–16.

25. Poirier 2021, 14.

26. For an overview of the sociology of categories, see Harrits and Møller 2011; for a more recent contribution focused on categories in computational systems, see Kiviat 2023. On categorization schemas of race and gender in discrimination law, see Crenshaw 1989. For work that connects these sociological and legal literatures, see Collins 1990.

27. Bowker and Star 1999.

28. On datasheets, see Gebru et al. 2018; on dataset nutrition labels, Holland et al. 2020 (orig. pub. 2018); and on data documentation, Fabris et al. 2022. For a survey of other efforts related to this work, see Paullada et al. 2020.

29. Denton et al. 2021, 2.

30. Creel and Hellman 2022, 36.

31. Creel and Hellman 2022, 36.

32. See the discussion of values in data interoperability in Caplan and Koopman, forthcoming.

33. For a related effort, focused of course only on algorithms but also acknowledging the provisional nature of any such mapping, see Mittelstadt et al. 2016.

34. See Suresh and Guttag 2021; and Baker and Hawn 2022.

35. See Mulligan, Koopman, and Doty 2016; and Nissenbaum 2009.

36. See Koopman et al. 2022.

37. See Jablonka 2024.

38. Bates, Lin, and Goodale 2016. Their approach to *sites* bears comparison to my discussion of *moments* above insofar as sites are often the physical correlates of the logical moments in the flow of data usage.

Chapter Seven

1. Berners-Lee 2018.

2. Stefansky 2017.

3. For a view of personalization as a wider cultural phenomenon dating back to the 1980s, see Selwyn 2016, 54.

4. Blanco 2022.

5. Chocano 2023, 46. For an interesting profile of another EdTech (education technology) entrepreneur, Khan Academy's Sal Khan, see Kessler 2023.

6. Chocano 2023, 50.

7. Chocano 2023, 50.

8. Chocano 2023, 50.

9. See early statements in UK white papers Gilbert et al. 2006, 7; an OECD report by Hopkins (2006, 17; cf. 115), later policy implementations of personalized learning in the US (in the 2015 Every Student Succeeds Act), Obama-era agency white papers from the US Department of Education (2010, 2017), statements from the Biden-era White House (US White House 2023), and ongoing efforts by the Chinese government as documented by Yang (2019) and Liu (2022).

10. On IBM's efforts in this space, see Williamson 2017, 164–69. Other major corporate pursuits of personalized learning are underway at SAS, Pearson, Wiley, Macmillan Learning, startup players like Duolingo, and Big Tech firms like Google.

11. See Saxberg 2018, viii; Saxberg was at the time of writing a vice president of learning sciences at the Chan Zuckerberg Initiative. For a discussion of philanthropy funding in education technology, see Williamson and Eynon 2020, 227. On the enormous levels of funding that philanthro-capitalist organizations are directing toward personalized learning, see reporting by Barnum and Zhou (2018) and Watters (2017). For an overview of how philanthropy-backed personalization in education tends to play out on the ground, see Boninger, Molnar, and Saldaña 2020.

12. See Wolf et al. 2018, 177; and a summary in Dumont and Ready 2023, 1. Some even claim a Deweyan precedent for personalized learning, including Dumont and Ready (2023, 2); Shemshack and Spector (2020, 3); and Herold (2019). For reasons articulated below, I find the asserted connection to Dewey reliant on a simplified interpretation of his educational theory as merely student-centered education.

13. Worth noting is that the high-profile tidal push for personalized learning may be shifting even as I write. In the summer of 2023, the Chan Zuckerberg Initiative pulled much of its funding (and cut much of its staff) for its education projects, as documented by Barnum (2023). Other projects have dissolved, such as the once-touted Knewton personalized-learning system deployed in partnership with Pearson, effectively sold off for scrap parts to Wiley in 2019. But will the new boom in artificial intelligence lead to a reinvigoration of personalized-learning applications? The demand is clearly immense. Whether personalized learning is currently in an ascendent or descendent status, it presents a valuable case for consideration from the perspective of data equality. If personalized learning has begun its decline, the analysis to follow can be read as an explanation of why we ought to view its demise as an opportunity to finally shift our energies away from personalization in education. But if personalized learning is booming again by the time these pages are in your hands, then the argument to follow shows why we ought to be concerned.

14. Dewey 1988a (orig. pub. 1939), 229.

15. Dewey 1980 (orig. pub. 1916).

16. Dewey 1980 (orig. pub. 1916), 93.

17. Dewey 1980 (orig. pub. 1916), 93.

18. Dewey 1980 (orig. pub. 1916), 93. For a similar argument about the role of education in democratic liberalism, see Dewey's later *Liberalism and Social Action* (1987 [orig. pub. 1935], 44).

19. Dewey 1980 (orig. pub. 1916), 93.

20. Dewey 1980 (orig. pub. 1916), 25; cf. 93.

21. Dewey 1980 (orig. pub. 1916), 25.

22. Dewey 1980 (orig. pub. 1916), 93.

23. See Anderson 1999.

24. Dewey 1980 (orig. pub. 1916), 7.

25. D. Allen 2016, 3, 4; for the key sections of the argument I have described, see 43–49.

26. Kitcher 2021, 297.

27. See, for example, Kozol 1991.

28. Downey 2020.

29. Eynon 2022, 30.

30. On format pathways in biomedicine, see Koopman et al. 2022; in psychometric datafica-tion, see Koopman 2019, 66–107; and in racialized real estate accounting, see Koopman 2019, 108–50.

31. For a summary overview of data-driven EdTech, see Williamson 2017.

32. For overviews of the emergence of learning analytics in relation to educational data min-ing, see Romero and Ventura 2020; Piety, Hickey, and Bishop 2014; Siemens 2013; and Siemens and Baker 2012.

33. For one of numerous observations of the field's porousness, see Baker, Gašević, and Kar-umbaiah 2021, 2.

34. Siemens and Gašević 2012, 1.

35. Gašević, Dawson, and Siemens 2015, 65.

36. On these three steps of learning analytics, see Chatti et al. 2012, 5.

37. See Abyaa, Idrissi, and Bennani 2019, 1116–22; Baker and Siemens 2014; Chrysafiadi and Virvou 2013, 4717–22; Desmarais and Baker 2012, 16ff.; and Baker and Yacef 2009.

38. On the rise of AIEd, see Chen et al. 2022, 32; and Prahani et al. 2022, 173, fig. 2. On the increased focus on machine-learning techniques for pattern discovery in learner data, see Sani and Bichi 2016; and Abyaa, Idrissi, and Bennani 2019, 1123.

39. Besides personalized learning, another major purpose of learning-analytics research that is especially prominent in higher education involves predicting student success. Many con-clusions I draw about personalized learning apply to student success as well. On data-driven student success, see research by Smithers (2023).

40. Luckin, Holmes, et al. 2016, 11.

41. Williamson 2017, 108.

42. Shemshack and Spector 2020, 15.

43. This list is indicative, not exhaustive; the most detailed taxonomy I am aware of is pre-sented by Plass and Pawar (2020, 281–92); but see also Vandewaetere, Desmet, and Clarebout 2011, 125, table 2.

44. Xie et al. 2019, 7, fig. 6.

45. See Manouselis et al. 2011; as well as FitzGerald et al. 2018, 2095; Buder and Schwind 2012; and Greller and Drachsler 2012. For a critical take on this corporate-academic connection, see Hartley 2009, 429. For a defense of AIEd in response to this criticism, see du Boulay 2019, 2906–11.

46. On the Austen Peay University Degree Compass project as inspired by consumer recom-mendation engines, see Whitten, Sanders, and Stewart 2013. On personnel transfer between tech firms and education personalization projects, see Rieland 2016.

47. Bloom 1984. For one example, see the opening of Roll and Wylie 2016, 582.

48. See Van Schoors et al. 2021, 1806; Bernacki, Greene, and Lobczowski 2021, 1679; and Shemshack and Spector 2020.

49. Zhang, Yang, and Carter 2020, 259.

50. Zhang, Yang, and Carter 2020, 254.

51. Pane et al. 2017, 6.

52. Herold 2019.

53. Wong, Li, and Cheung 2022, 13. See also Wong and Li 2020, 12, table 4.

54. Vandewaetere and Clarebout 2014, 426.

55. Valdés Aguirre, Uresti, and du Boulay 2016, 933.

56. See Valdés Aguirre, Uresti, and du Boulay 2016.

57. For "heart," see Vandewaetere and Clarebout 2014, 427; and Sani and Bichi 2016, 747; "pillar," Abyaa, Idrissi, and Bennani 2019, 1106; "base," Chrysafiadi and Virvou 2013, 4715; "core component," El Aissaoui, Oughdir, and El Allioui 2022, 759; "core," Chatti et al. 2012, 5; "first step," Bellarhmouch et al. (2023, 4248); and "key element," Pelánek 2017, 313.

58. For a criticism of abstract "data doubles" of learner models, see Perrotta and Williamson 2018, 7.

59. Plass and Pawar 2020, 278.

60. See Bernacki, Greene, and Lobczowski 2021, 1684, observing a lack of theoretical grounding in personalized learning; Wong and Li 2020, 9, on the same in learning analytics; and Zawacki-Richter et al. 2019, 22, on the same in AIEd. Additionally, Hew et al. 2019, 962, finds that only one-third of a sample of empirical research articles in education technology journals made explicit reference to theory while two-fifths referred to no theory whatsoever. A more optimistic perspective about the role of theory in learning analytics is presented by Khalil, Prinsloo, and Slade (2023b); yet their data show that only 74 out of 395 articles exhibited a strong theoretical basis (fig. 1), and that an overwhelming number of these citations refer to a single theory, namely, "self-regulated learning" theory (figs. 2 and 3).

61. Bernacki, Greene, and Lobczowski 2021, 1694. For a similar criticism, see Plass and Pawar 2020, 278; and for literature reviews evidencing extensive employment of learning styles as a feature variable in learning-analytics research, see Abyaa, Idrissi, and Bennani 2019, 1113; and Nakic, Granic, and Glavinic 2015, 472. For a potential explanation in terms of disciplinary backgrounds of learning-analytics researchers, see Bernacki, Greene, and Lobczowski 2021, 1695; Zawacki-Richter et al. 2019, 9; and the unsettling observation by Luckin and Cukurova that "most commercial AI developers know little about learning sciences research, indeed they often know little about learning or teaching" (2019, 1). For a critical account of the historical development and current status of the learning style idea, see Fallace 2025.

62. Peirce 1998 (orig. pub. 1905), 335.

63. Peirce 1992 (orig. pub. 1892), 313.

64. A second point of clarification concerns a technical sense of discretization in applied mathematics, where this term refers to the process of translating continuous variables or models into discrete counterparts. *Discretization* as I use it here is not a process of translating, but rather a process of constituting, data.

65. See the notion of the "dividual" as contrastive with the "individual" in Deleuze 1995 (orig. pub. 1990). For an exemplary use of Deleuze's idea in the context of education analytics, see Smithers 2023.

66. Two prominent standards are the IEEE Standard for Learning Technology (2022) and the IMS LIP (or Learner Information Package) (2001) standards. On the relation between the IEEE and IMS standards, see Valdes-Aguirre et al. 2016, 967.

67. IEEE defines a *learner* as "an individual engaged with a learning technology system in order to acquire knowledge or skills" (IEEE 2022, 3.1, 12). IMS LIP defines data elements for "a collection of information about a Learner" (IMS/1EdTech 2001, 2.2, 14), where the "Learner" label refers to discrete individuals, as for instance in its enumeration of "typical sorts of learning information" such as education records, professional development records, and "life-long

learning records" forming "a cradle-to-grave record of the learning activities and achievements of an individual" (IMS/1EdTech 2001, 2.2, 14).

68. The IEEE standard is explicit in not specifying how learner identifiers or learner names are to be created (IEEE 2022, 5.1.11 and 5.1.12). The IMS LIP standard's concept of "Learner" is explicitly specified as flexible to accommodate either "individual or group learners" (IMS/1EdTech 2001, 2.2, 14).

69. Bernacki, Greene, and Lobczowski 2021, 1705.

70. Following taxonomies in Bernacki, Greene, and Lobczowski 2021, 1678; and Plass and Pawar 2020, 278.

71. Bernacki, Greene, and Lobczowski 2021, 1678.

72. Plass and Pawar 2020, 294.

73. Plass and Pawar 2020, 277. See further evidence for this in reviews by Bernacki, Greene, and Lobczowski (2021, 1696, table 4); and Chrysafiadi and Virvou (2013, 4717 and 4726, table 4).

74. On machine learning for emotion detection, see the review in Chrysafiadi and Virvou 2013, 4726, table 4; and discussion in El Aissaoui, Oughdir, and El Allioui 2022, 766.

75. See Williamson 2022, 212; and McStay 2020. On the prevalence of "affect models" over "skill models" as components in learner models, see a survey by Valdés Aguirre et al. (2016, 961).

76. See a company description of Microsoft's Face API at https://learn.microsoft.com/en-us/xamarin/xamarin-forms/data-cloud/azure-cognitive-services/emotion-recognition, accessed October 27, 2023.

77. Lester et al. 2023, 44. See also the brief discussion of collaborative-learning learning-analytics research in Desmarais and Baker 2012, 30.

78. Lester et al. 2023, 44.

79. See Bernacki, Greene, and Lobczowski 2021, 1697, table 5.

80. See Gašević, Dawson, Rogers, and Gašević 2016, 69; Siemens 2013, 1387; and Wong et al. 2023, 380. For similar (but not identical) taxonomies, see Chacón-Rivas, Santos, and Boticario 2015, 36; and Valdés Aguirre et al. 2016, 943.

81. Valdés Aguirre et al. 2016, 943.

82. See Pangrazio and Sefton-Green 2022; and Jarke and Breiter 2019.

83. Gašević, Dawson, et al. 2016, 70, table 1. See also a detailed set of eleven tables of more than fifty different data-input types for learner models in K G and Kurni 2021, 100.

84. Gašević, Dawson, et al. 2016, 75, table 4.

85. Saxberg 2018, viii.

86. See prior work on privacy in learning analytics and personalized learning by Rubel and Jones (2016); Regan and Jesse (2019); and Prinsloo, Slade, and Khalil (2022).

87. On privacy as a social good, see Kasper 2007; and earlier precedents by Regan (1995) and Post (1989).

88. See the dataset at https://dataverse.harvard.edu/dataset.xhtml?persistentId=doi:10.7910/DVN/26147, accessed November 17, 2023.

89. See the ASSISTments data dictionary at https://sites.google.com/site/assistmentsdata/an-explanation-on-how-to-interpret-our-data-sets?authuser=0, accessed November 17, 2023.

Chapter Eight

1. Zawacki-Richter et al. 2019, 10, 21.

2. Smuha 2023, 117.

3. For a recent survey of frameworks for learning-analytics ethics, see Kitto and Knight 2019, 2856, as well as the ethnographic survey conducted in Johanes and Thille 2019, which makes a rather uncompelling case on the basis of ascribing appropriate attitudes and intentions to education technology designers when what really matters are the structural drifts to which their designs are subject (as I argue above, in chapters 1, 3, and 5).

4. E. Cohen, Ben-Zvi, and Hod 2023, 136.

5. See Perrotta and Selwyn 2019, 263; Selwyn 2019, 12; Perrotta and Williamson 2018, 7; and Selwyn 2016, 96–94.

6. See Herold 2017.

7. Piety and Pea 2018, 223. See also Ferguson and Clow 2017; and Kitto and Knight 2019, 2857.

8. See Selwyn 2019, 15; Tsai, Perrotta, and Gaševic 2020, 556; Jarke and Macgilchrist 2021; and the related argument in Tschaepe 2021a developing Deweyan insights about the ways learner modeling imposes external values on curriculum and assessment rather than grounding its values in learner experience.

9. See Selwyn 2019, 14 (4.2); and Herold 2017; this critique resonates with the account in Zuboff 2019.

10. See Prinsloo, Slade, and Khalil 2022; Selwyn 2019, 13; Regan and Jesse 2019; Rubel and Jones 2016; and Slade and Prinsloo 2013.

11. Slade and Prinsloo 2013, 1518.

12. Ferguson, Hoel, et al. 2016, 10. See also Ferguson 2019, 27.

13. Khalil, Prinsloo, and Slade 2023a.

14. See Holmes and Porayska-Pomsta 2023.

15. See A. Nguyen et al. 2023; and Dumont and Ready 2023.

16. Preceding this more recent work, see also a paragraph on inequality in Selwyn 2019, 13.

17. Uttamchandani and Quick 2022, 205; Baker and Hawn 2022, 1076. For exhibits of this tendency, see Gardner, Brooks, and Baker 2019; Tsai, Perrotta, and Gaševic 2020; Kizilcec and Lee 2023; and Sha, Gašević, and Chen 2023.

18. For a related critique of the overreliance on fairness in AIEd research, see Madaio et al. 2023.

19. Selwyn 2016, 71–76.

20. For a description of the aspiration of equity analytics, see Essa 2019, 38–41, defending learning analytics against criticisms in Selwyn 2019. For the term *equity analytics*, see Reinholz and Shah 2018.

21. On the analytical concept of technological affordances, see Davis 2020.

22. For a counter-argument, see du Boulay 2019, 2911–13. What this counter-argument neglects are the actual institutional incentives in budget-starved public education environments where fiscal emergencies will surely lead to the discharging of teachers and purchasing of software despite the fact that, as du Boulay's empirical evidence attests, AIEd underperforms one-on-one collaborative tutoring with human instructors.

23. See Engzell, Frey, and Verhagen 2021.

24. Sha, Gašević, and Chen 2023. My hypothetical acceptance of procedural fairness here is a *ceteris paribus* assumption contingent on the presence of equity entry as a condition for procedural fairness.

25. On the failings of the testing and accountability movements, see Ravitch 2011.

26. On the failures of tracking from the perspective of racial inequality, see Darby and Rury 2018, 112–18, 129–34.

27. Holstein and Doroudi 2023, 159.

28. Holstein and Doroudi 2023, 159, citing Hardt 2014.

29. Ladd and Loeb 2013, 37.

30. For both the generalized form of this argument and its particular application to tracking, see Harris 2013.

31. On the detracking literature, see Blum and Burkholder 2021, 136. For a more recent empirical meta-analysis confirming that tracking both fails to yield learning-outcome efficiencies and increases inequality, see Terrin and Triventi 2023.

32. For a detailed argument for my premise that we cannot just slip out of our swaddling in data, see my earlier discussion in Koopman 2019.

33. Womack 2022, 49.

34. Järvelä 2006, 32.

35. For data on the recent growth of computer-supported collaborative learning in AIEd research, see Roll and Wylie 2016, 588, table 6.

36. For a joint industry-academic effort expressive of such co-optation, see the Pearson white paper by Luckin, Holmes, et al. (2016, 26, 38).

37. Wise, Knight, and Buckingham Shum 2021, 427.

38. Wise, Knight, and Buckingham Shum 2021, 436.

39. Wise, Rosé, and Järvelä 2023, 3.

40. Wise, Rosé, and Järvelä 2023, 6.

41. Wise, Rosé, Järvelä 2023, 1.

42. Stahl 2010, 25.

43. Stahl 2010, 26.

44. For two recent Deweyan perspectives, see Johnson and Schulkin 2023; and Gallagher 2017, 48-64.

45. On synechism, see Peirce 1992 (orig. pub. 1892), 313.

46. Kent and Cukurova 2020, 61.

47. Kent and Cukurova 2020, 61.

48. Zheng et al. 2023, 102.

49. Zheng et al. 2023, 103.

50. Martinez-Maldonado et al. 2021, 140.

51. Kent and Cukurova 2020, 63. On features of "synchrony" and "equality" in collaboration, see Luckin and Cukurova 2019, 2827.

52. Kent and Cukurova 2020, 62.

53. Zheng 2021, 36-39.

54. See Perkoff et al. 2024, describing work sourcing collaborative-learning data from classrooms.

55. Meta-analyses of computer-supported collaborative-learning interventions suggest moderate effects of beneficial learning outcomes for collaborative learning as compared to individuated learning; see Talan 2021; and Heisawn et al. 2019.

Conclusion

1. For an account of the agency's early history, see US FDA 2018.

2. For prominent calls for such regulation, see pieces by US Senator Kristen Gillibrand (2024) and by US Surgeon General Vivek Murthy (2024).

3. For a prominent analysis that is over-reliant on the claim that data tech operates in an unregulated environment, see Zuboff 2019, 101–7.

4. On technology firm uses of trade-secrecy and contract law, see Kapczynski 2020, building on J. Cohen 2019. On the legal regime of §230 immunizing platforms from the responsibilities typically assigned to content publishers, see Citron and Franks 2020.

5. On anti-trust for tech firms, see Khan 2017. For an overview of social media regulation, see Balkin 2021.

6. On values in technology, see Flanagan, Howe, and Nissenbaum 2008. On technological affordances, see Davis 2020.

7. For a compelling account of the virtues needed for data-driven societies, see Vallor 2016.

8. Dewey 1980 (orig. pub. 1916), 93.

9. Dewey 1980 (orig. pub. 1916), 3, 200, 341.

10. For a genealogy of the informational person, see my prior work in Koopman 2019.

11. On the administrative state as a context for Dewey's thought, see Livingston 1997 (orig. pub. 1994); and Kloppenberg 1986.

12. Other significant structuring tendencies emerging in these decades include the twin forms of corporate and consumer capitalism.

13. Lippmann 1997 (orig. pub. 1922).

14. Lippmann 1997 (orig. pub. 1922), 234.

15. Lippmann 1997 (orig. pub. 1922), 173.

16. Lippmann 1997 (orig. pub. 1922), 247.

17. These three strands can be mapped to a well-known categorical trichotomy (canonized in the critical philosophy of Immanuel Kant) between language (or reason), experience (or perception), and action (or willing).

18. Dewey 1984b (orig. pub. 1927), 340, 350.

19. For criticism of communicativist democracy in Dewey and others, see my argument in Koopman 2019, 173–95.

20. Dewey 1984b (orig. pub. 1927), 368.

21. For criticism of communitarian strains in Dewey and others, see my argument in Koopman 2009, 186–90.

22. Dewey 1984b (orig. pub. 1927), 371, 372.

23. Dewey 1980 (orig. pub. 1916).

24. Dewey 1988b (orig. pub. 1938), 26. See also Dewey 1986b (orig. pub. 1933), 77.

25. On the actionistic perspective central to pragmatism, see my discussion of conduct pragmatism in Koopman 2014; on actionistic pragmatism in education, see discussion in Koopman and Garside 2019.

26. For a pragmatist statement of this liberal politics of humility, see Rorty 1989.

Bibliography

Abyaa, Abir, Mohammed Khalidi Idrissi, and Samir Bennani. 2019. "Learner Modelling: Systematic Review of the Literature from the Last Five Years." *Educational Technology Research and Development* 67, no. 5 (January): 1105–43.

Alfano, Mark, J. Adam Carter, and Marc Cheong. 2018. "Technological Seduction and Self-Radicalization." *Journal of the American Philosophical Association* 4, no. 3 (Fall): 298–322.

Allen, Amy. 2016. *The End of Progress: Decolonizing the Normative Foundations of Critical Theory*. New York: Columbia University Press.

Allen, Barry. 2004. *Knowledge and Civilization*. Boulder: Westview Press.

Allen, Barry. 2008. *Artifice and Design: Art and Technology in Human Experience*. Ithaca: Cornell University Press.

Allen, Barry. 2020. *Empiricisms: Experience and Experiment from Antiquity to the Anthropocene*. Oxford: Oxford University Press.

Allen, Danielle. 2016. *Education and Equality*. Chicago: University of Chicago Press.

Allen, Danielle. 2023. *Justice by Means of Democracy*. Chicago: University of Chicago Press.

Allen, Danielle, and Glen Weyl. 2024. "The Real Dangers of Generative AI." *Journal of Democracy* 35, no. 1 (January): 147–62.

Amoore, Louise. 2011. "Data Derivatives." *Theory, Culture and Society* 28, no. 6 (November): 24–43.

Amoore, Louise. 2013. *The Politics of Possibility: Risk and Security beyond Probability*. Durham: Duke University Press.

Amoore, Louise. 2020. *Cloud Ethics: Algorithms and the Attributes of Ourselves and Others*. Durham: Duke University Press.

Anderson, Elizabeth. 1999. "What Is the Point of Equality?" *Ethics* 109, no. 2 (January): 287–337.

Anderson, Elizabeth. 2007. "Fair Opportunity in Education: A Democratic Equality Perspective." *Ethics* 117, no. 4 (July): 595–622.

Anderson, Elizabeth. 2008. "Expanding the Egalitarian Toolbox: Equality and Bureaucracy." *Proceedings of the Aristotelian Society, Supplementary Volumes* 82 (1): 139–60.

Anderson, Elizabeth. 2010a. *The Imperative of Integration*. Princeton: Princeton University Press.

Anderson, Elizabeth. 2010b. "The Fundamental Disagreement between Luck Egalitarians and Relational Egalitarians." *Canadian Journal of Philosophy* 36, supp. vol.: 1–23.

Anderson, Elizabeth. 2012. "Race, Culture, and Educational Opportunity." *Theory and Research in Education* 10, no. 2 (July): 105–29.

Anderson, Elizabeth. 2015. "Moral Bias and Corrective Practices." *Proceedings and Addresses of the APA* 8:21–47.

Anderson, Elizabeth. 2017. *Private Government: How Employers Rule Our Lives (and Why We Don't Talk about It).* Princeton: Princeton University Press.

Anderson, Elizabeth. 2018. "Dewey's Moral Philosophy." *The Stanford Encyclopedia of Philosophy*, edited by E. N. Zalta. https://plato.stanford.edu/archives/win2019/entries/dewey -moral/.

Anderson, Elizabeth. 2021. "How to Be a Pragmatist." In *Oxford Handbook of Practical Reason*, edited by R. Chang and K. Sylvan, 83–94. Oxford: Oxford University Press.

Anderson, Elizabeth. 2022. "Can We Talk? Communicating Moral Concern in an Era of Polarized Politics." *Journal of Practical Ethics* 10, no. 1 (March): 67–92.

Angwin, Julie, Jeff Larson, Surya Mattu, and Lauren Kirchneret. 2016. "Machine Bias." *ProPublica*, May 23. https://www.propublica.org/article/machine-bias-risk-assessments-in -criminal-sentencing.

Arendt, Hannah. 1968. *The Origins of Totalitarianism*, rev. ed. New York: Harcourt Books. Originally published in 1951.

Arendt, Hannah. 1998. *The Human Condition*, 2nd ed. Chicago: University of Chicago Press. Originally published in 1958.

Arendt, Hannah. 2006. "Truth and Politics." In *Between Past and Future*, 223–59. New York: Penguin. Originally published in 1967.

Aristotle. 1985. *Nicomachean Ethics*. Translated by Terence Irwin. Indianapolis: Hackett Publishing. Originally appeared circa 350 BCE.

Badano, Gabriele. 2022. "Are Numbers Really as Bad as They Seem? A Political Philosophy Perspective." In *Limits of the Numerical: The Abuses and Uses of Quantification*, edited by C. Newfield, A. Alexandrova, and S. John, 161–77. Chicago: University of Chicago Press:

Baker, Ryan, and Aaron Hawn. 2022. "Algorithmic Bias in Education." *International Journal of Artificial Intelligence in Education* 32:1052–92.

Baker, Ryan, and Kalina Yacef. 2009. "The State of Educational Data Mining in 2009: A Review and Future Visions." *Journal of Educational Data Mining* 1, no. 1 (October): 3–17.

Baker, Ryan, and George Siemens. 2014. "Educational Data Mining and Learning Analytics." In *The Cambridge Handbook of the Learning Sciences*, 2nd ed., edited by R. K. Sawyer, 253–72. Cambridge: Cambridge University Press.

Baker, Ryan, Dragan Gašević, and Shamya Karumbaiah. 2021. "Four Paradigms in Learning Analytics: Why Paradigm Convergence Matters." *Computers and Education: Artificial Intelligence* 2, no. 1 (May): 1–9.

Balkin, Jack M. 2021. "How to Regulate (and Not Regulate) Social Media." *Journal of Free Speech Law* 1, no. 1 (January): 71–96.

Bandy, Jack. 2021. "Problematic Machine Behavior: A Systematic Literature Review of Algorithm Audits." *Proceedings of the ACM, Human-Computer Interaction* 5, CSCW1, article 74 (April): 1–34.

Barnum, Matt. 2023. "Mark Zuckerberg Tried to Revolutionize American Education with Technology. It Didn't Go as Planned." *Chalkbeat*, October 4. https://www.chalkbeat.org/ 2023/10/4/23903768/mark-zuckerberg-czi-schools-personalized-learning-technology -summit.

Barnum, Matt, and Amanda Zhou. 2018. "Mark Zuckerberg's Education Giving So Far Has Topped $300 Million." *Chalkbeat*, September 6. https://www.chalkbeat.org/2018/9/6/21105640/mark-zuckerberg-s-education-giving-so-far-has-topped-300-million-here-s-a-list-of-where-it-s-going.

Barocas, Solon, Moritz Hardt, and Arvind Narayanan. 2023. *Fairness and Machine Learning: Limitations and Opportunities*. Cambridge: MIT Press.

Barocas, Solon, and Andrew D. Selbst. 2016. "Big Data's Disparate Impact." *California Law Review* 104, no. 3 (June): 671–732.

Bates, Jo, Yu-Wei Lin, and Paula Goodale. 2016. "Data Journeys: Capturing the Socio-material Constitution of Data Objects and Flows." *Big Data & Society* 3, no. 2 (July): 1–12.

Battle-Baptiste, Whitney, and Britt Rusert, eds. 2018. *W. E. B. Du Bois's Data Portraits: Visualizing Black America*. New York: Princeton Architectural Press. Originally exhibited in 1900; collected, edited, and reprinted in 2018.

Beer, David. 2016. *Metric Power*. New York: Palgrave Macmillan.

Behrent, Michael. 2013. "Foucault and Technology." *History and Technology* 29, no. 1 (May): 54–104.

Bellarhmouch, Youssra, Adil Jeghal, Hamid Tairi, and Nadia Benjelloun. 2023. "A Proposed Architectural Learner Model for a Personalized Learning Environment." *Education and Information Technologies* 28:4243–63.

Bengston, Andreas, and Lippert-Rasmussen, Kasper. 2023. "Relational Egalitarianism and Moral Unequals." *Journal of Political Philosophy* 31, no. 4 (December): 387–410.

Benjamin, Ruha. 2019. *Race after Technology*. Medford: Polity.

Benn, Claire, and Seth Lazar. 2022. "What's Wrong with Automated Influence." *Canadian Journal of Philosophy* 52, no. 1 (January): 125–48.

Berg, Dag-Erik. 2023. "Zooming in on Dewey, Democracy, and Subjectivity in Postdigital Education." *Postdigital Science and Education*, September. https://doi.org/10.1007/s42438-023-00422-8.

Berk, Gerald, and Dennis Galvan. 2009. "How People Experience and Change Institutions: A Field Guide to Creative Syncretism." *Theory and Society* 38, no. 6 (November): 543–80.

Berlin, Isaiah. 1969. "Two Concepts of Liberty." In *Four Essays on Liberty*. Oxford: Oxford University Press. Originally published in 1958.

Bernacki, Matthew, Meghan Greene, and Nikki Lobczowski. 2021. "A Systematic Review of Research on Personalized Learning: Personalized by Whom, to What, How, and for What Purpose(s)?" *Educational Psychology Review* 33:1675–715.

Berners-Lee, Tim. 2018. "One Small Step for the Web . . ." *Medium*, September 29, accessed April 12, 2024. https://medium.com/@timberners_lee/one-small-step-for-the-web-87f92217d085.

Bivens, Rena, and Oliver Haimson. 2016. "Baking Gender into Social Media Design: How Platforms Shape Categories for Users and Advertisers." *Social Media and Society* 2, no. 4 (October): 1–12.

Blanco, Cindy. 2022. "2022 Duolingo Language Report." Duolingo blog, December 6, accessed December 14, 2023. https://blog.duolingo.com/2022-duolingo-language-report/.

Bloom, Benjamin. 1984. "The 2 Sigma Problem: The Search for Methods of Group Instruction as Effective as One-to-One Tutoring." *Educational Researcher* 13, no. 6 (June/July): 4–16.

Blum, Lawrence, and Zoë Burkholder. 2021. *Integrations: The Struggle for Racial Equality and Civic Renewal in Public Education*. Chicago: University of Chicago Press.

Bohman, James. 1999. "Democracy as Inquiry, Inquiry as Democratic: Pragmatism, Social Science, and the Cognitive Division of Labor." *American Journal of Political Science* 43, no. 2 (April): 590–607.

Bonilla-Silva, Eduardo. 2014. *Racism without Racists*. Lanham: Rowman and Littlefield.

Boninger, Faith, Alex Molnar, and Christopher Saldaña. 2020. *Big Claims, Little Evidence, Lots of Money: The Reality behind the Summit Learning Program and the Push to Adopt Digital Personalized Learning Platforms*. Boulder: National Education Policy Center.

Bostrom, Nick. 2005. "A History of Transhumanist Thought." *Journal of Evolution and Technology* 14, no. 1 (April): 1–25.

Bouk, Dan. 2015. *How Our Days Became Numbered: Risk and the Rise of the Statistical Individual*. Chicago: University of Chicago Press.

Bowker, Geoffrey. 2005. *Memory Practices in the Sciences*. Cambridge: MIT Press, 2005.

Bowker, Geoffrey, and Susan Leigh Star. 1999. *Sorting Things Out: Classification and Its Consequences*. Cambridge: MIT Press.

Brighenti, Andrea Mubi. 2018. "The Social Life of Measures: Conceptualizing Measure–Value Environments." *Theory, Culture and Society* 35, no. 1 (January): 23–44.

Brock, André Jr. 2020. *Distributed Blackness: African American Cybercultures*. New York: New York University Press.

Browne, Simone. 2015. *Dark Matters: On the Surveillance of Blackness*. Durham: Duke University Press.

Bucher, Taina. 2018. *If . . . Then: Algorithmic Power and Politics*. Oxford: Oxford University Press.

Buckingham Shum, Simon, and Ruth Deakin Crick. 2016. "Learning Analytics for 21st Century Competencies." *Journal of Learning Analytics* 3, no. 2 (September): 6–21.

Buder, Jürgen, and Christina Schwind. 2012. "Learning with Personalized Recommender Systems: A Psychological View." *Computers in Human Behavior* 28, no1. (January): 207–16.

Burrell, Jenna. 2016. "How the Machine 'Thinks': Understanding Opacity in Machine Learning Algorithms." *Big Data & Society* 3, no. 1 (January): 1–12.

Calloway, Thomas. 1901. "The Negro Exhibit." In *Report of the Commissioner-General for the United States to the International Universal Exposition, Paris, 1900*, vol. 2, 463–67. Washington: GPO.

Caplan, Asher, and Colin Koopman. Forthcoming. "The Ethics of Data Interoperability: Mapping Problems and Strategies in Biomedical Data and Beyond." *Big Data & Society*.

Carmichael, Stokely, and Charles V. Hamilton. 1967. *Black Power: The Politics of Liberation in America*. New York: Vintage.

Castillo, Wendy, and Nathan Babb. 2024. "Transforming the Future of Quantitative Educational Research: A Systematic Review of Enacting QuantCrit." *Race, Ethnicity, and Education* 27 (1): 1–21.

Caton, Simon, and Christian Haas. 2024. "Fairness in Machine Learning: A Survey." *ACM Computing Surveys* 56, no. 7, article 166.

Chacón-Rivas, Mario, Olga Santos, and Jesus Boticario. 2015. "Modeling Learner Information within an Integrated Model on Standard-Based Representations." *Proceedings of the 5th Workshop on Personalization Approaches for Learning Environments*, in *UMAP/CEUR 2015 Workshop Proceedings* 1388:31–38.

Chang, Emily. 2018. *Brotopia: Breaking Up the Boys' Club of Silicon Valley*. New York: Portfolio.

Chatti, M. A., A. Dyckhoff, U. Schroeder, and H. Thüs. 2012. "A Reference Model for Learning Analytics." Special issue, *International Journal of Technology Enhanced Learning*, "State-of-the-Art in TEL," 1–22.

Chen, Xieling, Di Zou, Haoran Xie, Gary Cheng, and Caixia Liu. 2022. "Two Decades of Artificial Intelligence in Education: Contributors, Collaborations, Research Topics, Challenges, and Future Directions." *Educational Technology & Society* 25, no. 1 (January): 28–47.

Chocano, Carina. 2023. "The Language Game: Duolingo in the Age of Generative A.I." *New Yorker*, April 24 and May 1, 44–51. https://www.newyorker.com/magazine/2023/04/24/how-much-can-duolingo-teach-us.

Chouldechova, Alexandra. 2017. "Fair Prediction with Disparate Impact: A Study of Bias in Recidivism Prediction Instruments." *Big Data* 5, no. 2 (June): 153–63.

Chouldechova, Alexandra, and Aaron Roth. 2022. "A Snapshot of the Frontiers of Fairness in Machine Learning." *Communications of the ACM* 63, no. 5 (May): 82–89.

Chrysafiadi, Konstantina, and Maria K. Virvou. 2013. "Student Modeling Approaches: A Literature Review for the Last Decade." *Expert Systems with Applications* 40:4715–29.

Chun, Wendy Hui Kyong. 2006. *Control and Freedom: Power and Paranoia in the Age of Fiber Optics*. Cambridge, MA: MIT Press.

Chun, Wendy Hui Kyong. 2021. *Discriminating Data: Correlation, Neighborhoods, and the New Politics of Recognition*. Cambridge, MA: MIT Press, 2021.

Ciston, Sarah, Mike Ananny, and Kate Crawford. 2025. "A Critical Field Guide for Working with Machine Learning Datasets." Preprint, arXiv, January 26. https://doi.org/10.48550/arXiv.2501.15491.

Citron, Danielle Keats, and Mary Anne Franks. 2020. "The Internet as a Speech Machine and Other Myths Confounding Section 230 Reform." *University of Chicago Legal Forum* 2020:45–75.

Coeckelbergh, Mark. 2022. *The Political Philosophy of AI*. New York: Polity.

Cohen, Etan, Dani Ben-Zvi, and Yotam Hod. 2023. "Visions of the Good in Computer-Supported Collaborative Learning: Unpacking the Ethical Dimensions of Design-Based Research." *International Journal of Computer-Supported Collaborative Learning* 18, no. 1 (March): 135–43.

Cohen, G. A. 2013. "Notes on Regarding People as Equals." In *Finding Oneself in the Other*, edited by M. Otsuka, 193–200. Princeton: Princeton University Press.

Cohen, Julie. 2019. *Between Truth and Power: The Legal Constructions of Informational Capitalism*. Oxford: Oxford University Press.

Collins, Patricia Hill. 1990. *Black Feminist Thought: Knowledge, Consciousness, and the Politics of Empowerment*. New York: Routledge.

Cooper, A. Feder, Katherine Lee, Madiha Zahrah Choksi, Solon Barocas, Christopher De Sa, James Grimmelmann, Jon Kleinberg, Siddhartha Sen, and Baobao Zhang. 2023. "Arbitrariness and Prediction: The Confounding Role of Variance in Fair Classification." Paper presented at Association for the Advancement of Artificial Intelligence, Vancouver, British Columbia, February 2024.

Creel, Kathleen, and Deborah Hellman. 2022. "The Algorithmic Leviathan: Arbitrariness, Fairness, and Opportunity in Algorithmic Decision-Making Systems." *Canadian Journal of Philosophy* 52, no. 1 (January): 26–43.

Crenshaw, Kimberlé. 1989. "Demarginalizing the Intersection of Race and Sex: A Black Feminist Critique of Antidiscrimination Doctrine, Feminist Theory and Antiracist Politics." *University of Chicago Legal Forum* 1:139–67.

Currah, Paisley. 2022. *Sex Is as Sex Does*. New York: New York University Press.

Darby, Derrick, and John Rury. 2018. *The Color of Mind: Why the Origins of the Achievement Gap Matter for Justice*. Chicago: University of Chicago Press.

Darwall, Stephen. 2006. *The Second-Person Standpoint: Morality, Respect and Accountability*. Cambridge: Harvard University Press.

Davis, Jenny. 2020. *How Artifacts Afford: The Power and Politics of Everyday Things*. Cambridge: MIT Press.

Dawson, Michael. 2001. *Black Visions: The Roots of Contemporary African-American Political Ideologies*. Chicago: University of Chicago Press.

Deleuze, Gilles. 1995. "Postscript on Control Societies." In *Negotiations*, translated by Martin Joughin, 177–82. New York: Columbia University Press. Originally published as "Postscriptum sur les sociétés de contrôle" in 1990.

Denton, Emily, Alex Hanna, Razvan Amironesei, Andrew Smart, and Hilary Nicole. 2021. "On the Genealogy of Machine Learning Datasets: A Critical History of ImageNet." *Big Data & Society* 8, no. 2 (September): 1–14.

Desmarais, Michael, and Baker, Ryan. 2012. "A Review of Recent Advances in Learner and Skill Modeling in Intelligent Learning Environments." *User Modeling and User-Adapted Interaction* 22, no. 1-2 (April): 9–38.

Dewey, John. 1980. *Democracy and Education*. In *The Collected Works of John Dewey, The Middle Works, Volume Nine*, edited by Jo Ann Boydston et al. Carbondale: Southern Illinois University Press. Originally published in 1916.

Dewey, John. 1981. *Experience and Nature*. In *The Collected Works of John Dewey, The Later Works, Volume One*, edited by Jo Ann Boydston et al. Carbondale: Southern Illinois University Press. Originally published in 1925.

Dewey, John. 1982. *Reconstruction in Philosophy*. In *The Collected Works of John Dewey, The Middle Works, Volume Twelve*, edited by Jo Ann Boydston et al. Carbondale: Southern Illinois University Press. Originally published in 1920.

Dewey, John. 1983. *Human Nature and Conduct*. In *The Collected Works of John Dewey, The Later Works, Volume Fourteen*, edited by Jo Ann Boydston et al. Carbondale: Southern Illinois University Press. Originally published in 1922.

Dewey, John. 1984a. *Individualism Old and New*. In *The Collected Works of John Dewey, The Later Works, Volume Five*, edited by Jo Ann Boydston et al. Carbondale: Southern Illinois University Press. Originally published in 1930.

Dewey, John. 1984b. *The Public and Its Problems*. In *The Collected Works of John Dewey, The Later Works, Volume Two*, edited by Jo Ann Boydston et al. Carbondale: Southern Illinois University Press. Originally published in 1927.

Dewey, John. 1986a. "Radio's Influence on the Mind." In *The Collected Works of John Dewey, The Later Works, Volume Nine*, edited by Jo Ann Boydston et al., 309–10. Carbondale: Southern Illinois University Press. Originally published in 1934.

Dewey, John. 1986b. "The Underlying Philosophy of Education." In *The Collected Works of John Dewey, The Later Works, Volume Eight*, edited by Jo Ann Boydston et al., 77–104. Carbondale: Southern Illinois University Press. Originally published in 1933.

Dewey, John. 1987. *Liberalism and Social Action*. In *The Collected Works of John Dewey, The Later Works, Volume Eleven*, edited by Jo Ann Boydston et al. Carbondale: Southern Illinois University Press. Originally published in 1935.

Dewey, John. 1988a. "Creative Democracy—the Task before Us." In *The Collected Works of John Dewey, The Later Works, Volume Fourteen*, edited by Jo Ann Boydston et al., 224–30. Carbondale: Southern Illinois University Press. Originally published in 1939.

Dewey, John. 1988b. *Experience and Education.* In *The Collected Works of John Dewey, The Later Works, Volume Thirteen*, edited by Jo Ann Boydston et al. Carbondale: Southern Illinois University Press. Originally published in 1938.

Dewey, John. 1988c. *Freedom and Culture.* In *The Collected Works of John Dewey, The Later Works, Volume Thirteen*, edited by Jo Ann Boydston et al., 62–187. Carbondale: Southern Illinois University Press. Originally published in 1939.

Dewey, John, and James Hayden Tufts. 1985. *Ethics.* In *The Collected Works of John Dewey, The Later Works, Volume Seven*, edited by Jo Ann Boydston et al. Carbondale: Southern Illinois University Press. Originally published in 1932.

Dourish, Paul. 2016. "Algorithms and Their Others: Algorithmic Culture in Context." *Big Data & Society* 3, no. 2 (December): 1–11.

Downey, Douglas B. 2020. *How Schools Really Matter: Why Our Assumption about Schools and Inequality Is Mostly Wrong.* Chicago: University of Chicago Press.

Du Bois, W. E. B. 1900. "The American Negro at Paris." *American Review of Reviews*, November, 575–77.

Du Bois, W. E. B., ed. 1904. *Some Notes on Negro Crime, Particularly in Georgia.* Atlanta: Atlanta University Press.

Du Bois, W. E. B. 1915. "The Immediate Program of the American Negro." *Crisis* (of the NAACP), April, 310–12.

Du Bois, W. E. B. 1944. "My Evolving Program for Negro Freedom." *Clinical Sociology Review* 8, no. 1 (January): 27–57.

Du Bois, W. E. B. 1955 (circa). "Equality of the Races." W. E. B. Du Bois Papers (MS 312), Special Collections and University Archives, University of Massachusetts Amherst Libraries, online at https://credo.library.umass.edu/view/full/mums312-b207-i018.

Du Bois, W. E. B. 1996. *The Souls of Black Folk.* New York: Penguin. Originally published in 1903.

Du Bois, W. E. B. 1999. *Darkwater: Voices from within the Veil.* New York: Dover. Originally published in 1920.

Du Bois, W. E. B. 2007. *The Philadelphia Negro: A Social Study.* Oxford: Oxford University Press. Originally published in 1899.

du Boulay, Benedict. 2019. "Escape from the Skinner Box: The Case for Contemporary Intelligent Learning Environments." *British Journal of Educational Technology* 50, no. 6 (November): 2902–19.

DuBrin, Rosie, and Ashley Gorham. 2021. "Algorithmic Interpellation." *Constellations* 28, no. 2 (June): 176–91.

Dumont, Hanna, and Douglas Ready. 2023. "On the Promise of Personalized Learning for Educational Equity." *NPJ Science of Learning* 8, article 26.

Dworkin, Ronald. 1977. *Taking Rights Seriously.* Cambridge: Harvard University Press.

Dworkin, Ronald. 2000. *Sovereign Virtue: The Theory and Practice of Equality.* Harvard: Harvard University Press.

Ebers, Martin, and Susana Navas, eds. 2020. *Algorithms and Law.* Cambridge: Cambridge University Press.

Edenberg, Elizabeth. n.d. "Algorithmic Fairness and Institutional Justice." Unpublished manuscript.

El Aissaoui, Ouafae, Lahcen Oughdir, and Youssouf El Allioui. 2022. "A Literature Review on Student Modeling Purposes." In *Advanced Intelligent Systems for Sustainable Development*

(AI2SD 2020, AISC 1417), edited by J. Kacprzyk, V. E. Balas, and M. Ezziyyani, 758–85. Switzerland: Springer Nature.

Engzell, Per, Arun Frey, and Mark Verhagen. 2021. "Learning Loss Due to School Closures during the COVID-19 Pandemic." *Proceedings of the National Academy of Sciences* 118, no. 17 (April): 1–7.

Essa, Alfred. 2019. "Is Data Dark? Lessons from Borges's 'Funes the Memorius.'" *Journal of Learning Analytics* 6, no. 3 (December): 35–42.

Eubanks, Virginia. 2018a. *Automating Inequality: How High-Tech Tools Profile, Police, and Punish the Poor.* New York: Macmillan.

Eubanks, Virginia. 2018b. "The Digital Poorhouse." *Harper's Magazine*, January. https://harpers .org/archive/2018/01/the-digital-poorhouse/.

Eynon, Rebecca. 2022. "Datafication and the Role of Schooling: Challenging the Status Quo." In *Learning to Live with Datafication: Educational Case Studies and Initiatives from across the World*, edited by L. Pangrazio and J. Sefton-Green, 17–34. Routledge: New York.

Fabris, Alessandro, Stefano Messina, Gianmaria Silvello, and Gian Antonio Susto. 2022. "Algorithmic Fairness Datasets: The Story So Far." *Data Mining and Knowledge Discovery* 36:2074–152.

Fallace, Thomas. 2025. *You Are Not a Kinesthetic Learner: The Troubled History of the Learning Style Idea.* Chicago: University of Chicago Press.

Fazelpour, Sina, and David Danks. 2021. "Algorithmic Bias: Senses, Sources, Solutions." *Philosophy Compass* 16, no. 8 (August): 1–16.

Fazelpour, Sina, Zachary Lipton, and David Danks. 2022. "Algorithmic Fairness and the Situated Dynamics of Justice." *Canadian Journal of Philosophy* 52, no. 1 (January): 44–60.

Feenberg, Andrew. 1991. *Critical Theory of Technology.* New York: Oxford University Press.

Feenberg, Andrew. 2006. "Replies to Critics." In *Democratizing Technology: Andrew Feenberg's Critical Theory of Technology*, edited by T. Veak, 175–210. Albany: SUNY Press.

Ferguson, Rebecca. 2019. "Ethical Challenges for Learning Analytics." *Journal of Learning Analytics* 6, no. 3 (December): 25–30.

Ferguson, Rebecca, and Doug Clow. 2017. "Where Is the Evidence? A Call to Action for Learning Analytics." *LAK '17 Proceedings of the Seventh International Learning Analytics & Knowledge Conference, ACM International Conference Proceeding Series*, ACM: 56–65.

Ferguson, Rebecca, Tore Hoel, Maren Scheffel, and Hendrik Drachsler. 2016. "Guest Editorial: Ethics and Privacy in Learning Analytics." *Journal of Learning Analytics* 3, no. 1 (April): 5–15.

Finn, Ed. 2017. *What Algorithms Want.* Cambridge: MIT Press.

FitzGerald, Elizabeth, Ann Jones, Natalia Kucirkova, and Eileen Scanlon. 2018. "A Literature Synthesis of Personalised Technology-Enhanced Learning: What Works and Why." *Research in Learning Technology* 26:2095–111.

Flanagan, Mary, Daniel Howe, and Helen Nissenbaum. 2008. "Embodying Values in Technology: Theory and Practice." In *Information Technology and Moral Philosophy*, edited by J. van den Hoven and J. Weckert, 322–53. Cambridge: Cambridge University Press.

Floridi, Luciano. 2011. *The Philosophy of Information.* Oxford: Oxford University Press.

Floridi, Luciano. 2013. *The Ethics of Information.* Oxford: Oxford University Press.

Floridi, Luciano. 2023. *The Green and The Blue: Naive Ideas to Improve Politics in the Digital Age.* New York: Wiley.

Flowers, Johnathan. 2023. "Pragmatism and AI: A Critical Approach." In *Handbook of Critical Studies of Artificial Intelligence*, edited by S. Lindgren, 141–51. Cheltenham: Edward Elgar Publishing.

Flowers, Jonathan and Kevin Taylor, eds. 2021/2022. "Deweyan Approaches to Contemporary Issues at the Intersection of Data and Technology." Special issue series, *Education and Culture* 37, nos. 1–2, and 38, no. 1.

Forestal, Jennifer. 2022. *Designing for Democracy: How to Build Community in Digital Environments*. New York: Oxford University Press.

Forster, E. M. 1986. *A Room with a View*. New York: Vintage. Originally published in 1908.

Foucault, Michel. 1978. *The History of Sexuality, Volume 1: An Introduction*. Translated by Robert Hurley. New York: Vintage Books. Originally published as *La volonté de savoir: Histoire de la sexualité I* in 1976.

Foucault, Michel. 1995. *Discipline and Punish: The Birth of the Prison*. Translated by Alan Sheridan. New York: Vintage Books. Originally published as *Surveiller et punir: Naissance de la prison* in 1975.

Foucault, Michel. 2000. "The Subject and Power." In Power, *Essential Works, Volume 3: Power*, edited by J. Faubion and P. Rabinow, translated by R. Hurley and others.Vol. 3 of Essential Works of Michel Foucault, 1954–1984. New York: New Press. Originally published in English in 1982.

Fraser, Nancy. 1995. "From Redistribution to Recognition? Dilemmas of Justice in a 'Postsocialist' Age." *New Left Review*, no. 212, July/August, 68–93.

Frisby, Michael B. 2024. "Critical Quantitative Literacy: An Educational Foundation for Critical Quantitative Research." *AERA Open* 10, no. 1 (January/December): 1–13.

Gabbidon, Shaun L. 2000. "An Early American Crime Poll by W. E. B. Du Bois." *Western Journal of Black Studies* 24, no. 3 (Fall): 167–74.

Gabriel, Iason. 2020. "Artificial Intelligence, Values, and Alignment." *Minds and Machines* 30, no. 3 (October): 411–37.

Gallagher, Shaun. 2017. *Enactivist Interventions: Rethinking the Mind*. Oxford: Oxford University Press.

Galloway, Alexander. 2004. *Protocol: How Control Exists after Decentralization*. Cambridge: MIT Press.

Galloway, Alexander, and Eugene Thacker. 2007. *The Exploit: A Theory of Networks*. Minneapolis: University of Minnesota Press.

Galton, Francis. 1888. "Co-relations and Their Measurement, Chiefly from Anthropometric Data." *Proceedings of the Royal Society of London* 45 (December): 135–45.

Galton, Francis. 1892. *Hereditary Genius: An Inquiry into Its Laws and Consequences*, 2nd ed. London: Macmillan. Originally published in 1869.

Gansky, Ben, and Sean McDonald. 2022. "CounterFAccTual: How FAccT Undermines Its Organizing Principles." In *FAccT '22: 2022 ACM Conference on Fairness, Accountability, and Transparency*, June, 1982–92.

Gardner, Josh, Christopher Brooks, and Ryan Baker. 2019. "Evaluating the Fairness of Predictive Student Models through Slicing Analysis." In *Proceedings of the 9th International Conference on Learning Analytics and Knowledge*: 225–34. New York: Association for Computing Machinery.

Gašević, Dragan, Shane Dawson, Tim Rogers, and Daniela Gašević. 2016. "Learning Analytics Should Not Promote One Size Fits All: The Effects of Instructional Conditions in Predicting Academic Success." *Internet and Higher Education* 28:68–84.

Gašević, Dragan, Shane Dawson, and George Siemens. 2015. "Let's Not Forget: Learning Analytics Are About Learning." *TechTrends* 59, no. 1 (January): 64–71.

Gebru, Timnit, Jamie Morgenstern, Briana Vecchione, Jennifer Wortman Vaughan, Hanna M. Wallach, Hal Daumé, and Kate Crawford. 2018. "Datasheets for Datasets." *Communications of the ACM* 64:86–92.

Gerrie, Jim. 2003. "Was Foucault a Philosopher of Technology?" *Techné: Research in Philosophy and Technology* 7, no. 2 (Winter): 66–73.

Gilbert, Christine, et al. (aka Teaching and Learning in 2020 Review Group). 2006. *2020 Vision: Report of the Teaching and Learning in 2020 Review Group.* Nottingham: Department for Education and Skills.

Gillborn, David, Paul Warmington, and Sean Demack. 2018. "QuantCrit: Education, Policy, "Big Data" and Principles for a Critical Race Theory of Statistics." *Race, Ethnicity and Education* 21 (2): 158–79.

Gillespie, Tarleton. 2014. "The Relevance of Algorithms." In *Media Technologies*, edited by T. Gillespie, P. Boczkowski, and K. Foot, 167–93. Cambridge: MIT Press.

Gillespie, Tarleton. 2016. "Algorithm" in *Digital Keywords*, edited by B. Peters, 18–30. Princeton: Princeton University Press.

Gillibrand, Kristen. 2024. "It's Open Season on Personal Data: We Need a Data Protection Agency Now." *The Hill*, February 6, accessed March 7, 2024. https://thehill.com/opinion /technology/4448949-its-open-season-on-personal-data-we-need-a-data-protection -agency-now/.

Gitelman, Lisa, ed. 2013. *"Raw Data" Is an Oxymoron.* Cambridge: MIT Press.

Goldsby, Jacqueline. 2006. *A Spectacular Secret: Lynching in American Life and Literature.* Chicago: University of Chicago Press.

Gould, Stephen Jay. 1996. *The Mismeasure of Man*, rev. ed. New York: W. W. Norton. Originally published in 1981.

Greller, W., and H. Drachsler. 2012. "Translating Learning into Numbers: A Generic Framework for Learning Analytics." *Journal of Educational Technology & Society* 15, no. 3 (July): 42–57.

Grgić-Hlača, Nina, Muhammad Bilal Zafar, Krishna P. Gummadi, and Adrian Weller. 2018. "Beyond Distributive Fairness in Algorithmic Decision Making: Feature Selection for Procedurally Fair Learning." *Proceedings of the AAAI Conference on Artificial Intelligence* 32, no. 1 (February): 51–60.

Hacking, Ian. 1995. "The Looping Effects of Human Kinds." In *Causal Cognition*, edited by D. Sperber, D. Premack, and A. Premack, 351–83. Oxford: Oxford University Press.

Hacking, Ian. 2002a. "Five Parables." In *Historical Ontology*, 27–50. Cambridge: Harvard University Press. Originally published in 1984.

Hacking, Ian. 2002b. "Historical Ontology." In *Historical Ontology*, 1–26. Cambridge: Harvard University Press.

Haidt, Jonathan. 2024. *The Anxious Generation: How the Great Rewiring of Childhood Is Causing an Epidemic of Mental Illness.* New York: Penguin.

Hampshire, Stuart. 1983. *Morality and Conflict.* Cambridge: Harvard University Press.

Handerer, Fritz, Peter Kinderman, Carsten Timmermann, and Sara J. Tai. 2021. "How Did Mental Health Become So Biomedical? The Progressive Erosion of Social Determinants in Historical Psychiatric Admission Registers." *History of Psychiatry* 32, no. 1 (March): 37–51.

Harcourt, Bernard. 2007. *Against Prediction.* Chicago: University of Chicago Press.

Harcourt, Bernard. 2015. *Exposed: Desire and Disobedience in the Digital Age.* Cambridge: Harvard University Press.

Hardt, Moritz. 2014. "How Big Data Is Unfair." *Medium*, September 26. https://medium.com/@mrtz/how-big-data-is-unfair-9aa544d739de.

Harris, Angel. 2013. "Can Members of Marginalized Groups Remain Invested in Schooling? An Assessment from the United States and the United Kingdom." In *Education, Justice, and Democracy*, edited by D. Allen and R. Reich, 101–32. Chicago: University of Chicago Press.

Harrits, Gitte Sommer, and Marie Østergaard Møller. 2011. "Categories and Categorization: Towards a Comprehensive Sociological Framework." *Distinktion: Scandinavian Journal of Social Theory* 12, no. 2 (August): 229–47.

Hartley, David. 2009. "Personalisation: The Nostalgic Revival of Child-Centred Education?" *Journal of Education Policy* 24, no. 4 (June): 423–34.

Hartman, Saidiya. 2019. *Wayward Lives, Beautiful Experiments: Intimate Histories of Riotous Black Girls, Troublesome Women, and Queer Radicals.* New York: W. W. Norton.

Hayek, Friedrich. 2011. *The Constitution of Liberty.* Chicago: University of Chicago Press. Originally published in 1960.

Hayles, N. Katherine. 1999. *How We Became Posthuman.* Chicago: University of Chicago Press.

Heidegger, Martin. 1977. "The Question Concerning Technology." In *The Question Concerning Technology, and Other Essays*, translated by W. Lovitt. New York: Harper & Row. Originally published as "Die Frage nach der Technik" in 1954.

Heilinger, Jan-Christoph. 2024. "The Distributive Demands of Relational Egalitarianism." *Ethical Theory and Moral Practice* 27 (August): 619–34.

Hellman, Deborah. 2020. "Measuring Algorithmic Fairness." *Virginia Law Review* 106, no. 4 (June): 811–66.

Henne, Céline. 2023. "John Dewey: Was the Inventor of Instrumentalism Himself an Instrumentalist?" *HOPOS* 13, no. 1 (Spring): 120–50.

Herold, Benjamin. 2017. "The Case(s) against Personalized Learning." *EducationWeek*, November 7. https://www.edweek.org/technology/the-cases-against-personalized-learning/2017/11.

Herold, Benjamin. 2019. "What Is Personalized Learning?" *EducationWeek*, November 5. https://www.edweek.org/technology/what-is-personalized-learning/2019/11.

Hew, Khe Foon, Min Lan, Ying Tang, Chengyuan Jia, and Chung Kwan Lo. 2019. "Where Is the 'Theory' within the Field of Educational Technology Research?" *British Journal of Educational Technology* 50, no. 3 (May): 956–71.

Hickman, Larry. 1992. *John Dewey's Pragmatic Technology.* Bloomington: Indiana University Press. Originally published in 1990.

Hickman, Larry. 2001. *Philosophical Tools for Technological Culture: Putting Pragmatism to Work.* Bloomington: Indiana University Press.

Hildebrand, David. 2024. "What Are Data and Who Benefits?" In *Framing Futures in Postdigital Education: Critical Concepts for Data-Driven Practices*, edited by A. Buch, 79–97. Cham: Springer.

Hildreth, Roudy. 2009. "Reconstructing Dewey on Power." *Political Theory* 37, no. 6 (December): 780–807.

Hobbes, Thomas. 1968. *Leviathan.* New York: Penguin. Originally published in 1651.

Hoffmann, Anna Lauren. 2019. "Where Fairness Fails: Data, Algorithms, and the Limits of Antidiscrimination Discourse." *Information, Communication, & Society* 22, no. 7 (May): 900–915.

Holland, Sarah, Ahmed Hosny, Sarah Newman, Joshua Joseph, and Kasia Chmielinski. 2020. "The Dataset Nutrition Label: A Framework to Drive Higher Data Quality Standards." *Data*

Protection and Privacy, vol. 12, edited by D. Hallinan, P. De Hert, S. Gutwirth, and R. E. Leenes, 1–26. New York: Bloomsbury. Originally published in 2018.

Holmes, Wayne, and Kaska Porayska-Pomsta, eds. 2023. *The Ethics of Artificial Intelligence in Education: Current Challenges, Practices and Debates.* New York: Routledge.

Holstein, Kenneth, and Shayan Doroudi. 2023. "Equity and Artificial Intelligence in Education." In *The Ethics of Artificial Intelligence in Education*, edited by W. Holmes and K. Porayska-Pomsta, 151–73. New York: Routledge.

Hopkins, David. 2006. Introduction to *Personalising Education*, 17–20. Paris: OECD (Organization for Economic Co-operation and Development).

Hsu, Brian, Rahul Mazumder, Preetam Nandy, and Kinjal Basu. 2022. "Pushing the Limits of Fairness Impossibility: Who's the Fairest of Them All?" Available at ArXiv, https://arxiv.org/abs/2208.12606.

IEEE (Institute of Electrical and Electronics Engineers). 2022. *IEEE Standard for Learning Technology—Data Model for Content Object Communication*, IEEE Std. 1484.11.1–2022. New York: IEEE.

Iliadis, Andrew, and Federica Russo. 2016. "Critical Data Studies: An Introduction." *Big Data & Society* 3, no. 2 (October): 1–7.

IMS/1EdTech. 2001. *IMS Learner Information Package Information Model, Version 1.0, Final Specification.* Lake Mary: IMS Global Learning Consortium.

Jabko, Nicolas, and Adam Sheingate. 2018. "Practices of Dynamic Order." *Perspectives on Politics* 16, no. 2 (June): 312–27.

Jablonka, Eva. 2024. "Reading Koopman's 'How We Became Our Data' as an Invitation to Resist the Formatting of the 'Informational Person' with the Support of Mathematics Education." *Journal of the American Association for the Advancement of Curriculum Studies* 16, no. 1 (February): 91–106.

Jackson, Jeff. 2015. "Dividing Deliberative and Participatory Democracy through John Dewey." *Democratic Theory* 2, no. 1 (June): 63–84.

Jackson, Jeff. 2018. *Equality beyond Debate: John Dewey's Pragmatic Idea of Democracy.* Cambridge: Cambridge University Press.

James, William. 1977. "The Moral Philosopher and the Moral Life." In *The Writings of William James: A Comprehensive Edition*, edited by J. McDermott, 610–29. Chicago: University of Chicago Press. Originally published in 1891.

Jarke, Juliane, and Andreas Breiter, eds. 2019. Special issue, "The Datafication of Education." *Learning, Media and Technology* 44 (1): 1–86.

Jarke, Juliane, and Felicitas Macgilchrist. 2021. "Dashboard Stories: How Narratives Told by Predictive Analytics Reconfigure Roles, Risk and Sociality in Education." *Big Data & Society* 8, no. 1 (June): 1–15.

Järvelä, Sanna. 2006. "Personalised Learning? New Insights into Fostering Learning Capacity." In *Personalising Education*," 31–46. Paris: OECD (Organization for Economic Co-operation and Development).

Jeong, Heisawn, Cindy Hmelo-Silver, and Kihyun Jo. 2019. "Ten Years of Computer-Supported Collaborative Learning: A Meta-analysis of CSCL in STEM Education during 2005–2014." *Educational Research Review* 28, 2019, document no. 100284.

Johanes, Petr, and Candace Thille. 2019. "The Heart of Educational Data Infrastructures = Conscious Humanity and Scientific Responsibility, Not Infinite Data and Limitless Experimentation." *British Journal of Educational Technology* 50, no. 6 (November): 2959–73.

Johnson, Khari. 2020. "AI Weekly: A Deep Learning Pioneer's Teachable Moment on AI Bias." *VentureBeat*, June 26. https://venturebeat.com/ai/ai-weekly-a-deep-learning-pioneers-teachable-moment-on-ai-bias/.

Johnson, Mark, and Jay Schulkin. 2023. *Mind in Nature: John Dewey, Cognitive Science, and a Naturalistic Philosophy for Living.* Cambridge: MIT Press.

Jonze, Spike. 2013. *Her.* Annapurna Pictures. 126 min. Film.

K G, Srinivasa, and Muralidhar Kurni. 2021. *A Beginner's Guide to Learning Analytics.* Germany: Springer.

Kapczynski, Amy. 2020. "The Law of Informational Capitalism." *Yale Law Journal* 129, no. 5 (March): 1460–515.

Kasirzadeh, Atoosa. 2022. "Algorithmic Fairness and Structural Injustice: Insights from Feminist Political Philosophy." In *Proceedings of the 2022 AAAI/ACM Conference on AI, Ethics, and Society (AIES'22)*, 349–56. New York: Association for Computing Machinery.

Kasper, Debbie V. S. 2007. "Privacy as a Social Good." *Social Thought and Research* 28:165–89.

Kearns, Michael, and Aaron Roth. 2020. *The Ethical Algorithm.* Oxford: Oxford University Press.

Kehlenbach, E. Stefan. 2022. "The Subatomic Person: A New Ontology of Big Data." *Theory & Event* 25, no. 4 (October): 851–72.

Kent, Carmel, and Multu Cukurova. 2020. "Investigating Collaboration as a Process with Theory-Driven Learning Analytics." *Journal of Learning Analytics* 7, no. 1 (April): 59–71.

Kessler, Andy. 2023. "AI's Education Revolution." *Wall Street Journal*, May 21. https://www.wsj.com/articles/ais-education-revolution-khan-academy-tutor-animation-schools-5aec9a5e.

Khaitan, Tarunabh. 2015. *A Theory of Discrimination Law.* Oxford: Oxford University Press.

Khalil, Mohammad, Paul Prinsloo, and Sharon Slade. 2023a. "Fairness, Trust, Transparency, Equity, and Responsibility in Learning Analytics." *Journal of Learning Analytics* 10, no. 1 (March): 1–7.

Khalil, Mohammad, Paul Prinsloo, and Sharon Slade. 2023b. "The Use and Application of Learning Theory in Learning Analytics: A Scoping Review." *Journal of Computing in Higher Education* 35, no. 3 (December): 573–94.

Khan, Lina M. 2017. "Amazon's Antitrust Paradox." *Yale Law Journal* 126, no. 3 (January): 710–805.

Kitcher, Philip. 2015. "Pragmatism and Progress." *Transactions of the Charles S. Peirce Society* 51, no. 4 (Winter): 475–94.

Kitcher, Philip. 2021. *The Main Enterprise of the World: Rethinking Education.* Oxford: Oxford University Press.

Kittler, Friedrich. 1999. *Gramophone Film Typewriter.* Translated by Geoffrey Winthrop-Young and Michael Wutz. Stanford: Stanford University Press. Originally published as *Grammophon Film Typewriter* in 1986.

Kittler, Friedrich. 2010. *Optical Media.* Translated by Anthony Enns. Cambridge: Polity. Originally published as *Optische Medien: Berliner Vorlesung 1999* in 2002.

Kitto, Kirsty, and Simon Knight. 2019. "Practical Ethics for Building Learning Analytics." *British Journal of Educational Technology* 50, no. 6 (November): 2855–70.

Kiviat, Barbara. 2023. "The Moral Affordances of Construing People as Cases: How Algorithms and the Data They Depend on Obscure Narrative and Noncomparative Justice." *Sociological Theory* 41, no. 3 (September): 175–200.

Kizilcec, Rene, and Hanson Lee. 2023. "Algorithmic Fairness in Education." In *The Ethics of Artificial Intelligence in Education: Current Challenges, Practices and Debates*, edited by W. Holmes and K. Porayska-Pomsta, 174–202. New York: Routledge.

Kleinberg, Jon, Sendhil Mullainathan, and Manish Raghavan. 2016. "Inherent Trade-Offs in the Fair Determination of Risk Scores." Available at ArXiv, https://arxiv.org/abs/1609.05807.

Kloppenberg, James. 1986. *Uncertain Victory: Social Democracy and Progressivism in European and American Thought, 1870–1920*. Oxford: Oxford University Press.

Knight, Jack, and James Johnson. 2011. *The Priority of Democracy: Political Consequences of Pragmatism*. Princeton: Princeton University Press.

Kolodny, Niko. 2014. "Rule over None II: Social Equality and the Justification of Democracy." *Philosophy & Public Affairs* 42, no. 4 (Fall): 287–336.

Kolodny, Niko. 2023. *The Pecking Order: Social Hierarchy as a Philosophical Problem*. Cambridge: Harvard University Press.

Koopman, Colin. 2006. "Pragmatism as a Philosophy of Hope: Emerson, James, Dewey, and Rorty." *Journal of Speculative Philosophy* 20, no. 2 (Summer): 106–16.

Koopman, Colin. 2009. *Pragmatism as Transition: Historicity and Hope in James, Dewey, and Rorty*. New York: Columbia University Press.

Koopman, Colin. 2013. *Genealogy as Critique: Foucault and the Problems of Modernity*. Bloomington: Indiana University Press.

Koopman, Colin. 2014. "Conduct Pragmatism: Pressing beyond Experientialism and Lingualism." *European Journal of Pragmatism and American Philosophy* 6, no. 2 (Fall): 145–74.

Koopman, Colin. 2016. "Unruly Pluralism and Inclusive Tolerance: The Normative Contribution of Jamesian Pragmatism to Non-ideal Theory." *Political Studies Review* 14, no. 1 (February): 27–38.

Koopman, Colin. 2017. "Contesting Injustice: Why Pragmatist Political Thought Needs Du Bois." In *Pragmatism and Justice*, edited by S. Dieleman, D. Rondel, and C. Voparil, 179–96. Oxford: Oxford University Press.

Koopman, Colin. 2018. "Infopolitics, Biopolitics, Anatomopolitics: Toward a Genealogy of the Power of Data." *Graduate Faculty Philosophy Journal* 39, no. 1 (Spring): 103–28.

Koopman, Colin. 2019. *How We Became Our Data: A Genealogy of the Informational Person*. Chicago: University of Chicago Press.

Koopman, Colin. 2022. "The Political Theory of Data: Institutions, Algorithms, & Formats in Racial Redlining." *Political Theory* 50, no. 2 (April): 337–61.

Koopman, Colin. 2024a. "From Galton's Pride to Du Bois's Pursuit: The Formats of Data-Driven Inequality." *Theory, Culture & Society* 41, no. 1 (January): 59–78.

Koopman, Colin. 2024b. "Artificing Intelligence: From Isolating IQ to Amoral AI." *AI & Society*.

Koopman, Colin, and Darren Garside. 2019. "Transition, Action and Education: Redirecting Pragmatist Philosophy of Education." *Journal of Philosophy of Education* 53, no. 4 (November): 734–47.

Koopman, Colin, Patrick Jones, Valérie Simon, Paul Showler, and Mary McLevey (coauthored under the group name Critical Genealogies Collaboratory). 2022. "When Data Drive Health: An Archaeology of Medical Records Technology." *BioSocieties* 17, no. 4 (December): 782–804.

Kozol, Jonathan. 1991. *Savage Inequalities: Children in America's Schools*. New York: Harper Perennial.

Kubin, Emily, and Christian von Sikorski. 2021. "The Role of (Social) Media in Political Polarization: A Systematic Review." *Annals of the International Communication Association* 45, no. 3
(September): 188–206.

Ladd, Helen, and Susanna Loeb. 2013. "The Challenges of Measuring School Quality: Implications for Educational Equity." In *Education, Justice, and Democracy*, edited by D. Allen and
R. Reich, 19–42. Chicago: University of Chicago Press.

Latour, Bruno. 2005. *Reassembling the Social: An Introduction to Actor-Network-Theory*. Oxford:
Oxford University Press.

Lazar, Seth. 2022. "Power and AI: Nature and Justification." In *The Oxford Handbook of AI Governance*, edited by J. Bullock, et al., 198–209. Oxford: Oxford University Press.

Lazar, Seth. 2023. "Communicative Justice and the Distribution of Attention." Knight First
Amendment Institute at Columbia University, October 10. https://knightcolumbia.org/
content/communicative-justice-and-the-distribution-of-attention.

Leonelli, Sabina. 2016. *Data-centric Biology: A Philosophical Study*. Chicago: University of
Chicago Press.

Lester, James, Anisha Gupta, Fahmid Morshed Fahid, and Jay Pande. 2023. "Learner Modeling
in Intelligent Tutoring Systems SWOT Analysis." In *Design Recommendations for Intelligent
Tutoring Systems*, vol. 10, edited by A. Sinatra, et al., 43–52. Orlando: US Army Combat
Capabilities Development Command.

Levine, Alexandra. 2022. "Suicide Hotline Shares Data with For-Profit Spinoff, Raising Ethical Questions." *Politico*, January 28, accessed July 10, 2024. https://www.politico.com/news/
2022/01/28/suicide-hotline-silicon-valley-privacy-debates-00002617.

Levy, Ro'ee. 2021. "Social Media, News Consumption, and Polarization: Evidence from a Field
Experiment." *American Economic Review* 111, no. 3 (March): 831–70.

Li, Dan. 2023. "Machines Learn Better with Better Data Ontology: Lessons from Philosophy of Induction and Machine Learning Practice." *Minds and Machines* 33, no. 3 (September): 429–50.

Li, Lin, Lele Sha, Yuheng Li, Mladen Raković, Jia Rong, Srecko Joksimovic, Neil Selwyn, Dragan
Gašević, and Guanliang Chen. 2023. "Moral Machines or Tyranny of the Majority? A Systematic Review on Predictive Bias in Education." *LAK23: 13th International Learning Analytics and Knowledge Conference* (March): 499–508.

Lippert-Rasmussen, Kasper. 2018. *Relational Egalitarianism: Living as Equals*. Cambridge: Cambridge University Press.

Lippmann, Walter. 1997. *Public Opinion*. New York: Free Press. Originally published in 1922.

Liu, Xiaoting (Maya). 2022. "Nurturing the Next-Generation AI Workforce: A Snapshot of
AI Education in China's Public Education System." Asia Pacific Foundation of Canada,
March 7. https://www.asiapacific.ca/publication/nurturing-next-generation-ai-workforce
-snapshot-ai-education.

Livingston, James. 1997. *Pragmatism and the Political Economy of Cultural Revolution, 1850–1940*.
Chapel Hill: University of North Carolina Press. Originally published in 1994.

Luckin, Rosemary, and Mutlu Cukurova. 2019. "Designing Educational Technologies in the Age
of AI: A Learning Sciences-Driven Approach." *British Journal of Educational Technology* 50,
no. 6 (November): 2824–38.

Luckin, Rose, Wayne Holmes, Mark Griffiths, and Laurie B. Forcier. 2016. *Intelligence Unleashed:
An Argument for AI in Education*. London: Pearson.

Lum, Kristian, and William Isaac. 2016. "To Predict and Serve?" *Significance* 13, no. 5 (October):
14–19.

Macfarlane, Kirsty. 2018. "Education, Sufficiency, and the Relational Egalitarian Ideal." *Journal of Applied Philosophy* 35, no. 4 (November): 759–74.

Madaio, Michael, Su Lin Blodgett, Elijah Mayfield, and Ezekiel Dixon-Román. 2023. "Beyond 'Fairness': Structural (In)justice Lenses on AI for Education." In *The Ethics of Artificial Intelligence in Education: Current Challenges, Practices and Debates*, edited by W. Holmes and K. Porayska-Pomsta, 203–39. New York: Routledge.

Mader, Mary Beth. 2011. *Sleights of Reason: Norm, Bisexuality, Development*. Albany: SUNY Press.

Malabou, Catherine. 2019. *Morphing Intelligence: From IQ Measurement to Artificial Brains*. Translated by Carolyn Shread. New York: Columbia University Press. Originally published as *Métamorphoses de l'intelligence: Que faire de leur cerveau bleu?* in 2017.

Manolev, Jamie, Anna Sullivan, and Roger Slee. 2018. "The Datafication of Discipline: ClassDojo, Surveillance and a Performative Classroom Culture." *Learning, Media and Technology* 44 (1): 36–51.

Manouselis, Nikos, Hendrik Drachsler, Riina Vuorikari, Hans Hummel, and Rob Koper. 2011. "Recommender Systems in Technology Enhanced Learning." In *Recommender Systems Handbook*, edited by F. Ricci, L. Rokach, B. Shapira, P. Kantor, 387–415. Boston: Springer.

Martinez-Maldonado, Roberto, Dragan Gašević, Vanessa Echeverria, Gloria Fernandez Nieto, Zachari Swiecki, and Simon Buckingham Shum. 2021. "What Do You Mean by Collaboration Analytics? A Conceptual Model." *Journal of Learning Analytics* 8, no. 1 (April): 126–53.

McAfee, Noelle. 2004. "Public Knowledge." *Philosophy and Social Criticism* 30, no. 2 (March): 139–57.

McLuhan, Marshall. 1994. *Understanding Media*. Cambridge: MIT Press. Originally published in 1964.

McNeil, Joanne. 2022. "Crisis Text Line and the Silicon Valleyfication of Everything." *Vice*, February 10, accessed November 24, 2022. https://www.vice.com/en/article/wxdpym/crisis-text-line-and-the-silicon-valleyfication-of-everything.

McNeil, Joanne. 2023. *Wrong Way*. New York: Farrar, Straus & Giroux.

McStay, Andrew. 2020. "Emotional AI and EdTech: Serving the Public Good?" *Learning, Media, and Technology* 45 (3): 270–83.

Mehrabi, Ninareh, Fred Morstatter, Nripsuta Saxena, Kristina Lerman, and Aram Galstyan. 2021. "A Survey on Bias and Fairness in Machine Learning." *ACM Computer Surveys* 54, no. 6 (July), article 115.

Metaxa, Danaë, Joon Sung Park, Ronald E. Robertson, Karrie Karahalios, Christo Wilson, Jeff Hancock, and Christian Sandvig. 2021. "Auditing Algorithms." *Foundations and Trends in Human-Computer Interaction* 14, no. 4 (November): 272–344.

Metcalf, Jacob, Emanuel Moss, Elizabeth Anne Watkins, Ranjit Singh, and Madeleine Clare Elish. 2021. "Algorithmic Impact Assessments and Accountability: The Co-construction of Impacts." In *Proceedings of the 2021 ACM Conference on Fairness, Accountability, and Transparency (FAccT '21)*, 735–46. New York: Association for Computing Machinery.

Miceli, Milagros, and Julian Posada. 2022. "The Data-Production Dispositif." in *Proceedings of ACM Human-Computer Interaction* 6, CSCW2, article 460.

Microsoft Corporation. 2022. "Microsoft Responsible AI Standard, v2." June, accessed July 3, 2024. https://www.microsoft.com/en-us/ai/principles-and-approach/.

Miller, David. 1997. "Equality and Justice." *Ratio* 10, no. 3 (December): 222–37.

Mills, Charles. 2018. "W. E. B. Du Bois: Black Radical Liberal." In *A Political Companion to W. E. B. Du Bois*, edited by N. Brommell, 19–56. Lexington: University Press of Kentucky.

Mitchell, Shira, Eric Potash, Solon Barocas, Alexander D'Amour, and Kristian Lum. 2021. "Algorithmic Fairness: Choices, Assumptions, and Definitions." *Annual Review of Statistics and Its Application* 8:141–63.

Mittelstadt, Brent Daniel, Patrick Allo, Mariarosaria Taddeo, Sandra Wachter, and Luciano Floridi. 2016. "The Ethics of Algorithms: Mapping the Debate." *Big Data & Society* 3, no. 2 (December): 1–21.

Montemayor, Carlos. 2023. *The Prospect of a Humanitarian Artificial Intelligence: Agency and Value Alignment*. New York: Bloomsbury.

Morris, Aldon. 2020. "The Sociology of W. E. B. Du Bois as a Weapon of Racial Equality." *Quaderni di Sociologia*, 83-LXIV:11–24.

Motchoulski, Alexander. 2021. "Relational Egalitarianism and Democracy." *Journal of Moral Philosophy* 18 (6): 620–49.

Muhammad, Kahlil Gibran. 2010. *The Condemnation of Blackness*. Cambridge: Harvard University Press.

Mulligan, Deirdre, Colin Koopman, and Nick Doty. 2016. "Privacy Is an Essentially Contested Concept: A Multi-dimensional Analytic for Mapping Privacy." *Philosophical Transactions of the Royal Society A* 374 (2083): 1–17.

Mulligan, Deirdre, Joshua Kroll, Nitin Kohli, and Richmond Wong. 2019. "This Thing Called Fairness: Disciplinary Confusion Realizing a Value in Technology." *Proceedings of ACM Human-Computer Interaction* 3, issue CSCW, article 119 (November): 1–36.

Murakawa, Naomi. 2021. "Ida B. Wells on Racial Criminalization." In *African American Political Thought*, edited by M. Rogers and J. Turner, 212–34. Chicago: University of Chicago Press.

Murthy, Vivek H. 2024. "Surgeon General: Why I'm Calling for a Warning Label on Social Media Platforms." *New York Times*, June 17, accessed July 2, 2024. https://www.nytimes.com/2024/06/17/opinion/social-media-health-warning.html.

Nakic, Jelena, Andrina Granic, and Vlado Glavinic. 2015. "Anatomy of Student Models in Adaptive Learning Systems: A Systematic Literature Review of Individual Differences from 2001 to 2013." *Journal of Educational Computing Research* 51, no. 4 (January): 459–89.

Nath, Rekha. 2020. "Relational Egalitarianism." *Philosophy Compass* 15, no. 7 (July). https://doi.org/10.1111/phc3.12686.

Newfield, Christopher, Anna Alexandrova, and Stephen John, eds. 2022. *Limits of the Numerical: The Abuses and Uses of Quantification*. Chicago: University of Chicago Press.

Nguyen, Andy, Ha Ngan Ngo, Yvonne Hong, Belle Dang, and Bich-Phuong Thi Nguyen. 2023. "Ethical Principles for Artificial Intelligence in Education." *Education and Information Technologies* 28, no. 4 (October): 4221–41.

Nguyen, C. Thi. 2020. "Echo Chambers and Epistemic Bubbles." *Episteme* 17, no. 2 (June): 141–61.

Nissenbaum, Helen. 2009. *Privacy in Context: Technology, Policy, and the Integrity of Social Life*. Stanford: Stanford University Press.

Noble, Safiya. 2018. *Algorithms of Oppression: How Search Engines Reinforce Racism*. New York: NYU Press.

Nussbaum, Martha. 2013. *Creating Capabilities: The Human Development Approach*. Cambridge: Belknap Press.

O'Neill, Onora. 1987. "Abstraction, Idealization and Ideology in Ethics." *Royal Institute of Philosophy Lecture Series* 22:55–69.

O'Neill, Onora. 2022. *A Philosopher Looks at Digital Communication*. Cambridge: Cambridge University Press.

Ochigame, Rodrigo. 2019. "The Invention of 'Ethical AI.'" *Intercept*, December 20. https://theintercept.com/2019/12/20/mit-ethical-ai-artificial-intelligence/.

Ochigame, Rodrigo. 2020. "The Long History of Algorithmic Fairness." *Phenomenal World*, January 30. https://www.phenomenalworld.org/analysis/long-history-algorithmic-fairness/.

Orwell, George. 1981. "Such, Such Were the Joys . . ." In *A Collection of Essays*. New York: Harvest Books. Originally published in 1947.

Panagia, Davide. 2017. "#datapolitik: An Interview with Davide Panagia," by Çağlar Köseoğlu. *Contrivers' Review*, November. http://www.contrivers.org/articles/40/Davide-Panagia-Caglar-Koseoglu-Datapolik-Interview-Political-Theory/.

Panagia, Davide. 2019. "On the Political Ontology of the Dispositif." *Critical Inquiry* 45, no. 3 (Spring): 714–46.

Panagia, Davide. 2021. "On the Possibilities of a Political Theory of Algorithms." *Political Theory* 49, no. 1 (February): 109–33.

Panagia, Davide. 2024. *Sentimental Empiricism: Politics, Philosophy, and Criticism in Postwar France*. New York: Fordham University Press.

Pane, John, Elizabeth Steiner, Matthew Baird, Laura Hamilton, and Joseph Pane. 2017. *Informing Progress: Insights on Personalized Learning Implementation and Effects*. Santa Monica: RAND Corporation.

Pangrazio, Luci, and Julian Sefton-Green, eds. 2022. *Learning to Live with Datafication: Educational Case Studies and Initiatives from across the World*. New York: Routledge.

Parfit, Derek. 2000. "Equality or Priority?" In *The Ideal of Equality*, edited by M. Clayton and A. Williams, 81–125. New York: St Martin's Press. Originally presented orally in 1991, then first published in 1995.

Pariser, Eli. 2011. *The Filter Bubble*. New York: Penguin.

Patton, Paul. 2010. "Foucault and Normative Political Philosophy: Liberal and Neo-liberal Governmentality and Public Reason." In *Foucault and Philosophy*, edited by T. O'Leary, C. Falzon, and J. Sawicki, 204–21. Hoboken: Wiley-Blackwell.

Patton, Paul. 2014. "Foucault and Rawls: Government and Public Reason." In *The Government of Life: Foucault, Biopolitics, and Neoliberalism*, edited by V. Lemm and M. Vatter, 141–62. New York: Fordham University Press.

Paullada, Amandalynne, Inioluwa Deborah Raji, Emily Bender, Emily Denton, and Alex Hanna. 2020. "Data and Its (Dis)contents: A Survey of Dataset Development and Use in Machine Learning Research." *Patterns* 2, no. 11 (November). https://www.sciencedirect.com/science/article/pii/S2666389921001847.

Pearson, Susan. 2021. *The Birth Certificate: An American History*. Chapel Hill: University of North Carolina Press.

Peirce, Charles Sanders. 1992. "The Law of Mind." In *The Essential Peirce: Selected Philosophical Writings, Vol. 1 (1867–1893)*, edited by N. Houser and C. Kloesel, 312–33. Bloomington: Indiana University Press. Originally published in 1892.

Peirce, Charles Sanders. 1998. "What Pragmatism Is." In *The Essential Peirce: Selected Philosophical Writings, Vol. 2 (1893–1913)*, edited by N. Houser and C. Kloesel, 331–45. Bloomington: Indiana University Press. Originally published in 1905.

Pelánek, Radek. 2017. "Bayesian Knowledge Tracing, Logistic Models, and Beyond: An Overview of Learner Modeling Techniques." *User Modeling and User-Adapted Interaction* 27, no. 3–5 (December): 313–50.

Perkoff, Margaret, Emily Doherty, Jeffrey B. Bush, and Leanne Hirshfield. 2024. "Crafting a Responsible Dialog System for Collaborative Learning Environments," presented at *AAAI 2024*, Vancouver, February 2024.

Perrotta, Carlo, and Neil Selwyn. 2019. "Deep Learning Goes to School: Toward a Relational Understanding of AI in Education." *Learning, Media and Technology* 45 (3): 251–69.

Perrotta, Carlo, and Ben Williamson. 2018. "The Social Life of Learning Analytics: Cluster Analysis and the 'Performance' of Algorithmic Education." *Learning, Media and Technology* 43 (1): 3–16.

Peters, John Durham. 1999. *Speaking into the Air*. Chicago: University of Chicago Press.

Phillips, Whitney, and Ryan Milner. 2021. *You Are Here: A Field Guide for Navigating Polarized Speech, Conspiracy Theories, and Our Polluted Media Landscape*. Cambridge: MIT Press.

Piety, Philip J., Daniel Hickey, and M. J. Bishop. 2014. "Educational Data Sciences—Framing Emergent Practices for Analytics of Learning, Organizations, and Systems." In *Learning Analytics and Knowledge 2014, Association for Computing Machinery*, 193–202. New York: Association for Computing Machinery.

Piety, Philip, and Roy Pea. 2018. "Understanding Learning Analytics across Practices." In *Learning Analytics in Education*, edited by D. Nieme, R. Pea, B. Saxberg, and R. Clark, 215–32. Charlotte: Information Age Publishing.

Plass, Jan, and Shashank Pawar. 2020. "Toward a Taxonomy of Adaptivity for Learning." *Journal of Research on Technology in Education* 52, no. 3 (June): 275–300.

Poirier, Lindsay. 2021. "Reading Datasets: Strategies for Interpreting the Politics of Data Signification." *Big Data & Society* 8, no. 2 (July): 1–19.

Porter, Theodore. 1986. *The Rise of Statistical Thinking, 1820–1900*. Princeton: Princeton University Press.

Post, Robert C. 1989. "The Social Foundations of Privacy: Community and Self in the Common Law Tort." *California Law Review* 77, no. 5 (October): 957–1010.

Prahani, Binar Kurnia, Iqbal Ainur Rizki, Budi Jatmiko, Nadi Suprapto, and Amelia Tan. 2022. "Artificial Intelligence in Education Research during the Last Ten Years: A Review and Bibliometric Study." *International Journal of Emerging Technologies in Learning* 17, no. 8 (April): 169–88.

Prewitt, Kenneth. 2018. "The Census Race Classification: Is It Doing Its Job?" *Annals of the American Academy of Political and Social Science* 677, no. 1 (May): 8–24.

Prinsloo, Paul, Sharon Slade, and Mohammad Khalil. 2022. "The Answer Is (Not Only) Technological: Considering Student Data Privacy in Learning Analytics." *British Journal of Educational Technology* 53, no. 4 (July): 876–93.

Rabinow, Paul. 1996. "Galton's Regret," in *Essays on the Anthropology of Reason*, 112–28. Princeton, NJ: Princeton University Press. Originally published in 1992.

Rahman, K. Sabeel. 2017. *Democracy against Domination*. Oxford: Oxford University Press.

Ravitch, Diane. 2011. *The Death and Life of the Great American School System: How Testing and Choice Are Undermining Education*, rev. and expanded ed. New York: Basic Books.

Rawls, John. 1999. *A Theory of Justice*, rev. ed. Cambridge: Belknap Press. Originally published in 1971.

Rawls, John. 1999. "Two Concepts of Rules." In *Collected Papers*, edited by S. Freeman, 20–46. Cambridge: Harvard University Press. Originally published in 1955.

Rawls, John. 2001. *Justice as Fairness: A Restatement*, edited by E. Kelly. Cambridge: Belknap Press.

Regan, Priscilla. 1995. *Legislating Privacy: Technology, Social Values, and Public Policy*. Chapel Hill: University of North Caroline Press.

Regan, Priscilla M., and Jolene Jesse. 2019. "Ethical Challenges of Edtech, Big Data and Personalized Learning: Twenty-First Century Student Sorting and Tracking." *Ethics and Information Technology* 21, no. 3 (September): 167–79.

Reinholz, Daniel L., and Niral Shah. 2018. "Equity Analytics: A Methodological Approach for Quantifying Participation Patterns in Mathematics Classroom Discourse." *Journal for Research in Mathematics Education* 49, no. 2 (March): 140–77.

Reisman, Dillon, Jason Schultz, Kate Crawford, and Meredith Whittaker. 2018. "Algorithmic Impact Assessments: A Practical Framework for Public Agency." Report, *AI Now*. https://ainowinstitute.org/publication/algorithmic-impact-assessments-report-2.

Rieland, Randy. 2016. "How AltSchool Is Personalizing Education by Collecting Loads of Data on Its Students." *Smithsonian Magazine*, September 14. https://www.smithsonianmag.com/innovation/how-altschool-personalizing-education-by-collecting-hordes-data-on-students-180960463/.

Risse, Mathias. 2023. *Political Theory of the Digital Age: Where Artificial Intelligence Might Take Us*. Cambridge: Cambridge University Press.

Rogers, Melvin. 2009. "Democracy, Elites and Power: John Dewey Reconsidered." *Contemporary Political Theory* 8, no. 1 (February): 68–89.

Roll, Ido, and Ruth Wylie. 2016. "Evolution and Revolution in Artificial Intelligence in Education." *International Journal of Artificial Intelligence in Education* 26, no. 2 (February): 582–99.

Romero, Cristóbal, and Sebastián Ventura. 2020. "Educational Data Mining and Learning Analytics: An Updated Survey." *WIREs Data Mining and Knowledge Discovery* 10, no. 3 (May/June).

Rondel, David. 2018. *Pragmatist Egalitarianism*. Oxford: Oxford University Press.

Rondel, David. 2021. "Introduction: The Unity of Richard Rorty's Philosophy" in Rondel (ed.), *The Cambridge Companion to Richard Rorty*, 1–18. Cambridge: Cambridge University Press.

Rorty, Richard. 1979. *Philosophy and the Mirror of Nature*. Princeton: Princeton University Press.

Rorty, Richard. 1989. *Contingency, Irony, and Solidarity*. Cambridge: Cambridge University Press.

Rorty, Richard. 1999a. "Pragmatism as Anti-authoritarianism." *Revue Internationale de Philosophie* 53, no. 207 (1) (March): 7–20.

Rorty, Richard. 1999b. *Philosophy and Social Hope*. New York: Penguin.

Rose, David. 2001. "Universal Design for Learning: Deriving Guiding Principles for Networks That Learn." *Journal of Special Education Technology* 16, no. 2 (Spring): 66–67.

Rubel, Alan, and K. M. L. Jones. 2016. "Student Privacy in Learning Analytics: An Information Ethics Perspective." *Information Society* 32, no. 2 (March): 143–59.

Sandvig, Christian, Kevin Hamilton, Karrie Karahalios, and Cedric Langbort 2014. "Auditing Algorithms: Research Methods for Detecting Discrimination on Internet Platforms." Paper presented at Data and Discrimination: Converting Critical Concerns into Productive Inquiry, Seattle, May 2014.

Sani, Salisu, and Abdullahi Bichi. 2016. "Artificial Intelligence Approaches in Student Modeling: Half Decade Review (2010–2015)." *International Journal of Computer Network and Information Security* 5, no. 5 (October): 746–54.

Saxberg, Bror. 2018. Preface to *Learning Analytics in Education*, edited by D. Nieme, R. Pea, B. Saxberg, R. Clark, vii–x. Charlotte: Information Age Publishing.

Scanlon, T. M. 1998. *What We Owe to Each Other*. Cambridge: Harvard University Press.

Scanlon, T. M. 2000. "The Diversity of Objections to Inequality." In *The Ideal of Equality*, edited by M. Clayton and A. Williams, 41–59. New York: St. Martin's Press. Originally published in 1996.

Scanlon, T. M. 2018. *Why Does Inequality Matter?* Oxford: Oxford University Press.

Scheffler, Samuel. 2003. "What Is Egalitarianism?" *Philosophy & Public Affairs* 31, no. 1 (Winter): 5–39.

Scheffler, Samuel. 2015. "The Practice of Equality." In *Social Equality*, edited by C. Fourie, F. Schuppert, and I. Williman-Helmer, 21–44. Oxford: Oxford University Press.

Schuster, Nick, and Jenny Davis. 2024. "Role-Taking Skill and Platform Marginalization." Paper presented at American Philosophical Association, Portland, OR, March 2024.

Seaver, Nick. 2018. "What Should an Anthropology of Algorithms Do?" *Cultural Anthropology* 33, no. 3 (August): 375–85.

Seidman, Louis Michael. 2003. *Constitutional Law: Equal Protection of the Laws.* New York: Foundation Press.

Selwyn, Neil. 2016. *Is Technology Good for Education?* Cambridge: Polity Press.

Selwyn, Neil. 2019. "What's the Problem with Learning Analytics?" *Journal of Learning Analytics* 6, no. 3 (December): 11–19.

Selwyn, Neil, and Kari Facer. 2013. "The Need for a Politics of Education and Technology." Introduction to *The Politics of Education and Technology*, edited by N. Selwyn and K. Facer, 1–17. New York: Palgrave Macmillan.

Sen, Amartya. 1992. *Inequality Reexamined.* Cambridge: Harvard University Press.

Sha, Lele, Dragan Gašević, and Guanliang Chen. 2023. "Lessons from Debiasing Data for Fair and Accurate Predictive Modeling in Education." *Expert Systems with Applications* 228, document 120323.

Shannon, Claude. 1949. "The Mathematical Theory of Communication." In *The Mathematical Theory of Communication* by Claude Shannon and Warren Weaver. Urbana: University of Illinois Press. Originally published as "A Mathematical Theory of Communication" in 1948.

Sheehey, Bonnie. 2019. "Algorithmic Paranoia: The Temporal Governmentality of Predictive Policing." *Ethics and Information Technology* 21, no. 1 (March): 49–58.

Shemshack, Atikah, and Jonathan Spector. 2020. "A Systematic Literature Review of Personalized Learning Terms." *Smart Learning Environments* 7 (33): 1–20.

Siemens, George. 2013. "Learning Analytics: The Emergence of a Discipline." *American Behavioral Scientist* 57, no. 10 (October): 1380–400.

Siemens, George, and Ryan Baker. 2012. "Learning Analytics and Educational Data Mining: Towards Communication and Collaboration." In *Proceedings of the 2nd International Conference on Learning Analytics and Knowledge*, 252–54. New York: Association for Computing Machinery.

Siemens, George, and Dragan Gašević. 2012. "Guest Editorial: Learning and Knowledge Analytics." *Educational Technology & Society* 15, no. 3 (July): 1–2.

Simon, Valérie. 2023. "Making Sense of the Practical Lesbian Past: Towards a Rethinking of Untimely Uses of History through the Temporality of Cultural Techniques," PhD dissertation, University of Oregon.

Simondon, Gilbert. 2017. *On the Mode of Existence of Technical Objects.* Translated by Cecile Malaspina and John Rogove. Minneapolis: University of Minnesota Press. Originally published as *Du mode d'existence des objets techniques* in 1958.

Slade, Sharon, and Prinsloo, Paul. 2013. "Learning Analytics: Ethical Issues and Dilemmas." *American Behavioral Scientist* 57, no. 10 (October): 1510–29.

Smithers, Laura. 2023. "Predictive Analytics and the Creation of the Permanent Present." *Learning, Media and Technology* 48 (1): 109–21.

Smuha, Nathalie A. 2023. "Pitfalls and Pathways for Trustworthy Artificial Intelligence in Education." In *The Ethics of Artificial Intelligence in Education: Current Challenges, Practices and Debates*, edited by W. Holmes and K. Porayska-Pomsta, 113–45. New York: Routledge.

Spinoza, Benedict de. 1994. *Ethics*. In *A Spinoza Reader: The Ethics and Other Works*, translated by Edwin Curley. Princeton: Princeton University Press. Originally published posthumously as *Ethica* in 1677.

Stahl, Gerry. 2010. "Group Cognition as a Foundation for the New Science of Learning." In *New Science of Learning: Cognition, Computers and Collaboration in Education*, edited by I. Saleh and M. Khine, 23–44. New York: Springer.

Stark, Luke, Daniel Greene, and Anna Lauren Hoffmann. 2020. "Critical Perspectives on Governance Mechanisms for AI/ML Systems." In *The Cultural Life of Machine Learning*, edited by J. Roberge and M. Castelle, 257–80. London: Palgrave Macmillan.

Stefansky, Emma. 2017. "Mark Zuckerberg Asks Forgiveness for His 'Mistakes' on Facebook." *Vanity Fair*, October 1. https://www.vanityfair.com/news/2017/10/mark-zuckerberg -facebook-mistakes-apology.

Sterne, Jonathan. 2012. *MP3: The Meaning of a Format*. Durham: Duke University Press.

Sunstein, Cass. 2018. *#Republic: Divided Democracy in the Age of Social Media*. Princeton: Princeton University Press.

Superfine, Benjamin. 2013. *Equality in Educational Law and Policy, 1954–2010*. Cambridge: Cambridge University Press.

Suresh, Harini, and John Guttag. 2021. "A Framework for Understanding Unintended Consequences of Machine Learning." *Proceedings of the 1st ACM Conference on Equity and Access in Algorithms, Mechanisms, and Optimization*, article 17.

Swist, Teresa, and Kalervo Gulson. 2023. "School Choice Algorithms: Data Infrastructures, Automation, and Inequality," in *Postdigital Science and Education* 5, no. 1 (January): 152–70.

Symons, John, and Ramón Alvarado. 2022. "Epistemic Injustice and Data Science Technologies." *Synthese* 200, no. 2, article 87.

Talan, Tarik. 2021. "The Effect of Computer-Supported Collaborative Learning on Academic Achievement: A Meta-analysis Study." *International Journal of Education in Mathematics, Science, and Technology* 9 (3): 426–48.

Taylor, Paul. 2011. "William Edward Burghardt Du Bois." In *The Wiley-Blackwell Companion to Major Social Theorists*, edited by G. Ritzer and J. Stepinsky, 426–47. Chichester: Wiley.

Taylor, Paul. 2021. "W. E. B. Du Bois." In *African American Political Thought*, edited by M. Rogers and J. Turner, 235–59. Chicago: University of Chicago Press.

Tenen, Dennis. 2017. *Plain Text: The Poetics of Computation*. Stanford: Stanford University Press.

Terrin, Éder, and Moris Triventi. 2023. "The Effect of School Tracking on Student Achievement and Inequality: A Meta-analysis." *Review of Educational Research* 93, no. 2 (April): 236–74.

Thompson, Debra. 2016. *The Schematic State*. Cambridge: Cambridge University Press.

Thylstrup, N. B. 2022. "The Ethics and Politics of Data Sets in the Age of Machine Learning: Deleting Traces and Encountering Remains." *Media, Culture & Society* 44, no. 4 (May): 655–71.

Tiisala, Tuomo. 2021. "Foucault, Neoliberalism, and Equality." *Critical Inquiry* 48, no. 1 (Autumn): 23–44.

Tocqueville, Alexis de. 1990. *Democracy in America*. Translated by Henry Reeve. New York: Vintage Books. Originally published as *De la démocratie en Amérique* in two parts in 1835 and 1840.

Tsai, Yi-Shan, Carlo Perrotta, and Dragan Gašević. 2020. "Empowering Learners with Personalised Learning Approaches? Agency, Equity and Transparency in the Context of Learning Analytics." *Assessment & Evaluation in Higher Education* 45 (4): 554–67.

Tschaepe, Mark. 2021a. "Data without Democracy: The Cruel Optimism of Education Technology and Assessment." *Education and Culture* 37 (1): 7–24.

Tschaepe, Mark. 2021b. "Pragmatic Ethics for Generative Adversarial Networks: Coupling, Cyborgs, and Machine Learning." *Contemporary Pragmatism* 18, no. 1 (May): 95–111.

Tschaepe, Mark. 2023. "Philosophical Tools for Educational Culture: Reconstructing Data and Assessment Practices." *Contemporary Pragmatism* 20, nos. 1–2 (April): 140–49.

Turkle, Sherry. 2011. *Alone Together: Why We Expect More from Technology and Less from Each Other.* New York: Basic Books.

US Department of Education, Office of Educational Technology. 2010. *Transforming American Education: Learning Powered by Technology.* Washington, DC: Education Publications Center.

US Department of Education, Office of Educational Technology. 2017. *Reimagining the Role of Technology in Education: 2017 National Education Technology Plan Update.* Washington, DC: Information Resource Center.

US Food and Drug Administration (FDA). 2018. "Food Standards and the 1906 Act," accessed March 7, 2024. https://www.fda.gov/about-fda/histories-product-regulation/food -standards-and-1906-act.

US White House. 2022. "Blueprint for an AI Bill of Rights: Making Automated Systems Work for the American People." White paper from the Office of Science and Technology Policy, October 4. https://www.whitehouse.gov/ostp/ai-bill-of-rights/.

US White House. 2023. "President Biden Issues Executive Order on Safe, Secure, and Trustworthy Artificial Intelligence," October 30. https://www.whitehouse.gov/briefing-room/ statements-releases/2023/10/30/fact-sheet-president-biden-issues-executive-order-on-safe -secure-and-trustworthy-artificial-intelligence/.

Uttamchandani, Suraj, and Joshua Quick. 2022. "An Introduction to Fairness, Absence of Bias, and Equity in Learning Analytics." In *The Handbook of Learning Analytics,* edited by C. Lang, G. Siemens, A. Wise, D. Gašević, and A. Merceron, 205–12. Vancouver: Society for Learning Analytics Research.

Valdés Aguirre, Benjamin, Jorge Ramírez Uresti, and Benedict du Boulay. 2016. "An Analysis of Student Model Portability." *International Journal for Artificial Intelligence in Education* 26, no. 3 (September): 932–74.

Valdivia, Ana, and Martina Tazzioli. 2023. "Datafication Genealogies beyond Algorithmic Fairness: Making Up Racialised Subjects." In *2023 ACM Conference on Fairness, Accountability, and Transparency (FAccT '23),* 840–50. New York: Association for Computing Machinery.

Vallor, Shannon. 2016. *Technology and the Virtues: A Philosophical Guide to a Future Worth Wanting.* Oxford: Oxford University Press.

Vallor, Shannon. 2024. *The AI Mirror: How to Reclaim Our Humanity in an Age of Machine Thinking.* Oxford: Oxford University Press.

Van Schoors, Rani, Jan Elen, Annaleis Raes, and Fien Depaepe. 2021. "An Overview of 25 Years of Research on Digital Personalised Learning in Primary and Secondary Education: A Systematic Review of Conceptual and Methodological Trends," in *British Journal of Education Technology* 52, no. 5 (September): 1798–822.

van Wietmarschen, Han. 2022. "What Is Social Hierarchy?" *Noûs* 56, no. 4 (December): 920–39.

Vandewaetere, Mieke, and Geraldine Clarebout. 2014. "Advanced Technologies for Personalized Learning, Instruction, and Performance." In *Handbook of Research on Educational Communications and Technology*, edited by J. Spector, M. Merrill, J. Elen, and M. Bishop, 425–37. New York: Springer.

Vandewaetere, Mieke, Piet Desmet, and Geraldine Clarebout. 2011. "The Contribution of Learner Characteristics in the Development of Computer-Based Adaptive Learning Environments." *Computers in Human Behavior* 27, no. 1 (January): 118–30.

Verma, Sahil, and Julia Rubin. 2018. "Fairness Definitions Explained." *ACM Fairware '18*, May, 1–7.

Viehoff, Daniel. 2014. "Democratic Equality and Political Authority." *Philosophy & Public Affairs* 42, no. 4 (September): 337–75.

Viehoff, Daniel. 2019. "Power and Equality." In *Oxford Studies in Political Philosophy, Volume 5*, edited by D. Sobel, P. Vallentyne, and S. Wall, 3–38. Oxford: Oxford University Press.

Vismann, Cornelia. 2008. *Files: Law and Media Technology*. Translated by Geoffrey Winthrop-Young. Stanford: Stanford University Press. Originally published as *Akten: Medientechnik und Recht* in 2000.

Vredenburgh, Kate. 2022. "Fairness." In *The Oxford Handbook of AI Governance*, edited by J. Bullock et al., 129–48. Oxford: Oxford University Press.

Watters, Audrey. 2017. "'Personalized Learning' and the Power of the Gates Foundation to Shape Education Policy," *Hack Education*, July 18. https://hackeducation.com/2017/07/18/personalization.

Weber, Max. 2004. "Politics as a Vocation." In *The Vocation Lectures*, edited by D. Owen and T. Strong, translated by Rodney Livingstone. Indianapolis: Hackett. Originally published as "Politik als Beruf" in 1919.

Wells, Ida B. 1997. *A Red Record*. In Wells, *Southern Horrors and Other Writings: The Anti-lynching Campaign of Ida B. Wells, 1892–1900*, edited by J. Royster, 73–157. Boston: Bedford Books. Originally published in 1895.

Westbrook, Robert. 1998. "Pragmatism and Democracy: Reconstructing the Logic of John Dewey's Faith." In *The Revival of Pragmatism*, edited by M. Dickstein, 128–40. Durham: Duke University.

Whitehead, Alfred North. 1955. *Adventures of Ideas*. New York: Mentor. Originally published in 1933.

Whitten, Leah, Anthony Sanders, and J. Gary Stewart. 2013. "Degree Compass: The Preferred Choice Approach," in *Journal of Academic Administration in Higher Education* 9, no. 2 (Fall): 39–43.

Williams, Bernard. 2005a. "The Idea of Equality." In *In the Beginning Was the Deed*, 97–114. Princeton: Princeton University Press. Originally published in 1962.

Williams, Bernard. 2005b. *In the Beginning Was the Deed: Realism and Moralism in Political Argument*, edited by G. Hawthorn. Princeton: Princeton University Press.

Williamson, Ben. 2017. *Big Data in Education: The Digital Future of Learning, Policy, and Practice*. Los Angeles: Sage.

Williamson, Ben. 2022. "Afterword: The Future of Datafication in Education? Clouds, Bodies, and Ethics." In *Learning to Live with Datafication: Educational Case Studies and Initiatives from across the World*, edited by L. Pangrazio and J. Sefton-Green, 209–15. New York: Routledge.

Williamson, Ben, and Rebecca Eynon. 2020. "Historical Threads, Missing Links, and Future Directions in AI in Education," in *Learning, Media and Technology* 45 (3): 223–35.

Wing, Jeanette. 2020. "Ten Research Challenge Areas in Data Science." *Harvard Data Science Review* 2, no. 3 (September). https://doi.org/10.1162/99608f92.c6577b1f.

Winner, Langdon. 1980. "Do Artifacts Have Politics?" *Daedalus* 109, no. 1 (Winter): 121–36.

Wirth, Niklaus. 1976. *Algorithms + Data Structures = Programs*. Englewood Cliffs: Prentice-Hall.

Wise, Alyssa Friend, Simon Knight, and Simon Buckingham Shum. 2021. "Collaborative Learning Analytics." In *International Handbook of Computer-Supported Collaborative Learning* (Computer-Supported Collaborative Learning Series, vol. 19), edited by U. Cress, C. Rosé, A. Wise, and J. Oshima, 425–43. Switzerland: Springer Nature.

Wise, Alyssa Friend, Carolyn Rosé, and Sanna Järvelä. 2023. "Nine Elements for Robust Collaborative Learning Analytics: A Constructive Collaborative Critique." *International Journal of Computer-Supported Collaborative Learning* 18, no. 1 (March): 1–9.

Wittgenstein, Ludwig. 2001. *Philosophical Investigations*. Translated by G. E. M. Anscombe. Oxford: Blackwell. Originally published posthumously as *Philosophische Untersuchungen* in 1953.

Wolf, Mary Ann, Rachel Jones, Sara Hall, and Bob Wise. 2018. "Policies and Capacity Enablers and Barriers for Learning Analytics." In *Learning Analytics in Education*, edited by D. Nieme, R. Pea, B. Saxberg, R. Clark, 175–214. Charlotte: Information Age Publishing.

Wolff, Jonathan. 1998. "Fairness, Respect, and the Egalitarian Ethos," in *Philosophy & Public Affairs* 27, no. 2 (April): 97–122.

Womack, Autumn. 2022. *The Matter of Black Living: The Aesthetic Experiment of Racial Data, 1880–1930*. Chicago: University of Chicago Press.

Wong, Billy Tak-Ming, and Kam Cheong Li. 2020. "A Review of Learning Analytics Intervention in Higher Education (2011–2018)." *Journal of Computers in Education* 7, no. 1 (March): 7–28.

Wong, Billy Tak-ming, Kam Cheong Li, and Simon K. S. Cheung. 2023. "An Analysis of Learning Analytics in Personalised Learning." *Journal of Computing in Higher Education* 35, no. 3 (December): 371–90.

Xie, Haoron, Hui-Chun Chu, Gwo-Jen Hwang, and Chun-Chieh Wang. 2019. "Trends and Development in Technology-Enhanced Adaptive/Personalized Learning: A Systematic Review of Journal Publications from 2007 to 2017." *Computers and Education* 140, 103599.

Yang, Xiaozhe. 2019. "Accelerated Move for AI Education in China." *ECNU Review of Education* 2, no. 3 (September): 347–52.

Young, Iris Marion. 1990. *Justice and the Politics of Difference*. Princeton: Princeton University Press.

Yu, Mingyi. 2021. "The Algorithm Concept, 1684–1958." *Critical Inquiry* 47, no. 3 (Spring): 592–609.

Zack, Naomi. 1998. *Thinking about Race*. New York: Wadsworth.

Zawacki-Richter, Olaf, Victoria Marín, Melissa Bond, and Franziska Gouverneur. 2019. "Systematic Review of Research on Artificial Intelligence Applications in Higher Education—Where Are the Educators?" *International Journal of Educational Technology in Higher Education* 16 (39): 1–27.

Zhang, Ling, Sohyun Yang, and Richard Allen Carter. 2020. "Personalized Learning and ESSA: What We Know and Where We Go." *Journal of Research on Technology in Education* 52, no. 3 (June): 253–74.

Zhang, Marilyn. 2022. "Affirmative Algorithms: Relational Equality as Algorithmic Fairness." In *2022 ACM Conference on Fairness, Accountability, and Transparency (FAccT '22)*, 495–507. New York: Association for Computing Machinery.

Zheng, Lanqin. 2021. *Data-Driven Design for Computer-Supported Collaborative Learning: Design Matters*. Singapore: Springer Nature.

Zheng, Lanqin, Miaolang Long, Jiayu Niu, and Lu Zhong. 2023. "An Automated Group Learning Engagement Analysis and Feedback Approach to Promoting Collaborative Knowledge Building, Group Performance, and Socially Shared Regulation in CSCL." *International Journal of Computer-Supported Collaborative Learning* 18, no. 1 (March): 101–33.

Zimmermann, Annette, and Chad Lee-Stronach. 2022. "Proceed with Caution." *Canadian Journal of Philosophy* 52, no. 1 (January): 6–25.

Zuboff, Shoshana. 2019. *The Age of Surveillance Capitalism*. New York: PublicAffairs.

Index

The irony of a manual index in an age of relentless machine searchability could not be lost on the writer, but this tool was not constructed as an exhaustive database of terms (which most readers already have access to via typical text search functionality); rather, it maps and catalogs key concepts, their key locations, and some of their more obscure references.